Brain-Based Therapy with Adults

Brain-Based Therapy with Adults

Evidence-Based Treatment for
Everyday Practice

By

John B. Arden
Lloyd Linford

WILEY

John Wiley & Sons, Inc.

Library of Congress Cataloging-in-Publication Data

Arden, John Boghosian.
     Brain-based therapy with adults: evidence-based treatment for everyday
practice / by John Arden, Lloyd Linford.
          p.   ;   cm.
     Includes bibliographical references and index.
     ISBN 978-0-470-13890-8 (pbk.: alk. paper)
1. Neuropsychiatry. 2. Psychotherapy. I. Linford, Lloyd. II. Title.
     [DNLM: 1. Mental Disorders—therapy. 2. Psychotherapy—methods.
3. Evidence-Based Medicine—methods. 4. Psychophysiology. WM 420 A6763b
2009]
     RC341.A736 2009
     616.8—dc22
                                                                 2008022832

Printed in the United States of America

10 9 8 7 6 5 4 3 2 1

Contents

Acknowledgments

This book is sometimes extravagant in its praise of the human brain. If you need a reminder about the brain's limitations, we recommend you try writing a book like this one. It quickly becomes obvious that no one person (or even two) can do this on their own. *Brain-Based Therapy* would not have come into existence without the support and contributions of many people. First and foremost, we are indebted to our wives, Vicki Arden and Pam Valois, for their encouragement, insightful editorial comments, and good-hearted willingness to sacrifice countless evenings and weekends to the project. For too long both of us have gone to bed and woken up talking about BDNF and the DLPFC. Vicki and Pam had the good grace to refrain from pointing out we had developed OCD or ADHD, or some other alphabetical psychological disorder.

This book came out of our good fortune in meeting and talking with colleagues in Kaiser's Northern California Best Practices and Post-Doctoral Training programs, and with presenters at Kaiser's Annual Northern California Psychiatry and Chemical Dependency Conference. We would like to thank the other members of the Conference planning group—Stephen Miller, Marion Lim-Yankowitz, Marilyn McPherson, Debby Mendlowitz, Caryl Polk, and John Peters—who for each of the last 16 years have brought these experts to talk with our colleagues in San Francisco. Among many outstanding academics and clinicians who contributed to this book through the ideas they articulated on the conference podium, we'd like to single out our friends Jim Grigsby, who helped create the idea for this book and edited the first three chapters of this volume, and Lou Cozolino, who has set a high standard for integrating neuroscience and psychotherapy in his own work and writing. Conversations with Dr. Cozolino led to the idea for the BASE, a mnemonic that condenses our ideas about brain-based treatment into a practical and teachable form. Michael Lambert, the dean of psychotherapy researchers, finally got us to see that *people* trump technique in psychotherapy.

Like a tripod, this book is supported by three legs of approximately equal importance: neuroscience, attachment studies, and psychotherapy research into evidenced-based treatment for specific psychological disorders. Regarding the latter, we have received heart-warming and brain-changing support from the members of Kaiser's Best Practices Steering Committee, to whom we express our thanks. In particular we must acknowledge Elke Zuercher-White's generosity in sharing her scholarship and insight into the origins of anxiety disorders and evidenced-based treatment for OCD, panic, and social anxiety disorder. Anna Wong, the leader of Kaiser's ADHD Best Practices Workgroup and the coauthor of its clinical recommendations, changed our minds about ADD in two or three brilliant conversations about brain-based attentional disorders. Dr. Zuercher-White's and Dr.Wong's readings and comments on chapters in the book resulted in critical changes and improvements. Margaret Schadler and Jim Ballenger also provided critical input on various chapters (as did, unwittingly, Joel Meresman, whose work on depression has influenced us both). Conversations with another member of the Best Practices Steering Committee, John Peters, have been indispensable in formulating our ideas about outcomes management and the "common factors" that make psychotherapy work. Charles Vella helped us with matters pertaining to neuroscience and edited the chapter on memory. Rex Bierly and Daniel Dalcorso reviewed the whole manuscript. Tom Cohen's support and close reading of the ADHD chapter only deepened a debt that's been accruing over 30 years of friendship; likewise Patricia Saar's support and comments about the book helped reshape our orientation to the reader.

Finally, we would like to thank the great team at Wiley, whose professionalism and commitment to clinically relevant books is exemplary. Peggy Alexander, Marquita Flemming, Kim Nir, and Katie DeChants at Wiley have been generous and helpful throughout this project.

In short, many excellent brains have been involved in the creation of this book and its companion volume. It's only fair to restate the obvious: these contributors can't be held responsible for the book's shortcomings or any errors of fact we have inadvertently committed to print. We are solely responsible for the contents.

—John Arden, Sebastopol, California
—Lloyd Linford, Piedmont, California

Preface

This is the first of two books on evidence-based psychotherapy grounded in neuroscience. In this first book, we focus on the treatment of adults; volume 2 focuses on *Brain-Based Therapy with Children and Adolescents*. If our proposed project of integrating psychotherapy research and neuroscience sounds like cross-breeding apples and oranges, let us explain why you may find this new hybrid to your taste.

The idea for *Brain-Based Therapy* emerged from some career-changing developments in the setting where both of us practice, the Kaiser Permanente Medical Centers in Northern California. Our clinical and executive roles in the organization expose us to many young therapists looking for training and to leading researchers in psychotherapy and neuroscience. Our jobs allow us to communicate with some of the luminaries of psychology and psychiatry, scientist-clinicians who are building a new model for clinical psychology and psychiatry. Our work also keeps our feet on the ground through exposure to the needs and ideas of psychotherapists new to the field and through our own clinical work in a setting that is noteworthy for its diversity and intensity.

The brain sciences from which psychology has been separated for the last 100 years have not been idle during the break. Since the 1980s, pharmaceutical research has offered wealth and fame to explorers looking for chemically-based solutions to common human problems. The advent of advanced imaging technology has allowed researchers to gaze in wonder at the brain as an unfolding process, whether that brain is thinking about something sad or something sexy. Studies of neuroscience are fast taking us out of the Prozac era, which has tended to encourage the view that all there is to psychopathology is chemical imbalance. Even psychosurgery is making a comeback, but it is a different breed from the hammer-handed approaches of the past. Many neuroscientists continue to be skeptical that psychotherapy's awakening interest in their work is for real. Will psychotherapists make the intellectual investment necessary to appreciate the subtleties of the neuroscientific view of the mind? Many neuropsychological scientists (such as our friends Jim Grigsby and Lou Cozolino) think the answer is yes. They are as optimistic as we are about rebuilding psychology on an understanding of the brain and moving neuroscience into areas of vital interest to psychotherapists.

Our work has also brought us into contact with some of the legendary figures of the science of psychotherapy, researchers participating in a critically important conversation. One side of this discussion is led by clinicians such as Christine Padesky (Greenberger & Padesky, 1995), who honor particular technical approaches to working with patients, the other by psychotherapy researchers such as Michael Lambert (Lambert & Bergin, 1994), who value the therapeutic relationship over any one method. And from the neuroscience area, Helen Mayberg and Nancy Andreason have contributed valuable information about how the brain functions during psychopathology. These forms of research have yielded important lessons about how we can get better outcomes from the treatments we offer.

At some point in listening to these astute and creative voices in our field, a lightbulb went off over our heads. It occurred to us that by bringing these ideas together between the covers of a book, we might achieve some of the excitement we feel every year in helping create Kaiser's annual psychiatry conference. Bringing together the divergent views of biological and psychological scientist-clinicians leaves us feeling that there has never been a more exciting era in our field, or one more promising for the future. That is our reaction at the end of these gatherings, and we hope we have been able to capture some of this excitement in these pages.

The essence of this new apple-orange integration is that something that must be thought of as brain-mind is cocreated by genetic potential and experience—by interpersonal experience in particular. Interactions between neurons and the interpersonal environment drive development. Psychotherapy is a special kind of relationship we talk about with literally hundreds of therapists within the Kaiser Permanente system. Knowing something about the brain's architecture and how it manages to be both an organ with various functional modules and a system of almost infinite adaptability has changed how we listen to patients. How does the visual cortex of a blind man transform itself into a network sensitized to sound? How does a woman who has been through hell come to see the experience as a gift? Understanding some answers to these questions and utilizing them in treatment is the primary goal of *Brain-Based Therapy*.

About This Book

We start with some basics: in Chapters 1 and 2, we examine how neurons work, how they communicate, and how groups of them develop into functional modules. We also compare recent neuroscientific discoveries with psychotherapeutic theories about change. In discussing neuroscience, we face a paradox: the brain is a system made up of many functional parts and is an infinitely complex system in which the parts are subsumed by their relationship to the whole. We deal with this paradox by being inconsistent. Sometimes we write as if we believe in the localization hypothesis, whereby particular areas of the brain (e.g., Broca's area) give us certain functions (speech); at other times we are able to see these parts as elements of a larger self-organizing whole. The reader is advised to recall that the latter view is the more accurate one and that localization is only a matter of analytic convenience.

Chapters 3 and 4 examine the second element in our synthesis, the "apple" of psychotherapy research. Again, we try to do justice to a complex intellectual tradition full of lively controversy. We believe that it is a good thing to know where we have come from as therapists, and that means, among other things, examining the political–monetary influences that have created our field as it is today. The 1970s—when the third edition of the *Diagnostic and Statistical Manual of Mental Disorders*, the first antidepressants, and cognitive-behavioral therapy came together to form an era we will refer to as the *pax medica*—is when psychotherapy grew up. We see that era as just ending, with a bright promise of what the field will look like in its maturity.

The remaining chapters of *Brain-Based Therapy with Adults* bring the apples and oranges together. The neuroscience of memory and emotion and the psychopathological effects of dysregulation are examined in Chapters 5 and 6. We take up evidence-based approaches to specific disorders using this integrated perspective in Chapters 7 through 10. For those involved in the teaching and learning of psychotherapy, we include vignettes based on using the neurodynamic model in supervision.

The acronym BASE—for *b*rain-based, *a*lliance-oriented, *s*ystematic, *e*vidence-based therapy—is used for heuristic purposes. A final chapter provides some tips on helping patients reregulate such neurodynamically important processes as sleep and the mind–body relationship.

Throughout the book we try to do justice to the work of investigators in diverse fields who have created a complex and self-defining body of work in their own disciplines. We have approached this project like detectives, looking for clues to what will enhance your practice with patients. The result is, of course, only one take on the material, and we encourage you to look at the original sources.

CHAPTER 1

How We Change

The average species on Earth lasts for only about four million years, so if you wish to be around for billions of years, you must be as fickle as the atoms that made you. You must be prepared to change everything about yourself—your shape, size color, species affiliation, everything—and to do so repeatedly. . . . So at various periods over the last 3.8 billion years you have abhorred oxygen and then doted on it, grown fins and limbs and jaunty sails, laid eggs, flicked the air with a forked tongue, been sleek, been furry, lived underground, lived in trees, been as big as a deer and as small as a mouse, and a million things more. The tiniest deviation from any of these evolutionary shifts, and you might now be licking algae from cave walls or lolling walruslike on some stony shore or disgorging air through a blowhole in the top of your head before diving sixty feet for a mouthful of delicious sandworms.

—Bill Bryson, *A Brief History of Almost Everything*

As PSYCHOTHERAPISTS, WE think a lot about how people change. Our ideas on the subject shape how we practice our professional arts. In many psychotherapies, there is a moment when the patient looks at us and poses the question directly: "Do you think people can change?" This is usually a way of asking "Do you think I can, and that I will?" Some evidence suggests that the average psychotherapist has more than the usual level of conflict or unhappiness in his or her own family background. Maybe that is what inspires us to try to transform a little of other people's unhappiness into security and contentment and to believe that the answer to the question about can I and will I change is yes.

In our time, three or four relatively independent traditions in science are converging on clinical psychology. By being aware of their intersection,

1

psychotherapists can back up their optimism with solid evidence that people do change and that therapy is effective in helping them do so. Neuroscience, genetics, attachment studies, psychotherapy research, and studies of mindfulness meditation all play a part. In this book we rely on research in neuroscience, psychotherapy research, cognitive and psychodynamic psychology, attachment research, and evidence-based psychotherapeutic practices. The model we present incorporates many assumptions on which psychotherapy has been based for the last 100 years or so—about the importance of the therapeutic alliance and particular techniques with specific disorders. What is relatively new is the emphasis we place on attachment and neuroscience. We argue that a personal and rather mysterious decision by Sigmund Freud separating psychology from biology has had long-lasting and deleterious effects.

Some commentators (Cozolino, 2002) have suggested that psychotherapy could not have survived as a branch of neurology, which is to say that Freud had to cut the umbilical cord uniting the two. The point is well taken. However, Freud's decision also led to a schism in the mental health field, in which psychology has viewed the mind as an entity independent of the brain and biological psychiatry tends to see the brain as if the mind were just a "ghost in the machine." The latter view has been the dominant one in the "Pax Medica Era," which we believe may be coming to an end. In this book, we would like to advance the assumption that the mind and the brain are different manifestations *of a single set of processes*—that mind and experience shape the brain's structure. That is how we change.

NURTURED NATURE

In contemporary neuroscience, the causes of even basic psychological phenomena are often far from simple ones. The genetic contribution to brain functioning is a case in point. Genes commonly are taken as the most deterministic, least environmentally influenced element in our lives—for all intents and purposes as "nature." In fact, this is a serious overstatement, because the gene itself, while influencing behavioral potential, is in turn endlessly shaped by the environment. An obese patient who says "I got the gene for my waist size from my father!" means to say he is not responsible for his eating habits any more than he is for his brown eyes. His alibi needs updating. While genes influence our vulnerability not only to obesity but to various psychological disorders as well, people's *experience* typically determines whether pathogenic genes are expressed and result in an actual disorder.

Every cell in the human body contains the same set of genetic instructions found in the fertilized egg's DNA. What makes one cell become a neuron and another a part of the bones in the hand? To be expressed, the DNA molecule must be opened up so that it can be copied and transmit its genetic information into proteins within the cell. In practice, the cell's DNA is selectively "unpacked," and accordingly, only some genes are expressed. The chemical regulators of the DNA form an *epigenetic* system that determines what role (if any) a particular gene will have. Animal studies have shown that epigenetic factors are affected by environmental influences such as early abuse or neglect by a parent (Higgins, 2008) and in humans, reactions to environmental trauma such as famine can be transmitted from one generation to another.

Genes are an important factor in understanding how we change. Under certain conditions, they constitute a major influence in the development of such psychological disorders as schizophrenia (where estimates of the heritability of this disorder range as high as 80%), autism, obsessive-compulsive disorder, and social anxiety disorder, among other disturbances. This happens where the individual carries the necessary gene or genes and where the epigenetic system permits the gene to be expressed. The unpacked part of the DNA string is copied, producing a complementary molecule of messenger RNA (mRNA) through a process called *transcription*. The RNA in turn produces proteins in the cell through *translation*. Through transcription and translation, information in an expressed gene becomes the template for the cell's functions. But whether the gene is allowed to express itself is subject to environmental influences.

Like Escher's famous lithograph of a hand drawing itself, genes and environmental responsiveness are cocreating processes. Minor changes in either the environment or the transcription and translation processes may result in significantly altered functioning. Gene expression is fundamental to synaptic plasticity, the process that allows the brain to remodel itself, to change how it functions in order to adapt to novel or changing conditions (Black, 1998; Kandel, 2000). Recent science suggests an übergenetic, or epigenetic, system that changes in response to environmental exposure (e.g., to famine) and has the power to switch the expression of specific genes on or off. Although the percentage varies widely depending on the precise gene, roughly speaking, genes control about 50 percent of the variance in most traits. People who carry a gene that influences the trait of shyness are much more likely to feel shy and behave accordingly than people who lack this predisposition *if* their shy gene gets expressed. Inevitably the gene's expression will be moderated by environmental influences. A child with a tendency to be shy may learn to modulate her shyness through the support and encouragement of her parents (Kagan, 1998); and adults can modify such a disposition through many different kinds of experiences, including therapy. A person with a family history of affective disorders, who carries a gene that predisposes him to psychopathology, may never develop depression or bipolar disorder and can enjoy a reasonably happy life. A child growing up in an extended and encompassing family of shy people who struggle with a high incidence of major depression, however, will be challenged on both the nature and nurture fronts.

Early studies of heredity assumed that siblings reared in the same families are exposed to highly similar environments and that differences between siblings must be caused by genetic variation. More recent research shows that things are not that simple. Dunn and McGuire (1994) compared family environments and noted unique factors that often exerted significant influence on development, such as different friends and school experiences. Siblings, even identical twins, do not inhabit the same environments, and even shared experiences may be interpreted quite differently, which in turn may prompt the influential people in their environment—including their parents—to interact with them differently than with their siblings (Pike & Plomin, 1996).

Each step of the way, genetics and experience mutually influence development. Genes set the range of possible developmental paths; experience stimulates the individual to react in ways that are based on learning; and learning changes the likelihood of genetic expression (Guzowski et al., 2001). For example, the manner in which parents respond to their child's temperament produces feedback that results in shaping the growth, interconnections, and massive "pruning" (or programmed cell death) of the child's neurons. When a newborn baby first emerges from his mother's womb, he's likely to have twice as many neurons as the obstetrician or midwife assisting in the delivery. Over the course of childhood and through adolescence, these excess neurons die off based in part on how often they are stimulated by the external environment and other neurons. In this way, interplay between a child and parent changes the child's behavior and the influence of gene expression. We explore the interactions and effects of temperament and attachment in this book's companion volume, *Brain-Based Therapy with Children and Adolescents*.

Gene expression, experience, mental activity, and behavior are intertwined and form a transactional set of processes (Rutter et al., 1997). The growth of new synapses (and even new neurons) gives us the capacity to nurture nature—because the functional relationships between neurons play such an important role in determining who we are and how we behave (LeDoux, 2002). In other chapters we explore some of the subtle ways that nature and nurture interplay to produce the kinds of problems found in the panoply of mental disorders cited in the fourth edition of the *Diagnostic and Statistical Manual of Mental Disorders*. For the time being, let us turn to an examination of how these interactions between genes and environmental "triggers" produced the human brain in the first place.

EVOLUTIONARY BACKGROUND

Our genes are the historical record of minute changes in the DNA of our evolutionary ancestors passed down from one generation to another. Comparative studies of human and nonhuman genomes suggest that we share an enormous amount of this heritage with other mammals and almost all of it with the nonhuman primates. Human DNA is 96% identical to the DNA of chimpanzees (Lovgren, 2005). In the awesome timeline of evolutionary history, *Homo sapiens* arrived only recently. Although the common ancestors of humans, the great apes and the Old World monkeys, are believed to have made their first appearance 63 million years ago (and were still around as recently as 13 million years ago), humans have been on the scene for a small fraction of that time. *Homo sapiens idaltu*, dating from about 160,000 years ago, is the oldest known anatomically modern human.

According to one model (known as the Lake Toba Catastrophe theory), between 50,000 and 70,000 years ago a super-volcanic event reduced the world's human population to as few as 1,000 breeding pairs (Ambrose, 2001). With only a few thousand individuals surviving, humans became an endangered species on the brink of extinction. This radical restriction of the breeding population may be why human DNA is remarkably homogenous across different settings. Tumultuous environmental change would have favored genetic shifts in our ancestors' capacities for rapid learning and adaptation. The capacity for rapid adaptation to changing conditions—the capacity for flexible change—was privileged.

Even before the Lake Toba volcanic event, our ancestors' brains had begun to expand, especially the prefrontal cortex. The growth of the neocortex and associated structural and functional changes in the subcortical brain centers took place relatively slowly from about 400,000 years ago until about the time of the Lake Toba events. From 50,000 years ago onward, the record of fossils and cultural artifacts shows startlingly rapid change, suggesting either a dramatic genetic shift or the cumulative effects of interactions between genetically mediated brain potential and an environment in which human culture in itself started to play a dominant role in human evolution. Our ancestors relatively suddenly began producing ever more refined human artifacts, beyond the early fashioning of stone tools. After 50,000 years ago, there is evidence that our progenitors began burying their dead, making animal hides into clothing, and painting symbolic art on the walls of their dwellings. The essential capacities of the modern human brain rather suddenly came on line for creatures confronting massive environmental change.

Paleoanthropologists believe this "great leap forward" could only have come about as a result of changes in the neural architecture underlying our ancestors' behavior and capacity for internalized thought in the human neocortex. Of all animal species, humans have the largest prefrontal cortex as a proportion of total brain volume. About 20% of the human brain is comprised of *frontal lobes*; by contrast, frontal lobes comprise about 3.5% of feline brain volume. The most recent addition to our evolutionary development, the frontal lobes are also the last to mature in individual humans, with development not complete until sometime in the third decade of life. The *prefrontal cortex* (at the forefront of the frontal lobes) gives us many of our most complex human cognitive, behavioral, and emotional capacities. It endows us, for example, with the ability to develop and act on a moral system (Dolan, 1999). The prefrontal cortex (PFC) lets us set aside our own agendas and reflect on the needs of others. It is associated with our subjective experience of empathy. When the PFC is damaged, people are likely to engage in behaviors that are antisocial and impulsive or not engage in purposeful behavior at all. At a time when human populations were dispersing out of Africa, a larger PFC constituted an indispensable asset in enhancing the richness of social bonds and attachment.

Underneath the cortex there were other changes in the brains of our immediate ancestors. "Lower brain" centers, such as the limbic areas and the cerebellum, changed to support the growth of the human behavioral and emotional repertoire. The cerebellum, an area specialized for motor control in other mammals, also performs sophisticated organizing functions in the human brain, working in tandem with frontal lobes (Grigsby & Stevens, 2000).

The motor area of the brain adjacent to the tongue and lips in the left frontal lobe (now called Broca's area) coevolved with the ability to produce speech (Fuster, 1997), enriching social relationships and internal cognitive processes. Like a new tool, speech changed what the brain could do, and, as we later demonstrate, heightened brain activity leads to further changes in neural architecture.

As our ancestors were subjected to radical new pressures from sudden climate change and as genetic shifts made new behaviors possible, the advantages of social life became even more pronounced for humans. The human brain has a vested interest in the expression of our genetic endowment for empathy, the human ability to "feel" what others are thinking and feeling, because mindsight is prerequisite to the brain's very existence. Human infants have very large heads and are born with brains that require, as it were, much home assembly. To survive, the brain must have relationships with caring, attentive, and deliberate caregivers who see the needs of their young as more important than their own. Loving, appreciating the development of those we love, and resolving interpersonal problems with those we are closest to has survival value for the brain. Human evolution has favored the development of these qualities over almost all others, because the survival of the brain itself depends on them.

John Bowlby (1969) applied this evolutionary perspective to observations of infants and children with their caregivers. Looking at the human infant as a young creature whose world is, for all intents and purposes, the maternal environment, Bowlby showed that newborns adapt out of Darwinian necessity to their mothers' personality and circumstances. The infant's capacity for creating and using relationships is carried in the brain's genetic makeup. Within minutes of birth, infants show a preference for gazing at the human face and can imitate facial expressions such as opening the mouth and sticking out the tongue (Meltzoff & Moore, 1998). The infant's hand grasps when something (such as another hand) is placed in its palm. Replete with clever neurodynamic mechanisms for intuiting the mental state of those around us, we are born to be shaped in the context of relationships. The cold evolutionary rationale for this phenomenon may well be that our ancestors faced catastrophic environmental change. Those endowed with a brain that could change rapidly, learn quickly, and maximize the advantages of social networking survived.

The ability to decipher subtle social cues is a contribution of the expanded PFC. The *orbitofrontal cortex* (OFC)—that part of the prefrontal lobes that lies directly above and behind the eyes—enhances the human capacity for social appraisal, allowing us to give complex social interactions an emotional value and think over the likely consequences of risky social moves before we act. Language lets us tell someone who was not there what we witnessed or what we *heard* from someone else about what *he or she* witnessed, vastly expanding the generalizability of individual experience. Together these faculties let us learn from other people's stories as well as our own.

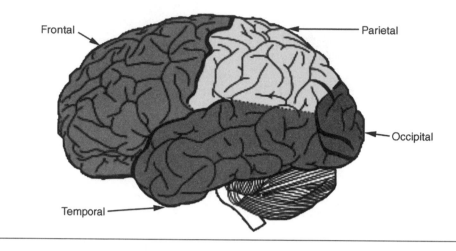

Figure 1.1 Lobes of the Human Brain

Astonishingly, the brain embodies within it the power to be *changed* by these stories, and this may be the human brain's most valuable legacy. Elsewhere in this book we return to the discussion about the interplay of genes and evolutionary history and the difference that the frontal lobes have made in human history. Affect regulation, decision making, and attention are topics of enormous relevance to psychotherapy. But before launching into a more detailed account of what contemporary neuroscience has to tell us as psychotherapists about the brain, let us consider why we *need* to have this discussion at all. How did psychology and brain sciences become estranged in the first place?

REDISCOVERY OF THE BRAIN

Awareness of the astonishing adventure of our evolutionary past was lost to humanity until the late nineteenth century, when Charles Darwin's *Descent of Man, and Selection in Relation to Sex* (1871) exhumed it. Darwin's careful cataloging of how species such as the finches of the Galapagos adapted to food supplies and other environmental variables laid the foundation for our understanding of gene–environmental interactions in biological systems—a model that is at the heart of modern neuroscience. Similarly, his later theory that man and the nonhuman primates descended from common stock opened new fields of inquiry into our history as a species and the selective advantages bestowed by the human brain.

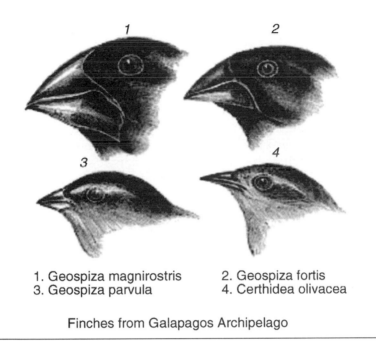

1. Geospiza magnirostris   2. Geospiza fortis
3. Geospiza parvula   4. Certhidea olivacea

Finches from Galapagos Archipelago

Figure 1.2 Environmental Selection of Biological Fitness

Darwin's insights permeate modern biological thought, neuroscience included. His most enduring contribution is the idea that the environment and existing diverse life forms interact to favor the most "fit." As he put it in *On the Origin Species:*

> As many more individuals of each species are born than can possibly survive; and as, consequently, there is a frequently recurring struggle for existence, it follows that any being, if it vary however slightly in any manner profitable to itself, under the complex and sometimes varying conditions of life, will have a better chance of surviving, and thus be *naturally selected.* From the strong principle of inheritance, any selected variety will tend to propagate its new and modified form. (Darwin, 1859, p. 5)

Darwin's theory is sometimes referred to as *selectionism,* and the neuroscientific version of this perspective as "neural Darwinism" (Edelman, 1987). Selectionists see the individual brain as a kind of "second nature" in which each neuron is subjected to the test of fitness all across the course of development (Edelman, 2006). Operating on neurons and the neurodynamic networks that support thinking and feeling, it is natural selection that ultimately drives enduring psychological change.

EARLY PSYCHOANALYSIS

Sigmund Freud was a younger contemporary of Darwin's. A neurologist by training, he moved from bench work in the laboratory to clinical work with patients with complex somatic symptoms. In 1885, Freud left Vienna for Paris to study with the most renowned neurologist of his day, the great Jean-Martin Charcot, who was using hypnosis to treat hysteria. Compared to the abiding popular view that hysterical phenomena were products of the uterus's wanderings inside the body, Charcot's ideas about the treatment of this disorder were revolutionary. He demonstrated that hysterical symptoms were products of "reminiscences" and that even very ill patients could get better through the power of belief in a cure. Charcot's effect on the 29-year-old Freud was electric. When he returned to Vienna, Freud and his mentor, Joseph Breuer, developed a method for treating hysteria that became known as the talking cure.

Victorian hysterical phenomena ran the gamut from simple conversion paralysis to the appearance of subcutaneous markings on the patient's skin that looked like symbols or words. Unlike their colleagues, who presumed these symptoms were the result of malingering or fakery, Breuer and Freud developed a theory that the genesis of hysteria lay in repressed memories of childhood. By bringing these early experiences into awareness via hypnosis, Breuer and Freud believed they could release repressed psychic energy and bring about a cure. One of Breuer's patients, Bertha Pappenheim (or "Anna O."), called the technique "chimney sweeping" and lovingly attributed unusual powers to her physician (Mitchell & Black, 1995). Breuer modestly said that he deserved no credit for his patient's recovery; the patient had to cure herself. In terms of the later history of psychotherapy, Breuer's idea was prescient; but Freud believed that Breuer had missed a central element in psychoanalysis by denying the reality of his patient's transferential feelings.

Freud continued to do both detailed neurological studies and clinical work. Between 1877 and 1900, he published more than 100 scientific pieces on neurology and neuroscience, only seven of which have appeared in English (Solms & Saling, 1990). Building on his studies of the nervous system of crayfish, nineteenth-century neuroscience, and his own clinical experience with hysterics, in 1895 Freud developed what he called the "Project for a Scientific Psychology" (1895/1958). The project set no less a goal than linking the dawning understanding of how the brain functions with Freud's emerging observations about psychopathology. Santiago Cajal and Heinrich Waldeyer had recently dubbed nerve cells "neurons," and Freud added the very important point that the "contact barriers" between these cells make mental activities possible (Solms & Saling, 1990). A decade later, Sir Charles Scott Sherrington gave these contact barriers the name *synapses* (Kusurkar, 2004).

Despite these remarkable insights, Freud became discouraged with brain science. His appetite for clinical work and theorizing about the greater meaning of psychological phenomena supplanted his goal of a scientific psychology grounded in brain science. The ambitious "Project" fell by the wayside and was never published in his lifetime (Solms & Saling, 1990); yet for the rest of his career Freud seemed to harbor regrets about the decision. In his final work on psychoanalytic theory, published at the end of his life, he said:

> The future may teach us to exercise a direct influence by means of particular chemical substances on the amounts of energy and their distribution on the mental apparatus. (Freud, 1895/1958)

From brain science, Freud gravitated toward a case study method based on mutual introspection. This decision was to have profound effects on the mental health sciences for almost a century afterward.

While Breuer and Freud were elaborating their psychical theories, Darwinian views were taking hold in more general scientific circles, and the two views had much in common. Like psychoanalysts, Darwin and his party took the position that we are as much a product of the drive to mate and survive as are other living creatures. Freud's maturing view of human nature was as dark as Darwin's view of animal life—under the starched petticoats of Victorian Europe, mankind, no less than the naked mole rat, was driven by an instinctual need for sexual success. No doubt Freud would have agreed with Darwin's observation that despite our "exalted" and "noble" qualities, "man still bears in his bodily frame the indelible stamp of his lowly origin" (Darwin, 1871, p. 405). In the psychoanalytic model, change arises from individuals' capacities to look at themselves, "lowly" qualities and all. With the help of the relationship with the analyst, successful analysands temper the infantile aspects of their harsh superego judgments about themselves, and go on to live gratifying, less conflicted lives as adults.

Whatever one makes of the specifics of classical psychoanalytic theory, Freud doubtless introduced or synthesized some spectacularly important neurodynamic ideas: that mental life is a product of cellular activity; that nerve cells communicate across the synapses that separate them through a special kind of biological energy; that mental life is a compromise wrought from the interaction of modules in the mind with conflicting agendas and cognitive strategies; that fundamentally important parts of our mental life never attain consciousness; and that our minds, shaped by early relationships, can nevertheless change as a result of a special kind of conversation. That we can change as a product of a relationship is, of all Freud's many contributions, perhaps his most enduringly important one for our profession.

Freud is, if not the father then at least the elderly uncle of modern neurodynamic therapy. In the century since his most important contributions, we have learned more about the brain than was known in all of human history up to that time. For all his provocations of Victorian pretensions to virtue, Freud, more than Darwin, envisioned a brain that was quite different from that of other mammals. Modern neuroscience only partially shares Freud's conception of human consciousness. From the modern perspective, Freud underestimated both the extent of our unconsciousness and how profoundly tied we are to our evolutionary history. Because he had no knowledge of the relationship between the cortex and the subcortical brain, and the architecture of fear in particular, he tended to misunderstand why we are such an anxious species. His respect for our capacity to make conscious what was unconscious led Freud to place undue confidence in introspection and insight as a sufficient basis for therapeutic change. Most impactfully, however, Freud's separation of psychology from its roots in biology had lasting detrimental effects. It helped create a schism in the mental health professions, with psychologists concerned only with the mind, neurologists only with the brain, and psychiatrists unsure (at least until the 1970s) where they belonged in this dualistic perspective. Early in the twentieth century, other psychologists called psychoanalysis to account for some of these shortcomings.

BEHAVIORISM

By the 1920s, behaviorism began redressing the excesses of introspection as a method of scientific inquiry and the fanciful speculations of those who offered up the products of introspection as universal truths. Behaviorists held that psychology must avoid hypothetical constructs in studying human experience and must instead hold fast to empirical observations of what was visible and measureable. We can't see thoughts and feelings; all we can see is what we *do*; thus behavior is the proper subject for science. Behaviorism was attractive to many academics and therapists because of its scientific rigor, empirically based change strategies, and replicable findings (Watson, 1919).

Some early behaviorists asserted that if they had control of all the contingencies in a learning situation, they could change almost any desired behavior or personality characteristic (Watson, 1930). Compared to the dark picture of a human nature at the mercy of instincts and the unconscious, behaviorism's stance seems one of cheerful environmentalism. By focusing on the apparently mundane phenomena of conditioned reflexes and learning, the behaviorist B. F. Skinner taught pigeons Ping-Pong and rats to play basketball. Behaviorists wasted no time speculating on what the rodents were feeling or thinking while they waited for reinforcement. They got things done. One of behaviorism's founders, John B.Watson, was so successful at applying the technology to people that after leaving a successful career in academia, he went to work in advertising, where he helped condition several generations of Amer icans to associate sophistication and sexual success with smoking cigarettes.

COGNITIVE PSYCHOLOGY

An effective change strategy, behaviorism's insistence on dealing with the observable products of psychological life puts vital parts of the brain—and the mental experience associated with them—outside its sphere of study. Cognitive psychologists, like the behaviorists, rejected Freud's reliance on introspection, and for the same reason: it was too unreliable. However, in contrast to the classical behaviorists, who tended to regard the skull as a black box or as a stimulus-response machine, cognitivists were interested in internal mental states and were clever in designing experiments to elucidate them.

Although its roots go back to the great European gestalt psychologists Max Wertheimer, Wolfgang Kohler, and Kurt Kofka, the term *cognitive psychology* first appeared in the title of a 1967 book by Ulrich Neisser. Neisser characterized people as dynamic information-processing systems and described mental operations in computational terms. Computational models envision the mind as an information processor, and symbols, such as words, as by-products of neurodynamic patterns that contain information and create affect (Pinker, 1997). Perception, memory, decision making, and psycholinguistics are primary topics of interest. Language in particular was a kind of Trojan horse that effectively smuggled "the self" inside the laboratories of cognitive psychologists. Looking at language reintroduced a vital part of the subjective mental life that had been until then the province of psychologists championing introspection.

In the late 1980s, cognitive researchers and theorists began to address the existence of "hidden units" in human cognition. As the term implies, hidden units are aspects of the cognitive process that are not available to consciousness. Their "discovery" reestablished unconscious mental process as a topic of interest, but on different terms from those set by Freud. From a cognitive perspective, nonconscious processing is a matter of necessity. The task of processing sensory and perceptual stimuli is so vast that it proceeds more efficiently if we do not pay attention to it. Consciousness would add nothing to the final product, while nonconsiousness conserves conscious resources needed for executive functions such as decision making and for working memory.

The father of cognitive-developmental psychology, Jean Piaget, seems to have assumed the existence of an unconscious all along. His "assimilative processes" can be conscious or unconscious, or somewhere in between on a spectrum of awareness. But for many American cognitive scientists, this "cognitive unconsciousness" opened a seemingly new domain of study (Kihlstrom, 1987). Psychological laboratories documented the multitude of perceptions, decisions, and behaviors that occur outside of conscious awareness. Studies showed that familiar input is associated with pleasurable affect, while unfamiliar sensory stimuli frequently are experienced as less pleasing or even unpleasant. Other research showed that where there is dissonance between an old perceptual or cognitive construct and new experience, there is a drive to reduce it (Wexler, 2006; Zajonc, 1968). In neither instance is the subject's bias a matter of conscious choice; it is simply part of how the mind processes the data. The first defense against dissonance is avoidance. Thus, we gravitate toward what is familiar and when we cannot avoid dissonance, we move to reconcile the differences by favoring what we already know. If the new information is not yet overwhelming and consistent, we tend to discredit, deny, reinterpret, or even forget it. Generally, we look for agreement with our long-standing beliefs and perceptions.

Many behaviors (and the cognitive protocols that make them possible) simply run on autopilot. We can make ourselves aware of the behaviors and perhaps some part of the protocols, but we do not need to. Driving down Interstate 80 talking to our spouse, we make decisions about how fast to go, what lane we want to be in, and whether the car in the next lane may try to merge, all the while considering and responding to our spouse's complaints about our driving. This is an example of a kind of nonconscious functioning that can be brought to consciousness readily. If the driver of the tractor-trailer ahead of us unexpectedly hits his brakes, we are jarred out of the discussion with our partner and compelled to consider what we must do to keep ourselves intact. Should we veer off the road? Are there cars to either side of us? Is the driver behind us aware of what's happening? Other mental processes can never become conscious—for example, how we maintain an upright posture while walking, how we chew and swallow our food, or how we coordinate the several neural systems involved in uttering a word and how we put words together to make a grammatically correct and properly pronounced sentence. One of the reasons it is exhausting for nonnative speakers to speak a foreign language is that they have to think about things native speakers do nonconsciously when speaking their own tongue.

BRAIN-BASED THERAPY

Darwinism, psychoanalysis, behaviorism, cognitive science: each generates its own theory about how people change. Darwin's perspective on how we change may be the most durable of the four we have examined. But few clinicians think of themselves as looking at a microcosm of natural selection sitting in the chair opposite them. Of the purely psychological approaches, each began by taking a stance that was provocatively innovative and at odds with prevailing psychological theory. Psychoanalysts emphasized unconscious process, behaviorists focused on conditioned learning, and cognitive psychologists concerned themselves with conscious and nonconscious thought. Each school, over time, has had to move back toward the center—psychoanalysis acknowledging its subjectivity, behaviorists accepting the importance of an internal mental life, and cognitive science coming to terms with the fact that thought is closely intertwined with emotion.

In the 1950s, in what must at the time have seemed a development unrelated to the lofty concerns of the three dominant theoretical schools, researchers began to explore the question of how one specific change process—psychotherapy—worked. Surprisingly, they found common factors underlying therapies conducted on very different theoretical principles, factors that pointed to principles of change that were more important than the surface differences between antagonistic schools of practice (Lambert & Barley, 2002). Similarly, psychologists such as Piaget and Mary Ainsworth (1969) highlighted important commonalities in the cognitive and emotional development of children. The work of these psychologists laid the cornerstone for a new consensus in approaching clinical work with our patients.

Most recently, neuroscience has started to exert a unifying influence on theories about how we change. It might occur to a neuroscience graduate student these days that the three dominant psychological schools of the last half of the twentieth century all made the same kind of error: each looked at a circumscribed aspect of the brain-mind and denigrated the significance of the remainder, mistaking a part for the whole. A contemporary doctoral student would understand that in complex systems such as the brain, the functional transactions *between* parts are more important than the parts themselves in determining what happens. Moreover, it might strike the young neuroscientist as testimony to the enduring influence of Freud over our field that psychotherapists seemed to stop thinking about the brain after 1895 and did not pay much attention to it for the next 100 years. Now we are back to being able to think in an integrated way about what the brain and the mind have to do with each other.

As the model of embodied mind has emerged, integration across disciplines has acquired momentum. Modern cognitive science has converged with behaviorism to create *cognitive behavioral therapy*, and with neuroscience to produce *cognitive neuroscience*. *Neurodynamics* is a hot topic in psychoanalytic training centers. After decades of cacophony, there is suddenly the possibly of harmonizing major theories. A new perspective, *affective neuroscience*, places the roots of emotional experience in the brain at the center of this synthesis (Panksepp, 1998). Similar approaches focusing on the *sociophysiology* of the doctor–patient relationship (Adler, 2002; Gardiner, 1997), and the *social neuroscience* (Adolphs, 2003) of development have also emerged. An entire recent issue of the journal *Archives of General Psychiatry* (2006) was devoted to the effect of psychotherapy on the brain. And according to neuropsychiatrist Nancy Andreason:

> We can change who and what we are by what we see, hear, say, and do. It is important to choose the right activities for our brain to be well trained. . . . [B]rain plasticity explains how and why psychiatric treatments that are not "biological," the various types of psychotherapy, can be effective for relieving the symptoms of illnesses such as depression or anxiety. These treatments, which we tend to think of in the false polarity between physical and psychological (or brain and mind), help people reframe their emotional and cognitive responses and approaches. This reframing can only occur, however, as a consequence of biological processes in the brain—a form of activity-dependent learning. (2001, p. 50)

In a happy coincidence (and perhaps more than that, a sign of a sea change in the mental health professions), advances in imaging technology now allow us to *see* the effects of psychotherapy on the brains of depressed patients before and after treatment (Goldapple et al., 2004). These images of the effects of psychological treatment indicate that psychotherapy and antidepressant therapy work in different and complementary ways to help the patient. Evidence that talk therapy results in measurable neurodynamic change in the brain has the potential for creating a different way of diagnosing psychological distress and building bridges between psychology and the more biologically oriented disciplines, almost a century after Freud inadvertently severed the two. These images suggest a new perspective on the question "how do people change?" They suggest we have inherited the capacity to do so. They demonstrate that we cannot alter the pattern of our thoughts and feelings without changing the brain, and our brains are exquisitely adapted to changing in response to the attuned and compassionate interest of another human being.

CHAPTER 2

Neuroscience: The Fantastic Voyage

"Ninety percent of the game is mental, the other half is physical."

—Yogi Berra

NEUROSCIENCE SEEMS TO be everywhere these days—on CNN, in Hollywood movies, on the back of your favorite magazine. Advertisers have embraced what some call *neuromarketing*, and *neuroeconomics* is now an emerging field. An ad for insurance on the back of *Newsweek* asks: "Why do most 16-year-olds drive like they're *missing a part of their brain*? Because they are." The ad goes on to give wary parents and older drivers an oversimplified but more or less accurate account of adolescent brain development: "It's because their brain hasn't finished developing. The underdeveloped area is called the dorsal lateral prefrontal cortex."

The brain drives (and is driven by) the evolutionary history of our species, not to mention our personal histories. Because of the size and relative immaturity of the human brain, humans require a longer period of dependency and caretaking than do other species. It can be argued that not only childhood but the romantic love that leads us to bond as pairs are dictated by the brain's unique features and manufacturing requirements. It behooves us to know as much about its workings as possible; and in this chapter, we provide a sort of basic owner's manual for "brain-based" therapists.

THE SOCIAL NEURON

The cerebral cortex is composed of one hundred billion cells called *neurons* and many more cells known as *glia*. Although we are only beginning to understand the importance of glial cells, neurons have been studied for more than 100 years and have revealed many of their secrets. Neurons consist of a cell body (or *soma*) in which are found a nucleus (containing genomic DNA and organelles related to its functioning) and other *cytoplasmic* cellular subcomponents outside the nucleus. Extending from this cell body are two types of extensions, *dendrites* and *axons*. Dendrites (from the Greek dendrone, or "tree") are branched projections of a neuron that act to conduct the electrical impulses received from other neurons. An axon (or nerve fiber) is a long, slender projection of a neuron that conducts impulses away from the neuron's cell body.

If any cell can be said to have a social life, it is the neuron. Neurons always come in groups, requiring the stimulation and interaction of myriad colleagues to survive. In the human brain, the average neuron forms connections with as many as 10,000 other neurons in large, widely distributed networks. Neural cells connect with one another at the gaps, or *synapses*, between them. Although their membranes do make physical contact with one another, the real communication between cells (as the young Freud first observed) occurs *across* these microscopic gaps. The

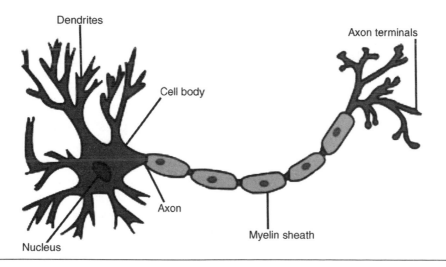

Figure 2.1   A Neuron with Cell Body, Axons, and Dendrites *Source:* LifeART image © Wolters Kluwer Health, Inc. Lippincott Williams & Wilkins. All rights reserved.

presynaptic neuron is the cell on the giving end of a transmission, and the *postsynaptic* neuron is the receiving cell.

As early as the 1800s, some scientists held the idea that neurons generated tiny amounts of electrical current. Subsequently it was observed that neurons generate this current through chemically induced changes in electrical potential. Changes in the distribution of positively and negatively charged ions (e.g., sodium, potassium, and chlorine) create electrical polarities between the inside of the cell and the extracellular environment. This differential puts the neuron's internal environment in an unstable equilibrium relative to the environment outside the cell, creating a kind of edginess, both electrically and chemically. The natural tendency of all chemical systems is to seek equilibrium, and neurons are no exception.

When a neuron receives *excitatory* stimulation from other neurons, it becomes *depolarized*, somewhat reducing the cell's negative electrical potential. Conversely, *inhibitory* stimulation received from other neurons tends to *hyperpolarize* the cell, increasing its negative potential. When the total input over a few milliseconds is sufficient to depolarize the neuron to a threshold level, the neuron *fires*. At this point, electrical and chemical changes cascade along the axon from the cell body. Axons are efficient conductors, and the cell's electrical depolarization races along them like fire following a trail of gasoline only infinitely faster. When the nerve impulse reaches the ends of the axon (the *terminal boutons*), it stimulates the release of a relatively fixed amount of a chemical neurotransmitter into the synapse. The transmitter substance crosses the synaptic gap (or cleft), binding transiently to receptors on the postsynaptic neuron and subsequently changing the electrical potential of the postsynaptic neuron's membrane. Such chain reactions between individual cells result in the construction of enormous neuronal networks (or "neural nets"). This is how neurons talk to each other.

Neurons typically form synapses with thousands of their colleagues, receiving and sending action potentials. After firing, there is a very brief refractory period during which no nerve impulse is possible because of the active transport of ions back across the cell membrane, restoring the "resting" equilibrium. Some neurons excite their colleagues' depolarization while other neurons inhibit them. In still other cases, substances released from a presynaptic neuron modulate the activity of downstream cells, rather than producing or inhibiting an action potential per se.

The average neuron in the cerebral cortex receives stimulation from between 1,000 and 10,000 other neurons and passes this on to similar numbers of colleagues. In a cubic meter of cortex, the density of synapses is perhaps 800 million to 1 billion *per cubic millimeter* (Abeles, 1991). A cortical neuron receives input from about 100 neurons every millisecond; on average,

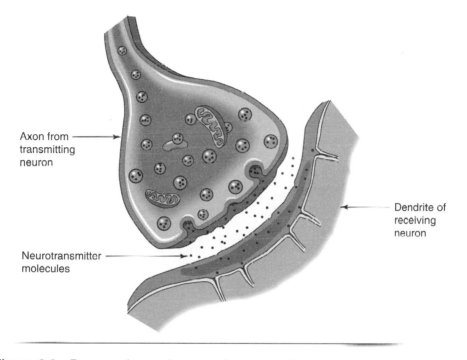

Axon from transmitting neuron

Dendrite of receiving neuron

Neurotransmitter molecules

Figure 2.2   Presynaptic membrane and postsynaptic receptors during transmission
Source: LifeART image © Wolters Kluwer Health, Inc. Lippincott Williams & Wilkins. All rights reserved.

if 25 additional excitatory inputs are received within a millisecond, it will fire. Cortical neurons spontaneously generate an average of about five action potentials per second, and they may discharge up to 100 times per second if receiving strong stimulation. Across the entire central nervous system, the appropriate activity of neural networks is dependent on a careful balance between inhibitory and excitatory neuronal behavior. A swing in this balance to a state far from equilibrium may lead the system into various dysfunctional states, with potentially profound psychological consequences, such as seizure or stupor (Grigsby & Stevens, 2000).

The research of Walter Freeman on the olfactory system (Freeman, W. I. 1987, 1992) suggests that both active and inactive neurons contribute to an overall pattern that conveys meaningful information. As Grigsby and Stevens (2000) describe it: "It is as though the brain has a resting 'hum' of background chaotic electrical activity, *out of which emerges highly organized, synchronized neural activity* yielding adaptive response to shifting conditions" (p. 134; emphasis added). Before the organized activity, there is noisy chaos; suddenly things quiet down and a coordinated event is occurring between neural modules. There is a constant background of spontaneous activity. If we could hear it, it might sound like the buzz of a capacity crowd at Fenway Park just before the first pitch—except that the number of neurons potentially making "noise" is in the tens of billions, somewhat in excess of Fenway's capacity.

Neuroscientists view the brain as a self-organizing system that is malleable, plastic. The brain continually pulls itself up by the bootstraps, becoming more organized and patterned over time. The firing of individual neurons doesn't mean much; it is the habit they have of organizing themselves into networks of thousands and even millions of cells that produces the more interesting psychological phenomena. *The more often the neural network organizes an event such as a memory, the more likely it is that this event will occur again, and when it does reoccur, it will take less energy to make it happen.* It is impossible to overstate the significance of this simple idea, for it constitutes the basis for such vital psychological functions as memory and for the development of those complex processes often referred to as psychic structure, ego, habit, and character. Fathered by the pioneering Canadian psychologist Donald Hebb, this concept is called *Hebbian learning.* As he hypothesized:

> [T]he persistence or repetition of a reverberatory activity (or "trace") tends to induce lasting cellular changes that add to its stability. The assumption can be precisely stated as follows: when an axon of cell A is near enough to excite a cell B and repeatedly or persistently takes part in firing it, some growth process or metabolic change takes place in one or both cells such that A's efficiency, as one of the cells firing B, is increased. (1949, p. 62)

Figuratively speaking, *neurons that fire together wire together.* Once the brain (or, more specifically, a network of neurons) does something, it is statistically more likely to do it again. Experience changes the probability of activating a given neural network by increasing or decreasing the strength of the synaptic ties among the individual neurons that comprise the network. Learning is based on this phenomenon of one event altering the probability of the event occurring again. This concept is fundamental to modern neuroscience. It plays a part in the brain's signal ability, *neuroplasticity,* the capacity to change itself. It is a concept we will return to at the end of this chapter.

NEUROCHEMICAL ORCHESTRA

For the last 40 years, biological psychiatry has focused on the one-factor model of "chemical imbalance" as an explanation for the psychopathology of some of the major psychiatric disorders. We are ready—actually overdue—for a broadened perspective. LeDoux (2002) has proposed that the one-factor model, encapsulated by the phrase "No twisted thought without a twisted molecule," be replaced by the concept that *synaptic changes underlie mental illness.* The old model involves the assumption that specific neurotransmitters affect the regulation of complex psychological functions, such as mood. In particular, a class of neurotransmitters called *monoamines* (which includes serotonin) is believed to affect cognitive and emotional functioning.

TRANSMITTERS AND RECEPTORS

For each specific neurotransmitter, there may be several different special-ized receptors on cells in a neurodynamic subsystem. There are two main categories of receptors, which have been described as "the faster and smaller," and "the slower and more complex." The faster and smaller recep-tors are ion-channel receptors. They include the glutamate and Gamma-aminobutyric acid (GABA) receptors. They are *fast* because they are asso-ciated with the ease with which charged ions are able to pass through the neuron membrane. GABA is the major *inhibiting* neurotransmitter in the nervous system. Glutamate is the major *excitatory* neurotransmitter. Together they account for much of the neurotransmission in the brain.

Table 2.1 shows the most important neurotransmitters, their functions, and their sites of origins.

Glutamate receptors tend to be located out on the dendrites of the neuron. GABA receptors usually are located closer to (or actually on) the neuron's cell body. Because each neuron receives both glutamate and GABA inputs, the chances of an action potential occurring in the neuron depend on the equilibrium between excitation and inhibition. This balance can tip one way or the other. Monosodium glutamate (MSG), which is used in some foods, can increase the amount of glutamate in the body and eventually cause headaches, ringing in the ears, and other symptoms. GABA-directed inhibition can be increased by taking ben-zodiazepines such as Valium, which bind to a specific site on a GABA receptor.

The "slower and more complex" receptors are called G-protein recep-tors. The *catecholomines*, such as dopamine, bind to these receptors. Upon binding, the shape of the receptor changes slightly, thereby activating an intracellular substance called a G-protein, which in turn leads to the release of a "second messenger" within the neurons. Second messengers help create proteins that regulate the expression of genes within the cells and enzymes that aid in the synthesis of neurotransmitters. Because G-proteins

Table 2.1
Principle Neurotransmitters, Their Targets and Effects

System	Targets	Effects	Important In
Noradrenaline system	Adrenergic receptors in: Spinal cord Thalamus Hypothalamus Striatum Neocortex Cingulate gyrus Hippocampus Amygdala	Excitatory Arousal Reward	Attention Alertness Anxiety Mood Regulation of the sympathetic nervous system
Dopamine system	Receptors at pathway terminations. (There are 5 varieties of this transmitter)	Excitatory *or* inhibiting, depending on receptor Reward Motor Cognition Endocrine	Pleasure Learning Bonding Attachment Attention Motivation
GABA	Receptors close to cell body	Inhibiting	Tranquility Calmness
Glutamate	Receptors on cell's dendrites	Excitatory	Arousal
Serotonin system	Receptors in: Thalamus Striatum Hypothalamus Nucleus acumens Cingulated gyrus Neocortex Amygdala Hippocampus	Increased introversion Mood regulation Body temperature Sleep	Anger Depression Aggression Sense of safety Satiety
Cholinergic system	M1 receptors in the brain stem Basal optic nucleus of Meynert Hippocampus	Learning Short-term memory Arousal Reward	Memory

act on gene expression, it takes time to see their effects and those effects wear off slowly. This may be one reason why antidepressant medications often take as long as four weeks to become effective—the neurotransmitter affects G-protein synthesis, and these proteins influence gene expression.

The neurotransmitter dopamine (DA) is produced in the brain stem and is associated with the reward system and motor activity. Stimulant street drugs, such as cocaine and methamphetamine, potentiate (that is, heighten the effects of) dopamine. Mild doses of these agents energize, but overdoses can lead not only to seizures but to psychosis. In fact, a theoretical association between schizophrenia and DA paralleled the development of a wide variety of drugs that blockade the DA receptor sites. After the initial development of drugs such as chlorpromazine (Thorazine) and haloperidol (Haldol), newer medications such as clozapine (Clozaril) and risperidone (Risperdal) were created as researchers gradually discovered that there were at least five (if not more) different types of DA receptors in two families, one excitatory and the other inhibitory, or modulatory, in effect. Dopamine is associated with activation in many neurodynamic modules and with experiences of reward and motivation. Many dopaminergic systems project (i.e., are connected) to the areas of the brain that are important in attachment behavior and the experience of closeness (Insel & Young, 2001).

Neurotransmitters are not confined to the brain. Approximately 95% of the body's serotonin (5-HT), for example, is processed in the digestive tract. There are several varieties of this neurotransmitter, and numerous different types of 5-HT receptors. Serotonin is produced in the raphe nucleus located in the brain stem and is operative throughout wide regions of the brain. It has been the focus of much attention in recent years because of its role in depression and anxiety. However, the one-factor theory linking serotonin defects to depression leaves out several important elements, including the specialized role of many receptor sites.

A theory that is replacing this one-factor view of depression is one that takes into account the genetic underpinnings of transmitter regulation. According to this view, SSRIs exert their effects by inducing genes inside the neuron to make proteins that become tools of synaptic transmission, such as new receptors. LeDoux (2002 p. 281) states that "a brain on antidepressants can be brought back from a state of isolation from the outside world and encouraged, even forced, to learn. The brain, in other words, *is duped into being plastic* by these treatments" (emphasis added). Many serotonin fibers terminate in a part of the brain called the amygdala, which encodes incoming perceptual data with emotional coloring. Serotonin actually excites the GABA cells—and GABA has an inhibitory effect—increasing the inhibiting influence of these cells on projection neurons. Medications such as fluoxetine (Prozac) may work in the amygdala to reduce the activity of the projection neurons and consequently modulate anxiety. Instead of the simple tune contemplated by the one-factor theory of mood, the complex interactions of different receptors and neurotransmitters (as well as other chemical messengers such as neurohormones) are more like a symphony.

Whereas monoamine neurotransmitters such as dopamine activate *exploratory* behavior, neuropeptides such as endorphins, vasopressin, and oxytocin mediate *bonding* behavior, such as fondling, nursing, and caretaking (Panksepp, 1998). When nonhuman primate parent and offspring come together for grooming or play, endorphin levels increase (Keverne et al., 1989). The neurohormone oxytocin seems both to increase feelings of intimacy and be increased by that psychological state. Oxytocin may broadly mediate positive social interactions and emotions (Uvnäs-Moberg, 1998). Increased physical contact through touch increases the level of oxytocin in the blood, and positive feelings result. Increased oxytocin also activates maternal behavior and decreases irritability and aggressiveness (Bartels & Zeki, 2004; Insel, 2003).

Another neurohormone, vasopressin, also facilitates attachment and pair bonding. Vasopressin levels are correlated with the maintenance of monogamy in several mammalian species (Young et al., 2001). The amygdala, most widely known for its fear-inducing potency, also plays some part in the bonding process. Both oxytocin and vasopressin have numerous binding sites on the amygdala. The neurohormones contribute to inhibiting fear and suppressing the stress-reactive hypothalamic-pituitary-adrenal axis (Carter, 2003).

One more factor in the neurochemistry of attachment are the *endogenous opiates* produced within the body. These natural painkillers are helpful in making the shock of physical injury bearable and in tempering the emotional pain of separation. A small dose of exogenous opium (too small to be sedating) quiets puppies in the throes of protesting separation from their mothers (Lewis, Amini, & Lannon, 2000). There are numerous opiate receptors in the central nucleus of the amygdala (Kalin, Shelton, & Snowdon, 1993). Given the fact that endogenous opiates are associated with bonding and nurturance, opiate addicts may be using the exogenous form of these substances to ameliorate both a deficiency in their internal opiate systems and the legacy of early separation and loss. Studies show that in subjects who abuse cocaine and other drugs, drug craving activates a part of the brain called the anterior cingulate, which is associated with bonding and nurturance (Wexler et al., 2001). Similarly, patients who cut themselves or otherwise inflict pain through self-injurious behaviors may (among other things) be trying to stimulate the release of endogenous opiates. "Chronic self-mutilators provoke the lesser pain in order to trick their nervous systems into numbing the unendurable one" (Lewis, Amini, & Lannon, 2000, p. 95).

When individuals who inflict self-harm are given naltrexone, a drug that blocks the effects of opiates, their self-injurious behavior decreases (van der Kolk, 1987). Conversely, research with rats has shown that morphine reduces maternal behavior (Kalin, Shelton, & Lynn, 1995), perhaps because it blocks the endogenous chemistry of attachment.

MODULES AND NETWORKS

A single neuron, by itself, is at risk. The only function of neurons is to connect and communicate with other neurons and other specialized cells (e.g., muscles and glands). The individual neuron and the thousands of colleagues to which it connects form complex networks of bundled neurons. Transactions with the ever-changing environment sculpt the raw material of the nervous system across the course of development until at one point we have an organ that takes (or produces) pleasure in reading a book, doing gymnastics, or listening to Beethoven's Fifth.

Midway through gestation, a fetus has many more neurons than it will ever need. Over time, and in large part as a result of certain types of experience, neurons that do not form viable, functional connections with others are weeded out. The technical term for this programmed cellular suicide is *apoptosis*. The most efficient neural networks are those that have been subjected to this Darwinian process and survived. Neural networks are enriched and made more efficient—in other words, they *learn*—through a process of forming connections with other neurons. Connections between neural networks are forged by use, in association with the stimulation from other neurons reaching out to them, forming new synaptic junctions. After birth, there is a massive establishment of new synaptic connections between neurons. Modifications of receptor density and sensitivity on both sides of the synapse enhance efficiency.

The brain is a hierarchical system, composed of widely distributed neural networks made up of modular components. Many of these modules are in turn aggregations of still other modular subcomponents, each highly specialized, each making different, specific contributions to neural and psychological functioning (Arbib, Érdi, & Szentágothai, 1998; Eccles, 1984; Gazzaniga & LeDoux, 1978; Globus, 1992; Globus & Scheibel, 1967; Hubel & Wiesel, 1963; Kaas, 1987, 1989; Szentágothai, 1975, 1979, 1980). It is tempting to associate certain areas of the brain with various psychological capacities (e.g., the amygdala as the site of emotional learning, or the orbitofrontal cortex as the "social brain"). Positron Emission Tomography (PET) imaging, with its fascinating multicolored pictures of the brain, and functional magnetic resonance imaging (fMRI), with its video-like documentation of brains

at work, encourage this way of thinking. But conceptualizing brain functioning too concretely in terms of specialized geography misconstrues the
complex relationship between neurodynamic structure and function. The
functional architecture of the central nervous system suggests that each
locale is very much affected by the operations of its neighbors, and by the
larger subsystem of which it is a part. We should try to avoid the error of
the nineteenth-century phrenologists, who drew maps of the brain showing
the precise location of various psychological functions—or at least, not
confuse our map with the territory.

What, exactly, *is* a neural module? Neural modules are more conceptual
than concrete entities. The concept is that these modules are communities
of cells involved in one or more specialized functions. Complex psychological activity typically involves the simultaneous processing of information by numerous modules and the sequential passing along of that
information to other nodes in a widely distributed array. Modules more
central in the hierarchical organization (could we say more *urban* modules?) mediate either a specific function or set of functions, or (in the case of
those in the suburbs or out in the country) subcomponents of such
functions (Grigsby & Stevens, 2000). Although each module operates
somewhat independently, it is also bound into the structural-functional
organization of the brain as whole. Those thinking in terms of the localization hypothesis like to speak of specialized functional regions (such as the
phrenologist's "speech area") or even multiple regions (e.g., Broca's area
and Wernicke's area, both of which are very involved in language). In fact,
psychological functions of any complexity involve a relatively large number of different subcortical and cortical regions throughout the brain.

In 1861, the French physician Pierre Paul Broca met a man who had been
nicknamed "Tan," based on the fact that this was the only syllable he
had had uttered for the previous 21 years. When Tan died, autopsy revealed
damage to an area of the left frontal lobe that was subsequently called
Broca's area. As we've noted, such strong linkages between modules
and specific functions incline us to think of the brain as a series of linked
but semiautonomous processors. The actual relationships are more complex and interdependent. Speech and language involve various relatively
independent psychological processes, such as perception of consonant
sounds, production of consonant sounds, understanding of tense, finding
words for objects and actions, grammar, gesture, inner speech, even fine-
muscle regulation of the tongue (to name only some of the elements
involved). In speech and in many other higher level functions, what is
important is the overall pattern of activity across large groups of neural
networks involved in behavior and learning.

The brain as a whole is organized into dynamic assemblies of networks distributed throughout different regions of the brain, in something like the way a personal computer is connected through a network server to the Internet. Sometimes the connection is active, and sometimes it is not; but when it is "on," the connection makes a huge difference in what the individual computer can do. Network factors can change the function of subsystems and even individual neurons. For example, when a very young individual goes blind, the visual cortex may be reorganized in such a way that it becomes part of the auditory cortex, with a corresponding improvement in the acuity of the individual's sense of sound.

NEURAL NETWORKS

Changes in the synapses between neurons result in changes in the probability that a network will respond to a certain level and type of neural input. The network's sensitivity can vary, and as we noted, so can its efficiency. With more practice, the network becomes more efficient, and less energy is required to activate it. In other words, learning changes the likelihood that someone will engage in a particular psychological activity (whether perceptual, emotional, cognitive, or motor) in the future. The behavior that occurs is an *emergent property* of the specific neural pathways involved and of the constantly changing interactions between the internal and external environment of the organism (Globus, 1992; Grigsby & Osuch, 2007). Even what seems to be a minor change in a person's environment may produce a very different pattern of activity. This is a major reason why people are so responsive to change.

Neuronal development and the formation of networks of neurons proceeds hand in hand with psychological and physical development. Burgeoning neurodynamic organization goes on in the brain of an infant in the first few months of life as a result of interactions with the environment, especially with the external environment's most important feature—the baby's caregivers (Lewis et al., 2000). We intuitively appreciate the critical importance of these early relationships in healthy development—and contemporary imaging studies allow us to see the difference that loving interaction, or the lack of it, makes in the human brain. The sprouting dendrites and axons of young neurons—the organs of its relatedness, as it were—are stimulated on the macrolevel by the emotional quality of the relationships with parents and siblings: the smiles and cooing, the frowns and teasing, the pleasure and pain of having one's needs met or frustrated. As organization proceeds, babies will drink in not only what nutrients they need for survival, but durable lessons about the caring relationship itself and neurodynamic routines for imagining how another person *feels*.

BRIEF TOUR OF THE BRAIN

Networks of neurons behave, for the most part, in statistically predictable ways, performing specific functions in the brain. Yet neurons in almost any network are capable of influencing their colleagues in far-removed regions. In fact, seemingly trivial events in one area of the brain can produce massive changes in the whole system—and in the blink of an eye. Although there are no simple causes for complex psychological functions, it is heuristically valuable to talk about the functions of the most important neurodynamic modules.

SUBCORTICAL PROCESSING

The brainstem houses several important modules. At the lowest level of the brain stem is the *medulla*, which plays an essential role in the regulation of such basic physiologic processes as respiration and heart rate. The vagus nerve (which we will describe later) begins in the medulla. The medulla also carries sensory nerve fibers from the body below to the thalamus and higher centers above, and motor neurons descending from the cortex through the spinal cord to the muscles. At the base of the medulla, fibers to and from the left hemisphere cross over to the right side of the spinal cord (and from there to the periphery), and fibers to and from the right hemisphere make their way to the left side of the cord. Accordingly, many functions on the right side of the body are actually controlled by the left hemisphere of the brain, and vice versa.

The pons and midbrain structures sit on top of the medulla. The pons is involved in relaying sensory information between the cerebrum and cerebellum, controls arousal, regulates respiration, and initiates REM sleep. The midbrain which sits on top is involved in vision, hearing, eye movement, and body movement.

The *thalamus* is a kind of upward extension of the brain stem, split into symmetrical structures in each hemisphere. Its structure and function are quite complex, but in simplified terms, it relays and processes all manner of sensory information, as well as some motor information, between the cortex and subcortical structures. The thalamus is very important in most theories of how the brain produces consciousness (Edelman, 2006). Like the pons below, the thalamus is involved in sleep, wakefulness, and arousal generally. Some strokes affecting the thalamus may cause Déjerine-Roussy syndrome. Also called thalamic pain syndrome, it involves episodes of severe burning pain.

Here we might also mention the *cerebellum*, long thought to be involved solely in motor functioning. Sure enough, cerebellar injury or degeneration often leads to uncoordination and unsteadiness (*ataxia*), tremor associated with movement (*action tremor*), and abnormalities of muscle tone. However, more recently it has been found that lesions of certain areas of the cerebellum can affect high-level cognition as well, including the executive cognitive functions and the crucial capacity to learn through classical conditioning. If an elderly patient has motor-control problems diagnosed as an effect of cerebellar degeneration and also shows signs of other psychological problems (such as late-onset hoarding), it is good practice to look for cognitive problems as well.

The basal ganglia are a group of functionally related nuclei located on both sides of the thalamus. They include the corpus straitum which include the caudate nucleus (discussed in the section on OCD) and the putamen. Still other parts of the basal ganglia are the globus pallidus, substantia nigra, and subthalamic nucleus. Finally, there is the nucleus accumbens, which plays an important role in pleasure and pain.

The *amygdala* (actually there are two of them, one on either side of the brain) is an almond-shaped structure in the temporal lobe, considered to be part of the *limbic system*. It is a complex group of nuclei involved in emotion, learning, memory consolidation, autonomic nervous system regulation, facial expression, arousal, and other functions. As a result of the research of LeDoux, McGaugh, and others, it has gained notoriety as a sort of panic button in the brain. Actually, the amygdala is activated by both positive and negative emotional experience, but unequally. It registers negative/fearful experiences more than positive/pleasant ones (Zald, 2003). While the amygdala contributes to the coding of emotional memories, the *consolidation* of certain types of emotional memories (especially those involving lower levels of arousal) may not involve this module (Kensinger & Corkin, 2004; LaBar, 2007).

Although it is responsive to both sad and happy faces, the amygdala is especially primed to activate in response to fearful or potentially threatening inputs (Yang et al., 2002). In fact, amygdala activation decreases when a stimulus is understood as nonthreatening (Whalen, 1998). Electrical stimulation of the amygdala (which may induce fear) enhances the startle reflex, whereas lesions of the amygdala can completely block fear-potentiated startle.

Nature has endowed us with two routes in and out of the amygdala: a fast route running to the thalamus and a slower one that leads first to the thalamus, then to the cortex, then back to the amygdala. LeDoux (1996) has dubbed these two routes the "low road" and the "high road." *The low road is quick and imprecise.* It is the pathway involved in fear conditioning. In classical conditioning, this occurs when a conditioned stimulus (or *CS*; the bell in Pavlov's famous experiments) is associated with an unconditioned stimulus (*UCS*; the dog food). As every psychology undergraduate learns, once a CS ("ring! ring!") is reliably paired with a UCS ("chow!"), it is very hard to extinguish the conditioned response ("drool!"). Given the high arousal of the feeding situation, it is the amygdala that helps code this learning into the brain's memory system.

The amygdala's low road serves an adaptive function. If a distant human ancestor saw what he took to be a hunting lion and it actually *was* a lion, the amygdala kick-started the appropriate action. False positives—"Oh, that was just a bush that looked like a lion"—are no-harm situations; but false negatives—"Oh my god, that thing I thought was a bush is coming after me!"—are not. A speedy reaction on the part of the amygdala is more important than fine-grained distinctions.

The downside of the amygdala's speed and sensitivity is that its fast track can terrify us when there is no adaptive reason for it. We can in fact be having this reaction without consciously knowing its cause or being able to verbalize much of what is going on. LeDoux and his colleagues have shown that the amygdala can be conditioned to elicit a fear response without any involvement on the part of the cortex and without ever achieving consciousness. Conditioned fear is mediated by subcortical pathways projecting from the thalamus to the amygdala. This circuit is a robust, nonconscious, subcortical regulator of emotional learning. The amygdala seems to play no significant role in most conscious memory processes. Pavlov's findings regarding the recurrence of "extinguished" conditioned responses long after the conclusion of active reenforcement are a reminder that the neural pathways of the fear response remain intact even after consciousness has helped "extinguish" them. Our amygdalas can also facilitate conditioned responses to *internal* stimuli, such as perspiration or quickened respiration. By interpreting these internal reactions as threatening on the same level as a man jumping out at us on a dark night, the amygdala can set off an escalating, self-reinforcing cycle of stimulation that results in a panic attack.

The high road out of the amygdala is slow and more complex. It is associated with conscious thinking about the situation at hand and with reality testing. "Come to think of it, the last five times that bell rang I didn't get the chow."

In the high-road circuitry, the amygdala interacts with the *medial prefrontal cortex* and the *anterior cingulate*. In conjunction with the amygdala and other regions, areas of the prefrontal cortex serve as a regulator of emotional processes and our behavioral responses to them. The amygdala responds to fear; the prefrontal cortex integrates this emotion with conscious sources of information and plans our physiological and behavioral responses to the situation. The cortex can disrupt amygdala-induced fear responses through the high-road circuitry that links the cortex with the limbic areas and the two hemispheres of the cortex with each other. This allows the person to subdue inappropriate emotional responses. As we noted, the elimination (extinction) of classically conditioned responses appears to require the participation of the cortex. For better or worse, however, the amygdala is quite capable of ignoring or bypassing top-down reassurance and can go right on stimulating the autonomic nervous system to respond as if the bush were indeed a lion.

In contrast to the hippocampus (described below), the amygdala may be further sensitized by the neurochemistry of stress, becoming, as it were, more and more efficient. As a result, chronic stress may modify the system so we react rapidly to danger rather than thinking about it. In essence, *the connections are stronger going from the amygdala to the cortex than they are going from the cortex to the amygdala*. Perhaps because of this, fearful feelings affect our conscious thoughts more easily than our thoughts can dampen them (a factor that prolongs or dooms many psychotherapies, whether cognitive-behavioral or insight-based approaches).

There appears to be a reciprocal relationship between the amygdala and cortex. McGaugh (2004), for example, has developed the *memory modulation* hypothesis, which asserts that following an arousing emotional experience, corticosteroid and adrenergic systems are activated by the amygdala, leading to enhanced consolidation of memory by the cortex. Similarly, the prefrontal cortex appears capable of modulating the release of stress hormones (Diorio, Viace, & Meany, 1993), but when the amygdala ignores or overrides it, this inhibitory function of the cortex is less efficient, in effect taking the brakes off the amygdala and setting off a reaction pattern that leads to escalating stress hormones and "new learning" that is more resistant to extinction (LeDoux, 1996).

The *hippocampus* (from the classical Greek name for "seahorse" because it is so shaped) is a complexly organized limbic structure. It has much to do with consolidation of conscious memories and cognitive navigation and less involvement in emotion or emotional learning. The hippocampus links widely dispersed neuronal networks that allow us to remember facts and autobiographical events consciously. The connections between the amygdala and the hippocampus are quite rich. In some ways they are the "Odd Couple" of the brain, with the amygdala playing the part of the uptight Felix and the hippocampus the role of the more relaxed journalist, Oscar. The shared pathways between them allow for the long-term storage and retrieval of emotionally based memories.

It has been suggested that the hippocampus may be impaired by prolonged stress (an idea we return to in Chapter 10). Some argue that persons with smaller hippocampi may be more vulnerable to posttraumatic stress disorder, while others have proposed the reverse: it is stress that leads to hippocampal atrophy. Importantly, the hippocampus is the site of new cell growth in the adult brain (*neurogenesis*), a process that appears to be decreased in reaction to stress or depression and that may be stimulated or potentiated by SSRIs.

Temporal lobe neurons degenerate relatively early in the course of Alzheimer's disease, and especially in the hippocampus, which lies in the medial temporal lobe. This may be why one of the earliest and most profound symptoms of the disease is forgetfulness. The hippocampus seems to be less important than the amygdala in the experience of early childhood. Research suggests that the amygdala is more active than the hippocampus in the young of many species, including our own. It has been shown that rats can learn tasks that require the amygdala but not the hippocampus at a younger age than they can learn tasks requiring the hippocampus but not the amygdala (Rudy & Morledge, 1994). The same appears to be true of children in regard to skills based on conditioned learning and emotional memory. If a childhood event occurs before the age at which the hippocampus matures and comes online (a gradual process that accelerates after the age of one year), the explicit recall of that event is likely to be impossible (Grigsby & Stevens, 2000).

Table 2.2 presents some important subcortical brain processing areas and their functions.

Anterior Cingulate

In addition to the amygdala and hippocampus, there is a third major module in the so-called limbic area of the brain—the *cingulate gyrus*. The cingulate gyrus is approximately in the medial cortex of the brain. It partially wraps around the *corpus callosum*, the central neurodynamic fiber that links the left and right hemispheres of the brain. The anterior (front) part of the cingulate gyrus has a complex and interesting functional-anatomical organization, playing a role in such tasks as error detection and determining the focus of our attention and in experiences such as the personal sense of urgency and social interactions (Rudebeck, Buckley, Walton, & Rushworth, 2006). The anterior cingulate cortex (ACC) acts

Table 2 2

Brain Processing Areas and Their Functions

Major Module	Location	Functions
Limbic Areas		
Amygdala	Bilateral, temporal lobe	Vital in facial recognition, encoding of implicit emotional memories; activation of startle and fear responses; activation of hypothalamic-pituitary-adrenal axis and sympathetic nervous system.
Hippocampus	Bilateral, temporal lobe	Critical to encoding of explicit emotional memory, contextualization of experience, and emotion regulation.
Thalamus		"Relay station" to cerebral cortex.
Pituitary gland	below hypothalamus	Secretes hormones regulating homeostasis.
Hypothalamus	below thalamus	Regulates autonomic nervous system via hormone production and release; affects and regulates blood pressure, heart rate, hunger, thirst, sexual arousal, and the sleep/wake cycle.
Cerebellum	Behind the pons of the brain stem	Regulates and coordinates motion and balance and sequencing of complex cognitive tasks.

as a sort of alarm system for physical pain and perhaps for the emotional pain of threatened rejection, exclusion, or ostracism (Eisenberger & Lieberman, 2004). From an evolutionary point of view, exclusion or outright banishment from the social group could result in pain or ultimately death (Eisenberger & Lieberman, 2004). The ACC probably plays a part in social anxiety disorder, a common psychiatric disturbance (Kaiser, 2008), and it appears to be important in various forms of depression as well (Mayberg, et al., 2005). Because recognizing and correcting problems and mistakes (social and otherwise) is part of what the ACC does, over- or underactivation is likely to produce distortions in the appraisal of one's own behavior and that of others. We will be referring to the ACC throughout this book.

The amygdala has robust connections to the ACC and less robust connections from it. This helps explain why the conscious thought that "everything looks okay, I don't need to be afraid" is often insufficient to calm anxious feelings because it's insufficient to inhibit the amygdala. The amygdala's continued activation leads anxious people to question and reevaluate their conscious perception of what the true situation is—sets up dissonance often resolved in favor of the stronger inputs from the amygdala to the cortex. And it helps explain why therapy takes repetitive exposure to fear-inducing stimuli rather than just insight, to be effective, as we will discuss Chapter 7, on anxiety disorders. Unlike the amygdala, however, the ACC is involved in both working memory and the functional system associated with the sense of self (e.g., Lenartowicz & McIntosh, 2005; Moran, Macrae, Heatherton, Wyland, & Kelley, 2006). Moreover, connections between the ACC and orbitofrontal cortex are thought to be involved in formulating "high-road" responses and response flexibility. In some studies of subjects whose ACC has been compromised, behavioral changes typical of "low-road" unmodulated anger and impulsivity have been reported.

CORTICAL PROCESSING

The *cerebral cortex*, atop the brain stem, medulla, and cerebellum and covering the hippocampus and amygdala in the limbic areas, occupies most of the brain's total volume. The cortex is a six-layered sheet of neurons ranging from 1.5 to 4.5 millimeters (about a quarter of an inch) in depth. It is folded in a series of *gyri* (the plural term for the exposed areas of cortex) and *sulci* (singular *sulcus*, the fissures or furrows between the gyri). These bulges and folds give the brain its distinctive appearance, with the folding serving to increase the cortical surface area packed into the skull case. Table 2.3 lists important areas of the cortex and their functions.

Table 2.3

Important Areas of the Cortex and Their Functions

Major Module	Location	Functions
Anterior cingulate	Between limbic areas and cortex, just above corpus callosum which connects left and right hemispheres	Error recognition, emotion formation and regulation, anticipating rewards, decision making, and empathy. Contains spindle neurons, specialized cells that play a part in mirroring the responses of others.
Frontal Lobes		
Prefrontal cortex (PFC)	At front of frontal lobes, anterior to motor and premotor sections of frontal lobes	Probably the seat of personality; involved in almost every problem therapists work with: relationships, depression, anxiety, obsessive-compulsive disorder, schizophrenia, attention deficit disorder.

Home of the executive functions that plan complex actions, orchestrate thoughts and actions in accordance with internal goals, differentiate among conflicting thoughts, make qualitative and moral judgments, predict outcomes and future consequences of current activities, and exercise social "control" (ability to suppress urges that could otherwise lead to unacceptable outcomes). |
Orbitofrontal cortex (OFC)	In frontal lobes behind eyes	Required for emotional decision making; its influence on personality and behavior is virtually ubiquitous.
Dorsolateral cortex (DFC)	In frontal lobes on top and to the side	Involved in working memory and executive functions.
Temporal Lobe		Includes auditory cortex and medial temporal lobe, which includes *amygdala* (important in facial recognition, coding of implicit emotional memory, and activation of the HPA axis) and *hippocampus* (critical in coding explicit memory, contextualizing experience, and emotion regulation).
Parietal Lobe		Spatial cognition, mathematical thought (in the left hemisphere), and imagery of movement are strongly dependent on this region. The experience of the self in space (in the right hemisphere).
Occipital Lobe		Contains primary visual cortex.

Hemispheric Specialization: The cortex is highly differentiated, with different regions playing varying roles as modular subcomponents of the brain's functional systems. The columns of cortical neurons in the right hemisphere (RH) appear to be organized differently from those in the left. Right-hemisphere neurons are organized in columns that appear to have more *horizontal* linkages, providing more cross-modal (i.e., highly integrated) representations. This architecture endows the RH with a special sense of context and a capacity for perceiving the "big picture" relative to the more detail-oriented left hemisphere (LH). The more *vertical* columnar organization of the LH seems to facilitate detailed and problem-focused processing. This may constitute the neurodynamic basis for the LH's facility for in-depth and analytic analysis of facts, in contrast to the RH's proclivity for thinking contextually and quickly grasping the gist of a situation. In both hemispheres, the six cortical layers are organized to handle input, output, and bi-directional information flow. The lower levels take in sensory information to be processed up to higher levels, where they will be "perceived." The middle levels blend both types of information (Hawkins & Blakeslee, 2004).

The cortex is asymmetrical, with each hemisphere having somewhat different anatomy and function and developing at slightly different rates. A legacy of our genetic and evolutionary history, we see this asymmetry in most mammals, and it is visible even in the human fetus. During the course of evolution, the cerebral hemispheres have grown increasingly dissimilar and specialized (Gerschwind & Galaburda, 1985). The *corpus callosum* that connects the two cerebral hemispheres undergoes a growth spurt between the ages of one and four years. It continues to mature through childhood, integrating the two hemispheres so that they function less like autonomous processors and more like large aggregations of nodes in a widely distributed network (Galin, Johnstone, Nakell, & Herron, 1979).

Even into maturity, however, the hemispheres retain distinctive functioning without the integrating role of the corpus collosum. The neuroscientist William Wolcott Sperry, working with his Caltech graduate student Michael Gazzaniga, studied subjects who had undergone a surgical procedure for intractable epilepsy that involved severing the corpus collosum. Sperry won the 1981 Nobel Prize for this research. He concluded that "both the left and the right hemisphere may be conscious simultaneously in different, even in mutually conflicting, mental experiences that run along in parallel" (Sperry, 1974). Gazzaniga went on to do pioneering work on hemispheric specialization. His research (e.g., Gazzaniga, 1985;

1995; Gazzaniga & LeDoux, 1985) suggests our explanations for what we do (even among those of us with an intact corpus collosum) have a confabulatory quality—an observation that generated a chorus of "amens" in psychoanalytic circles.

Hemispheric controls of specific behaviors, although based on tentative findings, is clinically thought provoking. For example, a reflective gaze to the left (activated by the RH) may connote the pessimism that some studies have associated with the RH; while a gaze to the right (activated by the LH) may be associated with an optimistic perspective (Drake, 1984; Thayer & Cohen, 1985). The RH controls the musculature on the left side of the face, dominating the expression of emotion on that side. Some studies suggest that the left side of the face is more emotionally expressive than the right (Johnsen & Hugdahl, 1991; Sergent, Ohta, & MacDonald, 1992). People tend to look to the left when recalling autobiographical memories (Wheeler, Stuss, & Tulving, 1997), possibly reflecting activation of right-hemispheric circuits. These data are not conclusive; individual differences abound; and there are sex differences in hemispheric lateralization and specialization; nevertheless, these studies suggest beguiling clinical hypotheses.

In general, the RH processes novel experiences, and the LH routine ones (Goldberg, 2001). For example, musically naive people process music predominantly with their RH because of the novelty of the stimuli. Trained musicians process music mostly with their LH (Bever & Chiarello, 1974). Similarly, Alex Martin and colleagues from the National Institute of Mental Health used PET (positron emitted tomography) scans to demonstrate that as individuals learn tasks, the information is initially processed by the RH until the novelty wears off; when it becomes familiar and routine, it is lateralized to the LH (Martin et al., 1997). Interestingly, this appears to be the case for both verbal and nonverbal information. Novel faces are processed by the RH, familiar ones mostly by the LH (Henson et al., 2000; Marzi & Berlucchi, 1977).

One's sex plays a significant role in determining the relative contribution of the two hemispheres to different aspects of functioning (Springer & Deutsch, 1998, and these differences begin to appear early in gestation (Trevarthen, 1996). It has been established that, on average, girls develop language earlier than do boys; whereas boys, on average, have greater upper body strength, motor coordination, and visual-spatial abilities than do girls (see Kimura, 1999, and Ullman, Miranda, & Travers, 2008, for reviews). In addition to verbal fluency, females typically test stronger in skills such as grammar, speed of articulation, verbal memory, and verbal fluency; males perform better on tests requiring the duplication of block designs, maze performance, and mental rotation (Hampson, 2008; Kimura, 1999; Maitland, Herlitz, Nyberg, Backman, & Nilsson, 2004).

It is tempting to say that men show stronger RH abilities in the visual-spatial areas and women stronger language abilities and attention to detail related to the LH, but the research does not support such definitive sex differences in lateralization. Recent research calls into question findings about sex differences in such functions as mental rotation, on which males are often thought to have a neurally-based advantage. Feng, Spence, and Pratt (2007), for example, found that giving both male and female under-graduates 10 hours of practice on an action video game reduced sex difference in performance on the standard test of mental rotation (Vanden-berg & Kruse, 1978). In general, *females demonstrate less lateralization* and greater interhemispheric flexibility than do males. Females appear to have more *bilaterally distributed* processes and perhaps a thicker corpus callosum linking the two hemispheres as well. Cerebral blood flow findings support greater bilaterality—the brain equivalent of being ambidextrous—in women.

In any case, the attempt to assign functions to one or the other hemisphere, whether by gender or not, often fails to consider the fact that the networks mediating most "right-hemisphere tasks" involve processing nodes in the LH, and the converse is true as well. The brain stubbornly refuses to conform to our desire to find simple answers to complex questions. Following the activity in even the simplest neural networks may lead one all over the brain. Having said this, let us indulge ourselves once more in some further tentative generalizations about the right brain and the left brain.

The right cerebral cortex (for the vast majority of right handers and a large percentage of left handers) is the so-called nondominant or subordi-nate hemisphere because it lacks a capacity for language. This is not to say that the RH is completely devoid of language; there is evidence that it appreciates a good paradox and a well-chosen metaphor. It plays an important role in that aspect of language referred to as *pragmatics*, which include prosody (poetry and the rhythms and inflections of speech), non-verbal behaviors, and perceptions. Although semantic and syntactic lan-guage functions are generally found in the LH, it has long been believed that the RH is better able to comprehend emotionally laden language, such as cursing (Searlman, 1977). It also is more adept at reading emotions in the facial expressions of others, irrespective of whether these expressions are congruent with the speaker's semantic meaning (Ahern et al., 1991). When the LH is cut off from communication with the RH, it is unable to read and interpret facial expressions. In contrast, the RH readily processes facial communication and tone of voice (Heller, Etienne, & Miller, 1995; Ross et al., 1994). Similarly, patients with LH damage are impaired in their ability to read emotionally expressive body language (Blonder, Bowers, & Heilman, 1991). In perceiving emotional meaning in the language of others, in maintaining the sense of a corporeal and emotional self, and in appraising the dangerousness of others, the RH plays a role that is dominant to that of the LII (Devinsky, 2000).

Some authors (Schore, 1997) assert that the RH is tightly coupled with the subcortical emotional and cognitive centers in the "limbic area" and may be the home of the psychodynamic unconscious. Minimally, the RH's emotional sensitivity seems to be the product of a largely nonconscious appraisal process (Fischer, Shaver, & Carnochan, 1990). The RH maintains rich connections with the subcortical areas associated with emotional processes and attachment and is also involved with the endocrine and autonomic nervous system (Wittling & Pfluger, 1990). Accordingly, the RH seems to be more influential in regulating states of body arousal (Damasio, 1994). There are also indications that the RH is more receptive to the emotional nuances of a relationship. Some believe that it mediates withdrawal in social situations while the LH mediates approach. The literature suggests that patients with greater RH arousal have difficulty regulating negative emotion, moods, and withdrawal behaviors.

Greater activation of the RH has also been associated with lower self-esteem in adults (Persinger & Makarec, 1991) as well as with depression (Nikolaenko, Egorov, & Frieman, 1997). A growing body of research supports the idea that shifts in the equilibrium of activation of the two hemispheres is involved in whether one is experiencing a positive or negative affect. For example, greater activation of the RH is associated with uncomfortable and negative emotions such as sadness, anxiety, and anger; activation of the LH is associated with emotions such as contentment and happiness (Davidson, 1992). Several studies have found links between affective style and baseline levels of asymmetric activation in the prefrontal cortex. Generally, the right PFC is associated with more negative emotion and the left PFC with more positive feelings (Hugdahl & Davidson, 2003).

The capacity to recover from negative emotional states is an important aspect of resiliency. Richard Davidson (2000), a pioneering contributor to research on cerebral asymmetry and mood states, has proposed that individuals who *practice* positive mood states and well-being—for example, through mindfulness meditation—become more resilient. They easily bounce back to what may be regarded as their neuropsychological default mode of functioning. In one study, Davidson put a Tibetan monk through an extensive electrophysiological assessment while the monk engaged in meditations thought by Buddhists to promote "virtuous" (i.e., positive) emotions. Compared to both this subject's resting state and the records of many other subjects Davidson and colleagues have tested, marked shifts in activation of the monk's RH and LH occurred during the meditations. The ratio of LH to RH activation tilted dramatically to the left (Goleman, 2003), a pattern Davidson has previously found to be typical of subjective happiness, well-being, and contentment. Cultivating traits such as optimism, hopefulness, tenacity, positive self-perception, and a good sense of humor promotes resiliency. As these mind states become part of an individual's routine, we can be sure that the neural architecture that supports them is being strengthened too.

There is evidence that the tendency toward resilience is more a left- than a right-hemispheric function. For example, infants who are crying or sad show greater right frontal electroencephalogram (EEG) activity, while infants displaying the "approach emotions," such as happiness, show more left frontal EEG activity (Bell & Fox, 1992). Consistent with the research that people with right frontal asymmetry tend to be more negative and withdrawn, Schmidt (1999) found that female undergraduates who rated themselves high in shyness showed right frontal EEG asymmetry and left frontal hypoactivation. Their more socially oriented counterparts, by contrast, displayed more left frontal asymmetry. In addition to amygdalar activation, primate research shows that fear and anxiety are associated not only with elevations in stress hormones but also heightened RH activity (Kalin, Larson, Shelton, & Davidson, 1998). Raw and intense emotions are represented in the right hemisphere (Porges, Doussard-Roosevelt, & Maiti, 1994; Ross, Homan, & Buck, 1994). Socially mediated feelings such as guilt seem to be processed by the LH.

During the first two years of life, the RH develops more rapidly than the LH (Chiron et al., 1997; Thatcher et al., 1987). Schore (1994) argued that the data support the idea that the LH is mediated by the dorsolateral prefrontal cortex, while the RH is mediated by the orbitofrontal cortex (hence the RH is more closely integrated with the limbic system). This asymmetric pattern may in turn be associated with the early maturation of social-emotional attachment schemas. Infants get intimately acquainted with their world on an affective level very early on. Basic patterns of attachment and the processes underlying foundational identifications are encoded in memory systems that are nonconsicous to begin with and never attain consciousness.

Conscious coping and problem-solving may have become the fiefdom of the LH because verbal language also developed in that hemisphere (Corina, Vaid, & Bellugi, 1992). At about 15 months of age, the left side of the brain undergoes a growth spurt associated with the child's burgeoning speech capacity. By the third year of life, the corpus callosum has matured further, accelerating cross-talk between the respective functions of the two hemispheres. Children under 3 years of age show the effects of less hemispheric integration between the hemispheres, and some authors have argued that prior to age 3, children are a bit like split-brain subjects (Siegel, 1999), an interesting analogy that should be taken with a grain of salt. Four-year-old children clearly are better able to process information and use words to describe their inner states and impulses than are younger children.

Viewed through the eyes of a champion of right-brain functioning, the left hemisphere might look chatty, glib, loose with the truth, and boringly linear. More neutrally, the LH is more outwardly directed than is its colleague on the right, more interested in engagement with and interpretation of the world. The LH processes information differently from the RH. It tends not only to be detail-oriented and linear but to favor sequential and time-dependent information. These characteristics seem consistent with the LH's specialization for language. Gazzaniga (1995) views the LH as having an interpretive function, struggling to make sense of what it experiences. The LH specializes in "spin," the generation of narratives that assemble a coherent version of what has happened to us or what is about to occur. In this sense, the LH functions as a sort of White House press secretary, making authoritative pronouncements that sometimes rest on very shaky premises. This positive spin may serve to regulate our moods. Patients sometimes become pessimistic and depressed in association with LH damage or decreased activation, suggesting that the press secretary may be slacking off. The LH is active in response to appetitive stimuli that evoke positive affect (Urry et al., 2004). The left-sided tendency to initiate approach behaviors complements the tendency of the RH to initiate withdrawal.

Is it time to remind the reader again that despite the emphasis in this chapter on modules and systems specializing in specific functions, it is more accurate to conceive of the brain as an integrated and dynamic system. Giving too much credence to the localization hypothesis oversimplifies the actual state of affairs in the brain. In the decades after Sperry's groundbreaking work with split-brain subjects, people became fond of referring to themselves or others as right brained or left brained. We agree with Springer and Deutsch (1998) who warned against "dichotomania," a disorder characterized by overgeneralizing a little scientific information. In discussing the renaissance of the localization hypothesis in the 1980s, Goldberg (2001) wryly stated that "Gall and his Phrenology enjoyed an odd revival in the name of modularity." He went on:

In reality the modular theory explains very little, since by lacking the ability to reduce multitudes of specific facts to simplifying general principles, it fails the basic requirement of any scientific theory. Like the belief systems of antiquity, it merely labels its domain by inventing a new notation; it has the seductiveness and illusory appeal of instant explainability—by introducing a new module for every new observation. (pp. 56–57)

Goldberg's analysis may be set side by side with the evidence that supports localization and the paradox simply acknowledged that the brain is both modular and a system that is nothing if not widely distributed in nature.

PREFRONTAL CORTEX

Dubbed the "Executive Brain" by Goldberg (2001) and the executive control system by his teacher, the great Russian neuropsychologist Alexander Luria, the frontal lobes are a kind of brain within the brain. These neurodynamic modules direct much activity in the rest of the brain. The *prefrontal cortex*—the very front regions of the frontal lobes—mediates attention, planning, decision making, inhibition, and initiation of goal-directed behavior. It makes up a considerable portion of the frontal lobes. The *orbitofrontal cortex* (OFC) (see Figure 2.3) can inhibit the emotional and autonomic reactivity of subcortical structures such as the amygdala.

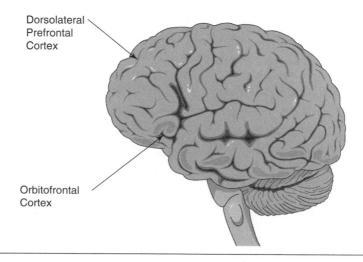

Dorsolateral
Prefrontal
Cortex

Orbitofrontal
Cortex

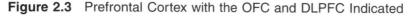

Figure 2.3 Prefrontal Cortex with the OFC and DLPFC Indicated

It's inhibiting function alone gives the OFC a major part to play in the "social brain." A cascade of stimuli and neural information is released by contacts with the environment, especially interactions with other people. The ability to ignore and modify some nonconscious reactions probably came in to play as an important part of establishing a stable and cooperative group life for our ancestors. Social cooperation in finding and sharing food, group security arrangements—not to mention status and the intricacies of the social expression of sexual and aggressive impulses—are mediated in part by the OFC. The OFC allows us to be flexible in response to shifting contexts and perspectives (Nobre et al., 1999). It helps us deal with changing conditions and in formulating new responses in novel contexts (Freedman et al., 1998). In addition to its other roles, the OFC is involved in regulation of the autonomic nervous system, modeling the emotional state of others, predicting their behavior, and interpretating social interaction. Moral judgment, self-awareness, and autobiographical memory are other OFC functions.

Without these capacities, our behavior toward others would be much more erratic, emotionally labile, and combative than it already is. People with OFC damage are subject to driving recklessly, shoplifting on impulse, and overreacting if caught or corrected. The unfortunately notorious Phinias Gage is a case in point. On September 13, 1848, Gage, foreman of a railway workgang, was placing explosives to clear the way for a new rail line. An explosion shot a steel rod through his head, skewering his OFC but leaving his brain otherwise intact. Gage largely retained his premorbid cognitive abilities, but he lost much of his ability to inhibit impulses. Once a respected supervisor, after the blast he was labile, erratic, rude, and hard to get along with. Later in life, Gage was reduced to doing a stint in a circus "freak show," and he died penniless in San Francisco 20 years after the injury. (His skull, however, is on display at Harvard.)

The dorsolateral prefrontal cortex (DLPFC) areas of the prefrontal cortex contribute to working memory as well as the executive cognitive functions just discussed. In fact, working memory—the 30 to 60 seconds of consciousness we have to remember how this sentence began so it will mean something when we get to its end—is largely a function of the DLPFC. Although working memory is directed by the frontal lobes, actual memories are stored in more widely distributed networks.

Mediated not by synaptic remodeling but by transient neurochemical changes in the synaptic environment, working memories are essentially the brief contents of consciousness. The limited capacity of this memory system is one reason that most processing at any given time must occur nonconsciously. Some observers (Ramin, 2007) argue that other species—

notably chimpanzees—have more working memory than we do, perhaps because the acquisition of language preempted prefrontal cortical real estate that previously had been devoted to working memory. In any event, the limited capacity of working memory in our species would be swamped by the processing demands required to carry out the most mundane tasks.

The OFC is activated when we make decisions based on emotional information (Teasdale et al., 1999). Its role in affect regulation is vital. For example, say you are driving to your 6-year-old son's school to pick him up as usual. As other kids come tumbling out of the school and are greeted by their parents, walk off together, or board the school bus, you do not see your son. After a few more minutes, you start getting the familiar sensations of anxious arousal. Where could he be? Maybe he is talking to his teacher about something. Going into the school, you notice the halls are empty. His classroom is locked; and looking through the little window in the door, you can see no one is in there. *Where is he*? The story you saw on the news last week about a stranger abduction in a nearby community flashes through your mind. Your breathing and pulse quicken and you feel a twinge of panic. Then it occurs to you that maybe this is the wrong day. You get out your PDA and sure enough, he is on a field trip and is not due back for a half hour. Your longer-term memory has come into play; the OFC tells your amygdala to stop overreacting. It signals the parasympathetic nervous system to put the brakes on the physical symptoms of anxiety.

One way that emotions become conscious is that nonconscious affective responses coming up from subcortical regions get connected to the OFC (LeDoux, 1996). The OFC maintains critical connections to limbic structures and to other cortical areas involved in complex thought. The OFC is therefore very much involved in making plans based on emotion and motivation (Damasio, 1994). It can access explicit memory through its rich connections with the hippocampus. A complex integrating region, the OFC is an essential part of the network involved in assigning emotional valence to events and people. For these reasons, Schore (1994) has identified it as the principal cortical area involved in emotion regulation. Trauma negatively impacts this cortical-subcortical regulatory process. Invigorating the neural networks in the OFC underlies the psychotherapeutic treatment of patients who have trauma in their histories (as borderline patients, e.g., frequently do).

NEUROPLASTICITY

Neurodynamic modules—components of the brain such as the OFC that specialize in particular types of cognitive and/or emotional processing—are best thought of as subsystems functioning within a hierarchy of increasingly more complex systems. The brain is exquisitely sensitive to environmental change and relentless in reorganizing itself to meet the next challenge. It achieves this environmental sensitivity through individual neurons and cellular networks that can almost instantaneously create large waves through the whole brain. The brain's resting state is one of near-chaotic activity (Grigsby & Stevens, 2000) that actually subsides as organized activity begins. Edelman (2006) sees the resting-state hum as reflective of "reentry," the constant signaling from one brain area to another, and believes that consciousness emerges from it. The signal paths change with the speed of thought.

The brain is made to increase our everyday "fitness" in the environment. For example, a neighbor loses her dachshund and posts a sign offering a reward for Hilda's return under a picture of Hilda at her most appealing. You are out on a walk. Because the visual system in the brain reacts to minute changes in the visual field, you notice something small, horizontal, and brown moving at the end of the block. Data regarding this change in the visual field is fed to your visual cortex, which consolidates it into a form that registers elsewhere in the brain as "dog" after it meets the demands of the invariant category that defines dogs in general, from great Danes to miniature terriers. From here on, other neural networks recalling memories of Hilda herself or the picture you just saw come into play and a decision is made based on how closely the data from the various networks match up. All this happens nonconsciously, in the blink of an eye, because the brain hovers near chaos, is quickly affected by environmental change, and is capable of organizing itself in reaction to it. The Hilda experience does not reside in the brain (or in reality either) but *emerges* from the interaction of environmental stimulation with neurodynamic potentials.

For the person finding the lost dog, the Hilda experience is the product of hundreds of thousands of interactions over the years between the neurons involved in seeing, building mental images, classifying them, and deciding what to do about them. As we noted earlier, the now-famous paraphrase "Cells that fire together wire together" describes how our brain reorganizes as we have new experiences. Hebbian learning sculpts psychological infrastructure in such a way that *states* of mind that are repetitively activated can become *traits* (Perry et al., 1995). Therapeutically, the more often a patient does something new—whether that is losing his temper or trying to subdue it—the greater the effect on the underlying neurodynamic structures.

Repeated activities (or states, or moods) become neurodynamic attractors through Hebbian learning. Each time the brain generates a positive mood, the networks in the OFC become a little more efficient at generating such states. PET scan studies show that as proficiency in a particular skill increases, the associated brain regions work progressively less hard with each repetition. This is both a grossly generalized principle and a fine-tuned and detailed one. It holds true dendrite to dendrite, whereby tiny bits of information are transferred, and module to module (see Andreason, 2001, for overview). Nobel laureate Eric Kandel (1997) demonstrated that axons branch out and new synapses are formed in the course of advancing development and learning. More synapses mean increased chances of neurodynamic efficiency and integration.

Neurogenesis involves the growth of new neurons. Ongoing learning is thought to stimulate the production of neurogenesis in the neocortex of adult primates (Gould et al., 1999). Neurogenesis is both cutting edge and still quite controversial in terms of differing views of how widespread a phenomenon it is in the brain. Aerobic exercise stimulates neurogenesis in the hippocampus and the olfactory bulbs (Gould et al., 1999; Erickson et al., 1998). Overall, neuroplasticity is about not just the promise of change but the everyday reality of it as part of normal functioning. It is one of the brain-based capacities that makes psychotherapy effective.

CHAPTER 3

Psychotherapy and the *Pax Medica*

Few areas of social concern have generated the kind of charged atmosphere that hovers over the field of psychological problems. The dearth of solid knowledge and of indisputable treatments has formed a vacuum that has drawn in an assortment of competing ideologies, movements and fads.

—Aaron Beck, *Cognitive Therapy of Depression*

NEUROSCIENCE AND THE scientific study of psychotherapy are like identical twins separated at birth and reared unaware of one another. Once intimately connected in the work of Joseph Breuer and Sigmund Freud, neuroscience after Freud turned its gaze back to bench work and experimental psychology, for the most part regarding psychotherapy as sloppy and unscientific. For our part, psychotherapists have tended to view neuroscience as focusing on minutiae with little relevance for clinical work. More recently, some excellent texts by therapists have appeared with the goal of helping us understand more about the brain in the context of clinical theory and experience (Cozolino, 2002; Score, 1997; Siegel, 1999). But a comparable effort has yet to be made to integrate neuroscience with the scientific study of psychotherapy. Coming not from the tradition of biological science but from that of social science, this literature ultimately focuses on what makes psychotherapy work. In this chapter, we review how contemporary psychotherapeutic theory got to where it is today and why we believe our field is on the threshold of a new era in which brain science will resume its natural relationship with clinical practice.

AN ENDANGERED SPECIES

In the heady atmosphere of contemporary psychotherapy, it is difficult to imagine that the field once hovered on the verge of extinction. Half a century ago, however, in an important review of the then-sparse outcome literature, the formidable psychotherapy researcher Hans Eysenck (1952) questioned whether psychotherapy had any positive effects at all. Timothy Leary, before his psychedelic period, conducted a study comparing psychotherapy patients to those put on a wait list. He found that the "waiters" did as well as the patients. As dark clouds were gathering on the psychotherapy front, imipramine (Tofranil), the first tricyclic antidepressant, made its appearance. In the 1950s and through the era of fluoxetine (Prozac), biology came back into the mental health field with a vengeance—and at the same time psychotherapy outcome studies were questioning the effectiveness of "talk therapy."

Eysenck's critics attacked his conclusions on technical grounds—his sample was too small and he arbitrarily classified all dropouts as treatment failures—but the silver lining of his work was that it forced a complacent field to reexamine itself. The value of the technical rebuttals mattered less than the cumulative intellectual energy invested in trying to understand how therapy worked. In the ensuing years, literally thousands of outcome studies were undertaken. Along the way, some relatively dirty laundry came to light:

- About 4 in 10 of our patients would get over their problem without therapy (Andrews & Harvey, 1981).
- We are very biased judges of evaluating our own successes and failures.
- Psychotherapy can and does hurt people, and some therapists contribute more than their share of the damage (Lambert & Ogles, 2004).

But 50 years of vigorous inquiry have also produced some good news:

- Our patients are better off than 80% of untreated controls (Lambert & Baley, 2002).
- A large percentage of patients who drop out after only a few sessions do so because they have met their own goals (Pekarik, 1992).
- Most therapists get good results consistently (Lambert & Baley, 2002).

Perhaps the most productive aspect of the research is that it has identified the factors linked to successful outcomes. Research since Eysenck has not only established psychotherapy as an empirically validated treatment, it has moved us to a point where we can identify ways of improving almost every therapist's practice (Norcross, 2002).

From the very beginning, there have been controversies about what determines therapeutic success or failure. Debate has centered on three contrasting assertions:

1. Specific *methods* (or agents) produce particular results.
2. It is not the method; it is the *patient* who makes them work.
3. Neither of the above—the really effective ingredient is the *therapeutic alliance*.

Each of these assertions has a long and interesting pedigree.

FROM TECHNIQUE TO TWO-PERSON PSYCHOLOGY

Joseph Breuer, arguably the father of the "talking cure," championed the theory that the patient alone brings about change. Freud entertained seemingly contradictory views about the most potent agent of change. He agreed with his mentor that patient factors—for example, how diligently patients were willing to struggle with their resistances—were critical to outcome. But Freud also argued that the therapist's skill in employing *methods* that could illuminate esoteric unconscious processes was indispensable to analytic success. Freud placed great importance on the technical education of analysts. Even becoming a neophyte analyst required a personal analysis, close supervision of cases, and intensive study of psychoanalytic authorities. The experimental rigor Freud demonstrated in his scientific work (and partially abandoned after the "Project for a Scientific Psychology") was to be compensated for by the analyst's scientific attitude. The analytic attitude "consists in making no effort to concentrate the attention on anything in particular, and maintaining in regard to all that one hears the same measure of calm, quiet attentiveness—of 'evenly hovering attention'" (Freud, 1912/1958). Similar rigor was required of the analytic patient: an uncensored openness to the productions of the mind as they came into consciousness.

Eventually, classical psychoanalysis came to be hamstrung by its lack of engagement with biological science and by its devotion to the technical aspects of analysis. Analysts tended to talk only to other analysts, not to other psychologists. Orthodoxy was established, attacked, and reestablished in different partisan schools. Especially in the United States, the psychoanalytic profession fell victim to a medical elitism that excluded some of the best minds in psychology. The "two-person psychology" of modern psychoanalytic thought has largely liberated itself from these constraints. In its deviation from classical theory, however, two-person psychology highlights the foibles of the classical tradition from which it emerged, where the analyst is a source of esoteric knowledge, good outcomes are a product of analytic technique, and the mind is something to be studied as if it were a disembodied object.

In the 1940s, the lay analyst Melanie Klein tacitly deconstructed the view that the therapeutic encounter was a one-way street. Like Freud, Klein was more interested in the patient's fantasies than in the actual give-and-take of therapeutic interaction. But in insisting on the importance of projection and introjection of psychic content in development, Klein took a large step toward a two-person model of therapy. Moreover, it was hard to avoid the inference from Klein's work that she believed infancy to be a more important critical period in human development than the oedipal stage. Nevertheless, Klein remained relatively uninterested in the *real* parent-child bond, and it was left to others to bring this primary relationship into clearer focus in psychoanalytic developmental theory.

A major pioneer in this endeavor was Klein's analysand, D. W. Winnicott. A pediatrician before he became a psychoanalyst, Winnicott had an intuitive grasp of the mutually influencing interactions between mothers and babies. From this perch, it was not a great leap to appreciating the similarities between parenting and therapeutic relationships. It seemed obvious to Winnicott that there were two people present in the therapeutic encounter and that they influenced one another in ways beyond erotic or defensive "transference" and "countertransference" reactions. Another analyst, John Bowlby, felt the influence of both Klein and Winnicott. Although supervised by Klein, Bowlby all but abandoned theory in favor of studies of infant attachment that employed social science research methods and invited empirically based replications across diverse situations and cultures.

ROGERS, THE PATIENT, AND THE RELATIONSHIP

Outside the fortress of psychoanalysis, mainstream psychology was moving in a parallel direction toward two-person psychology and empiricism. Whereas Bowlby's methods were more those of an anthropologist than a psychoanalyst, Carl Rogers at the University of Chicago brought to psychotherapy the methodological rigor of the social sciences (Rogers, 1951). More remembered for his easily parodied reflective interpretations than for his research, Rogers in fact conducted pathbreaking science on what makes psychotherapy effective. Rogers's work subordinated the importance of therapeutic methods and patient factors to a third element, *the therapeutic relationship,* as the critical element in successful treatment. Bowlby (1969) and his followers reached a similar conclusion about normal development in closely observing the ways babies accommodated to the personalities and personal circumstances of their mothers. Both Rogers and Bowlby focused on the *attunement* between individuals and their caregivers, whether in the nursery or the therapist's office.

Rogers's empirically supported insights were repeated and replicated, and the gathering professional reaction of many researchers to the critics of psychotherapy was published in a new volume. *The Handbook of Psychotherapy and Behavior Change* (Bergin & Garfield, 1971) appeared at the outset of a momentous decade in the history of psychology.

RISE OF THE SELECTIVE SEROTONIN REUPTAKE INHIBITORS

As psychotherapy was gradually turning toward empiricism and the recognition that methods mattered less than patients and relationships, a massive shift was taking place in psychiatry. As noted, the first antidepressant appeared in the 1950s. However, it was really the advent of Prozac in 1974 (Wong, Horng, Bymaster, Hauser & Mulloy, 1974) that most profoundly affected psychiatry. Prozac shifted psychiatry away from interests in meaning, personality, or psychodynamics and toward an interest in neurotransmitters, in some measure reestablishing ties between clinical practice and brain science. On the basis of outcome studies, quite suddenly biological psychiatry became the "gold medal" treatment for depression, one of the most common psychiatric disorders.

The media trumpeted the news. Currently more than 20 million prescriptions are written annually for fluoxetine (generic for Prozac) alone, and fluoxetine is only the third most commonly prescribed antidepressant in the United States. One in 20 men, and almost 1 woman in 10, in the United States takes an antidepressant (Barber, 2008). By contrast, about 5 out of every 100 people in the U.S. population is engaged in psychotherapy with a psychologist, psychiatrist, or social worker. The number of patients treated for depression with psychotherapy actually declined between 1987 and 1997, a decade during which prescriptions for antidepressants doubled (Barber, 2008).

COGNITIVE BEHAVIORAL THERAPY

From the 1960s on, an American psychiatrist, Aaron Beck (1972; Beck et al., 1979), constructed a therapeutic establishment very different from the Freudian one. Whereas the Freudians were "all in their heads" as far as science was concerned, for the most part scorning outcome research, Beck devoted himself to such studies. Beck and his colleagues welcomed psychologists and social workers as fully qualified practitioners, in contrast to the psychoanalytic establishment, which often admitted them into training programs only by prior agreement that they would not practice clinical psychoanalysis. Beck made the most modest claims about how the mind worked, but even more than Freud, he championed the view that technique is what matters. For all their differences, Beck and Freud were both physicians and both came from a tradition in which psychotherapy was viewed as a mental health *treatment*. John Norcross (2002) summarizes some of the elements of this tradition concisely:

> This "treatment" or "medical model" inclines people to define process in terms of technique, therapists as providers trained in the application of techniques, treatment in terms of the number of contact hours, patients as embodiments of psychiatric disorders, and outcome as the end result of a treatment episode. (p. 12)

Beck sought to cut through what he considered the self-serving mystifications of psychoanalysis and Rogers's "personal growth" movement to bring to psychotherapy the kind of experimental rigor brought to the vetting of new medications and surgical procedures. Beck's genius was to change overly complex definitions of mental disorders into a simple checklist of affective and behavioral symptoms. Treatment plans, based on change strategies that are logically derived from these checklists, were standardized across therapies and therapists. Beck was able to make treatment planning consistent with evolving psychiatric thinking about diagnosis during the 1970s—and not coincidentally, this thinking was far more conducive to empirical validation than the esoteric concepts of many psychoanalysts.

Cognitive behavioral therapy (CBT) has been a survival kit for psychotherapy in an era of pressing challenges from biological psychiatry. Its methods make sense, it is usually brief, and it has been demonstrated effective in so many controlled trials that it is all but unassailable by critics. Moreover, as we explain later in this book, its methods are consistent with basic brain-based therapy principles. Pure CBT—as opposed to the elements of it many of us employ in our practices—has five components:

1. Psychoeducation
2. Breathing retraining
3. Cognitive restructuring

4. Exposure
5. Relapse prevention

PSYCHOEDUCATION

CBT therapists teach patients about the nature of their disorder, the principles of conditioned learning, and the relationship between cognition and mood. Therapy is especially concerned with "false beliefs," unrealistic ideas that exert strong effects on our emotions and on the kinds of choices we make in life. Psychoeducation also includes information about how CBT works and assurance that patients can expect that it will help. Many CBT therapists encourage their patients to read books that give good overviews of this material, such as David Burns's *Feeling Good: the New Mood Therapy* (1999). Practitioners such as Michelle Craske at the University of California at Los Angeles have for many years also included information about the neurophysiology underlying disorders such as panic.

RELAXATION TRAINING

Relaxation training of various kinds is also part of CBT, especially in the treatment of anxiety disorders. More recently, research has failed to substantiate the idea that relaxation techniques make enough of a contribution to outcome to continue including them in treatment (Kaiser Permanente, 2007b). Other studies (e.g., Segal, Williams, & Teasdale, 2002) have shown significant benefits from making instruction in mindfulness-based meditation a part of the treatment. Mindfulness includes training in diaphragmatic breathing. This technique influences some biochemical features of psychological state—such as the blood levels of oxygen and carbon dioxide—as well as shifting attention away from distressing thoughts. Some behavioral purists, however, emphasize only extinction of conditioned learning and oppose focusing on the breath because it can readily be used as a distraction from facing anxiety.

COGNITIVE RESTRUCTURING

The *c* in the term "CBT" stands for *cognitive*, and given the importance accorded thought in this form of therapy, it is appropriate that *c* comes first. A main task of the CBT therapist is to assist patients in restructuring core beliefs about their disorder—for instance, that patients will continue to be depressed no matter what they do or what else happens to them.

Homework is a prominent part of the work. Patients are encouraged to gather "data" about their internal lives, using structured thought records between sessions. Using a form called a *thought record* furthers the goal of grasping the relationship between important parts of a distressing experience:

- Environmental triggers ("My wife didn't remember that I hate broccoli.")
- Thoughts ("She always forgets this!")
- Feelings ("I don't want to be married to this insensitive ditz anymore.")
- Distress ("I'm trapped.")
- Alternative ideas ("Maybe I should just ask her why this is hard to remember.)

By examining the thought record together over time, patient and therapist get a sense of what repetitive themes are most closely tied to distress. Transcripts of excellent CBT treatments, in the clarity they bring to the thinking processes and the power this can have for patients, have the elegance of a Socratic dialogue. Christine Padesky's work (Greenberger & Padesky, 1995) exemplifies this kind of CBT virtuosity.

EXPOSURE

CBT therapists use exercises that require patients to face situations that they would, because of their disorder, usually avoid, such as taking an elevator, eating in public, or having dirty hands. Called *desensitization* or *exposure*, these exercises create an opportunity for patient and therapist to examine unrealistic false beliefs about the terrible things that might happen and the strong affective or somatic reactions that are associated with these ideas. A special technique for anxious patients, *interoceptive exposure*, involves provoking the somatic symptoms of anxiety and then challenging the thoughts associated with the patients' core beliefs about the meaning of these symptoms. For example, a patient's thought that rapid pulse and perspiration are indicators of imminent cardiac arrest could be challenged with the alternative explanation that these somatic experiences are symptoms of many different kinds of arousal. A closely allied technique used with depressed patients is *behavioral activation*. Together patients and therapists consider activities patients used to enjoy and note how much less often they engage in them since the onset of the depression. Then patients and therapists agree on an experiment: patients will go back to the (for example) salsa dance class, recording how they felt about the activity before and after the class. Assessing how far the pre- and postactivity mood state deviate from the patients' predictions typically generates something to think about with the therapist.

RELAPSE PREVENTION

The two most common psychological problems treated with CBT are depression and anxiety. Once people are diagnosed with one of these disorders, it is statistically significantly more likely that they will have recurrent episodes. The causes of relapse have to do with how the brain works and state factors, such as increased stress, illness or excessive fatigue, and a tendency to forget the lessons learned in psychotherapy. Relapses are demoralizing and can lead to abandonment of the self-care behavior learned in therapy. Part of CBT treatment is letting patients know their problem may reoccur and that it is a good idea to make plans for that eventuality at the termination of treatment. A plan may include tapering therapy over a period of time and booster sessions scheduled at regular intervals for some period after treatment ends.

PSYCHIATRY'S BIBLE

Beck's work dovetailed seamlessly with that of Robert Spitzer, the psychiatrist who took over the job of creating the third edition of the *Diagnostic and Statistical Manual of Mental Disorders* (*DSM-III*) for the American Psychiatric Association in 1974. Although its predecessor, the *DSM-II*, had done its work in 150 pages, Spitzer's opus was 900 pages long. He replaced vague and general ideas such as "anxiety neurosis" in the *DSM-II* with what have become some of psychiatry's "greatest hits": panic disorder, attention deficit hyperactivity disorder (ADHD), and major depression.

Completed in 1980, the *DSM-III*, together with Beck's work, launched a revolution in psychiatry and psychotherapy. With historical hindsight, Spitzer's *DSM* may be seen as part of a broad response to several major events in the culture of mental health: the fright created by outcome studies denigrating talk therapy, the waning of psychoanalytic dominance in psychiatry, the burgeoning of the psychopharmacological establishment, and an increasingly fragmented healthcare delivery system. In a field fraught with complexity and ambiguity—and a world where enormous amounts of money were at stake—Spitzer offered mental health professionals some peace, simplicity, and the comfort of a renewed faith in authority. His tome rapidly became the bible of psychiatry for insurance companies, the disability and criminal justice systems, and researchers interested in obtaining Food and Drug Administration (FDA) approval for drugs designed as specialized treatments for specific psychiatric disorders. Psychotherapists by and large accepted the "evidence-based" terms of the pharmaceutical and insurance companies if for no other reason than to stay competitive with the alternative treatments.

PAX MEDICA

Spitzer, along with Beck and the pharmaceutical manufacturers, produced a compromise in the mental health field that has worked reasonably well for more than 35 years. This *pax medica* stipulates that in psychotherapy, as in dermatology, *diagnosis* is fundamentally important in treatment. Treatment should be targeted at *symptoms*. Both pharmacological treatment and psychotherapy are viewed as effective; but when push comes to shove, psychopathology is best considered within the context of the medical model—and the mental health team should be led by a physician.

Beck's demand for "indisputable" evidence of efficacy could, in his view, be met only by a specific research methodology: the randomized controlled trial. Using this design, researchers began demonstrating the superiority of CBT, and both the American Psychiatric and the American Psychological associations issued guidelines for "evidence-based" psychological treatment. Therapists started seeing brochures in their mailboxes hailing specific treatments for depression, anxiety, eating disorders, and ADHD among other disorders, and a major transformation of psychotherapy was under way. In the era since the 1980s, 80 to 90% of research in psychotherapy has been aimed at documenting the efficacy of specific methods for specific disorders (Bohart, 2000).

The final critical element in the *pax medica* was the emergence of the managed care delivery system. Managed care thrived in the newly demystified and empirically validated world of *DSM*, the selective serotonin reuptake inhibitors (SSRIs), and short-term CBT. Utilization managers used "evidence-based" algorithms to limit the scope and duration of treatment. Changes in reimbursement, diagnosis, and therapeutic method went hand in hand with the boom in psychotropic medications that began with Prozac. Several therapists of our acquaintance in practice in those days threw up their hands and changed professions.

BEST PRACTICES

In the early 1990s, the leadership of the Permanente Medical Group of Northern California, the organization for which we, the authors, work, made an executive decision to try to make psychiatry services more effective and more responsive to our health plan members and large-group purchasers. A team of senior clinical managers was brought together to redesign psychiatry services to meet challenges posed by managed care behavioral healthcare systems. In 1992, one of us (LL) was assigned to direct a group that came to be called Kaiser Psychiatry and Chemical Dependency Best Practices—or "Best Practices" for short.

Given the zeitgeist prevalent in mental health treatment at the time, discussions about whether to focus on treatments designed for a specific disorder or on treatments that seemed to work *across* disorders were short-lived. In the contest between Carl Rogers and Aaron Beck, generic psychotherapy seemed guilty as charged of unempirical behavior. Moreover, an earlier effort to define "best practices" had already gone down the *DSM*/CBT road and produced an excellent clinical practice guideline based on panic disorder (under the direction initially of John Peters and later of Elke Zuercher-White).

Kaiser's Best Practices group is now almost 20 years old. Clinical practice guidelines have been published not only for panic, but for obsessive-compulsive disorder, social anxiety disorder, and depression. Where the research evidence does not warrant a practice guideline, clinical recommendations and clinical resources have been published to help clinicians understand an expert consensus approach. Clinical recommendations have been published on attention deficit and hyperactivity disorder in children, on adolescent depression, adolescent and adult eating disorders, work stress problems, intimate partner abuse, and cultural diversity.

MENTAL HEALTH AFTER THE *PAX MEDICA*

Four years after the publication of the *DSM-III*, three little-known researchers once again turned the spotlight of social science research methodology on the question of psychotherapeutic benefit, and their work effectively ended the debate about whether psychotherapy does anything at all for the patients who engage in it. Smith, Glass, and Miller, in *The Benefits of Psychotherapy* (1980), applied *meta-analysis* to a wide array of outcome studies. Meta-analysis allowed investigators to combine hundreds of smaller methodologically robust studies of psychotherapy into one large sample, increasing the power and credibility of their findings. Insofar as their meta-analysis included studies conducted in different settings, by different individuals, using a variety of methods, Smith and colleagues could lay claim to addressing the general problem of efficacy in psychotherapy.

Although Smith, Glass, and Miller's analysis demonstrated robust effects for psychotherapy and suggested that the method employed by therapists seemed to have no significant effect on outcome, their findings were largely ignored outside of academic circles. Between the ghost of Eysenck and the advent of the market forces that eventuated in managed care, studies aimed at demonstrating the superiority of particular therapeutic *methods* with particular *disorders* seemed—particularly in CBT quarters—to have taken on a momentum of their own.

In 1995, David Barlow, a distinguished researcher in the field of panic disorder and president of the American Psychological Association's Division 12, the Society of Clinical Psychology, established a task force on empirically validated treatments (Norcross, 2002). In the task force's view, earning the designation "empirically validated" was like winning a gold medal; like winning three stars from the *Michelin Guide*, it was not easy to achieve. To earn this distinction, a treatment had to be shown as superior to placebo or comparable treatment in two separate randomized clinical trials. Moreover, manualized forms of the treatment technique (i.e., versions reduced to a clear and teachable set of written procedures) must have been utilized in these trials, and outcomes determined by psychometrically robust measures. Initially, eight treatments passed this test; almost all were CBT. Eighteen *DSM-III* disorders were seen as candidates for this type of "best practice" process. It seemed that a virtual coronation of CBT as the queen of evidence-based treatments was about to occur.

But this is not what actually came to pass. At about the same time that Best Practices teams began working at Kaiser, the first cracks in the *pax medica* began to appear. The research base supporting the superiority of CBT attracted the scrutiny of other groups within the American Psychological Association. CBT, like psychoanalysis, has a specialized therapeutic language, but its critics maintain that the method's core processes differ only slightly from those of other effective therapies. For example, Fritz Perls, the founder of gestalt therapy in the 1950s, used the term *safe emergency* for the type of intervention CBT therapists call *exposure* (Perls et al., 1951). Something like exposure goes on in many forms of treatment. Patients are exposed to unintegrated and troubling thoughts and feelings with the assurance that accommodating and integrating these experiences will lead to feeling better. "All forms of successful therapy," according to Lou Cozolino, "strive to create these safe emergencies in one form or another" (2002, p. 32).

Within the American Psychological Association, the "evidence-based" party tended to congregate in David Barlow's Division 12; its critics massed in Division 29. The latter group has been led by two other estimable psychotherapy researchers, John Norcross and Michael Lambert, editor of the current edition of *The Handbook of Psychotherapy and Behavior Change* (2004). Barlow and his colleagues assembled a list of "evidence-based treatments"—therapies for which there was at least one controlled randomized trial demonstrating that it was superior to treatment as usual for a specific problem. Since the 1980s, Lambert had been conducting studies showing that diagnosis was *not* a significant factor in outcome and that specific treatment methods were only slightly more important. According to Lambert, *the most salient factor affecting outcome is who the patient is and what he or she brings to the treatment.* So-called "common factors" such as the warmth, confidentiality, and support found in virtually all psychotherapeutic approaches, are the next most powerful elements in the outcome of treatment. Trailing behind the patient and common factors (and basically in a dead heat with each other) are elements such as the therapeutic alliance, the impact of Barlow's "evidenced-based" methods, and the personality of the therapist. Norcross (1993) has suggested that we have more control over this personality variable than might be immediately obvious, because each of us has a range of ways we can "be" and still be ourselves.

The Norcross-Lambert school of thought asserts that many patients seeking therapy do not have a formal psychiatric diagnosis; they are just unhappy and distressed. Norcross (2002) wondered why the "evidence-based" school all but ignores anything *but* diagnosis and methods—factors such as the patient's coping style, functional impairment level, strength of resistance, treatment expectations, or stage of change. Time and again research has shown that these patient factors are highly related to the outcome of treatment. Given the finding that method per se is not as important as patient and "common factors" between therapies, Norcross also pondered why the CBTers continue to do studies that validate their particular therapeutic approach when the better question might be what approaches—or, better yet, treatment *relationships*—work for *whom*. Elements contributing to outcome are shown in Figure 3.1.

FACTORS IN OUTCOME

Figure 3.1 supports the position of the post-CBT empiricists that it is not a diagnosis that walks through the door of our offices, it is a *person*; and they are not greeted by a *method* but by another human being. Based on this reading of the outcome literature, the American Psychological Association's Division 29 convened a task force on evidence-supported *relationships*. Its goals were to reassert the importance of understanding who the patient is, beyond just his diagnosis, and secondarily to look at what

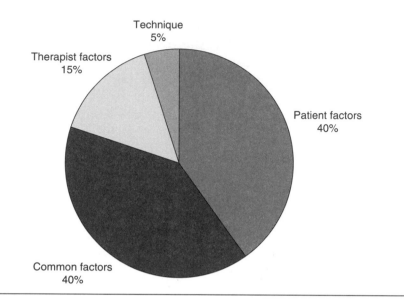

Figure 3.1 Factors Determining Outcome in Psychotherapy (After Lambert, 2006)

worked best for whom. The task force identified two patient factors as having particularly powerful effects on the outcome of psychotherapy:

- Level of the patient's functional impairment
- Level of the patient's resistance

Patients who come into treatment with impaired functional status are more likely to show important gains by the end of treatment. The higher their level of resistance to the process, however, the less likely they are to make gains. Results are mixed regarding other personal characteristics, such as gender and ethnicity. While there is currently insufficient evidence to support definitive appraisals of the importance of such patient characteristics as Axis II diagnoses, attachment styles, treatment preferences, and religious or spiritual practices, a number of studies suggest that these factors should be taken stock of in treatment.

In regard to the therapist variables, Orlinsky, Grave, and Parks (1994) identified several characteristics and behaviors that are consistently correlated with positive outcomes. These include the therapist's credibility, skill, empathic understanding, and his or her affirmation of patients. The capacity to engage with patients, focus on their problems, and convince patients to focus on the affective aspects of their issues are critical as well

(Orlinsky et al., 1994). All these issues have been found to correlate highly with good outcomes. Independent measures of the therapist's empathy, warmth, and genuineness seem to have only modest associations with therapeutic success. Orlinsky and colleagues found that what seems to matter most in outcome are the *patient's perceptions* of the relationship factors with the therapist rather than objective assessments of the alliance or the therapist's character.

The "common elements" underlie all therapeutic approaches. Collectively they blend into what we consider the quality of the therapeutic relationship. These relationship factors trump the combined impact of specialized techniques and diagnosis. The relationship—defined in terms of the therapeutic alliance, the patient's perceptions of the therapist's empathy, and consensus between the therapist and patient about treatment goals—earns the gold medal for being "demonstrably effective" in determining outcome (Norcross, 2002). Other common elements that have achieved this level of endorsement by the research are:

- Patients' awareness of the therapists' positive regard for them
- Patients' awareness of meaningful therapist-to-patient feedback and judicious self-disclosure on the part of the therapist
- The experience of successful repair of ruptures to the alliance
- The patient's sense that the therapist sensitively and effectively conveys his or her "countertransference" reactions to the patient
- The patient's sense that the therapist accurately interprets the undercurrents in the patient's relationships both with the therapist and significant others in the patient's life (Norcross, 2002)

Interestingly, none of the interventions or dimensions of treatment falling within the category of tailoring the relationship to fit the patient was found to be "demonstrably effective," but many were judged to probably be so. Also in the "probably effective" range are interventions designed to match the patient's stage of change and expectations about treatment. In Chapter 4 we look more closely at the interaction of patient variables with common factors, how they make sense in the context of brain functioning, and how to use these interactions in working with patients.

OUTCOMES MANAGEMENT

The report of the Division 29 task force does not assert that technique is unimportant. Observing the powerful effects of exposure with anxious patients or behavioral activation with depressed patients generally makes one wonder about the competence of colleagues who neglect such methods. Bohart (2000) argues persuasively that these technical practices become important *when patients engage them* in ways that actually help them solve problems. At bottom, the work of Lambert, Norcross, and others is an attempt to rebalance the current professional culture in which we practice—a culture that has been enormously impacted by the medicalization of psychological care. Neuroscientific hypothesizing about how psychotherapy works both supports and undermines the assumptions that underlie the compromises between psychology, medicine, and the marketplace that have been forged over the last 40 years.

Michael Lambert has carved out new directions in assessment and "best practices" in studies and interpretative essays written over the course of a long career. Referred to as *outcomes management,* Lambert's recent work (2004) assumes that patients come to therapy in order to change how they are functioning and feeling, not to get rid of an Axis I diagnosis. Lambert has shown that patients are best qualified to make the assessment of how the treatment is progressing. Based on decades of psychotherapy research, this method incorporates four research findings:

1. Psychotherapy is an effective, moderately powerful intervention.
2. It works well in many forms due to the common factors that underlie different schools.
3. The real "best practice" in individual psychotherapy is to ask the patient how things are going in the treatment on a regular basis (preferably at each visit).
4. When patients give this feedback to therapists, it minimizes the number of treatment failures and enhances the overall effectiveness and reliability of the therapist's practice (Lambert, 2006).

Researchers define the "patient factors" in Figure 3.1 primarily in terms of the patient's functional impairment and resistance. Beyond understanding these aspects of our patients' psychological functioning, there are important reasons for making sure we understand patients' goals, their view of the tasks we require of them, and their feeling about the therapeutic alliance (Safran & Muran, 2003). Psychodynamic therapists in particular are often attuned to these subtle, and often nonverbal, reactions in our patients.

RESOURCES AND THE *PAX MEDICA*

Because patient characteristics are preeminently important in the outcome of psychotherapy, and because our bridge to the patient is the therapeutic relationship, we need to remind ourselves frequently that "It's the relationship" that matters the most. Research demonstrates that most therapists, while we consider ourselves experts in interpersonal appraisal, make frequent misjudgments about what patients are thinking and feeling vis-à-vis the therapy (Lambert, 2004). The late prescient observer of the *pax medica*, Gene Pakarik (1992, 1993), spoke cogently to these issues. Like Scott Miller (Duncan, Miller, & Sparks, 2004) and other investigators of psychotherapeutic process, Pakarik honed in on the different (and often unspoken) expectations therapists and patients harbor about treatment. Instead of relying on what patients *say* about their expectations, Pakarik looked at patient *behavior*. His arena was the arguably naturalistic setting of public and semipublic clinics such as Kaiser, which offers open access to psychiatric services for large numbers of patients. In these settings, Pakarik argues, therapist patient differences about treatment become glaringly obvious. Therapists typically think many more visits will be required to attain good outcomes than do patients, and according to Pakarik, many patients drop out of treatment as a result. In routine clinic care, dropout rates approach 50%, and half of the patients terminate by the fourth visit. Across several studies, when patients were asked prior to treatment how many sessions they expected would be necessary to achieve their goals, 70% said they wanted 10 sessions or fewer; about half expected 5 sessions or fewer (Pakarik, 1993). What patients want from therapists may differ significantly from what many therapists want to provide. Most patients seek advice, problem definition, problem-solving, and lots of therapist interactivity (Pakarik, 1993).

In contrast to many patients, therapists put the number of sessions needed to achieve therapeutic goals at somewhere between 20 and 750. The "dose effectiveness" literature that has looked at thousands of cases is closer to the view of patients than of therapists; it indicates that most change occurs on average early on—70% by the seventh session (Howard et al., 1986). A small but significant cohort of patients expect therapy will take a long time to complete ("After all, it took me a long time to get this screwed up!"), but, in general, most patients want it short, sweet, and effective. The relationship between outcome and length of treatment aggregated from many studies of outcome is shown in Figure 3.2. Note the change in the steepness of the slope of improvement after session 10. Not coincidentally, most therapeutic gain is achieved by about session 7—close to the number most patients expect.

If the delivery of psychotherapy services is impaired by a chaotic healthcare system, an attachment to the idea that longer is always better (and the belief that one brand of psychotherapy is inherently better than another), psychopharmacology seems tainted by darker forces. In the *pax medica*, drug companies have tried to turn the prescribing relationship into

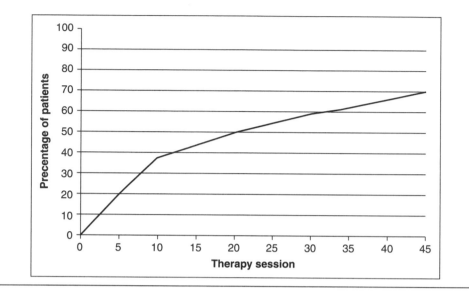

Figure 3.2 Session-by-Session Effectiveness of the "Dose" of Psychotherapy (After Lutz et al., 2001)

a commodity. In a development that bolsters our impression that this era is coming to an end, a group of researchers from the Oregon Health and Science University subpoenaed the FDA to release *all* the studies on antidepressant effectiveness it had considered in evaluating antidepressant efficacy. The FDA had received nearly as many unpublished studies as published ones; but few observers were aware of either the number or the conclusions of the unpublished ones. The report of the whole metasample, published in the *New England Journal of Medicine*, documents the fact that of the 74 studies originally reviewed, 38 were judged to be positive by the FDA (Turner, Matthews, Linardatos, Tell, & Rosenthal, 2008). All but one of these positive studies were published, while only *one* of the 40 negative studies made it into print. In other words, studies showing positive effects for antidepressants were 12 times more likely to be published than studies showing negative results.

Turner, who had once reviewed psychotropic drug data for the FDA, stated that he was motivated to undertake the study by colleagues who questioned the need for further clinical drug trials on the effectiveness of antidepressants. After conducting their study, he and his colleagues concluded that publication bias inflated the common impressions of the effectiveness of these medications by about a third overall; for some medications, the figure was as much as 69%. A *Wall Street Journal* story about these developments reported that:

"There is a view that these drugs are effective all the time," [Turner] said. "I would say they only work 40% to 50% of the time," based on his reviews of the research at the FDA, "and they would say, 'What are you talking about? I have never seen a negative study.'" Dr. Turner said he knew from his time with the agency that there were negative studies that hadn't been published (Armstrong & Winstein, 2008, p. D1).

As a "cost-saving measure," depression and other mental health problems are frequently treated by primary care physicians who see patients for 10 to 15 minutes and then write a prescription for an antidepressant. Harvard psychiatrist Joseph Glenmullen, in his book *Prozac Backlash*, states that SSRIs, with their ease of use and broad applicability, are both one of the blessings and one of the curses of the *pax medica*. Drug company ads prime millions to seek help for depression, panic, and obsessive-compulsive disorder, but utilization managers and treatment protocols pressure primary-care doctors to limit treatment to drugs, without regard to the availability of effective psychotherapeutic treatment (Pettus, 2006). This practice yields millions of dollars of ineffectual and misguided treatment.

Psychiatry in general seems to have lost contact with the importance of the therapeutic relationship, but the significance of this factor has not lessened because of that. Three enterprising researchers—McKay, Zac, and Wampold (2006)—reanalyzed treatment outcomes of patients who participated in the medication segment of the Treatment of Depression Collaborative Research Program of the National Institute of Mental Health (NIMH) (Elkin et al., 1989). The results bear eloquent testimony to the power of the prescribing relationship. The original NIMH study did not even include the relationship as a study variable, but focused instead on comparing the effects of the antidepressant imipramine with a placebo. Results heralded the power of the pill. In the study reanalysis, however, although medication controlled about 3.4% of the variance in outcome scores, the contribution attributed to the relationship with the psychiatrist was 9.1%. The authors concluded that "psychiatrist effects [on outcome] were greater than the treatment [antidepressant's] effects (p. 287)." The most effective psychiatrist actually got better results with placebos than the worst-performing psychiatrist got with antidepressants (McKay, Zac, Wampold, 2006).

The mess American mental healthcare finds itself in today, at the close of the era of the *pax medica*, is in no small measure a product of inequities resulting from competition among the mental health disciplines. A few patients are indulged with extravagant treatments, and many more are undertreated or receive no treatment at all. Literally billions of dollars are wasted on ineffective drug treatments, and the same is probably true of ineffective psychotherapy. Overall expectations of psychotherapy are diminished as a result of inappropriately rigid insurer-driven utilization policies (and the aggregated diminished expectations are used as justifications for further reductions in the funding for anything but evidence-based treatments). Far too many patients are convinced that just by taking a pill, their brain will bounce back into a healthy equilibrium. One promising development on the horizon is the emergence of a new model that balances respect for *both* brain and relationship factors in the treatment of major mental disorders.

THE ROAD AHEAD

If the uneasy truce between psychiatry and the other mental health professions that has held for 40 years is now on the threshold of change, what will a new model look like? In our view, neuroscience will play a leading role in a new synthesis. Both the psychotherapeutic professions and psychology have struggled since Freud severed neurology from psychology, leaving psychiatry mindless and psychology brainless. Contemporary psychiatry lacks both a solid connection to the mind and a solid foundation in physical medicine. There is even considerable controversy about how the most common psychiatric medications—SSRIs—work. Yet psychiatric problems are spoken of as "diseases" for which there are biochemical causes. Psychology and the other psychotherapeutic professions are entangled in a similar Cartesian dualism. We habitually speak of "mind" as if it were not embodied. Most psychotherapists lack basic knowledge about how the brain works. What is the way toward a model that heals this breach between brain science and the science of psychology?

Using the tools we have at hand—introspection, close observation of mother-infant attachment behavior, imaging studies of the brain, animal studies, studies of patients with neurological injuries and abnormalities, case studies of therapies in which deep-seated anxieties have been tamed, and the lessons of decades of psychotherapy outcome research—we have some strong clues about future directions. As we will see in Chapter 4, the foundation for a new model is likely to be based on an appreciation of how the brain is affected by the power of relationships in human development.

CHAPTER 4

The Therapeutic Relationship

There is no such thing as a baby, only a baby and a mother.
—D. W. Winnicott, *The Family and Individual Development*

GREAT OCCASIONS SUCH as wars or divorces may begin with events that in the present pass by almost unnoticed. Two such small moments in the history of psychology were Sigmund Freud's decisions to abandon neuroscience in favor of "pure psychology" in his theory-building work and to emphasize the technical features of treatment over the relational ones in his clinical practice (or at least in his writings about his cases). These two apparently minor decisions set the stage for a 100-years' war in the mental health professions. The idea that the relationship is part of the treatment has practically vanished from contemporary psychiatry. Battles within psychology over the importance of technique versus the therapeutic alliance have outlived the empirical justification for them. Relationships have been subordinated to the technical issues of selecting the right agent (or the right method) and making sure patients comply with the instructions on the bottle.

In this chapter we look at the therapeutic relationship: what makes it possible, how it produces change, and how its effectiveness can be maximized. Relationships may be the hottest topic in the psychological sciences today. Contemporary biological psychology, attachment theory, and research on the interaction of the relational and technical elements of treatment are changing the way therapists think and practice. Ideas from these differing perspectives provide the raw material for building a new model for psychological and psychopharmacological treatment that is likely to supercede the estimable but increasingly outdated assumptions of "evidence-based" treatment and the *pax medica*.

Early relationships in the family, particularly the parent-infant bond, are the crucible for later character. The limbic structures are crucial to all the behaviors that nurture an offspring through its initial dependency (Lewis et al., 2000). Mammals must have relationships to survive, and this characteristic reaches its most extreme in humans. The brain gives us the capacity to bond and empathize; and our attachment experiences, interacting with genes, build the neural networks that make us distinctively human. Changing the brain underlies all the effects of psychotherapy, regardless of the philosophy or methods used by the particular therapist.

Exploiting the brain's potential for neuroplasticity, empathy, and identification, patients use psychotherapy to modify memories and become less constrained by feelings from the past. Their curiosity is unleashed on current life and its real problems. Given the dominant role of fear and anxiety in subcortical memory systems, reducing anxiety and enhancing curiosity about the world are goals in all forms of psychotherapy. Talking integrates existing circuits and helps build new connections. It has the potential for increasing the power of the hippocampus and prefrontal cortex to inhibit and regulate subcortical activation. Using the relationship with the therapist as a base, patients can begin to rebuild old relationships and explore new ones.

PSYCHODYNAMIC VIEWS

Classical analysis contains within it the seeds of the controversies that would preoccupy psychotherapists for generations to come. What was of primary importance—the technique, the patient, the analyst, or the relationship between analyst and patient? In the classical view, technique seems to trump the personal factors. The relationship, at bottom, is a vehicle for remembering primary attachment experiences, which the patient projects, or "transfers," onto the therapist. These formative experiences have been forgotten, lost, or hidden because they are morally objectionable or emotionally dangerous. Some psychoanalytic authors (Klein, 1975) believe analysis of the transference accesses early infantile memories. Through projective identification, patients may harbor the belief that the therapist wants to destroy or seduce them, or that the therapist is cold and indifferent to their suffering. The therapist's job is to clarify that these are the *patient's* wishes and memories, and to interpret them as repressed and forgotten material. Roy Schaefer (1992) refers to this process as "retelling a life." Working within the transferential relationship, the therapist uses alternating interpretations and confrontations in the context of an emotionally supportive relationship (Weiner, 1998). Although some psychoanalytic authors tend to view everything that is thought, said, or withheld in the therapeutic relationship within this framework of unconsciously determined transference, others (such as Greenson, 1992) talk about the "working alliance" between therapist and patient.

Object relations theorists, such as W.R.D. Fairbarn, Margaret Mahler, and Stephen Mitchell, have elucidated the manner in which, through parental relationships, we build psychic structure. The object relations school takes the view that the person of the patient and the therapeutic relationship (or "analytic third") are the effective ingredients in psychotherapy. The therapeutic relationship parallels the original mother-infant dyad and spurs development in the same way. D. W. Winnicott's "good-enough" mother (Winnicott, 1958/1975/1992/1962/1972) not only nurtures us but also, through her imperfections, leads us to look outside the maternal orbit and begin exploring the world. According to Winnicott (1953), "The good-enough mother . . . starts off with an almost complete adaptation to her infant's needs, and as time proceeds she adapts less and less completely, gradually, according to the infant's growing ability to deal with her failure." By cocreating a loving "holding environment," mother and child share a neurodynamic symbiosis. As we venture out into the world, we take with us not only the emotional residue and the explicit memories of this experience, but the neurobiological structure that is its legacy. We carry within us the capacity to comfort ourselves to some extent and the ability to regenerate a good-enough relationship with friends and family members.

Therapists employing other perspectives, especially cognitive behavioral therapy (CBT), typically regard the psychodynamic emphasis on transference and the unconscious as overdone. Like classical analysts, however, CBT practitioners place more emphasis on technical rather than relational factors to get good outcomes. Certainly one of the factors underlying the dramatic rise of CBT is the recognition among many psychodynamic therapists that their patients must do more than just talk about the past and get to know themselves better—they must *do* something to change. However, by the 1980s, even cognitive scientists were discovering that most cognition occurs outside of awareness, that is to say, unconsciously (e.g., Kihlstom, 1987). Moreover, as CBT has become more concerned with core beliefs and schema analysis, it is moving into territory familiar to psychoanalysts.

ROGERS AND BEYOND

In the middle of the twentieth century, psychologists began to explore systematically the role of empathy in psychotherapy. The pioneering work of Carl Rogers (1942) emphasized empathy as the major effective agent in his patient-centered approach. Rogers held that "unconditional positive regard" was critical to building a therapeutic alliance and believed that through an atmosphere of acceptance, the therapist helps patients make positive changes. Unconditional positive regard meant that the therapist both empathized with the patient's suffering and accepted the patient as she was, without requiring her to meet treatment goals for approval. In Rogers's skilled hands, the technique produced a congruence regarding therapeutic goals and tasks. Like other humanistic theorists who followed him, Rogers asserted that given an optimum environment, the natural tendency for each of us is to grow to our full potential. His nondirective approach put the patient in the driver's seat with the therapist along for navigational feedback and emotional support. This approach often elicits less resistance and more self-efficiency in patients.

Psychotherapy exercises our empathic capacities in providing emotional support, consistency, firmness, and creating a coconstructed narrative. Both psychotherapy and the parenting relationship to which it is often compared enhance affect regulation, self-soothing, and mastery (Cozolino, 2002; Schore, 1994). Developing rapport involves shared attention, mutual positive feelings, and in-sync body language. Unconsciously coupled movements between the therapist and patient enhance positive shared feelings (Bernieri & Rosenthal, reported in Goleman, 2006). Two people in conversation develop better rapport by matching the rhythm of breathing (McFarland, 2001). During an empathetic encounter, our thoughts and emotions are in tune with those of the other person. We "get" their emotional experience and, in empathizing, may even develop neural firing patterns that are highly similar to those occurring simultaneously in the brain of the other person (Preston, Bechara, Grabowski, Damasio, & Damasio, 2002).

Establishing empathy can be a very challenging piece of work with some patients. Adults abused as children and depressed or very anxious adults present unique challenges to the therapist's empathizing. Technique is often helpful in these situations—a topic to which we return at the end of this chapter—but the change process is at its heart driven by empathy, consistency, and positive regard. Transference dynamics have much to do with deeply ingrained, nonconscious memories that are associated with character (Grigsby & Hartlaub, 1994). Occurring largely outside of awareness, the patient's reactions to the therapist contain implicit memories that are difficult to put into words but are habitually enacted or felt. Empathy and sustained gentle encouragement allow the patient to begin to find new patterns. New neurodynamic representations of self and others eventually supersede the old ones. Working with the transference means challenging and helping the patient to make adaptive changes. As we describe in more detail later, providing the "holding environment" for a "safe emergency" helps the patient move ahead productively.

ATTACHMENT

Every psychology undergraduate learns about Harry Harlow's primate studies. Harlow was carrying out research with rhesus monkeys when some of the animals began falling ill and dying of disease. Harlow isolated the newborn infants from their potentially infected mothers in hopes of saving the little ones. The strategy was successful in that the infants isolated in cages and bottle-fed by hand lived. But Harlow noticed that the babies kept in cages with cloth-lined floors survived more often than infants kept in cages with bare-wire floors (see Karen, 1998, for an interesting historical account of Harlow's work and his relationship with John Bowlby). The young monkeys became interested in (even fond of) the diapers lining their cages and used them for contact when stressed. Monkeys that lacked this nonhuman primate version of a transitional object often died within a few days of isolation. Harlow went on to demonstrate that early deprivation has long-lasting, even intergenerational effects. Studies of human infants make the same point. Premature infants given extra tactile and kinesthetic stimulation for just 45 minutes while in the hospital grow more quickly, reach developmental milestones sooner, are more alert, and can be discharged from the hospital sooner than controls (Field et al., 1986).

Harlow's studies played an important role in the origins of attachment studies. Later investigators studied the neurochemistry underlying attachment behavior, clarifying what happens in the brains of both infants and caretakers during the formation of these early and enduringly influential relationships. Oxytocin, a neuropeptide found only in mammals, is one important element in this neurochemistry. Oxytocin stimulates maternal behavior in mammals and facilitates bonding. For example, oxytocin injected into the brains of nonpregnant ewes activates maternal behavior (Insel & Young, 2001). Another neuropeptide, vasopressin, facilitates pair bonding. Injecting compounds that block vasopressin or oxytocin inhibits bonding in prairie voles. Adult animals separated at birth from their mothers have persistent neurotransmitter abnormalities. Both the expression of dopamine transporter genes and dopamine-mediated stress responses are altered. Abnormalities also appear in the individual's sensitivity to morphine and in the neurotransmitter receptors for serotonin, benzodiazepine, and the glucocortocoid receptors related to stress response (see Wexler, 2006, for a review).

Just as we are genetically equipped to produce the neuropeptides that elicit bonding behavior, we are also neurodynamically endowed from birth to attract the social attention of adults. The smiling response, for example, is so deeply wired into the human brain that it is seen in infants born with only brain stems (Herschowitz, Kegan, & Zilles, 1997). Although "endogenous" smiling fades with normally developing cortical inhibition, social smiling emerges at 2 to 3 months of age. Infants can distinguish their mothers' voices within 2 to 3 days after birth (Fifer & Moon, 1995). They are primed to look at and track faces within hours postpartum (Goren, Sarty, & Wu, 1975), and within the first 2 weeks they start demonstrating a preference for their mother's face over strangers' faces (Carpenter, 1974).

The neurochemical and early neurodynamic precursors of attachment play a significant role in organizing the brain in the first year of life. By 12 months of age, babies typically have developed durable attachment schema. In the pioneering work of the British psychoanalyst John Bowlby, attachment in infancy is seen as largely a matter of negotiating proximity with life-sustaining caregivers (Bowlby, 1969). Infants older than 6 months show pronounced attachment behavior. A student of Bowlby's who went on to become his major professional partner, Mary Ainsworth (Ainsworth, Blehar, Waters, & Wall, 1978), devised an experimental situation called the *strange situation*. A room in the psychology department at Johns Hopkins University, where Ainsworth was working at the time, was equipped with a one-way mirror, a table and chairs, and a handful of toys. Mothers and their babies were shown into the room, allowed to get used to things, and then a stranger entered the setting. Observations were made about how the baby handled this change in terms of seeking proximity to the mother or leaving her to continue exploring the toys. In another twist for the baby, the mother left the room and the baby was alone with the stranger for a few moments. The baby's reaction to the mother's return was of intense interest to the investigators. What did the baby do and how did she seem to feel when her mother returned and the stranger departed? In one more round, the mother left the room again, leaving the baby completely alone, and observations were made about how the baby reacted in her absence and to her return. "Infant Strange" has become one of the most significant and thoroughly replicated experiments in modern clinical and developmental psychology.

Ainsworth identified several common behaviors in the infants, along with corresponding behaviors in caretakers (Ainsworth, et al., 1978;

Karen, 1998), that she classified as *attachment styles*. In *secure attachment*, the child demonstrates displeasure at the mother's departure and quiets promptly on her return. The baby welcomes the mother's attempts to comfort her and quickly returns to exploring the environment. In *avoidant attachment*, the child seems indifferent to the mother's departure and exhibits muted if any response to her return. *Ambivalently attached* children typically show distress when the mother leaves, relate to the stranger, greet their mother on her return with signs of anger or coldness, and are hesitant to return to play (Ainsworth et al., 1978). An additional style, *disorganized attachment*, identified by Mary Main and colleagues at the University of California at Berkeley (Main & Hesse, 1990; Main & Solomon, 1986), is the most ominous of the four attachment schemas. The disorganized child reacts to the mother's return with stereotyped behavior, such as freezing for several seconds or rocking. These children appear to lack an organized schema or coherent coping strategy. Main also created a reliable way of assessing adult attachment, called the Adult Assessment Interview (Main & Goldwyn, 1994).

Attachment theorists maintain that infants do not construct their attachment schemas sui generis but in response to their impressions of their caregiver. Research shows that the child's attachment behavior is correlated with the behavior and communication styles of the primary caretakers. Moreover, attachment style as assessed in the strange situation with infants at 12 months of age tends to be a highly durable personal characteristic. Fonagy (quoted in Wallin, 2007) concludes from a review of longitudinal studies that the infantile model persists into adulthood in about three cases out of four (i.e., 68–75% of the time). Main's study of the reliability of attachment style in subjects from infancy to age 19 put the figure slightly higher, at over 80%.

The high concordance between the baby's and the parent's attachment styles lead researchers in the direction of looking at the attachment styles of parents. Main explored adult attachment using the Adult Attachment Interview and found that the parents' score on this interview predicts the child's security or insecurity 75% of the time (Wallin, 2007). This appears to hold true even when the parent is assessed *before the child's birth* (van Ijzendoorn, 1995). It may be that infants have a wider range of attachment options and greater capacity for adaptation than do mothers because of the superior plasticity of the infant brain. Parents have already structured early experience into durable patterns of remembering, regulating emotion, and "core beliefs" (to use the CBT term) about relationships—most of which are either nonconscious or only intermittently activated into conscious and self-critical awareness. The taxonomy of parental caretaking behavior has important implications for therapists vis-à-vis our patients:

- Mothers of *securely attached* infants accurately interpret their infant's communications, responding quickly and consistently to their child's needs; they balance, in a "good enough" manner, the conflicting requirements of being the child's secure base.
- Parents of children with an *avoidant attachment style* tend to remain unresponsive to their child's distress, discouraging crying and promoting separation.
- Parents who behave inconsistently, being sometimes tuned in and sometimes indifferent to the child's state of mind, tend to have children who are *ambivalently attached*.
- Abusive, impulsive, and depressed mothers tend to produce children who display *disorganized attachment*.

In a study with relevance to psychotherapy, Michael Rutter and his colleagues on the English and Romanian Adoptees Study Team (O'Connor et al., 1999) looked at healing early attachment traumas through enriched environments. The researchers reported generally optimistic conclusions, supporting the idea that the child's neuroplasticity—when exposed to "good enough" caretaking—can to some extent overcome earlier deprivations. However, children's resiliency appears to be contingent on obtaining remedial caretaking during the sensitive period of attachment. Resiliency of Romanian orphans generally varied as a product of their length of residence in the institution (See *Brain-Based Therapy with Children and Adolescents* for an extended discussion on this issue).

Many studies have looked at the application of attachment theory to adults. Mary Main's Adult Attachment Interview (Main & Goldwyn, 1994; Wallin, 2007) and related self-report questionnaires are used to assess adult attachment styles, and these styles correlate with psychosocial well-being. The interview consists of 36 questions covering basic life history, impressions of the major attachment figures, and focuses on experiences of loss or trauma. In effect, the attachment score is an assessment of the individual's patterns of emotion regulation. (Schore, 2003, refers to attachment as "the dyadic regulation of emotion" [p. 256]). Four styles of adult attachment have been identified: secure, preoccupied, dismissive-avoidant, and fearful-avoidant. Other studies have demonstrated that early attachment style affects the person's ability to cope with stress later in life (Mikulincer & Shaver, 2003) and competence in parenting (Siegel & Hartzell, 2004).

From the point of view of brain-based therapy, attachment schemas describe how the brain, through Hebbian learning, preserves repeating experiences by activating and reactivating neural networks across the course of development, changing the structure of the networks and bolstering their efficiency with each repetition. By the end of the first year of life, the infant is capable of imitating a person not physically present, and even to reference that object in ways that are separate from any of his or her physical features (e.g., through the word "mama") (Piaget, 1937; Beebe and Lachmann, 2002). Through coordinating vocalization, imitation of facial expressions, and the gradual build-up of expectancies, each partner in the interaction is able to enter into the feeling state of the other. Bebe and Lachman, in discussing the implications of how mothers imitate their infants' facial expressions, describe how we discover who we are through a relationship:

> The infant represents the experience of seeing the mothers' face continuously changing to become more similar to his or her own; the infant also represents the experience of his or her own face constantly changing to become more similar to the mother's own face. These "matching" experiences contribute to feeling known, attuned to, on the same wave length. Each partner affects the other so as to match affective direction, and this matching provides each with a behavioral basis for entering into the other's feeling state (2002, p. 98).

Beebe and Lachmann and other object-relations theorists agree with Winnicott that "there is no such thing as a baby." What is experienced in these defining interactions isn't a "self" or an "object" but an *interactional pattern characteristic of the two together*. Thus, by as early as six month of age, infants of depressed mothers show "depressed" behavior even in the company of optimally attuned, nondepressed caretakers (Field et al.1988). Other studies have demonstrated that events that evoke positive affective and behavioral responses and EEG records in babies of normal mothers, evoked in infants with depressed mothers negative behavior. The EEG records of these infants showed the heightened right-hemispheric activity associated with negative affect (Dawson, 1992a, 1992b).

Peter Fonagy and Mary Target have brought attachment theory and contemporary psychoanalysis into a closer relationship by focusing on the concept of *mentalization*, the ability to accurately estimate the beliefs and intentions of others (Robbins & Zacks, 2007). David Wallin (2007) has created a useful and thought-provoking approach for the application of attachment theory to psychotherapy more generally. He emphasizes the importance of Main's interpretation of attachment style as a set of cognitive-emotional rules that set the terms for what we are allowed to think (and what we must deny), what we are allowed to feel (and what must be defended against), and how vigilant or aggressive we must be to maintain a sense of inner security in our relationships.

NEURODYNAMICS

The neurodynamic networks activated during periods of social stress are reactivated in therapy when the therapist confronts maladaptive patterns. In the context of the therapeutic alliance, old representations and habitual patterns of behavior associated with conflictual past attachment relationships are reactivated. As Main discovered in interviewing her subjects, talking about these relationships seems to "prime" the implicit emotional and cognitive schemas underlying core relationship patterns.

For example, a mother of two young children comes in feeling guilty and ashamed about how angry she has been getting ("It's more like enraged") when her kids get tired and "act babyish." On several occasions, she has been so angry she has felt like hitting them and has had to leave the house to regain some self-control. In therapy, she begins the process of finding out where inside herself these reactions come from and what they have to do with a history—a daunting task given that "I don't remember anything before I was about 10." Therapy can help a patient like this begin to link her emotions and "high-road" impulse control centers in the prefrontal cortex. In the process, some childhood experiences may be recalled and become part of the patient's narrative, but memories are likely not so much to resurface or become conscious (as psychoanalysis would have it) as to be coconstructed with the therapist.

Whereas moderate stress facilitates cortical integration in the promotion of new learning, extreme stress may lead to dissociation. The role of psychotherapy is to integrate or modify dysregulated thoughts and feelings and to work against dissociation by integrating disparate states and self-representations (Cozolino, 2002; Grigsby & Stevens, 2000). A mild to moderate degree of stress usually is necessary to facilitate new learning and integration of cognitive and effective systems. It counters the Hebbian tendencies of the system to keep doing the same thing over and over again. During periods of overwhelming stress, however, the cortical systems supporting language, memory, and cognitive clarity may function in a less than optimal manner. The goal of therapy in such cases is to stabilize and shift the patient's state and facilitate improved functioning, relying on mechanisms of neuroplasticity to promote new and healthy traits.

In the case of the mother just mentioned, the combination of parental stress and the deep love she bore for her children motivated her to change the underlying attachment rules that had kept her in a state of unawareness about how she was feeling, how she felt about herself, and her implicit assumptions about what she could expect from other people. Through the relationship with the therapist, the patient was able to get something she had missed in the relationship with her alcoholic parents: a tolerance, in fact an interest, in emotions, the ability to reliably and accurately imagine what other people are feeling and why they react as they do, and improved confidence that relationships are an essential way of regulating our emotions. The supportive relationship with the therapist both elicited traces of the patient's emotional reactions that typically were kept out of awareness and provided an arena in which her "rules" could be clarified and changed. In the course of working with the therapist, the patient also learned and began to practice cognitive and behavioral techniques for managing her anger.

Cozolino (2002, p. 27) proposes that psychotherapy and neural growth and integration should include these six goals:

1. The establishment of a safe and trusting relationship
2. Gaining new information and experiences
3. The simultaneous or alternating activation of neural networks that are inadequately integrated or dissociated
4. Moderate levels of stress or emotional arousal alternating with periods of calm and safety
5. Developing a method of processing and organizing new experiences so as to continue ongoing growth and integration outside of therapy
6. The integration of conceptual knowledge with emotional and bodily experience through narratives that are coconstructed with the therapist

Whatever technical interventions are employed—free associations, dream journals, or CBT thought records—a brain-based approach provides a common denominator for guiding therapeutic work. Our need for and ability to use social appraisal and social relatedness is built into our brains. We utilize therapy just as we do parenting and partnering relationships—the same neurodynamic modules and processes are involved. As we discussed in Chapter 2, the limbic areas and both cerebral hemispheres are critical "wetware" in all social relationships, including the psychotherapeutic one.

MIRROR NEURONS

Recent neuroscience has identified a specialized cell that is associated with empathy. Dubbed *mirror neurons*, these cells respond to the movements (either seen or imagined) of another person, and possibly to many other aspects of social interaction as well. Giacomo Rizzolatti, the Italian neuroscientist who led the team who discovered mirror neurons, noted that they "allow us to grasp the minds of others not through conceptual reasoning but through direct simulation; by feeling, not by thinking." (quoted in Goleman, 2006). Their discovery gives us new insight into the generalized macroprocesses of "evidence-based" theories of psychotherapy and psychopharmacology that have dominated the field for the last 40 years. Mirror neurons are influencing the brain-based understanding and treatment of problems ranging from depression to autism. These cells were first discovered in the frontal cortex of monkeys (Rizzolatti, et al., 2001) watching other monkeys looking for food. Interestingly, mirror neurons seem responsive to another person's actions only when those actions are *intentional* and goal directed—for example, watching your 12-year-old daughter walk over to the refrigerator to get a snack typically would activate your mirror neurons. Watching her come in the front door after school, drop her books on the dining room table, and go into her room to change probably would not cause them to fire.

Mirror neurons are so named because they fire not only when we are observing intentional behavior in another person *but also when we engage in that same behavior ourselves*. Whether we are performing the act or watching someone else do it, mirror neurons are active. It is almost as if our brains are doing the same thing as the brain of the person we are watching, as if we are engaged in the same action. Mirror neurons are found not only in areas corresponding to movement but also vocal expressions and gestures (Gallese, Fadiga, Fogassi, & Rizzolatti, 1996).

We speculate that the development of the mirror neuron system must have played a key role in the evolution of our species. As the social world of hominids favored more sophisticated social adaptation, a brain elaborated to support this interpersonal functioning enhanced the "fitness" of the best-equipped individuals and groups. Rich and layered feedback loops developed in the cortex and bestowed enhanced powers to inhibit sub-cortically driven instinctual and automatic responses in social situations. A more balanced appraisal of the social context would be likely to increase survival potential, both in terms of controlling aggression and also by increasing the chances of reproductive success in complex social settings (Mesulam, 1998). Hominid success resulted in population growth and increased resource competition, redoubling the value of advanced communication skills. Mirror neurons, advantageous to begin with because they increased the capacity to learn from watching the food-seeking behavior of other individuals, later seem to have become coordinated with the neurodynamic systems involved in communicating through hand gestures. Rizzolatti and Arbib (1998), note that mirror neurons are found in Broca's area (important in language expression). They suggest that the mirroring system evolved from *watching the actions of others* to *listening to their communications*. This link between actor and observer became "a link between the sender and the receiver of each message" (p. 188). i.e., it strengthened the relationship between the two parties involved. Interestingly, just listening to the speech of another activates our tongue muscles. The feedback loop between social complexity and the evolutionary fitness of mirror neurons resulted in further social development, as hand gestures favored the human populations who used them and as mirror neurons gave other individuals the neurodynamic basis for advanced imitation (Gallese, 2001). Mirror neurons probably also played a part in the evolution of vocal communication, as vocalizations emerged as a sort of proto-language.

Goal-directed behaviors and planning for the future are functions of the prefrontal lobes (Chaminade et al., 2002). The expansion of these modules differentiated hominids from other apes. In monkeys, most of the early work on mirror neurons focused on an area of the frontal lobes (F5) analogous to Broca's area in the human brain. The discovery of mirror neurons in non-human primates suggests that our ability to perceive and express phonetic gestures and actions is a legacy to the nonhuman primates and to us from a common ancestor (Gallese et al., 1996). In humans, however, the evolution of phonetic gestural communication to actual words paralleled the expansion of the frontal lobes and mirror neuron system.

Mirror neurons presumably bestowed on us a capacity for carrying out adaptive functions that increased the chances of our survival and chances of reproductive success. We imitate the behavior of another person on the same side of our bodies as the behavior we observe in the other person (Koski et al., 2003). This has adaptive value insofar as it enables us to respond to a physical attack or threat more quickly. If someone were to move to strike you with their right hand, for example, your impulse would be to block it with your left.

Mirror neurons are part of the neurobiology of empathy (Iacoboni & Lenzi, 2002). They are probably an important component of the brain-based systems that let us "feel" for a person who looks sad and dejected. Watching a scene in which two girls are talking, and one makes a face, shrugs, and walks away toward another group makes us wonder if the girl who was left feels rejected. Good actors tap into this empathetic system, causing us to experience vicariously their trials and tribulations we are witnessing on the movie screen. Other brain-based cognitive and emotional systems are also involved in our response to drama— for example, the attachment system seems to get primed out of its neurodynamic latency by exposure to attachment themes, especially when they are emotionally powerful. There is increasing agreement, however, that our capacities for attachment also rest on the capacity of these cells to help us understand the intentions of others (Miller, 2005). Most writers who focus on the neurodynamic aspects of psychotherapy (e.g. Cozolino, 2006; Schore, 2002; Siegel, 2007) agree, and point to the importance of mirror neurons as part of the neural basis of the therapeutic alliance.

EMPATHY AND THEORY OF MIND

Other major neurodynamic elements underlie our capacity to feel empathy as well. Damasio (2003), for example, notes that empathy is associated with the right somatosensory cortices, a region also associated with integrated body mapping. Whereas damage to the parallel region in the left hemisphere results in no loss of empathy, damage to the right somatosensory cortex produces deficits in our ability to empathize. The actual commands for producing "as-if" body states are likely to come from a variety of prefrontal cortices related to mirror neurons. These and other neurodynamic elements play an integral role in the "theory of mind" (ToM) each of us carries within us.

Theory of mind is both a complex neurodynamic and cognitive-emotional process by which we try to understand and predict the behavior of others. Other nonhuman primates, such as baboons and chimps, can do this too (Grigsby & Stevens, 2000). Children develop aspects of ToM by age 5. The neural substrate of this capability is the same one we use when planning our future (Ramnani & Miall, 2004). ToM bolsters the individual's capability for formulating responses to the behavior anticipated in others. For example, one primate field observer watched an emerging competition for dominance shaping up between two males, one a young adult and the other a senior and more dominant one. The young male recruited a female to help chase the old fellow up a tree, where he looked down at the couple and expressed his displeasure by hooting and making gestures. Perhaps worried about how all this was going to turn out for him, the young male grinned widely—a sure signal of primate tension and stress—but first *placed his hand over his mouth* so the older animal could not see what he was signaling and discover that his brashness was mixed with fear (recounted in Grigsby & Stevens, 2000). The young animal used his ToM to carry off this deception by forecasting the consequences of his rival seeing weakness in his grin and trying to exploit it.

A variety of areas in the brain are associated with ToM, including the amygdala, insula, and anterior cingulate (Siegal & Varley, 2002; see Cozolino, 2006, for a review). The right orbitofrontal cortex is involved in decoding mental states, and the left specializes in reasoning about those states (Sabbagh, 2004). According to Frith and Frith (1999), there may be three major cortial nodes involved in ToM operations:

1. The medial prefrontal cortex for self-related mental states
2. The superior temporal sulcus for goals and outcomes
3. The inferior frontal area for actions and goals

ORBITOFRONTAL AND ANTERIOR CINGULATE CORTICES

If various modules of our brain are impaired either through underdevelopment (due, e.g., to insecure attachment) or through an insult such as traumatic brain injury, then the interpersonal process will be limited as well. For example, deficits in the functioning of the orbitofrontal cortex (OFC) appears to produce the social disconnect problems of autism (Baron-Cohen, 1995). An area of the OFC referred to as FI and area 24 of the anterior cingulate cortex (ACC) are rich in *spindle cells*. These areas are thought to be involved in our emotional reactions to others, especially instantaneous feelings of empathy. Hearing a baby cry, for example, makes us feel empathy for that baby. These neurodynamic modules have also been described as an important part of our biological basis for love because they activate when we find a person attractive or we see a picture of a person we love (Bartels & Zeki, 2000).

Spindle cells are a class of neurons that respond extremely quickly to incoming stimuli. There are more of these cells in the human brain than in the brains of any other species. The cells are spindly with a large bulb at one end and a long thick extension. It is thought that their overall large size, with a bulb about four times larger than that of other neurons, equips them for high-velocity transmission. The location of spindle cells in the brain and the connections they make between areas crucial to our conduct of relationships underscore their importance in the experience of emotion and even adaptation to therapy. Spindle cells have rich synaptic receptors for dopamine, serotonin, and vasopressin. These transmitters play a role in mood, valuing our emotional experiences, and bonding. These cells form connections between the cingulate cortex and the OFC (Allman, 2001).

In humans, spindle cells connect divergent bits of information quickly and efficiently in ways not seen in other species (Nimchinsky et al., 1995, 1999). Many theorists believe that their efficiency puts the "snap" in our snap judgements. They provide a unique interface between cognition and emotion. As such, they aid us in the ability to maintain sustained attention and self-control and give us the behavioral flexibility for quick problem solving in complex and emotionally stirring situations (Allman, 2001). Spindle cells appear after birth and seem to be dependent on experiential stimulation for growth and development. They may be vulnerable to the effects of negative life experiences such as neglect, abuse, and trauma, resulting in deficits in the abilities organized by the cingulate cortex (see Cozolino, 2006, for a review).

Several neural circuits important in social interactions seem to be "idling" all the time, ready to act or respond to social situations. These neural circuits seem to activate during our judgments about people. They include the dorsal and ventral parts of the medial prefrontal cortex, the right intraparietal sulcus, the right fusiform gyrus, the left superior temporal and medial temporal cortex, the left motor cortex, and parts of the occipital cortex (Mitchell et al., 2002). These idling areas become more active when we interact with or think about people. They have been called a default system for mulling over our relationships (Iacoboni et al., 2004).

The orbital medial prefrontal cortex (OMPFC) maintains connections with several subcortical structures, including the amygdala and the hypothalamus. Because of these connections, the OMPFC is an important motivational and emotional center (Fuster, 1997), one that is critically involved with affect regulation (Schore, 1994). The OMPFC helps us modulate and temper our emotions so that we can effectively achieve our goals, social and otherwise. Studies measuring OFC activity suggest that it is also involved in feelings of warmth and love. In brain imaging studies, the OFCs of mothers light up in reaction to pictures of their infants but not in reaction to pictures of other people. The higher the level of OFC activation, the more intense the subjective positive feelings, as the OFC essentially overwhelms the rest of the brain with warm feelings (Urry et al., 2004).

The cingulate cortex wraps around the corpus callosum the way a shirt collar encircles the neck. The cingulate plays an indispensable part in bonding, maternal behavior, and activities requiring social cooperation (Rilling et al., 2002). Its front portion, the *anterior cingulate cortex* (the ACC) helps integrate cognitive and emotional information from throughout the cortex (Bush, Luu, & Posner, 2000). The ACC is active when detecting emotional signals from others as well as ourselves (Critchley et al., 2004). Alexithymics—people who do not subjectively experience feelings and cannot describe them—have *smaller* than normal right ACCs; subjects who report more fearfulness and worry have *larger* right ACCs (Gundel et al., 2004). The ACC acts as a sort of alarm system for both physical pain and emotional distress (Eisenberger & Lieberman, 2004). The dorsal ACC (that is, it's top part) alerts other brain modules of harm and responds when there is a threat of interpersonal rejection (Lieberman, 2005). Damage to the ACC results in decreased empathy and maternal behavior (Brothers et al., 1996). When we or those we love experience pain or social ridicule, the ACC activates (Botvinick et al., 2005). Activation of the nearby posterior cingulate gyrus has been correlated with the subjective experience of autobiographical memories and emotional processing (Critchley et al., 2003).

Another neurodynamic module, the insula cortex, serves in part as a conduit between subcortical areas and the cortex. It provides information from the body, input from the amygdala, and input from the hypothalamus to the medial prefrontal cortex. Empathy is an emergent product of the interaction of the insula's body networks and its links with the medial prefrontal cortex. The insula seems to provide the neurodynamic foundation for the capacity to look inward; together with the medial prefrontal area, it helps interpret what it *feels* like to be another person. The insula links the mirror neuron system with internal body states. This "insula hypothesis" of empathy is supported by the introspective capacities of the prefrontal cortex (Carr et al., 2003).

Jaak Panksepp (1998), a distinguished biopsychologist who was for many years at Bowling Green University, coined the term "affective neuroscience" to describe the brain-based study of emotional experience. Panksepp has proposed that the neural circuitry that activates when adults flirt with each other is also activated in infants interacting with any friendly, smiling person. Panksepp speculates that the reward and circuits energized when we fall in love, crave our lover when she's away, and bond with our newborn baby are also ones activated during drug addiction and withdrawal. Cocaine addicts have been reported to have smaller cingulate, insula, and frontal cortices than controls (Franklin et al., 2002). It is not clear, however, whether these abnormalities preceded the cocaine abuse or resulted from it. Activation of these areas in the brain may represent the addict's attempt to relieve the pain of insecure attachment schemas (see Cozolino, 2006, for review). The PFC and subcortical areas are also involved in craving and drug abuse. Specifically, the OFC and the ACC activate when addicts crave, binge, and become intoxicated. During withdrawal, these areas deactivate. The overvaluing of the drug and the disinhibition of judgment when seeking out the drug involves the OFC (Goldstein, 2002).

THE TELLTALE FACE

In social encounters, the social brain especially values information conveyed by the facial expressions and expressive eye communications of the people with whom we interact. Research subjects were shown pictures of faces with differing pupil-to-sclera (the white part of the eye) ratios so rapidly that they were not consciously aware of what they were seeing. Nevertheless, the amygdalas of these subjects became activated after each exposure and in predictable directions, depending on whether the eye communication made the face look happy or threatening (Whalen et al., 2004).

The right hemisphere (RH) is more adept than the left at reading emotions in the facial expressions of others (Ahern et al., 1991). Patients with RH damage are impaired both in their ability to read emotional facial expressions and body language (Blonder, et al., 1991). The left hemisphere (LH) in most of us is clueless when it comes to reading emotionally expressive facial and body language cues. Lacking the RH's sensitivity to context and emotional nuance, the LH confabulates something specious to explain the available neurodynamic inputs.

Blushing is a uniquely human social communication—no other animal does it. We blush when we are embarrassed or anxious that others will find out that we are anxious. It has been described as an inadvertent apology or confession of guilt or shame (deJong et al., 2003). Blushing invites attention. In fact, many sufferers of social anxiety disorder fear it, a phobia referred to as erythrophobia (Bögels et al., 1996). Researchers have found that staring fixedly at one side of the face of a person in a performance situation results in the performer blushing more on the side of the face being scrutinized (Drummond & Mirco, 2004). Blushing is but one of many facial cues processed by the "social brain." The main neural networks specializing in faces are located in the fusiform gyrus, superior temporal sulcus, and (as mentioned) the amygdala (Gautheir et al., 2000; Puce et al., 1995). A variety of regions in the cortex become activated depending on whether the person is familiar to us and how we interpret his or her intent. In humans, these systems are activated only when images of faces are presented right-side up (Kilts, Egan, Gideon, Ely, & Hoffman, 2003), whereas chimps' brains activate when they are upside-down as well. In humans, neurodynamic systems associated with identifying *objects* activate when the subject is shown images of upside-down faces (Aguirre et al., 1999).

The face is a complex organ that inputs emotional communication from others, starts the process of empathizing with what the other person is feeling, and communicates our reactions to them. The face can operate more quickly than the conscious brain, and much of what it senses and expresses remains subliminal. People have an interpreting bias when viewing facial expressions. When we view a frown, we tend to become more negative; when we view a smile, we feel more positive (Larsen, Kasimatis, & Frey, 1992). Researchers have found that when an attractive woman directly gazes at a man, his brain activates dopamine circuits associated with pleasure (Blakemore & Firth, 2004). When our eyes lock eyes with another person, the social brain—including the amygdala, cingulate, insula, frontal cortex, and superior temporal gyrus (Kingstone, Tipper, Ristic, & Ngan, 2004; Pelphley et al., 2004)—activates. Amygdalar damage results in deficits in social judgment and difficulty reading faces, especially in estimating trustworthiness (Whalen et al., 2004). Some neuroscientists have stressed that we are primed to have a preference for happy faces (Leppanen & Hietanen, 2003). Cooperation and information sharing between the left and right hemispheres is very important in appraising facial expression, as a study comparing alexithymics and "normals" illustrates. Alexithymics process facial information more in their LHs and show less activation in the medial frontal regions and their cingulate gyrii than do normals (Berthoz et al., 2002).

The role of implicit racial bias has been the focus of some inquiry. One study showed that when European American subjects were shown pictures of African Americans, they exhibited more left-amygdala activation and even a startle response (Phelps et al., 2000). Yet for European Americans and African American subjects who are shown the pictures of people from the same race, there is greater amygdala habituation (Hart et al., 2000). Subjects who are in an angry mood have been shown to express more racial bias even when race had nothing to do with the cause of their anger (DeSteno et al., 2004).

Evolution and each person's experience-dependent neurodynamic development equip us for appraising the emotional state and social intent of the individuals around us. We are also endowed with a quick feedback system that links our own facial musculature with the emotional centers in our brains. Contracting the muscles on the right side of our face that are controlled by our LH increases the chances that we will experience positive affect. Contracting the muscles on the right side that are controlled by our RH increases the chances that we will feel one of the negative emotions (Schiff, Esses, & Lamon, 1992). Paul Ekman, a pioneer in the study of human emotion and facial expression, also noted the existence of this feedback process (Ekman, 1983; Ekman & Oster, 1979). Asked to frown or to smile, subjects are disposed to feel sad or happy, respectively. In the psychotherapeutic encounter, facial expression is one of many sources of nonverbal emotional communication. Through their mirror neuron systems, patients may nonconsciously mimic the facial expressions and moods of their therapists. The OFC, insula, ACC, and amygdala, among other modules, all play important roles in the social encounter that is psychotherapy.

Now that we are equipped with a better understanding of what is going on "behind the scenes" of the interpersonal encounter, we return for a second look at the characteristics of successful therapeutic relationships. As we discussed in Chapter 3, the American Psychological Association's Division of Psychotherapy Task Force on Empirically Supported Relationships (Norcross, 2002) summarized these elements. Three of the factors topping the list of characteristics that all successful therapies have in common are: a strong alliance between patient and therapist, warmth and empathy on the therapist's part, and a consensus between therapist and patient regarding the goals and tasks of treatment.

THERAPEUTIC ALLIANCE

Therapists whose work was marked by superior outcomes in studies reviewed by the Division 29 Task Force spent more time with difficult patients, used outside resources, were firm and direct, encouraged autonomy, implemented problem-solving skills, and had strong therapeutic relationships with the patients. Orlinsky, Grave, & Parks (1994) reviewed some 2,000 process-outcome studies since Eysenck (1952) and added to this list of virtues the therapist's credibility, skill, empathic understanding, and ability to affirm patients and direct their attention to their emotional experience. This list of virtues could also describe the characteristics of a "good-enough" parent. Whether we as therapists think we exhibit these sterling qualities, even the opinion of objective raters about whether we do so or not matters less than what our *patients* think.

In a review of the literature on therapeutic alliance and patient outcome, Lambert and Barley (2002) concluded that "client-perceived relationship factors, rather than objective raters' perceptions of the relationship" were the most powerful in predicting the overall success of the therapy (p. 22).

In the early stages of therapy, the strength of the alliance is linked with the patient's sense of being understood and supported by another person who engenders hope. The therapist's empathy, in particular, is likely to elicit implicit nonconscious attachment schemas, or transference. Wallin (2007) states that the early sessions often give the therapist a feel for the patient's attachment style. Goleman (2006) describes the complexity of empathy succinctly:

> The word empathy is used in three distinct senses: knowing another person's feelings; feeling what that person feels; and responding compassionately to another's distress. These three varieties of empathy seem to describe a 1-2-3 sequence: I notice you, I feel with you, and so I act to help you. (p. 58)

The more we know about the patient's *perception* of our empathic activity the better (Miller, Duncan, & Hubble, 2004). Clinicians in organized practice settings are moving to enhance overall outcomes through early identification of alliance problems. Patients are told that giving structured feedback is one of the tasks expected of them in treatment and are offered simple instruments to provide this input. Therapists discuss this input with patients when it indicates potential problems. Studies have documented the fact that our intuitive sense of how our patients are feeling, and how engaged they are in the therapy, can be way off target. As Hovarth and Bedi (2002, p. 60) state: "Therapists should anticipate that their initial assessment of the patient's relational capacities, preferences, and evaluation of the quality of the alliance may differ from the patient's." From the point of view of the attachment literature, it makes excellent sense that a major of arena of action in any psychotherapy will be exploring these differences, eliciting the patient's implicit affective responses to less than perfect alliances, and working together to improve the relationship. In this way, therapy can bring very deep attachment schemas to light and help the patient rework them.

PATIENT FACTORS

Recall from Chapter 3 that patient characteristics are the single most important factor in whether a therapy is successful. Three variables have been found to be "demonstrably effective" (the gold medal for empirical certainty): the type and intensity of a patient's resistance, her functional impairment, and her particular coping style. Gender and ethnicity have not been demonstrated to figure significantly in outcome. Bohart (2000) has shown that in many ways what happens in treatment depends on what the patient *wants* to happen. What we as therapists are called on to do is foster the optimum balance between supporting patients in attaining new traits (or neural attractors) while we appreciate their need to remain autonomous and in their current state. Resistance is often at the fulcrum of this balancing act.

Empirical studies have consistently found that tailoring technique to the patient's resistance enhances therapeutic success. Beutler and Harwood (2000) suggest three responses to these expressions of resistant states:

1. Acknowledgment and reflection of the patient's concerns and anger
2. Discussion of the therapeutic relationship
3. Renegotiation of the therapeutic contract regarding goals and therapeutic roles

Empirical support for tailoring technique to accommodate the patient's resistance is especially strong in regard to the use of directive and nondirective interventions. CBT is the prototype of the directive approach; psychodynamic methods are examples of nondirective approaches. In general, *directive interventions work best with patients with relatively low levels of resistance*, and *nondirective interventions work best with patients whose level of resistance is relatively high*. For example, Beutler, Engle, and colleagues (1991) demonstrated that CBT and nondirective interventions were differentially effective for depressed patients, depending on their initial level of characterological resistance. Patients who were less resistant did best with directive, CBT procedures.

Resistance often varies with how positively patient and therapist are feeling about the therapeutic team (aka "congruence" regarding the therapeutic alliance). Patients who are very positive about therapy and the therapist are also typically (but not always) highly receptive and engaged. This is one more reason why it is a good practice to inquire about how patients feel therapy is progressing and how they see the therapeutic relationship. Safran and Muran (2003) distinguish two important types of resistance—*withdrawal* and *confrontation*—that express differing and sometimes conflicting needs in the patient regarding the alliance.

Patients who are hamstrung by attachment schema that predispose them to see a conflict between getting emotional closeness and the demand to accommodate to not-good-enough caretaking are likely to *withdraw* from emotional closeness in the therapy. Other patients angrily *confront* or subtly denigrate therapy and the therapist because they react to indications that the therapist is not good enough by asserting their need for autonomy over their need for support. If we notice and ask about indications of withdrawal or declining hope or frustration and pessimism in patients, we may find alternating withdrawal and confrontation in the same patient. Safran and

Muran (2003) provide convincing evidence that just letting patients talk about the feelings that underlie such attachment schema helps. From a brain-based point of view, soliciting even quite negative appraisals of the therapy and the therapist is likely to enrich the OFC networks related to affective awareness and bolster patients' skills in repairing relationship ruptures.

Therapists committed to getting the results empirical studies now say are possible using outcome-driven and patient-centered methods will supply patients with formal means to provide feedback. Michael Lambert uses the Q45 questionnaire, an instrument that has provided data on an enormous number of cases. Lambert's system makes it possible to see exactly where the patient falls relative to the mean progress of thousands of other patients. These appraisals significantly increase the clinician's ability to predict when a therapy is likely to end in abrupt termination, or whether it is going so well the patient may want to consider terminating. Scott Miller and his colleagues (Miller et al., 2004) developed a shorter measure that has some of the same virtues.

CUSTOMIZING THE THERAPEUTIC APPROACH

In addition to selecting techniques suitable to the patient's level of resistance, James Prochaska's "stages of change" theory can help us accommodate our approach to patient variables (Prochaska & DiClemenete, 1983; Prochaska & Norcross, 2002). For example, Mr. F., a 42-year-old man, comes in for a consultation. After some preliminaries, he confides that he is spending several hours a day looking at pornography on the Internet. He is seeking therapy because his wife checked the computer's history and confronted him with the evidence of this pattern. She insisted he get help. Mr. F. admits his habit bothers him, "but it's not a big deal." He is not sure therapy ever works, especially with something like this.

In Prochaska's terms, Mr. F. is at a "contemplative" level of change. He is *thinking* about doing something but does not know what that might be and is not convinced that anything will work. An appropriate intervention would be to acknowledge both sides of Mr. F.'s ambivalence and tell him that he is experiencing a typical stage in the change process. Psychotherapy has helped people with similar problems, as have 12-step groups. The therapist may tell Mr. F. that the best thing he can do for himself at this stage is to get more information and think about the pros and cons of making a change rather than jumping into anything *before he has made up his mind*. Offering to help the patient think more about how pornography is affecting him and his marriage, and getting more information on what other people have done about it, are appropriate therapeutic interventions with contemplators.

Discussing the patient's expectations for the treatment and laying the foundation for assimilating problematic experiences have also been found to be "probably effective" customizing interventions. The evidence for the impact of customizing the treatment in terms of the patient's preferences, personality disorder, attachment style, religion, and cultural or ethnic factors is indeterminate.

OUTCOMES, THERAPY RELATIONSHIPS, AND ATTACHMENT

D. W. Winnicott (1941/1975) conducted a famous series of experiments with babies in the "set situation." Winnicott (a pediatrician before he became a psychoanalyst) saw the mother and the baby together in his consulting room and, in the course of general discussion, placed a shiny tongue-depressing spatula on the table. Typically, 1-year-olds looked at the spatuala from the safety of Mom's lap and then looked away, seemingly uninterested. Left to their own devices, babies would eventually look back at it, possibly look away several more times, but eventually grab the spatula and begin tasting, sucking, and whacking it on the table. Babies who did not feel secure in the situation never relaxed enough to get carried away with their own subjectivity. Mothers who were too anxious to let babies have the experience on their own terms typically made things go amiss (and sometimes alarmingly so; Winnicott saw interference sometimes provoke asthma attacks). The set situation convinced Winnicott that it takes time for a baby to make up his mind, "find the courage of his own feeling," and make the spatula the vehicle for an experience that fosters subjective autonomy (Winnicott, 1941/1975; for an interesting discussion of the set situation, see Phillips, 1993).

here are suggestive parallels here to the therapeutic setting. The therapist qualities called out by the literature—warmth, empathy, firmness, supportiveness, flexibility—are also a laundry list of Winnicott's good-enough mothering. Good-enough therapists undoubtedly elicit more positive transference and are also better prepared to deal with ruptures in the therapeutic relationship. Being a good-enough therapist means privileging the patient's perceptions of the relationship—struggling against whatever qualities we, as therapists, may have in common with the uninvolved mothers of avoidantly attached children and the inconsistent ones of the ambivalently attached. Brain-based therapy involves keeping an eye on how the patient is experiencing us and the treatment, using all the resources of our brain's social appraisal system. Is the patient hopeful or pessimistic? Does she feel the therapist "gets it" or not? Difficulties inevitably occur. Faced with the patient's (and our own) tendency to defensively obscure these difficulties by left-brain storytelling, our clarifying of these negative feelings and worries can unlock a gold mine of material. The therapist's capacity to identify and repair ruptures fosters developmental (and psychotherapeutic) success. Psychotherapy research, the attachment literature, and neurodevelopmental theory all converge on this point. Once again, Michael Lambert:

> It is imperative that therapists carefully observe patient behaviors for any indication of difficulties with the alliance . . . it is essential for therapists to inform patients that dialogue about the therapy relationship is a vital part of therapy and that expressions of negative feelings are allowed and appreciated. (Lambert and Barley, 2002, p. 27)

FIRMNESS AND CONFRONTATION

Psychotherapy, like other close personal encounters (and in fact all other forms of communication), affects the brain, but not all forms of psychotherapy affect the brain favorably. For example, therapy that supports existing neural networks may prolong dysfunction. If a patient asks for and gets sympathy from the therapist for self-perpetuating negative thinking based on self-pity, constructive change via the creation of new neural nets does not develop. Unless we therapists challenge these negative core beliefs and feelings, we may inadvertently reinforce the existing dysfunctional dynamics. Whereas moderate stress can facilitate cortical integration through neuroplasticity in the promotion of new learning, extreme stress and trauma can lead to dissociation. The role of psychotherapy, therefore, is to integrate neural networks and work against dissociation (Cozolino, 2002).

Effective psychotherapy utilizes a mild to moderate degree of stress to facilitate new learning and foster integration of cognitive and effective systems. The task of brain-based therapists (aka psychotherapists) is to get patients out of their neurodynamic ruts. Fritz Perls once said that people must be frustrated enough to change—a view that reflects the conservatism of many neuroscientists about the difficulty of changing deep-brain-motivated characteristics and behaviors. In Winnicottian terms, one of the reasons that "good enough" beats "perfect" parenting hands down is that it frustrates children and spurs the development of their own resources.

In therapy as in parenting, frustration must be combined with support. The therapist creates a "safe emergency" (Perls, Hefferline, & Goodman,

1951), challenging patients to get in touch with their frustration and encouraging change. Safran and Muran (2003) highlight the patient's defensive operations that are elicited in the ups and downs of the therapeutic alliance. Clarifying these defenses and the feelings underlying them counteracts the conservativism of the brain. It bolsters the patient's need to integrate and to invent new reactions to a relationship that is not a fantasy romance with an ideal mate but rather one that appears to be ideal for fostering changes in the brain: a good-enough and secure relationship with a committed and imperfect caretaker.

CHAPTER 5

Working with Memory
and Emotion

Memory-images and imagination-images do not differ in their intrinsic qualities, so far as we can discover. They differ by the fact that the images that constitute memories, unlike those that constitute imagination, are accompanied by a feeling of belief which may be expressed in the words "this happened." The mere occurrence of images, without this feeling of belief, constitutes imagination; it is the element of belief that is distinctive in memory.

—Bertrand Russell, 1921, *The Analysis of Mind*

MEMORY FORMS THE foundation of who we are as individuals. It is central to therapy and fundamental to who we are and what we experience. Distinctions among memory, consciousness, neuroplasticity, and emotional experience are neurodynamically less than clear cut. Authors of psychotherapy textbooks often have much to say about the importance of memory in psychotherapy but frequently overlook the fact that the brain has several different memory systems. Understanding how the memory systems interact is one of the keys to a brain-based understanding of therapeutic process, psychopathology, and treatment goals.

Much of human memory is nonconscious but mostly not for the dynamic reasons postulated by Freud. Some memories that originate in conscious experience—for example, remembering how to pour coffee into a cup—become nonconscious because the brain must conserve precious energetic and processing resources. Consciousness consumes more energy than nonconscious processing; and the neural networks associated with consciousness are slower, energy inefficient, and quite limited in capacity

(Grigsby & Stevens, 2000). As a general rule, as soon as a memory is firmly encoded and stored in longer-term storage, it becomes nonconscious. Because of the architecture of the neural memory systems, however, many memories never attain consciousness at all.

MODULARITY OF MEMORY

Different types of memory encompass a number of psychological and behavioral processes. Although all forms of memory depend on the plasticity of neurons and the formation of new synaptic connections, the neural networks that mediate different kinds of memory are relatively independent of one another. In people with certain neurologic disorders, one type of memory may be severely impaired while others are completely intact. In neurologically normal individuals, the types of memory function in an integrated manner, but neuroscientists have successfully delineated their differing contributions to psychological experience and human behavior.

WORKING MEMORY

Since Freud, investigators have parsed the various memory systems in a number of different ways. For example, researchers have long differentiated short-term memory from long-term memory. Whereas short-term memory is ephemeral, long-term memories can last a lifetime. Recently, short-term memory has been renamed *working memory* to more accurately capture the contribution and role of this system in the memory process (Baddeley, 1992). Working memory lasts from 30 to 60 seconds, holding the content of what we are "working on" in the present. Anything that we "had in mind" while we process it is an example of working memory. A stranger's face, the phone number of United Airlines, a kid on the curb who looks like he might dash in front of your moving car, or a fleeting emotional impression—all are prime subjects for working memory.

Working memory, which has been called the "chalkboard of the mind," is dependent on the dorsolateral prefrontal cortex (DLPFC). This part of the brain is believed to link items together in conscious awareness where they can be attended to or manipulated (Goldman-Rakic, 1993); it provides an "attentional spotlight" that largely defines the moment-to-moment scope of consciousness. Working memory does not involve synaptic plasticity but rather transient chemical changes at the synapses.

LONG-TERM MEMORY

In contrast to working memory, long-term memory is a more or less enduring archive. The localization hypothesis of brain functioning breaks down in regard to where long-term memories are stored; storage seems to be a product of dynamic activity in and across many different areas of the brain. However, the systems that seem crucial to encoding implicit and explicit memories are biased to particular neural structures. Whether an experience, a procedural motor schema, information, or an emotional impression becomes encoded into long-term memory depends on complex dynamics between various neural systems.

Freud thought of psychotherapy as fundamentally a way of *remembering*, and we agree with that formulation. The patient's memory, her capacity to learn, change her emotions, and even her consciousness—in short, the very things that therapists are most concerned with—are overlapping functions and concepts. Both parties come to the therapeutic encounter with separate identities shaped by unique memories and learning. As the therapeutic relationship deepens, personal memories are shared either in implicit enactments or explicit discussions, and new shared memories are consolidated. The patient discloses much about himself, and we as therapists in turn share something about our own histories (*declarative memory*) as well. Each party holds on to idiosyncratic but overlapping memories about what happens in therapy (*episodic memory*), and these are likely to involve strong affects at times (*emotional memory*). The longer the therapy, the more likely both we and our patients will develop a somewhat ritualized, habitual style of behaving toward each other that is different in certain respects from how we relate with our other patients (*procedural memory*). The functioning of semantic, episodic, emotional, and procedural memories all can be identified in the therapy relationship, and each may be the focus of attention separately from the others at any given time, depending on what we are trying to accomplish.

A recently developed distinction between two memory supersystems helps clarify how some of these separate memory systems overlap or differ from each other. Declarative, semantic, episodic, procedural, and emotional memory subsystems are all forms of long-term memory. Schachter (1996, 1987) and others have regrouped these subtypes into large long-term memory systems, *explicit* and *implicit* memories (Schachter, 1987, 1996), as summarized below:

Explicit Memory	Implicit Memory
Declarative	Procedural
Semantic	Emotional
Episodic	

Explicit Memory System: The content of some explicit memories are preserved virtually instantaneously (e.g., episodic memory, the recall of events), and others only with painstaking repetition (e.g., learning organic chemistry). *Declarative memory* involves the recall of events or information. Recall of personal events (*episodic* memory) and recall of information in the form of interior speech (*semantic* memory) are distinguishable from one another (Kapur et al., 1996). If you remember that you got a paper cut while turning the pages of this book, that memory is mediated by your episodic memory system. If you remember this discussion about modularity, that is an emergent property of your semantic memory system.

Largely responsible for encoding explicit memories, the hippocampus helps people make inferences from previous learning and temporal information. The patient H.M. a star in the firmament of neurology and neuropsychology, is an example of what life is like without a hippocampus. In an attempt to control medically intractable epilepsy, his right and left hippocampus were removed in 1953, before the role of these structures was well understood (Scoville & Milner, 1957; Smith & Kosslyn, 2007). H.M. lost the ability to consolidate new explicit memories about facts and events. Still alive today, H.M. chats amiably with a stranger on being introduced to him; but if the visitor goes into another room for a few minutes and then comes back, H.M. will not remember having ever seen this person before. H.M. does remember long-distant events, and he can still formulate implicit (procedural) memories. H.M. can walk around the block in the neighborhood where he has lived for many years and remember how to get home—not explicitly but in a procedural way. He can be taught a certain movement, and when asked to make that movement again later, H.M. repeats it with more facility than when he first learned it—but he will have no recollection of having ever performed the task before.

H.M. helped neuroscience discover that the hippocampus is centrally involved in the laying down and retrieval of records of past experiences in the temporal lobe declarative-explicit memory system. The hippocampus also creates cognitive maps of our physical location, often including this information as part of what will be recalled about an event later. Studies with rats show that there are hippocampal neurons called place cells, some of which fire when the rat is headed in a particular direction, others when the rat is in a known or anticipated location. Later in life there is a gradual atrophy of the hippocampus (Golomb et al., 1993). Many Alzheimer's patients lose declarative memory while retaining, like H.M., parts of their implicit (procedural) memory system. They continue to perform out of habit while showing increasing difficulty remembering facts.

Emotionally significant events are more likely remembered in the long term not only because they hold more personally meaningful themes (Ochs & Capps, 1996) but because they are associated with higher levels of arousal. Emotional events stir a physiological reaction including an increase in the level of blood glucose that promotes the process of memory consolidation (Buchanan & Adolphs, 2004). From a psychological perspective, emotional events are more important to us and call out the neurodynamic pathways of conscious attention. Attention is the bottleneck of memory. Emotional events resonate in our minds; we are prone to remember emotionally evocative events spontaneously or when we are in the same mood we were in when they occurred. Through Hebbian learning, the more often we remember the emotionally charged event, the more likely we will find ourselves remembering it again in the future, enhancing memory consolidation (Reisberg & Heuer, 2004).

Some therapists unknowingly access their patients' explicit memory systems hoping to tap into "repressed memories." In some unfortunate cases, therapists have overstepped their bounds in this endeavor and have ended up playing a subtle and inadvertent role in helping patients formulate false memories of childhood abuse (Loftus, 2003). Memory researchers have critically evaluated the concept of repressed memories (Loftus, Milo, & Paddock, 1995). Just as with accurate memories of the past, the more often a false memory is repeated, the more likely we are to recall it as a credible picture of an actual event.

Traumatic events often are remembered all too well, and victims may be plagued by vivid recollections of the painful event(s) for years after the fact (Goodman et al., 2003; Pope, Hudson, Bodkin, & Olivia, 1998). Certain factors affecting central state (e.g., sleep deprivation, head injury, alcohol, or drug abuse) can disrupt memory for specific events, even when the events are of a traumatic intensity (McNally, 2003). In some cases, during periods of extreme stress, the biochemical process needed to consolidate recall of an event is profoundly disrupted—so that there is actually no memory to be suppressed (Payne, Nadel, Britton, & Jacobs, 2004). Emotional arousal has a very powerful effect on memory coding. Historically, psychodynamic theorists have maintained that conscious memory is heavily biased in favor of what is acceptable and favorable to us and those we need to think well of. When conflicts with unconscious wishes exceed the superego's tolerance or involve us in unacceptable levels of conflict with attachment figures, we may recall an edited version of the troubling events (so this theory goes) or otherwise manipulate the memory.

Recent findings in neuroscience give us a somewhat different picture of this phenomenon. High stress levels cause the adrenal cortex to release high concentrations of the steroid stress hormone cortisol. Prolonged exposure to cortisol is destructive to the hippocampus, weakening our capacity to encode explicit memories for storeage (Sapolsky, 1987). The hippocampus is also vulnerable to impairment from traumatic insult or from developmental disruptions, such as hypoxia (a shortage of oxygen in the body). On one hand, emotional arousal promotes memory consolidation; but on the other, too much affect overwhelms our ability to consciously recall what happened. Arousal within bounds promotes retention. For example, American baby boomers and their elders remember where they were and what they were doing when John F. Kennedy was assassinated. Their offspring are likely to remember where they were on September 11, 2001 when the planes struck the World Trade Center. These vivid episodic memories are sometimes referred to as "flashbulb memories." They are facilitated by a release of epinephrine from the adrenal glands, which also plays a role in the flashbacks of traumatic memories. The more personally involved an individual was in either one of these events, and the more they experienced intense unmodulated affects in regard to what they witnessed or did at the time, the more likely their memory of the events will be in some way distorted. A sort of inverted-U pattern describes this relationship between emotional arousal and memory, with either tail of the curve likely to be associated with impairment. Moderate arousal works best to facilitate neuroplasticity and the coding of new memories.

Implicit Memory System: Whereas explicit memories of an event are associated with what we attended to during an event, implicit memories capture what escapes conscious attention. Implicit memories are about what we *do* and *feel* rather than what we consciously recall. Implicit memories are nonconscious. Various people "remind" us of someone else, but we do not quite know why and at times we do not know that we are responding to them based on implicit memories of someone else. Habitual emotional responses and behavioral patterns that we are likely to describe as "that's just how I am" are typically based on implicit memories. Much of what makes us who we are relates to implicit memories.

The amygdala is a star player in the formation of implicit memories. LeDoux (2002) demonstrated that the amygdala precipitates implicit emotional memories via the neurodynamic "low road" that circumvents the cortex. Forgetting the conditioned emotional memories (and implicit memories in general) is more difficult than forgetting memories learned through the "high road" of the hippocampus and cortex. Recall that these nonconscious memory processes come into play much earlier in our development than explicit and declarative processing. In 1920, John B.

Watson and a graduate student, Rosalie Rayner, engaged in a famous and controversial experiment that demonstrated the role of classical conditioning in early implicit memory (Watson & Rayner, 1920).

"Little Albert," a 9-month-old hospitalized orphan, was the experiment's only subject. The investigators showed Albert masks of a white rat, a rabbit, a dog, and a monkey; he reacted with normal infantile curiosity to all four. When an actual white rat was placed near him, he vocalized, reached out for it, and tried to play with it. Thereafter, each time they introduced the rat, Watson or Raynor also startled Albert by striking a large metal bar outside his visual field, scaring him and making him cry. After several pairings of the startling sound with the white rat, the experimenters presented the rat without the sound. Albert cried and tried to get away from it. His conditioned fear was the first recorded instance of inducing a phobic reaction in human subjects (Hock, 2005).

In Albert's brain, the rat had become a conditioned stimulus to which he responded with all the behavioral (and presumably physiological and emotional) reactions appropriate to the unconditioned stimulus (a loud noise). As often happens in phobic reactions, Albert started generalizing this response. He cried when presented with a white rabbit 17 days after the original experiment and subsequently when shown a toy dog and a seal-skin coat. When Watson came into his room wearing a Santa Claus mask with white cotton balls in his beard, the baby cried. Albert was discharged a month after the experiment began, before the researchers could begin their planned deconditioning of his phobic reactions, and his fate is unknown.

Roundly criticized initially on methodological—and later on ethical—grounds, the Little Albert experiment illustrates how vulnerable we are to emotional memory. Little Albert stored these memories implicitly and presumably had no recall of Watson or the experiment as an adult. Because of the amygdala's importance in coding implicit memory, these memories often contain an element of fear, which easily intrudes into working and long-term memory as well. Although basic to nonconscious anxious and phobic reactions, implicit memory also has other important functions. It can preserve a sensory motor skill set, such as remembering how to execute the series of dance steps that cumulatively equal the macarena. Implicit memories such as this are described as *procedural memories*, behavioral procedures that are nonconscious, sequential, and more or less indelible.

Procedural Memory: The fact that you are able to read this sentence as automatically and relatively effortlessly as you do—and perhaps to have the experience of reading a page or two without any of its content entering your consciousness—is a product of your history: you were fortunate enough to have the right kind of procedural learning system operating when you first struggled with understanding letters and words. Procedural memory is a form of learning that contrasts with declarative learning in some important respects. Whereas episodic memory allows us to remember *events*, procedural memory lets us recall how to repeat specific *processes*, including skills and habits such as juggling, gargling, typing, flying helicopters, being passive-aggressively provacative with our spouses, and so on. In procedural learning, there may be no content involved. Instead, we learn *how to do* things (Cohen, 1984; Cohen & Squire, 1980; Milner, 1962, 1965). With enough practice, procedural learning allows us to perform different actions or processes automatically and unconsciously. Procedural learning is also essential for the development of the aspect of personality often referred to as character—the remarkable behavioral, emotional, and cognitive consistency displayed by people over time (Grigsby & Stevens, 2000).

Emotional Memory: The second major component of the implicit memory system is the *emotional memory* neural networks, often associated with the experience of fear. This is the system Watson and Raynor tapped into with Little Albert. LeDoux and his colleagues (including a large number of postdoctoral and graduate student slave-researchers, without whom our field would advance much more slowly) have done extensive research in this area. Their work suggests that classically conditioned fear responses to auditory and visual stimuli are mediated by subcortical pathways projecting from the sensory nuclei of the thalamus to the amygdala (LeDoux, 1995; LeDoux, Sakaguchi, & Reis, 1984; LeDoux, Iwata, Cicchetti, & Reis, 1988; LeDoux, Romanski, & Xagorasis, 1989). In other words, "this circuit bypasses the . . . cortex and thus constitutes a subcortical mechanism of emotional learning" (LeDoux et al., 1989, p. 238).

Despite its importance in emotional learning, the amygdala appears to play no significant role in most declarative memory processes. An interesting finding from this line of research is that the cortex is unnecessary for the acquisition of conditioned fear but is likely to be essential for the extinction of conditioned fear responses (LeDoux et al., 1989). This is to say that fear conditioning may occur without awareness of certain stimuli, but without awareness, it may not be possible to eliminate a conditioned fear response. This finding is especially important in formulating treatment plans for treating anxiety, as we show in Chapter 7.

The power of emotional conditioning varies as a function of an animal's state. Rats that are already afraid, for example, acquire a startle response to neutral stimuli more quickly than do rats that are not in this state of mind (Davis, 1992). McGaugh and colleagues (McGaugh, 1990; McGaugh et al., 1993) found that if norepinephrine is administered at around the time of an electric foot shock, conditioning occurs more rapidly, and the conditioned response is not only learned more quickly but is more lasting. Other neuromodulators can block the acquisition of this conditioned response.

As we noted in our discussion of declarative memory, the development of the emotional memory system is independent of and occurs significantly before the development of conscious memories (Rudy & Morledge, 1994). The process of the myelination of cortical-hippocampal circuits that is necessary to achieve mature neurodynamic efficiency in the declarative memory system extends into late adolescence (Benes, 1989). This extended developmental calendar reflects the complex contributions of the hippocampus to our capacity to learn from experience as well as its close ties to the equally late-blooming prefrontal lobes.

Rats and other animals can learn tasks requiring the amygdala (but not the hippocampus) at a younger age than they can learn tasks requiring the hippocampus (but not the amygdala) (Rudy & Morledge, 1994). The amygdala is involved in activating generalized attention and mobilizing the whole brain-body system through its interactions with the hypothalamic-pituitary-adrenal system. The hippocampus, by contrast, is involved in attention even if the situation does not require mobilization (Sherry & Schacter, 1987). Hence we are able to store episodic memories even though emotional arousal is not a component of an incident. When our brains are working well, the amygdala helps set up the emotional state that is optimum for memory. Later, when we are once again in that emotional state, we are more likely to find ourselves remembering explicit material that is congruent with that feeling. This phenomenon of *mood-congruent memory* holds true for children as well as adults.

We typically have few explicit memories of the first three to five or so years of life. Freud believed this phenomenon was a product of "infantile amnesia." The contemporary scientific view is that the lack of explicit memories from early childhood, rather than a product of forgetting, is an artifact of the fact that the memory systems involved in the original coding are developmental and the earliest memories are destined to remain nonconscious. Early experience may be available to us consciously only as a feeling or sensorimotor response. The fact that the implicit memory system develops prior to our capacity to code explicit memories has profound effects on development—and significant implications for psychotherapy. Implicit memory is the basis for many emotional predispositions and cognitive habits. A preference for using withdrawal to deal with conflictual situations, for example, may get refined with cognitive development and experience; but its implicit function (maintaining limited attachment security) is likely to remain the same. A patient's defensive patterns and particular style of resisting painful content (see Safran & Muran, 2003, for an interesting discussion) typically are implicitly encoded. In situations in which fear conditioning and procedural learning occur concomitantly (possibly outside of awareness, but in any case prior to the maturation of episodic learning), very young children are likely to acquire habits and conditioned responses that are entirely dissociated from the context.

Contemporary infant research sheds light on the degree to which the formation of the brain's early memory systems requires the give-and-take of maternal infant interactions. The baby's capacity for recognizing patterns of action and developing *expectancies* about what usually happens, or what follows what (essentially, early implicit procedural memories) could not take place outside of these interactions. Early Hebbian learning requires repetition of these interpersonal experiences to stimulate growth in the parts of the brain that mediate the preservation of a record of experience. Without the development these networks, there would of course be no possibility of retaining the sensory-motor content of experience.

Along these lines, Kaminer (1999) studied interactions between mothers and babies by videotaping the face of each partner and then analyzing the interplay on a frame-by-frame basis. His sample consisted of mothers rated susceptible to depression, and a matched group without this vulnerability. In the videotapes, Kaminer was concerned with when the mother vocalized comments on the baby's movements and expressiveness, and how the baby reacted to this (and vice versa). "What are you looking at?" the mother would ask in reaction to the baby's directed gaze at a fist, or "You're smiling now!" The mothers who were more vulnerable to depression tended to make these "action/agency" comments when their babies looked *away* from them; the nondepressed mothers tended to make them while fully facially engaged with their infants. In reviewing Kaminer's results, Beebe and Lachmann (2005) speculate that:

"Infants [of the depressed moms] may learn that their agency is noted by the mother only when they are visually 'away' or more 'separate.' These more vulnerable mothers tended to frame their action/agency comments in terms of 'Where are you looking?' and 'You are not looking at me.' These babies may learn that their agency occurs only when they are more separate, or somehow 'against' the mother." (p. 31)

Implicit memories are habitual and not easily changed without consistent behavioral effort. They are not readily available through "insight," and insight typically does not change them. Because much of what we experience and respond to is based on implicit memories, nonconscious processes play an important role in all the relationships with the people in our lives. The therapeutic relationship is a unique opportunity for clarifying these implicit patterns through thought records, free associations, or interpretations of the latent affective side of the therapeutic relationship when it is revealed how the patient relates to the therapist and in other relationships and, most importantly, to change these habits. The important role of implicit emotional memory is what gives the psychodynamic technique of "analyzing the transference" great potential power. But actually changing implicit patterns frequently requires a concerted effort to alter behavior (as in, e.g., the behavioral activation methods employed in CBT). Implicit memories are often about what we do, not just what we think.

Often when an implicit procedural memory is "made conscious" in therapy, therapist and patient together have figured out how to simulate implicit memories by using a different memory system. Therapist and patient successfully provide new narratives to some part of the patient's troubling history, using the clues provided by the patient's life experience and subtle but important emotional memories that have been enacted and then made conscious in the therapeutic alliance. Reading nonverbal communication is extremely important (Beebe & Lachmann, 2002; Wallin, 2007). Using these clues, patient and therapist rely on their cortical gifts to piece together a better version of the patient's past history, one that has made implicit schemas and themes more explicit and subject to conscious consideration.

MEMORY AND THERAPY

Much of the surface of psychotherapy involves conscious memory systems, such as working memory and explicit long-term memory. Memories like Little Albert's of frightening rats bypass our cortex and hippocampus—which is to say, our consciousness—entirely. Because of his age, Albert could only have remembered the frightening coincidence of the rodent and loud noises implicitly, not explicitly. If he had been older, say age 7, he would have had a *better* chance of resisting the potency of his amygdala's coupling of unconditioned emotional responses and conditioned stimuli—but only if his conscious "high-road" pathways had been activated. The amygdala in a latency-aged Albert could easily have taken the "low road" instead, resulting in an implicit emotional memory that might have taken the consciously puzzling form of a phobia.

Part of the challenge in psychotherapy is overcoming the tendency that both we and our patients share of relying too much on one or another of the subsystems of explicit memory. When patients are trying to recall an event, they are likely to rely on their episodic memory; and in describing their social history, they will use episodic or semantic memory. Explicit memories are at least potentially accessible to awareness, corresponding to what Freud called conscious memories that are temporarily out of awareness. They may be organized and elaborated upon by language or visual systems and typically occur in a particular context. Explicit memories take on the unique qualities of a personal experience because of links with implicit (emotional) memory. In this sense, together the two systems play a fundamental part in our self-representations: I am that person who moved from Laramie, Wyoming, to Salt Lake City before I was 2—or the one who lived in the same house in Los Angeles all my life.

Research—notably Gazzaniga's and LeDoux's studies of split-brain patients—demonstrates that much of our conscious "understanding" of ourselves reflects left-brain confabulation. H.M. (the man without hippocampi) is a fascinating example of how flexible our concept of self actually is and how dependent it is on neurodynamic variables. H.M. believes he is doing fine, and his self-image is untainted by the knowledge that he has serious memory deficits. Gazzaniga (2008) has noted that in split-brain subjects, neither hemisphere appears to miss or even recall the relative omnipresence of "the other brain" and subjects carry on living as if nothing has happened to them. Much of our conscious "understanding" of ourselves, inside therapy or in the outside world, is based on left-PFC confabulation.

The challenge in therapy is to try to reharmonize the subsystems of memory to give patients a more integrated sense of identity and emotional regulation. Emotions are mediated especially by subcortical neural systems such as the amygdala, with less neocortical involvement. Hence our feelings are not organized by language and are relatively context free. Typically it is not a particular time or place that binds our feelings. In this boundless "timelessness," our emotions resemble Freud's unconscious memories. *Talking* about memories, however, engages parts of the brain that think differently and more contextually. For patients who are overly reactive emotionally, talking can help build the "high road" to more integrated cortical–subcortical coordination and improved emotional regulation.

When we are caught up in an explicit memory, it is as if we are watching a documentary, but in fact our memories reedit this video every time we watch it. The neurodynamics of memory are no less subject to the Hebbian principle of repetition than are other parts of the brain. Each time we feel afraid at the sight of a rat and do nothing to involve the higher cortical structures, the stronger that reaction becomes. Put slightly differently, but more optimistically, each time we recall an event from the vantage point and perspective of the present, we rewrite that memory. This is part of why therapy works.

The semantic memory system is usually the focus of attention in therapy, whether we intend it to be or not. Since we use language as the primary method of communication, memories organized by linguistic associations become the grist for discussion. When we try to encourage new learning by adopting more conscious and positive cognitive sets (as in CBT), we may bypass the entire system of implicit memories. On the other hand, behavioral practice in CBT is implicit memory. But if, regardless of what techniques are employed to harness explicit memories and engage the left PFC, the therapist also attends to the subtle enactments and expressions of affect, these memories can become part of the therapy. Safran and Muran (2003) report this vignette, which illustrates these points about implicit memory:

T: So it sounds like it's uncomfortable to ask for what you want from me.
R: Yeah.
T: Can you say anything more about your discomfort?
R: Well. . . . It's like I'm being unreasonable and expecting too much . . . but still . . . I have a tendency to blame myself when things aren't going well in a relationship. And I don't want to do that here.
T: Yeah. It's not really fair for you to have to take all the blame if things don't work out for you here . . .
R: If I'm not to blame. I'm asking you to be really honest and tell me if I go off and start talking about a crack in the ceiling or whatever. Actually, as I'm saying that, I'm feeling stronger.
T: Uh-huh . . . and the essence of what you're saying in feeling strong . . . is that you want me to take some of the responsibility for what's going on . . . and you don't want to feel blamed for something that's not your fault . . .
R: Yeah . . . and I just had the thought, "I want this time to be about me."
T: Uh-huh.
R: I don't want this to be kind of an academic observation . . . and I'm

demanding that you be engaged in whatever problems I have . . . as mundane as they may be, as repetitive as they may be.

T: That sounds important. What does it feel like to say that?

R: Well. . . . I fell like I'm stamping my feet in a way. You know . . . like "Goddamn it!" (*Laughs.*) You know . . . like "give me that!" (p. 191)

Notice how the therapist in this transaction consistently goes for the latent *emotional* response, as opposed to the explicit-memory or semantic-only content. He takes the role of a good-enough parent, letting the patient have her own feelings, as opposed to defensively interacting to combat or shape them. Much of what we experience and respond to is based on implicit learning, in this case the patient's implicit responses to the therapist's good-enough interactions. This is an example of using the transferential relationship to make implicit patterns more conscious through language. However, the psychotherapy outcome literature would remind us that this will occur only to the extent the patient wants it to; not all patients are looking for this kind of in-depth psychological approach.

A weakness in many CBT treatments is the tendency for both therapist and patient to neglect clues to the patient's implicit and emotional schemas as they are played out in the room. Skillful CBT therapists are aware of this pitfall, just as experienced psychodynamic therapists are wary of the transitory helpfulness of abreaction. Feelings elicited from the thought record can be amplified by persistent inquiry about evasion or minimization. Emotionally significant events are more likely to be remembered in the long term not only because they hold more personally meaningful themes (Ochs & Capps, 1996) but because they are associated with higher levels of arousal. The main emphasis of CBT is on building new skills and habits and extinguishing habits acquired through implicit learning and amygdalar conditioning that is so critical to implicit memory. Monitoring the emotional tone of the therapeutic alliance is no less a part of cognitive behavioral therapy than of other method-driven therapies. Events that elicit little emotion, such as a dry interpretation by the therapist, diminish the chances that the patient will even remember what was said, much less that an interpretation will result in changing the neurodynamics. Skillfully and sensitively used in a strong alliance, the cognitive aspect of CBT can be very helpful in getting the patient's left prefrontal cortex back in the game when he or she is overwhelmed by a low-road mood. One of the method's great strengths is its effectiveness in activating behaviors that will create new neurodynamic alternatives to the old implicit patterns.

Novel experiences establish new connections between the existing neurodynamic structure and the patient's cognitive, emotional, and behavioral repertoire. Working with patients who have traumatic histories or those inclined to be emotionally dysregulated requires the therapist to be mindful of finding an optimal level of emotional arousal. Memories, especially if processed by the amygdala, do not dissipate through catharsis; in fact, they are likely to be consolidated by it. Developing "insight" into the etiology of the disorder is equally limited. If, however, the insight leads to reframing these memories in a new, more constructive narrative (as described in the next section), patients can better integrate their memory systems and build new neurodynamic attractors.

Beatrice Beebe and Frank Lachmann have written about the use of non-verbal attachment-based material in therapy with adults in the form of a vignette about a patient named Karen, a young woman preoccupied with issues of early depression and abandonment.

> Karen's immobile face, flat voice, sitting with her coat on, not looking and having nothing to say required extraordinary measures. To reach her, the therapist had to restrict the range of affect and activity so that Karen's level of arousal remained tolerable to her. Speaking in a soft and even voice, and slowing the rhythm, increased Karen's tolerance for arousal. With a voice and face that were more alive, she began to talk about her life. . . . This . . . led to Karen's ability to report a dream and a hallucinatory asso-ciaton of "cars without drivers." Her inaccessibility and her world where no one was at the wheel could then be interpreted. (2002, p. 62)

Emotional arousal is a key in the therapeutic process. When therapists titrate the stress to optimize the balance between a supportive relationship and a "safe emergency"— an inverted-U experience—patients can move ahead with modifying implicit memories. Simply tapping into explicit memories is typically not effective in reconstructing formative experiences, especially those that are primarily implicit. When we perceive cues that activate a previous emotional state, whether explicit memories of the event were formed at the time or not, implicit memories are activated that reinforce those feelings.

The Hebbian principle of neurodynamic learning suggests that all forms of therapy can be risky and counterproductive by simply repeating the past, not changing it. From a brain-based perspective, psychotherapy in general risks remaining "all talk" and no action. Cathartic therapies risk merely deepening patient rage or traumatic experience of helplessness. Nevertheless, our own clinical experiences and the psychotherapy out-come research tells us that more times than not, therapists and patients find the right road to change. Behavioral techniques, sensitive awareness of nonverbal nuances, and the verbal, narrativizing skills of the left hemisphere help build new skills and lay the foundation for revised nonconscious emotional and relational "memories."

Therapists would be well advised to bear in mind the fallible nature of explicit memory. Patients may have forgotten various events from their past or feel certain that an event took place when in fact it did not. Memories are also malleable. It is a good practice, and often a challenging one, to take a neutral stance in regard to patient recollections. Reenforcing memories of events that never occurred can have serious, negative effects on patients. Even repeated questioning can influence the quality of recall, leading patients to believe that the therapist knows there is more, hidden in my unconscious mind because of intense feelings associated with traumatic experience, both real and imagined. Alternatively, if the therapist acts skeptical or changes the subject, patients are likely to get the message that the feelings and events surrounding the traumatic experience are unimportant. It is always easy for us to unconsciously act out patients' underlying attachment schemas with them, playing the part of a distant, preoccupied, or ambivalent parent. The job of the therapist and the patient is to take the past and formulate a different future for the patient.

COCONSTRUCTING NARRATIVES

In preliterate societies, storytellers served to "remind" individuals of their common origins and both their connectedness with and unique differences from others. The telling and retelling of these stories imbued the culture and its members with a sense of meaning. They provided a context in which each individual could view him- or herself as a participant and full member of that society. Although largely mythical, the stories were viewed by the community as holding truth. In literate societies as well, the stories we tell and are told serve multiple functions (Ochs & Capps, 1996). They define our common origins, mores, ethics, and customs. The result is a cohesive culture, which, from a Darwinian perspective, results in improved evolutionary group "fitness."

As narratives became concretized through the writing down of theologies and myths, members could refer back to them for guidance and perspective (Arden, 1998). Narratives provide a psychological and neurodynamic infrastructure for each of us as well as a context and description of the culture. The most important of these narratives have an implicit as well as an explicit dimension. That is, in addition to particular content, these narratives are also procedural ("Adam and Eve begot Cain and Abel who begot . . . ''). We have heard them so often and from such an early time in our lives that without further conscious repetition they become part of our worldview and response pattern.

Narratives also serve a fundamental role in the interaction between parent and child. As a consequence of such neurodynamic developmental events as the maturation of the hippocampus through childhood, the explicit memory system allows children and parent(s) to coconstruct narratives that make sense of their family history. Through the process of coconstructing narratives, children learn how to narrate their own experience and relate it to the family's story. These narratives become semantic memories within the explicit memory system and are integrated with autobiographic and episodic memories. They become part of the children's psychological infrastructure and experience of self.

Narratives serve to provide historical and cohesive meaning to our lives. From childhood on, our parents help us construct a story about our lives by telling us what we were like in infancy, who and where we were when we started school, and how all our family members fit into our life. Narratives provide a kind of linguistic infrastructure for how we explain ourselves *to* ourselves. They also provide a way to present ourselves to those whom we hope to get to know. They provide a map of where we have been and where we are going. As we move toward the future with some continuity with the past, narratives provide a way to organize our emotional experience. Just as was the case for our ancestors' tribal myths, these stories about our family and ourselves need not be true to serve this function.

Narratives can be a useful tool in therapy if we direct our efforts toward moving away from negativistic and maladaptive themes to positive and adaptive ones. Narrative therapists do this by listening to and retelling stories that reshape suffering into epochs of survival (White, 2007). Given the inherent malleability of memory, negative and maladaptive memories that form a narrative can be modified to positive and adaptive memories that support mental health. From a psychodynamic perspective, Roy Schaefer takes a similar view in *Retelling a Life* (1992).

Therapy that challenges the patient to make healthy changes stirs up affect. The supportive relationship that characterizes a productive therapeutic alliance involves the development of affective tolerance and integration. The therapist and patient coconstruct narratives that make integration possible, as typically happened to some degree between the patient and parents in childhood. These new narratives help patients solidify new and healthy behaviors and strengthen altered neural networks by building up layers of meaning.

Language serves as one of the basic tools to integrate multiple neural networks. It provides the text for narratives that organize our experience around an autobiographical memory. Therapists utilize language and its associated left-hemispheric neural nets to coconstruct positive and adaptive narratives (Cozolino, 2002). Originally, narratives are self-stories shaped by interactions with parents, peers, and the context of one's culture. When those narratives do not serve a person well in adolescence or adulthood, the therapist's job is to help the patient reconstruct those narratives so that he or she can live with diminished anxiety, depression, or other psychological problems.

Cognitive therapists identify negative thinking and negative self-statements as an important aspect of all the major psychological disorders (Beck, 1976; Ellis, 1962). As we noted, the left hemisphere, as the "interpreter," tends to put a positive spin on our experience. The therapist can help the patient exploit this potential. But narratives are not dependent on one hemisphere over the other. A narrative that is too left-sided has no context and sounds vaguely confabulatory or emotionally removed. A predominantly right-hemispheric narrative may be overly somber and not make sense. Like the best movies and books, good personal narratives explain our world and our place within it in an intellectually and emotionally coherent way.

Whether we use the term "resistance" in psychodynamic or Hebbian senses of the term, patients often demonstrate a need to keep on being the way they are, and that entails continuing to tell the same self-stories. Attempts to disrupt the old narrative call out defenses; patients assert that experience in the real world supports the old narrative, not the new one. If, in patients' old narratives, the world appears as cold and rejecting, and they themselves appear helpless or perhaps even worthy of being rejected, perceived slights or unsuccessful social experiences reinforce the old narrative and maintain its underlying neurodynamics. The therapist's job is to empathize with the inevitability of this kind of psychological conservativism while steadfastly maintaining that the old story is not necessarily true. An analysis of the defenses involved, behavioral experiments conducted outside the office, accurate empathy about nonverbal communication, transference interpretations, and cognitive analysis—any one of these techniques may be helpful, but only in the context of a strong treatment alliance. It is through the power of a reactivated attachment relationship with the therapist that patients, like toddlers, move out from their secure home base, and begin to own a new narrative. Narratives are an indispensable resource in the construction of autobiographical memories. They remind us of that time we stayed with Aunt Alice or how we behaved at our fourth birthday party. Although they may be preserved throughout a lifetime, like all memories, they are modified each time we remember them. Each recollection reinforces the neural nets supporting them and is modified by the mood and context in which we are remembering them now. In this way, other neurons are enlisted into memory's neurodynamic system.

Siegel (1999) describes how a child uses narratives to navigate through the world by tapping into both implicit and explicit memories:

> Narratives reveal how representations from one system can clearly intertwine with another, thus the mental models of implicit memory help organize the themes of how the details of explicit autobiographical memory are expressed within a life story. Though we can never see mental models directly, their manifestations in narratives allows us to get a view of at least the shadow they cast on the output of other systems of the mind. (p. 63)

Narratives are multilayered because we experience innumerable events in our lives. There is not one single narrative underlying our experience, but many. Interacting with multiple people calls out different and sometimes complex emotional reactions, which in turn may elicit particular versions of our personal narrative and identity. Context, the specifics of an interaction, and the expectations that are generated by our existing neurodynamic networks all play a role in the narratives that we use in the moment. Our self-representation, our model of who we are, changes with the fluid and changeable nature of our social experience. As the repetition of thematic motifs in a Beethoven symphony guides our expectations toward the music's conclusion, integrative narratives can give patients the sense that the overall pattern of their lives is the meaningful resolution of difficult themes. Such narratives require left prefrontal activations—and require *action* and *labeling*, not the right hemisphere's tendency to withdraw. Rather than joining patients in their tendency to bemoan the past, a coconstructed narrative can help them integrate historical content into a kind of constructive wisdom. Memory, in essence, is rewritten from the positive vantage point of the present potentiated by an empathetic and encouraging therapeutic relationship.

MANAGING AFFECT

More than a century ago, William James proposed that emotions result from responses to body sensations. Like Freud, James started out as a student of biological psychology, training with, among others, Hermann von Helmholtz and William Wundt in Leipzig. James also became expert in the neurology of his day, and like Freud, he abandoned it in favor of theorizing about the mind without reference to the brain. He suggested that psychology take as its "facts" the individual's thoughts and feelings and leave the brain to the neurologists and physiologists. He continued to insist, however, that the mind is very much grounded in biology. Our visceral and muscular responses to environmental stimuli, according to James, are the essence of emotion, and emotion informs our thinking (rather than the other way around). According to James: "We feel sorry because we cry, angry because we strike, afraid because we tremble" (1890/2007, vol. 2, p. 449).

James's *Principles of Psychology*, published while Freud was still in his hypnosis stage, includes detailed diagrams of the brain and reviews of Broca's, Wernicke's, and the other specialized areas, with descriptions of how certain ablations resulted in specific kinds of aphasia. James concluded:

> For practical purposes . . . and limiting the meaning of the word consciousness to the personal self of the individual, we can pretty confidently [state] that *the cortex is the sole organ of consciousness in man*. If there be any consciousness pertaining to the lower centres, it is a consciousness of which the self knows nothing. (pp. 66–67; italics in original)

James's feedback theory of emotion was critiqued by Walter Cannon, president of the American Physiological Society. According to Cannon (the author of the term "fight or flight"), the physiological changes that accompany emotion arise from common autonomic nervous system reactions, so James's feedback theory does not explain our experience of *differentiated* emotions (Cannon, 1915). Later, cognitive psychologists turned James upside down, asserting that we explain bodily reactions by attributing specific emotions to them. Other researchers (e.g., LeDoux, 1996) have pointed out that appraisal theories such as this one overemphasize the contribution of cognitive processes in emotion.

The work of infant researchers (Stern, 1985; Beebe & Lachmann, 2002) and students of attachment (Main, 1985; Fonagy, 1991) generally support LeDoux's stance regarding the importance of the bodily sensations in felt emotion. These investigators show us how the symbolic capacities we treasure as adults unfold developmentally from early sensory-motor reactions. Their findings are consistent with contemporary neuroscience's model of emotion. In this view, mind—including reason, emotion, and a felt sense of existing as a "self," among other functions—is *embodied*. Networks connecting the body to many different parts of the brain, and vice versa, are activated in formulating emotions that can be recognized consciously and owned as important experiences of the self. Though they may arise somatically, we can generate feelings by just thinking about something (as Beck and other cognitive theorists have pointed out); we can also start thinking about something without being aware that we are doing so as a result of inputs that originate somatically (a more psychodynamic view). In any event, to achieve consciousness, the somatic origins of affects must be integrated with other information-processing activities in the brain, especially the cortex.

Beatrice Bebee records an interaction with a five-week-old baby named Elliott, that exemplifies the complex biological-emotional-interpersonal dimensions of the origins of emotions and their regulation in the brain. At the beginning, Elliott is crying.

> I . . . begin by vocally matching the infant's cry rhythm. After a time, I slow it down and lower the volume, and Elliott calms right down with me (see Stern, 1985, for a similar description). It looks almost as if Elliott is hypnotized. He becomes alert and visually engaged. Then Elliott's arousal level goes too low, and he begins to look sleepy. It is now necessary to increase the stimulation. I provide more stimulation with my face but keep my vocal volume down. What is needed is a complex combination of soothing and arousing. (p. 88)

The interaction here illustrates the subtlety of the interactions between arousal and expectations in development, and it quite beautifully illustrates how profoundly interpersonal this development is in all of us. As a stand-in for Elliott's mom, Bebee lays the foundation for Elliott to come to expect a particular outcome when he gets distressed. He may recall the sensory-motor experience of Bebee imitating his cry and in turn imitate *her* in calming down. If so, the memory will be in the form of a simple expectancy that when he gets distressed, help is available. This is the foundation for secure attachment, and it doesn't need consciousness in an explicit LH sense in order to memorialize that. Later on, when Elliott begins to differentiate an affective component in his experience of various levels of arousal (or the lack of it), the experience of emotion will be shaped by these earlier interactions.

Interactions such as this one are the basis of early implicit memories and neurodynamic change. Through countless "good enough" experiences, the infant learns to identify emotions and mediate them through the primary attachment relationship. Feelings continue to be a part of every interpersonal encounter afterward. Early experiences are so formative because they literally become part of the brain's biology; and the memory of them will continue to exist in the form of direct physical sensation, just as James said. These early attachment experiences have an undifferentiated sensory-motor quality that emotions retain throughout life. As Safran and Muran put it, "we know things not just through our heads, but through our actions and our bodily-felt experience." (p. 49)

In psychotherapy, these experiences often get played out in the transference or in nonverbal communications. Our adult patients may have an LH-based rational and semantic understanding that they have "abandonment issues," but little consciousness of how they protect themselves from experiencing these issues in therapy. As therapists, with our own limitations and defenses against comprehending what we are reacting to when a feeling about the patient begins to develop, we may have trouble recognizing that we are reacting to someone who regards us warily, as if they were still in insecure hands. In order to integrate what is happening dyadically, both the therapist and the patient must experience the affect on the old level of bodily sensations.

Safran and Muran (2000) report this vignette about a young woman coming to the end-point of a time-limited therapy, which illustrates the close relationship between nonverbal implicit memory and affect in therapy:

T: It's like you're really struggling internally right now.
R: (*Sobbing in a controlled fashion and looking downward*) Yeah, I guess, you know, I just think . . . that for whatever reason this situation has brought out so much of my sadness and loss and disappointment, and that instead of me feeling like I'm going forward, I just feel like I keep on uncovering things that I'm not even that aware of. I mean, I know you're there, but . . . I don't know.
T: So a couple of things come to mind, but one is . . . you know . . . I'm very aware that in this moment *you're looking down . . . looking away from me*. Do you have a sense of that?
R: Well, yeah . . .
T: Yeah?
R: I mean I do . . . because I just . . . I want to push it back in, and it just feels so umm . . . I mean, I feel it's about nothing. It just seems like this endless self-pity or something and umm . . .
T: So what would happen if you didn't push your experience back in there?
R: I couldn't deal . . . I just (*brief pause*) would be blubbering and not even able to talk. You know, it's so embarrassing. It's not like . . . I mean, I know I'm not looking, and it's almost like I want to go away from you . . . like be by myself in a way. (p 195, initial emphasis added)

Note that the therapist in this transaction consistently goes for the latent emotional response, as opposed to the explicit-memory or semantic-only content. He takes the role of a good-enough parent, letting the patient have her own feelings, and being sensitive to the nonverbal cue of *not looking*. Because so much of what we experience and respond to is based on implicit memories and nonverbal emotional experience, the patient here may be responding as much to the therapist noticing her *gaze* as anything that's said in the hour. On the other hand, like Beebe imitating Elliott's crying and gradually lowering its level of intensity, this therapist uses the therapeutic dialogue, mediated by the LII, to enhance the patient's affect regulation. In this way, transferential aspects of the interchange can be used both to make implicit patterns more conscious and to advance the patient's neurodynamic development by putting nonverbal cues into language. This is an example of what is meant by the therapeutic enhancement of affect regulation. However, the psychotherapy outcome literature would remind us that this will *only* occur to the extent the patient wants it to. Not all patients are looking for this kind of in-depth psychological approach.

Effective therapy stirs up powerful emotions that can be contained and worked through in the context of a supportive therapeutic alliance. Indeed, one of the inevitable goals of therapy—whether the patient feels he is too anxious, depressed, or gets angry too often—is to help him change his management of emotional experience. Alan Schore (1994, 1996) has written extensively on the importance of aiding patients in affect regulation. This usually means helping our patients recognize and tolerate increasing levels of both positive and negative affect, and bolstering their prefrontal cortical resources for downregulating intense feeling and using narratives to frame it.

Diana Fosha (2000) argues that closely attuned therapeutic attention to affect is what produces change. Trauma, especially if experienced early in life, frequently overwhelms the brain's ability to maintain neural integration across various networks dedicated to emotion, sensation, and conscious awareness. Cozolino (2006) defines the task of psychotherapy as the "attempt to reintegrate these dissociated networks by consciously processing traumatic memories. This reintegration, in turn, allows the networks of conscious cortical processing to develop the ability to inhibit and control past traumatic memories" (p. 32). It is through this process that the patient's pieces of experiences can be organized into a coherent and meaningful narrative.

Behavior therapists help patients regulate emotions when they utilize graduated exposure to anxiety-provoking situations, such as a cat phobia or a fear of eating in public. Wolpe's (1958) systematic desensitization pairs exposure to a feared situation or object with relaxation training and therapeutic encouragement and emotional support. Affect regulation builds and integrates cortical circuits so that patients can develop the flexibility to adapt to the world successfully. Integrating neural systems involves regulating emotions with information.

Cognitive-emotional schemas are of increasing interest both to psycho-dynamic and CBT theorists (Padesky, 1994). Schemata allow the individual to assimilate new social and environmental information rapidly, by pro-viding an organizational infrastructure that organizes incoming stimuli. The creation of these neurodynamic patterns is heavily influenced by mood and subcortical emotional processing. Schemata provide feedback on behavior, as cognitive sets help the individual to reorganize experience. This experience is reinterpreted, and the schema fosters further accommo-dation to the environment or assimilates externally simulated experience and becomes neurodynamically strengthened.

Within the therapeutic relationship, the therapist teaches and supports the patient's ability to regulate affect. Systems that regulate sympathetic arousal and parasympathetic inhibition in the orbitofrontal cortex are enhanced. Recall that the sympathetic nervous system acts as an accelerator in relation to anxiety and the parasympathetic nervous system acts in a complementary way as a brake. In treatment, sufficient sympathetic arousal is required to disrupt equilibrium and power change, balanced with the expectation that the partner in the interaction remains mindful of the need for parasympathetic inhibition when necessary. This makes the emergency of facing old demons a safe one for patients.

"Supportive therapy," where it provides too much parasympathetic inhibition and reassurance of an anxious or depressed patient, misses the point. What is required for optimum development is a judicious balance between activation of troubling affects and sympathetic discomfort, and support at those moments when patients really need help in inhibiting these reactions. It is the effective balance between the two systems that promotes growth. Even Carl Rogers (1951; Rogers & Dymond, 1954), whose "unconditional positive regard" is sometimes taken as the epitome of anxiety-suppressive and supportive psychotherapy, carefully moni-tored this balance and insisted that patients find their own solutions.

We gain conscious control over our emotions by intentionally reapprais-ing them (Ochsner, 2006). Even the process of naming the emotions can alter the activity of the amygdala (Harira et al., 2000). Within the thera-peutic relationship, the therapist teaches and supports patients' ability to regulate their affect. Activating the neurodynamic systems related to affect regulation in the OFC puts the brakes on the amygdala's tendency to overreact. Patients wake to a less frightening world where new behavioral possibilities open for them. At its best, a newly coconstructed narrative can help patients find a fresh and more cohesive sense of self in a world that, although often unfair and cruel, is *meaningful* and includes the possibility of good-enough relationships (Fivush, 1998). Talking "in the transference" about the feelings produced by the therapeutic alliance—even if these feelings are negative and hopeless—promotes integration between the right frontal lobe's negative emotions and withdrawal strategies and the left hemisphere's proclivities for positive affects and action. In later chapters we revisit how therapeutic dialogue serves the goal of helping patients achieve better integration of the neurodynamically complex process that eventuates in felt emotion and mood.

CHAPTER 6

Dysregulations

BEFORE EXAMINING HOW brain-based psychotherapy changes our understanding of the causes of specific psychological problems (and the psychological approaches we use to modify them), we would like to address some behavioral and lifestyle factors that compromise the brain's ability to function optimally. Although most psychotherapists see these factors as beyond the boundaries of the therapeutic relationship, we argue that anything that potentially undermines successful outcomes in psychotherapy ought to be talked about. As we noted in Chapter 5, a fundamental premise of brain-based therapy is that the mind is an *embodied* function. Changing brain chemistry through particular nutritional and substance abuse patterns often is dismissed as a symptom of "a deeper problem." Actually the reverse is just as likely to be true: commonly practiced nutritional and substance abuse patterns are, on their own, a major cause of psychiatric symptoms. In our society, eating, drinking, and using drugs as if we did not have a brain produces the neurochemistry and subjective experience of anxiety and depression. Excessive stress, caused by any one of a number of elective behavioral choices or environmental circumstances, also sets the stage for the potential development of anxiety and depression.

NUTRITION

Food fuels the brain. Deprived of the chemical building blocks it needs for maintenance and ceroplastic construction, the brain begins to sputter and degenerate. In such instances, dysregulated thoughts and emotions are not caused by unconscious conflict or malignant core beliefs. Histories of trauma and loss may also be red herrings for the evaluating clinician. A patient's stress, anxiety, and depression will intensify in these cases; a brain

Table 6.1
Psychological Effects of Amino Acids and Neurostransmitters

Amino Acid	Neurotransmitter	Effects
L-glutamine	GABA	Decreases tension and irritability
L-phenylalanine	Dopamine	Reduces anger and increases feelings of pleasure
	Norepinephrine	Increases energy, feelings of pleasure, and memory
L-trytophan	Serotonin	Improves sleep and calmness and mood

without adequate nutrition or under siege from alcohol and drugs begins to show the effects of exogenously induced neurochemical dysregulation: thoughts and feelings that are distorted, exaggerated, and unstable. The best psychotherapy in the world will not help a patient like this until the actual causes of the neurodynamic disorder are addressed.

The amino acids found in many foods are crucial building blocks for neurotransmitters. Neurotransmitters are formed by synthesizing specific amino acids. For example, L-glutamine is an amino acid found in foods such as almonds and peaches. When digested, our body uses it to synthesize the neurotransmitter Gamma-aminobutyric acid, or GABA. Recall that GABA is one of the major inhibitory transmitters and is very much involved in our ability to stay calm. The amino acids important in the synthesis of neurotransmitters and the functions and states they affect are shown in Table 6.1.

Understanding the relationship between specific dietary deficits and their effects on the brain requires some technical discussion. The therapist who remembers just a few of these things will be in a position to provide better care than one who states "It's beyond my comptence or scope of practice." Building the neurotransmitter acetylcholine, for example, requires the B-complex nutrient choline, which is derived from food. Deficits in choline and the elements of the B-complex vitamin group can have an adverse effect on synthesis, release, and metabolism of acetylcholine (Zeisel & Blusztujn, 1994). Deficits in acetylcholine are associated with memory problems. Drugs such as donepezil (Aricept) are given to patients with Alzheimer's disease to bolster their acetylcholine levels.

Serotonin is derived from the essential amino acid tryptophan. Low levels of diet-derived tryptophan are associated with lowering the pain threshold and with depressionlike symptoms (Demeyer et al, 1981).

Dopamine, as you may recall, is a neurotransmitter associated with pleasure and reward. It is derived from the amino acid phenylalamine and its companion tyrosine. Deficits in these amino acids as well as tryptophan and insufficiency of vitamin B_6 can alter mood, sleep, and arousal (Wurtman et al., 1981). Dopamine is associated with neurodynamic activation. Many dopaminergic systems project to the areas of the brain that are important in attachment behavior and the experience of closeness (Insel, 2003).

Amino acids have relationships with three other major neurotransmitter systems: the NMDA (N-methyl-d-aspartate), kainate, and AMPA (alpha-amino-3-hydroxy-5-methylisoxazole-4-propionic acid) systems (Monaghan et al., 1989). NMDA is an excitatory pathway for neural activity. When overstimulated, the result can be "neuronal burnout" (Olney et al., 1991). The point here is that a poor diet with the wrong food can result in abnormalities.

Several studies have shown that nutritional deficits are associated with cognitive deficits and neuropsychological performance across all ages (Schoenthal et al., 1991). Deficiencies in B vitamins affect psychological and neuropsychological test results in the elderly (Tucker et al., 1990). Children with higher B vitamin levels do better in school than do children with lower levels (Benten, 1992). Stress depletes the supply of B and C vitamins and also potassium. It is a good practice to encourage patients who are under unusual stress to eat foods rich in these elements and perhaps even use vitamin supplements.

Vitamins are critical building blocks for the body. When deprived of them, we experience specific deficits in our ability to think clearly. Table 6.2 lists some of the psychological consequences of deficiencies of B vitamins. The B vitamins influence the manufacture of specific neurotransmitters. For example, thiamin (B_1) is needed for GABA synthesis, and B_6 is needed for the manufacture of dopamine through the amino acids phenylalanine and tyrosine.

Stress has been shown to increase the level of cholesterol. High cholesterol is associated with increased risk of cardiovascular problems, which in turn contributes to a variety of psychological symptoms. The pharmaceutical treatment for cardiovascular problems frequently produces side effects that mimic psychological symptoms. Where possible, therapists should gently encourage a healthy cholesterol intake. There are two types of cholesterol, high-density lipoprotein (HDL) and low-density (LDL) lipoprotein. HDL cholesterol clears excess cholesterol from artery walls, while LDL cholesterol builds up on artery walls. Although we cannot consume "good" HDL cholesterol—it is formed only in the body—we can watch our fat intake. It has been found that saturated fats increase LDLs and polyunsaturated fats increase HDLs.

Table 6.2
Psychological Consequences of B Vitamin Deficiencies

Low B$_1$	Low B$_2$	Low B$_6$	Low B$_{12}$	Folic Acid
Decreased alertness	Trembling	Nervousness	Mental slowness	Memory problems
Fatigue	Sluggish	Irritability	Confusion	Irritability
Emotional Instability Decreased reaction time	Tension	Depression	Psychosis	Mental sluggishness
	Depression	Muscle weakness	Stammering	
	Eye problems	Headaches Muscle tingling	Limb weakness	
	Stress			

Costs of Low Blood Sugar

High levels of sugar contribute to anxiety and depression. Patients present-ing with these psychological issues should know that consuming foods with processed sugars may briefly "boost" energy but unfortunately what goes up must come down. The pancreas releases insulin to counterbalance the high sugar level. After the momentary sugar high, energy dips or crashes. In other words, instead of going back to the level of energy we felt prior to the sugar high, we fall lower than baseline. To make matters worse, the crash is agitated by the feelings of anxiety. The end product of that candy bar may be symptoms of anxiety and depression.

Sugar is a simple carbohydrate that has no minerals, vitamins, or enzymes to aid in its digestion. When consumed, sugar actually extracts nutrient supplies, such as B vitamins, from the body. As noted earlier, deficiencies in B vitamins cause a variety of problems including anxiety, depression, and difficulty concentrating. It is not uncommon for people who have consumed too much sugar to overreact to stress and feel irritable and spacey. Not surprisingly, many people complain that they are not only more agitated and negatively biased, but also that their sleep is dysregu-lated by too much sugar.

Caffeine

Caffeine depletes B vitamins (especially thiamin) and raises stress hormone levels. Large amounts of caffeine put the body into a prolonged state of stress and hyperalertness. The fourth edition of the *Diagnostic and Statistical*

Manual of Mental Disorders contains a diagnostic category called caffeinism. People who consume in excess of 250 milligrams of caffeine per day may experience a wide range of anxiety symptoms.

Caffeine intoxication contributes to restlessness, panic attacks, diarrhea, stomach pain, rapid heartbeat, ringing in the ears, and trembling. The crash that occurs after the caffeine wears off can result in headaches, fatigue, and difficulty concentrating. Caffeine raises the levels of the activating neuro-transmitters dopamine and norepinephrine. Norepinephrine is closely related to adrenaline, which is why many associate caffeine with feeling "wired."

It has been shown that caffeine dampens the level of adenosine, a neurotransmitter that helps us calm down and feel sedated. The caffeine molecule is shaped like adenosine and sits on the receptor site for adeno-sine in the brain, thus blocking its absorption. Instead of absorbing adenosine and receiving its inhibiting effects, cells are stimulated to increase firing. High levels of caffeine, especially if consumed in the afternoon or evening, can promote insomnia and poor-quality sleep.

Caffeine has been found to suppress the deepest and most restful sleep stage, stage 4 sleep, which recharges our immune system. People who do not get enough stage 4 sleep wake up feeling less rested; their immune systems are also more susceptible to viral infection. Caffeine also sup-presses rapid eye movement (REM), or "dreaming," sleep, and REM deprivation has been associated with increased irritability and difficulty concentrating the next day.

Consuming coffee on an empty stomach in the morning can cause a variety of problems. Patients who skip breakfast may not notice their compromised concentration and emotional lability. Unfortunately, the activating attentional effects of caffeine do not promote mindfulness. In addition, the effects of drinking caffeine on an empty stomach may not become noticeable for 2 or 3 hours. Consuming caffeine on an empty stomach releases energy reserves stored in fat cells that are normally tapped only during periods of deprivation, such as fasting. Like coming down from a sugar high, this compromised energy spurt likely ends with patients feeling depleted and may also generate an experience of free-floating anxiety. Many caffeinated soft drinks (which also contain up to 5 tablespoonfuls of sugar in one 12-ounce serving) add the ill effects of sugar to the "buzz" and crash from caffeine.

SUBSTANCE ABUSE

Alcohol and most other drugs cause deficits in motivation, optimism, and energy level for several days and even weeks after consumption. People who overindulge or have an alcohol or drug problem often misread social cues and overreact to social stress. Patients who habitually use drugs may have little insight into the nuances of interpersonal relationships. Intoxication does not improve mindsight.

Many patients are unaware of the adverse effects of substance abuse biologically, psychologically, and in their social relationships. The "relief" they get from alcohol is short-lived but may be well defended. Their practice of drinking to take the edge off their anxiety results in a brief period of pleasure when they have the buzz, but the edge comes back with interest, sometimes not until as much as a week later.

ALCOHOL

Alcohol is toxic to the brain, as it damages dendrites. It decreases blood flow to the brain and interferes with the operation of neurotransmitters. The degradation of neurotransmitters causes numerous emotional and cognitive problems even weeks after the last drink, which may make it hard for patients to see the effects of alcohol on their behavior. Many of the neurotransmitters discussed in Chapter 2 become downregulated after drinking.

Alcohol contributes to these problems as much as several days after drinking:

- It increases stress and anxiety because it lowers the levels of the naturally inhibiting neurotramitters (e.g., GABA). It is quite common for people to have panic attacks precipitated by recent alcohol abuse.
- It increases depression, possibly by lowering the levels of the neurotransmitter serotonin for as much as a few weeks after the last drink.
- It impairs deep sleep. It is quite common for people to have alcohol-related insomnia. Alcohol interferes with stage 4 and REM sleep.

Having a nightcap produces mid–sleep cycle awakening, a classic symptom of drinking in the evening. This occurs because the effects of alcohol begin to wear off after approximately 3 hours, when there is a surge of anxiety and tension.

Among serious drinkers, alcohol may account for up to 50% of their total daily caloric intake, restricting the normal consumption of macronutrients: fats, carbohydrates, and proteins. In other words, drinking suppresses the body's ability to make full use of food consumed. At high levels and over time, alcohol can cause Wernicke's encepalopathy and Korsakoff's syndrome.

Overall, alcohol must be regarded as a major exogenous cause of anxiety and depression. As noted, drinkers are likely to be deprived of the calming effects of full-strength GABA; diminished dopamine levels result in fewer feelings of pleasure and motivation; and diminished norepinephrine levels result in more problems attending and concentrating. Alcohol also depresses the neuropeptides and the immune system. Finally, among drinkers who are suffering from chronic pain connected to an injury, the intensity of their pain will increase over the long term even though they may feel temporary relief after a drink.

Alcohol damages specific areas of the brain, particularly the hippocampus and the cerebellum. The hippocampus, as noted earlier, is critically important in the process of learning and laying down of memories. It is also the site-specific target for stress hormones. Glucocorticoids have a neurotoxic effect, which weakens the hippocampus. Alcohol can activate the hypothalamic-pituitary-adrenal axis, and elevated glucocorticoids activate the whole neurodynamic stress response. In other words, although alcohol induces feelings of temporary relaxation, it raises stress hormones over the long term. A progressive Berkeley professor once described it to us as "the perfect capitalist drug: It causes the problems it pretends to cure so you buy more and more of it."

Alcohol leads to "cognitive constriction"; in other words, among people who abuse alcohol, the capacities to think broadly tend to wither and narrow. This is partly because of dendritic degradation. Regular alcohol consumption leads to black-and-white frames of reference rather than appreciation of shades of gray. Alcohol also contributes to "affective constriction," contributing to feeling emotional extremes. It tends to promote feeling either bad or good, not in between.

One of the standard rules in neuropsychological testing with regard to people who have consumed alcohol on a regular basis is that you do not test a "wet" brain. People who drink on a regular basis have a variety of cognitive deficits, showing decreased:

- Performance on tests of visual and spatial perception
- Visual and spatial learning ability
- Ability to make fine motor movements
- Adaptive abilities
- Short-term memory
- Nonverbal abstract learning
- Abstract thinking ability
- Conceptual thinking ability

In addition to these personal deficits, the negative effects of substance abusers on the people around them must be considered. An estimated 40% to 80% of adults committing murder or violent assaults were drunk or high at the time of the offense (Pernanen, 1991; Roizen, 1997). Another estimate suggests that as many as 60% of those committing sexual assault were intoxicated (Roizen, 1997). Although our patients' drinking and substance abuse problems may not produce the rolling human tragedies these statistics suggest are common in the prison population, they do point to the magnitude of the contribution of alcohol and drugs to human suffering and psychological distress.

Given that a good alliance and patient-centered care are vital ingredients of treatment success—and given that many of our patients will not bring up their nutritional or substance abuse habits for discussion—what is a good practice for therapists to follow in this area? As part of the assessment process, therapists can inquire about psychological functioning most likely to be affected by nutritional and alcohol or drug habits. A patient with an anxiety or mood-related problem, or even a relationship problem, may present openings for discussion. Some therapists balance their concerns about the effectiveness of psychotherapy in treating what may be a primarily alcohol-driven problem against letting patients determine the scope of work in treatment by using Prochaska's stage of change model. If a patient does not want to address these issues, the therapist can state that more information is readily available (and have information available at the interview or be able to tell the patient where to find it). Down the road, it may be unethical—as well as a poor outcome management strategy—not to tell a substance-abusing patient that psychotherapy and cocaine are like oil and water: They do not mix.

Now let us consider how to handle pathogenic nutritional habits in a way that honors the special attributes and needs of both the patient and the brain.

JAKE AND THE BASE

Jake sought help after months of acute anxiety punctuated by periodic panic attacks and alternating periods of depression. The initial assessment was performed by one of our interns, Diane. Jake told Diane that during the past few years, "stress had messed me up" and that he "didn't even have the time or the stomach for food anymore." He added that "food makes me nauseated—I'd rather just drink coffee instead." Jake described how he could not relax and was getting only a few hours of sleep a night. He had begun to take a "nightcap" to unwind and get to sleep. When

---

(Continued)

Diane pursued this, it turned out the nightcap was "a few shots." This helped Jake doze off but after a few hours of sleep he woke up and could not get back to sleep.

During the day, Jake was bothered by free-floating anxiety and had trouble concentrating. About three months earlier he had had a panic attack followed by increasing feelings of depression. The attacks were now coming more days than not. Diane consulted with Madeleine, her supervisor, before making the referral for a medication evaluation appointment. Madeleine suggested that Diane first focus on the BASE, a mnemonic representing the terms *brain, alliance, systematic, evidence-based practice*. Starting with the *b*, Jake's brain chemistry was dysregulated by his poor diet and alcohol intake.

Diane responded by saying "Well, yeah, I can see that, but the guy is so wrapped up in trying to cope with his anxiety and moods that it's going to be really tough for him to let go of his self-medicating." "Right," Madeleine said. "That's what the *a* is about—it's for alliance. We won't get anywhere with Jake unless you can form a good one with him. Stay in touch with his feelings about how things are going. That's really important right now. Follow up with any indications of negative reactions, and pay attention to the nonverbal cues, not just what he says. This is the kind of case that can easily end in premature termination if we forget about relationship for one second."

Diane used a stages-of-change model with Jake initially, since the object in the first stage of treatment was to help him see how caffeine and alcohol were contributing to the problem. "Harm reduction" was something that Jake felt he could do for starters, but abstinence was too big a leap for him. He started by reducing his caffeine intake and eating a small breakfast of cereal and milk in the morning. When he actually got the sense that nutrition and caffeine intake could be causing his symptoms, he started to feel that perhaps he could get more control over his life. Jake and Diane tracked the incidence of his panic episodes, and they were diminishing. In supervision, Madeleine continued to advise Diane to maximize empathy while simultaneously educating Jake about shifting his dysregulated neurodynamics to restore his maximum potential for regulating mood and attention. Jake agreed he would try substituting some sleep hygiene methods (see Chapter 11) for the nightcaps. Diane assured him they would assess how well this plan was working as the experiment unfolded.

A month or so into this step-down process, Jake was feeling less anxious and more optimistic. "This is good," he told his therapist midway through, "but my moods didn't start with coffee or booze; I need to get over the stuff I've been carrying around since my brother's death. It's like I stopped living myself." Talking with Diane in supervision, Madeleine pointed out that the *s* in the BASE model stands for "systematic factors." They'd already introduced the *s* by ruling out the contributory effects of diet and alcohol before considering medication or trying to establish a clear diagnosis. Building the alliance (which was especially critical in this case) before considering the technical aspects of treatment was also thinking systematically. Diane's assessment at this point was that she and Jake had a good working alliance; he was willing and able to talk about his reactions to her and the process. He was feeling more optimistic, and his resistance to talking about his emotional and social problems seemed moderate and perhaps even mild. "I think now we're ready for the *e*," Madeleine said. "*E* is for evidence-based treatment. It's time to talk to Jake about behavioral activation to treat his depression and try introducing some other CBT methods with him like thought records."

ALLOSTASIS

As we adapt to changing situations and unpredictable events, our bodies need extra energy from endogenous stores of fat, glycogen, and protein. The capacity of the brain and our bodies as a whole to maintain stability through change has been called *allostasis* (Sterling & Ayer, 1998). McEwen and colleagues broaden the concept of allostasis to refer to neurobiological processes such as the secretion of cortisol and norepinephrine (McEwen & Stellar, 1993). Changes in internal set points to meet changing performance demands are one form of allostatic regulation that helps us to achieve or maintain stability (McEwen & Wingfield, 2003). When demands exceed our ability to control the balance of energy expenditure versus conservation and recuperation, we experience *allostatic load*.

A common name for this experience is, simply, stress. Stress is a product of having to work to maintain our equilibrium, and it effects us on many levels. The term allostasis tends to be applied to the more technical and biological aspects of this regulatory process. Whatever we call it—stress or allostatic load—its relationship to the development of medical problems has been well documented over the last 30 years. For example, the occurrence of myocardial infarction has been shown to be associated with the frustration of an important life goal by a stressor (Neilson, Brown, & Marmot, 1989). The onset of multiple sclerosis is correlated with reduced immune system functioning following severe life stressors (Cohen, Tyrell, & Smith, 1991). The experience of stressful events is associated with the development of nonspecific back pain (as opposed to organic back pain) (Craufurd, Creed, & Jayson, 1990). The onset of peptic ulcers is also correlated with the frustration of an important life event by a stressor (Ellard et al., 1990). Irritable bowel syndrome also has been correlated with a response to a serious environmental stressor (Brown & Harris, 1989).

Since George Solomon's groundbreaking paper in the mid-1960s (Solomon & Moos, 1965), the evidence of a psychological link to the immune system has increased. Indeed, a relatively new field, psychoneuroimmunology, has demonstrated a bidirectional relationship between psychological processes and physical health. During the late 1970s and 1980s, David Felton discovered norepinephrine and epinephrine nerve tracks terminating in the lymph nodes and the spleen (Felton et al., 1987). In another groundbreaking discovery, Gail Granger and her colleagues found that lymphokines (later renamed *cytokines*) had hormonal effects at sites far removed from the lymph nodes. Many studies have focused on how various individual psychological differences interact with the immune system (see Granger et al., 2006, for a review).

Cytokines (small protein molecules that act as cellular messengers) have multiple effects. The list of known cytokine molecules is large and growing. It includes interleukins, interferons, colony-stimulating and growth factors, tumor necrosis factor superfamily, and chemokines. A healthy person optimally regulates cytokine at moderate levels of activity. Too little activity can result in immunodeficiency, severe infection, and even death. Hyperarousal can also cause illness, tissue damage, shock, or death (Granger et al., 2006).

Cytokines can also affect neurotransmission. For example, interleukins can affect neurometabolism in such a way as to lower the concentration of serotonin. Cytokines influence neurostransmission in the limbic system and hypothalamus and affect memory and learning, emotional regulation, and the psychobiology of the stress response. Granger and colleagues (2006) describe the array of effects associated with the cytokines:

> In summary, the experimental studies provide strong support for the conclusion that cytokine production (or administration) is causally linked to the expression of change in psychological, emotional, behavioral, and cognitive function. The severity of the symptoms clearly extends to the clinical range. The symptoms linked to cytokines include internalizing disorders (such as cognitive processes, psychosis, anxiety, fearfulness, depression, and thoughts about suicide). Generally, the effects of cytokines at the behavioral surface are consistent with our knowledge about the effects of cytokines on the central nervous and neuroendrocine system[s]. (p. 690)

As we have noted elsewhere in this book, cortisol plays many roles in shaping neurodynamics. It contributes to the regulation of brain-derived neurotropic factors, upregulates activity in the amygdala, and targets prefrontal systems involved in stress and the emotions (Sullivan & Gratton, 2002; see Gunnar & Vazquez, 2006, for a review). On a positive note, cortisol helps facilitate adaptation and restores homeostasis through many allostasic processes, those that aim at maintaining stability through changing conditions and demands (McEwen, 1999). Cortisol has been reported to orchestrate allostatic adjustments by enhancing or inhibiting gene transcription in tissues in many organs throughout the body (Sapolsky, Romero, & Munck, 2000). Allostatic load involves chronic high levels of cortisol and catecholamines, such as norepinephrine, that take a toll on our health (including our mental health). Examples of these health effects include increased blood pressure, progression toward type II diabetes, atherosclerosis, abdominal obesity, neural atrophy, cognitive deficits, anxiety, and depression.

As with most things pertaining to the brain and self-regulation, relationships appear to play an essential role. Using data from the Wisconsin Longitudinal Study, Singer and Ryff (1999) found that the presence of positive social relationships was associated with resilience and lower allostatic load despite adverse economic conditions. Individuals who early in life have had to deal with abuse or neglect bear ongoing higher allostatic loads. Seeman and colleagues, using data from the MacArthur Study on Successful Aging, reported that emotional support was a predictor of better cognitive functioning at the 7.5-year follow-up (Seeman, Lusignolo, Albert, &, 2001). Similarly, using data from the Social Environment and Biomarkers of Aging Study in Taiwan, Seeman and colleagues found that men between the ages of 54 and 70 who had a spouse 6 to 8 years prior to the collection of the data had a lower allostatic load than men who were single at that time. Interestingly, this effect was not found with women. But in both men and women age 71 years and above, those with close ties to friends or neighbors had lower allostatic load (Seeman, 2004).

Elderly people who have a supportive and engaging social life were reported to have better cognitive abilities seven years later than those who were socially isolated (Seeman et al., 2001). Social support has been shown to have a therapeutic effect on people suffering from various medical conditions and mental health problems. Empathy and social support are critical aspects of the application of evidence-based treatment. Our brains, built and rebuilt through relationships all through life, would not have it any other way.

STRESS AND DYSREGULATION

More than a century ago, William James proposed that emotions result from responses to our body sensations. According to James: "We feel sorry because we cry, angry because we strike, afraid because we tremble" (1890/2007, vol. 2, p. 449). Hans Selye (1979) described what he referred to as the "general adaptation syndrome." An individual under great stress, whether he chooses to flee or to fight, is coping with a sympathetic nervous system that has kicked into high gear. Selye described three stages in the individual's high-stress experience: physiological alarm; adaptation to the stress; and exhaustion. During the alarm phase, all resources are put in hyperalert mode to deal with the impending threat. Many of the fight-or-flight responses first described by Walter Cannon (1915) come into play during this phase. In the adaptation phase, the individual struggles to gather his psychological and physiological resources to try to resolve the cause, or at least the effects, of the

Table 6.3

Adaptive versus Maladaptive Ways to Deal with Short-Term Stress

Adaptive	Maladaptive
Mobilization of energy	Energy depletion, lethargy
Increased cardiovascular tone	Hypotension, hypertension
Suppression of digestion	Ulceration, colitis
Suppression of growth	Psychogenic dwarfism
Suppression of reproduction	Low libido, impotence
Suppression of the immune system	More colds and flu
Sharpened thinking	Neuronal death

stress. The exhaustion phase occurs when the individual either completes the task or gives up.

There are healthy and unhealthy ways to deal with stress. Ideally, our body adapts to the stress rather than breaks down because of it. Table 6.3 presents two opposing lists representing two different ways of dealing with short-term stress, one adaptive, one maladaptive. If the stress is chronic, a wide spectrum of symptoms may emerge, including:

- Diarrhea
- Frequent urination
- Low self-esteem
- Difficulty concentrating
- Hostility and aggression
- Difficulty making decisions
- Distractibility
- Irritability
- Insomnia
- Feelings of doom and gloom
- Skin rashes
- Changes in the menstrual cycle
- Low sex drive
- Mood swings
- Increased daydreaming
- Insensitivity to others

Our nervous system has two major stress regulation systems, one automatic and the other under conscious control. Recall that one part of the automatic system, the sympathetic nervous system (SNS), regulates arousal; the other, the parasympathetic nervous system (PNS), regulates relaxation. The PNS helps us calm down by releasing acetylcholine, which dampens the effects of adrenaline. The SNS is responsible for the fight-or-flight response. It activates the release of norepinephrine and epinephrine, making us more alert. The SNS initiates a cascade of events, including the movement of blood away from our skin, liver, and digestive system toward our heart, muscles, and lungs. It also signals our liver to release fats such as cholesterol and triglycerides into the bloodstream to promote energy.

Since the liver receives less blood during stress, several problems emerge when the stress is chronic. Because one of the liver's main functions is to clear the blood of cholesterol, chronic stress can result in a buildup of cholesterol deposits in our arteries. Consequently, prolonged stress puts us at greater risk for strokes and heart problems. An extensive Kaiser study demonstrated the downside of neuroplasticity and the effects of stress on both brain health and the body generally. People who reported high-numbers of adverse childhood experiences, such as physical or sexual abuse, were found, as a group, to have disproportionately high incidences of medical and psychological problems. The statistical relationship was simple and straightforward: the greater number of adverse childhood experiences, the more serious medical and psychological problems the adult had to contend with (Felitti et al., 1998). Acuity was also found to vary directly with the number of negative childhood events.

Sheldon Cohen (2004) has performed a series of studies exploring the relationship between susceptibility to the common cold and stress. His findings suggest that stress can lower the immune system's effectiveness, making individuals more susceptible to catching a cold. Positive and exciting events, however, appear to bolster the immune system. A meta-analysis of studies looking at different cortisol-related stressors (including loud noises and confrontations with obnoxious people) found that the greatest stress resulted from being subjected to criticism and not being able to do anything about it (Dickerson & Kemeny, 2004).

Many adults spend most of their waking hours at work. Our jobs can be a source of joy or despair. An array of symptoms is related to the negative reponses to stress on the job (Arden, 2002). Work stress is widespread in societies that are materialistic and status oriented, such as the United States and Japan. In a study of healthcare workers in Britain, workers were exposed to two different supervisors on alternative days. On the days when a difficult, critical, and unpleasant supervisor was in charge, the average worker's systolic blood pressure rose from 113/75 to 126/81 overall. It normalized on days when the more agreeable supervisor was working (Wager, Feldman, & Hussey, 2001). Studies conducted in Sweden and the United Kingdom have shown that lower-level civil servants were four times more likely to develop cardiovascular disease than higher-level civil servants (Marmot & Shipley, 2000; Wamala, Mittleman, Horsten, Schenck-Gustafsson, & Orth-Gomer, 2000). Coronary heart disease is as much as 30% percent higher among workers who feel unfairly criticized by bosses (Kivimaki et al., 2005).

NEURODYNAMICS OF STRESS

NORMAL NEURODYNAMIC REGULATION

Stress is a key driver of mental life, one that involves neurochemical and neuroanatomical components such as the hypothalamic-pituitary-adrenal (HPA) axis. The HPA axis represents our body's principal stress response system; it is the physiological infrastructure of the fight-or-flight response. The HPA axis is activated by signals from the amygdala once a threat has been detected, and it returns to baseline once the amygdala is quieted by feedback regulatory loops connecting the amygdala with the orbitofrontal cortex and the hippocampus. The amygdala plays a central role in activating the HPA axis, and it has important effects on the brain and the body generally, regulating carbohydrate metabolism, blood pressure, and body temperature.

In the healthy brain, there is a distinctive daily cortisol cycle. An elevation occurs early in the morning, prompting us to get up and confront the challenges of the day. Around midday, cortisol levels gradually begin to decline; they rise again in midafternoon and then decline again, usually bottoming out at about midnight. When the amygdala reacts to something it regards as threatening, it signals for release of cortisol, and cortisol, in turn, activates the HPA axis. The HPA axis signals the hypothalamus, resulting in the release of two peptides, corticotrophin-releasing factor (CRF) and vasopressin. These neurohormones, in turn, signal the pituitary gland (which lies below the hypothalamus on the pituitary stalk) to secrete adrenocorticotropic hormone (ACTH) into the bloodstream. When ACTH reaches the adrenal glands, situated above the kidneys, the adrenal glands secrete epinephrine and norepinephrine, both activating neurotransmitters. If the stress lasts more than 15 or 20 minutes after the initial cortisol release, the cycle begins all over again and is repeated until the "all-clear" signal is sent.

Three neuroanatomical structures—the orbital medial prefrontal cortex (OMPFC), the amygdala, and the hippocampus—play critical roles in regulating our responses to stress. Although the hippocampus is always remodeling itself through neuroplasticity and neurogenesis, the amygdala is relatively stable over time. The amygdala, like a family watchdog, remembers and watches for stressful events. It helps formulate very durable emotional memories; the hippocampus, by comparison, remains flexible for new learning. When exposed to angry faces or fear-evoking situations, the relationship between the amygdala and the OMPFC shifts. As the amygdala becomes more activated, the OMPFC becomes less so (Nomura et al., 2004). Due to these dynamics, the amygdala becomes dominant in shifting our neurodynamic state into a fight-or-flight mode. Judgments and behaviors adjust accordingly (Drevets & Raichle, 1998). Normally, after the danger is over or cortical centers demystify a specious threat, the OMPFC reactivates, putting the brakes on an overactivated amygdala. Stress regulation is supposed to work this way: the reactivity of the amygdala can be overridden by the executive control of the prefrontal cortex (PFC). The PFC may recognize that although a course of action *is* dangerous, we decide to do it anyway because of possible gains, or just for the fun of it.

A healthy hippocampus provides a second major check on the amygdala's reactivity and fearful fast reactions. The hippocampus is equipped with a large number of cortisol and other receptors. When these receptors are fully occupied, the hippocampus puts out signals that normally result in the HPA system recalibrating downward. Functionally, the hippocampus is vital to our sense of context, an important ingredient in accurately interpreting the emotional valence of a situation. For example, a woman executive feeling socially anxious about presenting at a corporate meeting reminds herself that she met with this same group two months ago and enjoyed it. Without this kind of contextual information from the hippocampus, the fear response from the amygdala becomes decontextualized and can escalate into generalized anxiety or panic. Chronic stress can disrupt the delicate equilibrium between the brain's "odd couple"—the hippocampus and the amygdala—in favor of the amygdala. Under normal circumstances, however, when a sufficient number of cortisol receptors are occupied in the hippocampus, the hypothalamus is signaled to stop secreting CRF, which signals the pituitary to stop releasing ACTH, downregulating the adrenal glands and the release of cortisol. Then everything starts to return to "normal."

A third element important in the normal stress regulatory system is that a healthy amygdala itself has an internal set point that limits its tendency for fast and dirty appraisals. This set point can be altered neurochemically (for example by the levels of serotonin and GABA). Low serotonin levels tend to make the amygdala more reactive. Also, as serotonin levels go down, norepinephrine levels may rise, further increasing reactivity. High cortisol levels diminish the inhibiting effects of serotonin and GABA in the amygdala. But given a relatively normal neurochemical environment, the amygdala does not reach extremes of activation.

Although too much stress over too long a period has, as we have seen, very negative effects on the brain, moderate levels of stress foster our sense of well-being and our ability to perform well cognitively and socially. Without it, we might not be motivated to rise to life's challenges. Moderate stress actually stimulates neural growth hormones and the production of new cells (Pham, Soderstrom, Henriksson, & Mohammed, 1997). The levels of specific catecholamines, such as norepinephrine and dopamine, are very important regulators in this regard. Dopamine is associated with arousal and the reward system. Low levels of dopamine can produce anhedonia (the loss the capacity of experience pleasure), emotional numbing, and social disconnection. We need a moderate level of arousal to remember and think effectively. If stress is mild, memories are enhanced and our attention is stimulated and focused so that we can learn from experience (Cowan & Kandel, 2001). Healthy levels of cortisol energize us to engage in the task at hand (Abercrombie, Thurow, Rosenkranz, Kalin, & Davidson, 2003). When confronted by chronic stress, however, the amygdala continues to trigger the HPA axis, resulting in ongoing release of cortisol even after the hippocampus tells it to slow down. In the face of continued exposure to high cortisol levels, the hippocampus becomes functionally impaired and starts to deteriorate.

Effects of Chronic Stress

The negative impact of chronic stress is evident throughout the body. The HPA axis works very effectively for brief periods of time; if we experience severe and prolonged stress, however, our biological systems falter. Sustained stress inhibits protein production, negatively impacting the B&T cells and leukocytes that are the immune system's natural killers. Among people who experience chronic stress, the suppression of the capacity of the immune system to fight off illness results in increased susceptibility to infection or immune deficiencies of various sorts. Moreover, long-term stress affects the functioning of the HPA axis itself. The body's normal setpoint for CRF levels, for example, is raised as a consequence of early life stress (Bonne, Grillon, Vythilingam, Neumeister, & Charney, 2004). This elevated set point increases the individual's overall stress sensitivity. High levels of CRF are implicated in, among other things, hippocampal damage (Brunson, et. al., 2001).

Acute but nonchronic experiences of stress—such as an unexpected public embarrassment that causes us to replay situations and ruminate about how we handled them—increase the level of stress hormones. The neurodynamics associated with the triggering experience are kindled and rekindled, prompting consciousness to replay the embarrassing scene and its evoked emotions over and over again. A cascade of physiological, emotional, and cognitive reactions may persist with each rehearsal, and new events that would otherwise be taken in stride stimulate emotionally charged memories of the disturbing event (Bower & Siver, 1998). This self-reinforcing pattern of acute stress is built into our neurodynamics.

The self-regulatory processes of the stress response cycle do not always stand up well to the pace and complexity of modern life. In response to stress, the adrenal glands release epinephrine and norepinephrine. Epinephrine activates glucose metabolism for use as energy and stimulates an increased blood flow for fight-or-flight behavior by raising heart rate and respiration and dilating blood vessels. Norepinephrine is upregulated by chronic stress, activating the amygdala, which in turn signals for the release of norepinephrine in the PFC. With more norepinephrine active in the brain, the amygdala gets into a positive feedback loop, repeatedly signaling the PFC, which in turn releases yet more norepinephrine. The amygdala continues to reinforce the stress cycle after the environmental threat has subsided. It commandeers conscious attention and infiltrates working memory, contributing to the whole experience of anxiety and being "stressed out." Attention and working memory begin to falter (Chajut & Algom, 2003). Normally, the PFC would put the brakes on this snowballing effect; in a cycle of escalating stress, however, it acts as a reinforcer of the stress feedback loop. We see the results of this cycle in patients (if not in ourselves and our colleagues) who feel overwhelmed and whose problem-solving style has been reduced to black-and-white, fight-or-flight options.

Chronic stress induces contrasting patterns of dendritic remodeling in hippocampal and amygdaloid neurons (Vyas et al., 2002). Whereas the hippocampus becomes less active, the amygdala becomes even more sensitive to neurochemical manipulation of its set point. Robert Sapolsky (1990) has shown that significant stress can cause permanent damage to the hippocampus. Hippocampal dendrites shrink and hippocampal nerves eventually die (Sapolsky, 1996) because stress hormones deplete glucose, starving neurons and reducing their ability to function. Cortisol may also inhibit the growth of new synapses related to neuroplasticity in the hippocampus (Lombroso & Sapolsky, 1998; McEwen, 1999). Even temporary stress, as long as it is severe enough, can damage the hippocampus (McEwen, 1992). To make matters worse, cortisol results in decreased hippocampal production of new neurons (neurogenesis).

This combination of cell death and decreased cell birth produces hippocampal shrinkage (see LeDoux, 2003, for a review). Thus, two of the major brakes in the system that regulate anxiety and stress—networks in the prefrontal cortex and the hippocampus—become dysregulated under the impact of ongoing elevated cortisol levels. If the OMPFC is also pulled in to the loop, fear is overinterpreted and generalized, as is the case with anxiety disorders.

Generally, damage to neuroanatomical systems is reversible if the stress subsides. Under the impact of chronic stress, however, the damage may be permanent, destroying some of our capacity to code long-term explicit memories. Cortisol-induced damage to the hippocampus has been reported in patients with posttraumatic stress disorder (PTSD) (Bremner & Narayan, 1998), and stress hormones also adversely effect the frontal lobes. In disorders such as PTSD, this negative impact on the frontal lobes can lead to poor decision making. Hippocampal damage impacts both memory and the capacity for new learning; and if hippocampal atrophy occurs early in childhood, its effects reverberate throughout life (Bremner & Narayan, 1998). Children with hippocampal damage due to adverse childhood events often suffer in terms of later academic achievement. Many people with mood disorders have deregulated amygdalar-HPA-hippocampal-OMPFC circuits. In fact, many depressed and bipolar patients must contend with elevated cortisol levels that do not take the normal noontime dip. This may be one reason why these patients also have problems with sleep.

To bring patients out of rigidly engrained states of emotional dysfunction such as depression, we need to bring into play new energy to destabilize the old patterns. A new balance between continuity and flexibility that allows for emergent states of increasing complexity is required (Arden, 1996; Grigsby & Stevens, 2002; Siegel, 1999). As therapists, our job is to help the patient become "unstuck" from inflexible and maladaptive patterns of brain activation. The neurodynamic attractors that patients formed early in life may have been adaptive to conditions within the family, but currently they produce nonproductive and dysfunctional consequences. Interestingly, the long-term use of selective serotonin reuptake inhibitor antidepressants (SSRIs) appears to reduce the adrenal production of cortisol. The serotonergic neurons also have direct projections to the amygdala, where they block the excitatory inputs through their effect on GABA, thus reducing anxiety. In Chapter 7, we consider strategies for working therapeutically with the these complex elements to help dysregulated patients achieve optimal levels of allostatic balance—a state otherwise known as happiness.

Brain-Based Therapy for Anxiety Disorders

"We gain strength, and courage, and confidence by each experience in which we really stop to look fear in the face . . . we must do that which we think we cannot."

—Eleanor Roosevelt

B RAIN-BASED THERAPY IS a way of integrating neurodynamic information with lessons from the literature on what makes psychotherapy work. In considering how actually to apply this model, we start with the anxiety disorders, the most common of the psychological disturbances. Schizophrenia affects only 1% of the population; depression affects 15% to 20% (depending on who is counting); more than 25% of the population, however, suffers from some form of anxiety disorder (Kessler, et al., 2005). This is not surprising, considering that, in our evolutionary history, the quick appraisal of threat has had a persistent life-or-death importance. This history sculpted the human amygdala, the hippocampus, the circuitry linking the limbic areas to the neocortex, and the hypothalamic-pituitary-adrenal (HPA) axis—each of which is fundamentally important in the experience of anxiety.

Fear is the core emotion underlying all anxiety disorders (LeDoux, 1996). In panic disorder, there is an escalating anticipation that something terrible is happening. In generalized anxiety disorder (GAD), fear takes a free-floating form that something is just not right. In posttraumatic stress disorder (PTSD), fear is episodic, acute, associated with flashbacks, and can be triggered at the level of a panic attack by a stimulus like a car

139

backfiring. In obsessive-compulsive disorder (OCD), the fear may be that a catastrophe is waiting to happen and can be forestalled by putting things in a particular order or scrubbing the hands. Finally, with phobias, fear is associated with situations (e.g., giving a speech), or sensations (e.g., fear of falling), or animals or insects (cats are one of the most common phobic objects).

Fear-based memories encoded in the amygdala are highly resistant to forgetting. Although the amygdala plays a key role in both specific and generalized anxiety states, it projects to many other key neuroanatomical sites as well. One of these is the locus coeruleus (LC) in the brain stem, which itself has extensive projections throughout the brain (Aston-Jones, Valentino, Van Bockstaele, & Meyerson, 1994). The LC is our primary source of norepinephrine, the activating neurotransmitter that mediates the fight-or-flight response. Activation of the LC during trauma heightens the *memory* of that trauma. These memories get hyperpotentiated, which means that they become more easily triggered by stimuli that in some way resemble or are emotionally associated with the original trauma. A door slamming can put an Iraqi combat veteran with PTSD into a panic level of anxiety, for example.

For most species, part of the fear response involves freezing. The innate tendency to freeze in reaction to a fearful threat may be the best response to a predator that senses and is excited by movement. The freezing response has been observed both in human infants with dysregulated attachment schemas and in trauma victims. Animals with a damaged amygdala lose this freeze response in reaction to danger.

There appears to be a bias toward right-hemisphere processing among people with anxiety disorders. This right-hemispheric bias, coupled with an underactivation of the left frontal lobes and of Broca's area (important in expressive speech) explains why some people feel speechless when they are scared (Rauch et al., 1997). Greater right-frontal activation has been associated with social anxiety disorder (Davidson et al., 2000), GAD (Wu et al., 1991), and panic disorder (Reiman et al., 1989).

Because the symptoms of anxiety can be experienced mainly as a somatic event that the brain is only reacting to appropriately, anxious people often seek medical help for anxiety problems. It has been estimated that as many as 75% to 90% of primary care outpatient visits are prompted by problems that are actually psychological or stress related. Not everyone manifests the same symptoms of anxiety or experiences them in the same way. One person's neurodynamics may channel anxiety to the gastrointestinal tract and leave him with chronic diarrhea, stomachaches, or decreased appetite. Another may experience headaches, neck pain, or shoulder tension. A third may complain of racing thoughts, feeling "spacey" or dizzy, and free floating anxiety.

The treatment of anxiety must be broad-based and address biopsychosocial dimensions. As we discussed in Chapter 6, dietary habits, alcohol and drug abuse, and childhood trauma should all be considered in evaluating anxiety disorders. Certain features of some disorders, such as a hypersensitivity to bodily sensations or the physical sensations of normal anxiety, tend to be heritable. A biopsychosocial approach to the treatment of anxiety disorders provides a comprehensive model (Barlow et al., 1989). Patients may be predisposed to developing anxiety disorders because of their genetic makeup, temperament, early attachment experiences, trauma histories, or social models. As primates, our brains are designed to make anxiety communicable through conscious and nonconscious channels, and this can serve as a pathway for the intergenerational communication of trauma.

In its mildest form, anxiety is a feeling of uneasiness, free-floating distress and worry. Generalized anxiety disorder is a chronic and more intense variation on this theme. GAD is discomfortingly pervasive, and may include spikes of very distressing intensity and functional impairment. Panic disorder usually engenders much more intense distress than GAD but in more condensed episodes. In GAD, people worry that they could get mugged walking from their parking place to their office; people with panic disorder feel like the mugger barely missed them with that last swipe of the knife.

As discussed, the neurodynamic modules and brain chemistry associated with anxiety are fast and effective. The amygdala is wired directly into the sympathetic nervous system and to the neurodynamic modules, such as the LC, that produce the transmitters associated with activation. The amygdala reacts very quickly to anything it deems a threat, before we are aware of anything consciously. The "low road" path from the amygdala by-passes the cortex altogether; it is a main route for the imprinting of nonconscous emotional memories of frightening experiences.

GENERALIZED ANXIETY DISORDER

With GAD, patients feel anxious most of the time. They may be chronic worriers with a tendency to overreact to stress, torturing themselves with what-if thoughts throughout the day: "What if that rainstorm tomorrow jams the freeways and I miss my plane? I'll be fired!" People with GAD are often aware that they are more than usually anxious. GAD sufferers, according to the definition of the disorder in the fourth edition of the *Diagnostic and Statistical Manual of Mental Disorders* (*DSM-IV*), do not worry about having a panic attack, being publicly embarrassed, being contaminated, or committing perverse sexual or aggressive acts; nor are their worries focused on an animal or particular set of sensations (anxieties associated with other disorders). Just about anything else is fair game.

GAD: SOMATIC SYMPTOMS AND RULE-OUTS

As we discussed in Chapter 6, the psychological and somatic effects of stress are many and varied. A stressful relationship with a supervisor, for example, often produces episodic increases in blood pressure and sympathetic nervous system (SNS) activation, resulting in increased respiration, heart rate, and perspiration, and changes in the allocation of blood supply. There may be spikes in the blood level of cortisol. These reactions become something to contend with in themselves, especially if they reenforce activation of the amygdala. Vulnerability to GAD might be thought of as a deficiency in the individual's amygdalar-HPA-hippocampal-OFC loop that downregulates the cycle of fear and stress. When GAD is triggered, some of its common symptoms include:

- Muscle tension
- Restlessness or feeling keyed up or on edge
- Irritability
- Mind going blank or difficulty concentrating
- Fatigue
- Sleep disturbance
- Feeling like there is a lump in your throat
- Frequent urination
- Dry mouth
- Clammy hands
- Feeling shaky or trembling

However, these physical correlates to anxious states of mind can be produced by other factors as well and in evaluating a patient it is important to rule out the nonpsychogenic ones. Medical conditions such as mitral valve prolapse occur in 5% to 15% of the general population. About half of these people suffer from chest pains, breathlessness, and palpitation—symptoms also common in GAD. Some other medical conditions with somatic symptoms similar to those activated by the amygdala and the SNS are:

- Adrenal tumor
- Cushing's disease
- Hypoglycemia
- Hypothyroidism
- Menière's disease
- Parathyroid disease
- Postconcussion syndromes

Anxiety symptoms can also be the result of the metabolic and toxic effects of consuming or being exposed to toxic chemicals or compounds. Examples of this kind of exogenous induction of reactions that mimic those of anxiety are: exposure to environmental hydrocarbons, mercury, and carbon dioxide; withdrawal from alcohol, barbiturates, and benzodiazepines; and deficiencies in magnesium, vitamin B_{12}, potassium, and calcium.

Some people with hypoglycemia are unaware of the fact that their anxiety symptoms are the result of low blood sugar. If their blood sugar drops below 50 milligrams per milliliter, they may develop any or all of these symptoms:

- Free-floating anxiety
- Shakiness
- Light-headedness
- Irritability
- Rapid heartbeat
- Difficulty concentrating

Many medications have side effects that cause anxiety symptoms. Unfortunately, primary care physicians do not always warn patients. Over-the-counter medication can also be anxiety provoking. Some agents with known anxiety-related side effects are:

- Asthma medications
- Nasal decongestant spray
- Many decongestants
- Steroids

Ideally, it is possible to rule out somatic, environmental, and behavioral causes (e.g., a 6-cans-of-caffeinated-Diet-Coke-a-day habit) early in the treatment of patients with GAD and panic. This is not always easy to do, however, so it is a good idea to refer new patients for a medical workup and consider behavioral and environmental causes of anxiety in the evaluation phase of treatment. This way of proceeding can be reassuring to anxious patients who are focused on medical explanations of their psychogenic SNS symptoms. Alternatively, identification of a medical or behavioral cause of SNS symptoms can save months or even years of ineffective psychotherapy.

Diagnosis: As with many *DSM* diagnoses, GAD is not an especially useful way of categorizing patients for a general practice psychotherapist. Indicated treatments for GAD are identical with those used to treat subclinical levels of anxiety. Diagnosis becomes important, however, when working in medical or other settings where sufferers are likely to be misdiagnosed or mislabeled with a medical condition, when communicating with other clinicians treating the patient, or where there are reimbursement issues with insurance companies. GAD is a common and generally accurate description of many people who struggle with anxiety.

To warrant the diagnosis of GAD, a person must have been worrying excessively about everyday problems for at least 6 months. People with GAD have trouble relaxing, they startle easily, and have difficulty concentrating. GAD sufferers frequently have a sleep disorder, either at onset or later in the sleep cycle. Fatigue, headaches, muscle tension, muscle aches, difficulty swallowing, trembling, sweating, nausea, light-headedness, breathlessness, and hot flashes are common somatic complaints. Unlike panickers, GAD sufferers are not agoraphobic, avoiding certain situations as a result of their disorder; but the disorder can reach disabling proportions when conducting everyday business produces extreme stress. The *DSM* does not say so, but in our experience GAD sufferers also commonly have relationship problems because of their needs for reassurance, control, and safety. An estimated 6.8 million adult Americans have GAD, and about twice as many women as men are affected. Symptoms may appear at any time in the life cycle after middle childhood.

Treatment: GAD tends to be a chronic condition that fluctuates in reaction to a patient's exposure to situational triggers. For example, even though a patient may have felt anxious throughout the day, her anxiety peaks when her boss walks into the room. A variety of different methods can be effective for countering these tendencies, including both psychodynamic and cognitive-behavioral approaches.

Psychodynamic theorists cite the importance of understanding the *type* of anxiety experienced by patients. In the psychodynamic framework, unconscious enactments of early experiences of loss are viewed as one of the most frightening and intense forms of anxiety. Relational problems, such as insecure attachments, are also common and may produce characterological defensive patterns, such as a need to be artificially self-reliant in order to avoid anxiety-provoking experiences of dependency. Ambivalent attachments require that the individual track and perhaps try to control the emotional state and well-being of attachment figures. Infant and primate studies support the psychoanalytic emphasis on infancy and early childhood as crucial in the development of anxiety-regulating neurodynamics. The rapid growth of the neural networks in the first 2 years of life is a sensitive period for the emergence of attachment schema. Intense emotions and the mutual influences of the right hemisphere and the limbic areas shape how we manage anxiety for the rest of our lives. This sensitive period occurs before the emergence of either explicit memories or language. Abandonment or fear of rejection can plunge us into states of fear, anxiety, and shame.

One technique for determining the type of anxiety involved in GAD and for helping patients resolve it is analysis of links between patients' core attachment schema and the current relational context, especially in the transference with the therapist. Defense analysis helps patients see how and when they use avoidance and defensive aggression, and how these tactics limits or preclude resolution of the underlying causes of their difficulties. By allowing patients to experience the safety of the therapeutic relationship, unconscious conflict and object relational patterns can be clarified. Safran and Muran (2003) have developed a sensitive and empirically supported method for tracking the subtle enactments of attachment schema in the transference. Wallin (2007) buttresses a traditional psychodynamic approach with the wisdom of the attachment literature. He emphasizes the importance of attending to nonverbal communication during the hour and helping patients verbalize the implicit emotional memories that contain the fingerprint of early attachment experiences.

From the brain-based perspective, a weakness in conventional psychodynamic treatment of GAD patients is that this approach is often overly tentative about encouraging patients to try out novel or neglected behaviors. Activating behavior helps shift brain processing to the more positive, playful, and optimistic left prefrontal cortex and helps anxious people overcome their avoidance.

NEURODYNAMICS AND CBT

Recent breakthroughs in imaging let us visualize the brain wetware involved in the experience of higher-level anxieties such as guilt (Greene, Sommerville, Nystrom, Darley, & Cohen, 2001). Jonathan Cohen, the director of Princeton's Center for the Study of Brain, Mind and Behavior, studies the neurobiological mechanisms underlying cognitive control and their disturbance in psychiatric disorders. In one study, Cohen and his colleagues asked subjects to consider moral dilemmas while undergoing functional magnetic resonance imaging (fMRI). Neuroimaging allowed the investigators to see what areas of the brain were activated in thinking about complex moral issues and behavioral choices. One of the study's dilemmas required subjects to consider hurting someone with their bare hands. When thinking about this, subjects' medial frontal lobes (associated with emotions about other people) and dorsolateral prefrontal lobes showed heightened activity (Greene et al., in preparation; summarized in Pinker, 2008). The latter area is implicated in mental computation (including reasoning about such mundane issues as setting up schedules). In addition, subjects' anterior cingulate cortex (ACC) was activated. The cingulate, although older than the neocortex from an evolutionary point of view, seems to become active in resolving problems such as the resolution of conflicts between an urge originating in one part of the brain and an advisory from a higher center (Greene et al., in preparation; summarized in Pinker, 2008). In GAD, this loop can get stuck in an "attractor" pattern of overactivity, perhaps producing the experience commonly reported by GAD sufferers of "obsessing" about whether one mundane course of action or another is "right" or "wrong."

The neurodynamic model of GAD, in which the amygdala, the ACC, and the prefrontal cortex figure prominently, supports the use of both behavioral *and* cognitive interventions. The higher cognitive centers play an important role in most anxiety disorders. When working in an optimal way, they provide a brake on the amygdala's activation and provide historical context in assessing risk (e.g., fear of flying). When things are working in a less than optimal way in the cortex, several cognitive traps lead to anxiety. All share a tendency to lock in expectations of how things ought to be. These traps include:

- **Perfectionism.** People who regard themselves as perfectionists set themselves up to disparage the quality of their work. Consequently, they drive themselves into anxiety.
- **Rigidity.** Rigid thinkers have trouble thinking beyond black/white, either/or, and right/wrong possibilities. Rigid thinkers fail to see the shades of gray.
- **Control obsession.** People who feel an intense need to maintain a strict sense of control of the events in their lives set themselves up for serial rude awakenings.

Cognitive behavioral treatment is often a good practice to adopt in the treatment of GAD. It begins with educating the patient about the brain-based aspects of anxiety. This discussion presents the brain as a distributed network (similar to the Internet) that is capable of both stable repetitive schemas (or attractors) and changing in reaction to environmental inputs. The limbic areas and the left prefrontal cortex can be reprogrammed to function differently. The amygdala, of course, will be one of the stars of this presentation, and it is important that the patient grasps its susceptibility to conditioned learning.

The goal of psychoeducation is to help patients understand how their thoughts and neurodynamics interact to produce so much worry. Nonconscious subcortical modules activate, appraising threats, vigilant for errors, and interpreting the meaning of the nonverbal behavior of the people around us. The higher (but slower) cognitive centers in the cortex get involved in interpreting this data from lower in the brain. When all the parts of this whole neurodynamic loop are functioning well, we experience a satisfying reflectiveness and a sense of safety and well-being. When they are not, we easily become afraid of and worry about things that are not present or are not even dangerous.

In the course of introducing patients to some basic features of the brain, specifics of their developmental history—particularly any events such as trauma or unusual separation experiences—should be elicited. Once this history has been explored, and the importance of the limbic brain modules established, the therapist goes on to give the cortex its due in GAD. This is where our "narrative" of why we are anxious is created. While the narrative is usually what is front-and-center in the patient's consciousness during a GAD episode, the brain physiology of anxiety is typically faster than consciousness. What is in our minds in the anxiety-laden moment is often based on the quick and dirty appraisals of the amygdala and an aroused sympathetic nervous system. By the time the language-privileged left hemisphere gets involved, somatic and neurological events may be far down the road, and what we "think about" is likely to have little to do with either the internal reality in the brain or the external stimuli. The left hemisphere is a spin expert, making up a story to make sense of things that in fact do not add up.

Psychoeducation should be carried out in a way that promotes the therapeutic alliance and the patient's engagement in treatment—which, as we saw in Chapters 3 and 4, are keys to good outcomes in all forms of psychotherapy. In practice this means frequently checking in with patients about whether they are interested in understanding the underlying brain functions involved in mental life, whether the discussion is at the right level of detail, and allowing plenty of opportunities for questions. Psycho-therapy research also emphasizes the importance of discussing how the therapy works, the goals of treatment, and what therapist and patient must do to attain their objectives. After we educate patients about GAD, how therapy works, and what is expected regarding, (for example), practice between sessions, they may be ready for the second step: the analysis of the thoughts associated with spikes in anxiety.

At the Kaiser Permanente Medical Centers, we include a psychoeduca-tional component for the treatment not only of GAD but of panic and OCD as well. For reasons of economy and efficiency, this part of the treatment is usually conducted in a class or group setting. One of us (JA) teaches such a class with a heavy emphasis on the brain-based factors, highlighting the amygdala, the ACC, and frontal lobes. Although some patients are too anxious to attend the group sessions, those who do so tell us that learning about the neuroanatomical and neurochemical compo-nents of their experiences helped them feel more "normal" and increased their hopes of gaining mastery over their fears. Workbooks that highlight brain-based dynamics are helpful as a supplement to group or individual therapy (Arden, in press).

Cognitive Restructuring: The thought record is a good tool to facilitate this component of the treatment (Greenberger & Padesky, 1995). It can be used to capture episodes of anxiety that occur outside of the office (see p. 225, Table 10.2 for an example of the form). In the office, patients fill out a preprinted record form during an hour with the therapist, trying to capture important aspects about an anxious moment. Questions or problems can be addressed on the spot. Patients are given a supply of forms to take home and bring back to the next session. The ensuing discussions about the "data" from the thought record allow patients and therapist to move closer to the frontal lobe cognitive processes that are reinforcing, rather than putting the brakes on runaway moods. Filling out the forms and talking about them with the patient reactivates the regulatory functions of the left prefrontal cortex vis-à-vis the amygdala.

In the thought record, patients capture *where* they were when they became anxious, *what* they were doing, what they were *thinking* about, the *intensity* of their anxiety, and what they *fear if the thoughts are true*. Finally, patients develop some *alternative thoughts* about the original prob-lem content that are typically more realistic than those tightly coupled with the mood. It is important to let patients know that they will not feel better filling out the first several columns of the record. In fact, they may well feel worse as they clarify how dire their thoughts are after, for example, a fight with a loved one. Only when patients reach the "alternative" column is there likely to be any sense of relief (Padesky, personal communication).

Psychoeducation and cognitive analysis rely on communication links between the left prefrontal cortices of patient and therapist. Behavioral interventions, by contrast, are aimed "below the belt," at the amygdala and its conditioned responses. One way to approach deconditioning in GAD is through cue-controlled relaxation, where the therapist coaches patients to go back to the anxiety-provoking situation and experience and resensitize themselves to its positive (or at least neutral) aspects. Patients will be substituting positive cues that trigger relaxation for the negative ones that trigger anxiety.

A patient we will call Doreen came in with "so much anxiety at work I'm about to scream!" Doreen's anxiety started at the front door of her office building. Discussion focused on what Doreen's work worries were about, and she recognized they were largely a product of her own demanding performance standards. She agreed to try doing a thought record with the understanding that the intent was to rebalance neurodynamic activity in her anxiety loop. The therapist suggested that she also start working on "reconditioning the front door," and after some explanation, Doreen agreed. Approaching the front door repeatedly, practicing deep breathing, and focusing on muscle relaxation transformed it from a phobic object into a neutral stimulus. After this had been accomplished, the therapist supported Doreen in reconditioning the door as a cue to relax. Working together, the therapist and Doreen constructed relaxation exercises she could carry with her, and as she calmed down, she was better able to meet her standards at work.

Although CBT purists are cautious about suggesting anything that smacks of surrogate defensive activity to anxiety-prone patients, we would argue that, at least with GAD, developing more adaptive defenses is both practical and beneficial. Some therapists in cases analogous to Doreen's have suggested patients use a talisman, such as a ring worn on the right hand. Married patients can use their wedding ring, tapping lightly on it to practice relaxation. Because conditioned learning is so fast and efficient, it takes more trials to extinguish a conditioned response than it does to establish one in the first place. There is good evidence that many conditioned responses never go away altogether. For that reason, steps beyond using counterconditioning and behavioral interventions usually are necessary to help patients.

There are alternative treatments for GAD as well. Kaiser's Anxiety Best Practices team, led by Elke Zuercher-White (1997, 1998) has identified group treatment as effective in treating GAD. Groups give patients the opportunity to learn skills to combat worry. Patients work on strategies, hear and see what worries others have, are taught how to apply cognitive behavioral strategies, and learn from others in the group. Group members empathize with fellow suffers, enjoy support and honest feedback about their common plight, and experience more detachment from their own anxiety symptoms. Another technique helpful among GAD sufferers who are particularly inclined to rehearsal and worry is to suggest that they set aside a specified amount of time and a particular time during the day when they will worry and defer worrying until that time. This method may activate parts of the prefrontal cortex that are otherwise being bypassed in the worry loop.

Finally, nontraditional techniques such as mindfulness meditation that which have a generally beneficent effect on many forms of psychopathology are particularly helpful with the "busy mind" of GAD. Meditation practice encourages the improved coordination of limbic and cortical functions that can also be produced by successful psychotherapy. By focusing on the breath and getting some distance from the compelling qualities of the anxious mind state, mindfulness and other body-oriented relaxation practices can help patients develop better prefrontal control over an overactivated amygdala.

PANIC DISORDER

The comorbidity of panic disorder with other disorders is well documented (Kessler et al., 2005). As much as half of the population with panic disorder has another disorder as well. Common comorbidities include other anxiety disorders such as GAD, phobias, and OCD, as well as depression. Although GAD is one of the most common coexisting disorders, it can be treated concomitantly if the panic treatment is also CBT oriented (Otto & Whittal, 1995).

However, comorbid depression may complicate the treatment of panic disorder. Depressed patients may be less motivated to do homework; when they do make the effort, they tend to appraise it negatively. Also, since depression generally lowers physiological arousal, patients may not be able to make adequate use of interoceptive exposure (the technique of exposing the patient to the physiological arousal thresholds and internal sensations that closely resemble the autonomic experiences of panic; Laberge et al., 1992). We therefore recommend that the treatment of depression be conducted before or (second best) simultaneous with the panic treatment.

Conditioned Responses

The amygdala responds quickly and has a memory like an elephant's. It is not easily reconditioned. After only a few pairings of an arousing stimulus (e.g., an electric shock) with a second stimulus (e.g., the sound of a buzzer) the amgydala will react to the bell as if it is the shock itself. Pavlov referred to the shock as the *unconditioned stimulus* (US), because it evokes a built-in reflexive response (startling), and he called the buzzer the *conditioned stimulus*, because the organism has learned it and incorporated it into its innate physiological repertoire. The subject reacting to the buzzer as if it were the shock is referred to as the *conditioned response*. Pavlov first identified this form of virtually automatic learning in experiments he conducted at the end of the 1890s. He was awarded the Nobel Prize for his work in 1904. Pavlov's discoveries became a cornerstone of the whole edifice of behavioral psychology (see Chapter 5 for an account of "Little Albert," an infamous application of conditioning by two behavioral psychologists). It may be that the neurodynamics underlying conditioning also give even very young infants the capacity to respond to their attachment figures, and to develop expectations about what follows what in bi-directional regulatory activity between the two partners in the dyad. This capacity is fundamental to the development of attachment schemas (Beebe and Lachman, 2002).

The results Pavlov observed in his original canine subjects have been replicated in hundreds of other settings and across several species. We now understand that these reactions arise because of common features in the mammalian brain. Classical conditioning seems to be an important factor in several major mental disorders, and panic disorder is perhaps foremost among them. Part of our job as therapists treating patients with panic attacks is to extinguish conditioned responses (reactions to neutral stimuli in the environment) to stop them from lighting the fuse of the fear loop.

Some experts regard the biological origins of panic attacks as a relatively straightforward case of the amygdala overreacting; others see the causes of the disorder as more complex (Kaiser Permanente, 2007a). If people have a vulnerability to biological dysregulation under stress, combined with issues about unpredictability, *and* they are exposed to the particular stimulus their amygdala experiences as a strong conditioned stimulus, another panicker is born.

DIAGNOSIS

Panic *attacks* and panic *disorder* are somewhat different matters. Attacks are discrete periods of intense fear or discomfort in which four or more of these symptoms develop abruptly and reach a peak within 10 minutes:

- Palpitations, pounding heart, or accelerated heart rate
- Sweating

- Trembling or shaking
- Sensations of shortness of breath or smothering
- Feelings of choking
- Chest pain or discomfort
- Nausea or abdominal distress
- Dizziness, unsteadiness, lightheadedness or faintness
- Derealization or depersonalization
- Fear of losing control or going crazy
- Fear of dying
- Paresthesias
- Chills or hot flashes

People may begin experiencing these episodes at any age, but late adolescence to the early 30s is the typical period of onset. According to the *DSM-IV*, panic *disorder* consists of recurrent, unexpected panic attacks along with chronic apprehension about repeated attacks. Patient worries about future attacks center on their consequences (losing control, going insane, or dying are common fears), and patients may visualize extreme, risky, and irrational solutions to escape some anticipated consequence. The *DSM* definition of panic disorder requires that patients have experienced at least two attacks *unrelated to situational triggers* (e.g., getting on an airplane) and *chronic apprehension* about having another attack. Just as hearing a bell ring reflexively activated the salivary glands of Pavlov's dogs, activation of the neural networks required to think about another attack sets off a conditioned response in the amgydalas of panic patients.

Formal diagnostic criteria for panic disorder are shown in Table 7.1.

TREATMENT

It is important to evaluate panic disorder carefully in terms of its severity and possible etiologies and to provide treatment promptly. Given the role of conditioning in the disorder and the brain's Hebbian propensity to repeat what it has already done, it is important to curtail the attacks as rapidly as possible. The goals of treatment include:

- Reduction or elimination of the frequency and intensity of attacks
- Improved tolerance for the sensations of anxiety
- Reduction in avoidance behaviors and restoration of higher-level psychological defenses
- Reduced radiation of the disorder into comorbid conditions such as depression

Table 7.1

Diagnostic Criteria for Panic Disorder with or without Agoraphobia

A. Both 1 and 2:
1. Recurrent unexpected panic attacks (at least two)
2. At least one attack followed by one or more of the following, and lasting for at least one month:
   a. Persistent concern about additional attacks.
   b. Worry about the implications of the attack or its consequences (e.g., losing control, having a heart attack, going crazy).
   c. A significant change in behavior related to the attacks.
B. The panic attacks are not due to the direct physiological effects of a substance (e.g., a drug of abuse, medication) or a general medical condition (e.g., hyperthyroidism).
C. The panic attacks are not better accounted for by another mental disorder, such as social anxiety disorder, specific phobia (on exposure to a specific phobic situation), obsessive-compulsive disorder (an exposure to dirt in someone with an obsession about contamination), posttraumatic stress disorder (in response to stimuli associated with a severe stressor), or separation anxiety (in response to being away from home or close relatives).
D. Agoraphobia may or may not be present. If Agoraphobia is not present, diagnosis is panic disorder without agoraphobia. If present, diagnosis is panic disorder with agoraphobia,
E. Agoraphobia is the fear of being in places or situations from which escape is difficult because of physical (being on a bridge) or social (standing in line) constraints, or where help is not readily available in the case of a panic attack. The situations are avoided or endured with fear. Typical agoraphobic fears are being in crowds, traveling by car or public transportation, going out without a companion, etc.

Source: Adapted from American Psychiatric Association (1994), pp. 396, 402.

Therapists conducting more rigorous CBT treatments typically use psychometric instruments to support evaluation and check in with patients on their progress in treatment. Kaiser Best Practices recommends the use of the Apfeldorf's paper-and-pencil questionnaire to identify panic disorder (Apfeldorf, Shear, Leon, & Portera, 1994). A score of 11 or more discriminates panic disorder patients from other anxiety patients 75% of the time. In determining when treatment is urgently needed, clinicians should look for the presence of these features:

- Suicidiality (a definite risk factor in panic disorder)
- Rapid generalization of avoidance
- Threats to employment
- Threats to significant relationships caused by inappropriate defensive interactions

If any of these issues surface, more intensive treatment, medication, or specialized treatment should be considered.

Many researchers and anxiety specialists agree that multimodal integrated treatments are the most efficacious for the treatment of panic (Gould et al., 1995; Margraf, Barlow et al., 1993; Zuercher-White, 1997, 1998). Further, when panic disorder occurs with agoraphobia, the treatment should always include exposure. As in all psychotherapies, patients with panic and their therapists discuss and agree at the outset on goals and the tasks involved in completing them. This discussion may or may not include an agreement about the role of medication in panic treatment, as most panickers would like their disorder to be over yesterday. Taking a pill to accomplish this has great appeal. For many anxious patients, medication is more attractive than hearing that they will be asked to reexperience the dreaded sensations that led up to their attack in the first place. As part of the psychoeducational component of the treatment, patients should be told about new studies regarding integrated pharmacological and psychotherapeutic panic treatment. The prognosis for integrated care is different with panic than it is with depression. Although there is good evidence that integrated treatment improves outcomes for many a depressed patient, research on panic disorder suggests that combining medication with CBT treatment *decreases* the effectiveness of psychotherapy and *increases* the risk of relapse once the medication is withdrawn (Kaiser Permanente, 2007a).

Behaviorists attribute these findings to the blunting of the *physical sensations* of anxiety by the medication. These sensations have become conditioned stimuli for the amygdala's escalation of activity in the anxiety loop, and the association must be dealt with at full strength in psychotherapy. Moreover, by treating the bottom-up (i.e., amygdalar) aspects of the disorder, medication diminishes the amount of work required from the top-down (i.e., conscious cognitive) regulatory functions in the prefrontal cortex; that is, medication stalls real durable change.

Ameliorating panic from both the behaviorist and the neurodynamic points of view requires that the therapy create more of a "controlled emergency" than medicine allows for. The behavioral and brain-based perspectives predict what in fact seems to happen: When people who take medicine stop it, the panic disorder returns. Even when CBT is started before termination of pharmacotherapy, it does not mitigate relapse after medication is discontinued (Barlow, Gorman, Shear, & Woods, 2000). Kaiser concludes that *"At the present time . . . the evidence in the literature overwhelmingly indicates CBT is the psychotherapeutic treatment of choice. The* cognitive behavioral treatment should not merely be aimed at symptom reduction but at achieving marked cognitive change, i.e., *cessation of fear of panic"* (Kaiser Permanente, 2001a, p. 5; italics in original).

There is strong research support for this position. A panic control treatment protocol was assessed over a series of controlled studies (Barlow, 1990; Craske, 1991). Cognitive behavioral therapy with interoceptive exposure was shown to be superior to placebo, wait list, and medication (alprazolam [Xanax]) groups. At a two-year follow-up, the panic control treatment group continued to show gains over the other groups (see Kaiser Permanente, 2001a, for a review). CBT for panic is the most cost-effective and tolerable treatment when compared to pharmacological treatments (Gould et al., 1995). Although several psychotherapeutic treatments make claims and present convincing anecdotal evidence about effectiveness in alleviating panic, research supporting the use of CBT methods in particular with this disorder (Zuercher-White, 1997) seems to override the general conclusion of psychotherapy research that all treatments produce about equal results.

As in all other forms of psychotherapy, the therapist's skill in building a good working relationship with patients is a key success factor. Treatment begins with a conversation about ends and means. The patient's personal experience of the problem and her aims in seeking treatment should be fully explored. The therapist can ask about the presence of and explain the role of predisposing factors (such as heredity and trauma) and explain the neurodynamic model of what is going on in the brain that produces a panic attack. Dysregulation in functioning between the easily conditioned limbic brain components and the slower but wiser PFC figures prominently in this explanation. The model emphasizes the twin goals of brain-based treatment for panic: reconditioning the fast fear circuits of the limbic and right hemisphere and increasing the regulatory power of the slow left-hemisphere circuits so that a change in neurodynamic reactions to anxiety sensations is achieved.

Giving the patient an overview of the neurodynamic model sets the stage for a more delicate discussion of the tasks involved in the therapy, especially exposure. Undertaking the exposure component takes courage and perseverance on the patient's part, and it is therefore all the more important that the therapist monitor the patient's resistance and engagement. Although exposure is sometimes used in treating GAD, it is a primary weapon in panic treatment. It is the major focus of the elegant panic treatments conducted by David Barlow (Barlow, Craske, Cerny, & Klosko, 1989). In the view of Barlow and Craske (1994) and others, panic disorder is a learned fear of the uncomfortable physical sensations associated with panic attacks. The patient's amygdala changes neurodynamically and responds to such physiological signals as sweating, rapid breathing, and rapid heartbeat as if they were the precursors to a catastrophic event.

Avoidance and Agoraphobia: Because panic attacks generally are unpredictable and feel uncontrollable, patients often try to control the *context* in which they occur by avoidance behaviors. Avoidance perpetuates fear, and fear perpetuates avoidance. As fear builds around situations, objects, and physical sensations, panickers tend to avoid them. In doing so, they deprive themselves of opportunities to gain mastery over the fear-provoking situations. Avoidance does typically work to some extent; it leads to a reduction of fear. This benefit is a powerful short-term reenforcer of avoidant behavior and can make it exceedingly difficult for patients to change. But avoidance also tends to generalize and become increasingly elaborate. If patients are asked to stop using avoidant defenses, their first response is likely to be "Why would I stop doing something that helps?"

Part of the answer to this question can be grasped through rational discourse with patients: the acute feelings of fear accompanying a panic attack are a product of a failure of the brain's braking system in downregulating anxiety. The rational part of the problem can be addressed through the thought records and patients left-hemisphere-to-left-hemisphere conversations with the therapist. But the second part of the answer to the question is that these behaviors cannot be worked through verbally or rationally. As the amygdala becomes more and more sensitive, people start avoiding what sets it off almost as a matter of procedural memory. People begin to develop avoidant behavior independently, as if for its own sake (Parent et al., 1994). Avoidance may be associated with a setting where something could occur and escape might be difficult or embarrassing (e.g., crowds in a theater lobby at intermission, work meetings). Avoidance may also come to be associated simply with activities where the somatic signs of anxiety *might* occur (e.g., aerobic exercise). Because of the neurodynamics involved, these implicit action responses are not tightly coupled with verbal or rational faculties; changing them requires that patients stop the avoidant pattern and experience direct exposure to the setting or sensations they are avoiding in order to recondition the amygdala and initiate the process of extinction. Individuals with the type of panic disorder that includes pronounced avoidant strategies, or *agoraphobia*, have two problems rather than just one. Agoraphobia can reach such extreme forms of avoidance that sufferers become totally housebound.

Breathing: Hyperventilation has been considered a symptom of panic but not necessarily a contributor to it (Ley, 1985, 1989; Smoller et al., 1996). A product of rapid and sometimes shallow breathing or panting, hyperventilation can jump-start activation of the SNS fight-or-flight response. Without big-muscle activity to dissipate it, increased respiration dissipates the level of carbon dioxide in the blood. The loss of carbon dioxide, in turn, causes the blood to become more alkaline and less acidic (the pH level rises). Vascular constriction results in less blood reaching the tissues and the extremities. The paradox is that when too much oxygen is inhaled, less is available to the tissues. Hyperventilation can, but does not always, cause symptoms such as numbness or tingling in the hands, feet, and lips; light-headedness; dizziness; headache; chest pain; and slurred speech. Sometimes it even induces fainting. People prone to panic attacks often overrespond to these physiological sensations, causing the symptoms to intensify. Abnormally sensitive carbon dioxide receptors in the brainstem may lead to a "false alarm" of suffocation. This dyspnea—the feeling of not getting enough air—can spur a panic attack and more hyperventilation (Klein, 1993; Papp, Klein, et al., 1993).

Habitual tendencies to hyperventilate may carry over into sleep. Nocturnal panic attacks may be spurred by hyperventilation (Ley, 1988). The same neural nets, the same physiology, and the same tendency to hyperventilate are associated with daytime and nighttime panic attacks (Craske & Barlow, 1993). One study showed that nocturnal panic involves fearful misappraisals of physiological symptoms as similar to those involved in the daytime variety of the disorder (Craske & Freed, 1995).

The sensation of breathlessness or labored respiration may spur hyperventilation, especially in people with asthma (Carr, 1995, 1996). Zuercher-White (1997) demonstrated the links between hyperventilation and panic in her "over-breathing test," a technique that can be used with patients to help them grasp the connection between breathing and anxiety. The therapist and patient hyperventilate together and then talk about the physical and psychological sensations it produces. Typically, patients report feeling anxious or even on the verge of a panic attack. The therapist explains that hyperventilation can be interrupted and reversed in a variety of ways (Zuercher-White, 1997). They include:

- Holding your breath for 10 to 15 seconds. This temporarily prevents the dissipation of carbon dioxide.
- Breathing in and out of a paper bag. Carbon dioxide in the bag is inhaled, thus restoring the balance of oxygen and carbon dioxide.

- Exercising vigorously. Metabolism increases quickly to produce more energy. The inhaled oxygen is used up and a larger quantity of carbon dioxide will be produced.
- Deep diaphragmatic breathing extends the lungs to their full capacity, promotes a relaxation response and brings the body out of its oxygen-rich fight-or-flight pattern.

Although Barlow (1997) notes that breathing retraining is the least effective element in the CBT tool kit for panic disorder, patients frequently report that it is of great help, and it seems to assist them in gaining a sense of self-efficacy. We recommend including it as part of the treatment approach.

Exposure: Conditioning, Barlow recognized, is a very powerful form of learning. In order to decondition people, you have to show them (often over and over again) that the conditioned and unconditioned stimuli are not ineluctably (or even logically) related. Discussing the importance of exposure can be a make-or-break moment in the therapy. Years of psychotherapy outcome research suggests that if the therapist does not adequately explore and take stock of the patient's negative reactions (which are often unspoken), the therapy project may be doomed. The therapist must elicit any doubts or negative feelings about exposure or any other treatment task. Clarification is the beginning of working through the problem and increasing the patient's sense of confidence in the therapist as a guide. Exploring and working through resistance to exposure is often an opportunity for the kind of rupture repair that is a predicator of treatment success in all psychotherapies (Norcross, 2002).

If patients grasp the rationale for the task and agree to undertake it, exposure takes the form of such activities as spinning around or aerobic exercise. These activities mimic somatic symptoms and create the occasion for patients to observe that they do not in fact lead to cardiac arrest. Activity that produces the physical correlates of anxiety are repeated until the link between these sensations and anxiety fades. Therapists using exposure should notice whether patients begin using subtle forms of avoidance, such as relaxation, in the heat of the exposure session. Although in other contexts such activity might be considered indicative of healthy defensive functioning, here it undermines the effectiveness of the therapy. Begun in the office, the exposure exercises must be made portable, and homework assignments can be given to patients to be completed outside of treatment to generalize their effectiveness, optimally in the situations associated with previous attacks.

Interoceptive exposure (i.e., exposure to stimuli arising within the body) should be offered after cognitive restructuring has begun (Barlow & Craske, 1994; Craske, Meadows, & Barlow, 1994). The subsequent and simultaneous cognitive restructuring and interoceptive exposure works to challenge cognitions arising from exposure (Zuercher-White, 1997). Psychoeducation helps patients understand why exposure is necessary. Panic can be thought of as a *phobia of internal bodily sensations*. Interoceptive exposure helps patients habituate to these sensations. The cognitive component helps them restructure the self-talk and narratives that arise during interoceptive exposure to the physical sensations. From a brain-based perspective, this involves building or rebuilding neural circuits that support adaptive cognitions and letting the procedural schemas associated with avoidance and insecurity disappear through attrition. By restructuring cognitions during interoceptive exposure, patients can establish an increased sense of self-efficacy.

Exposure begins in the office or clinic but soon moves into the patient's outside world. To foster generalization, the exposure exercises should be practiced at home, work, and other places that panic occurs. Repetition is critical to maximize the potential for neural plasticity. When guiding patients through interoceptive exposure, it is best to lead by modeling. Do not tell the patient what to expect. Some examples of interoceptive exercises include:

- **Running in place** to increase heart rate and hyperventilation
- **Holding your breath** to tighten the chest and create sensations of suffocation
- **Spinning** leading to dizziness
- **Hyperventilation or breathing through a straw** creating light-headedness
- **Swallowing quickly** to cause a lump in the throat
- **Tensing the body** leading to chest constriction
- **Standing up quickly from lying on the floor** to cause dizziness
- **Staring at one spot** to increase the feeling of being trapped

Certain kinds of patients should not be worked with in this way. Do not use these exercise with patients with:

- Asthma
- Epilepsy
- Heart conditions
- Low blood pressure
- Pregnancy

In talking to patients about the exposure experience, ask when the symptoms of anxiety accompanying the physical sensations came up. Ask patients to rate the anxiety from 1 (no problem) to 10 (horrible). Encourage patients by informing them that the more intense the sensations and the anxiety they can tolerate in these exercises, the greater the changes in the panic loop in the brain. The exposures should be graduated in intensity and massed (versus intense and sporadic). As treatment progresses, the exposure should shift from therapist-directed to patient-directed. Applying coping skills such as breathing and self-talk during exposure is important. Also, staying focused maximizes the involvement of the four lobes and the various memory systems.

Whereas several relaxation techniques help people with mild to moderate GAD, these techniques seem to add little or nothing to the outcome of panic treatment (Kaiser Permanente, 2001a). Teaching diaphragmatic breathing and mindfulness, however, is another matter. In learning to breathe from the belly, patients also typically learn that they can indirectly affect their pulse rate and, by focusing on exhaling, limit the level of carbon dioxide in their blood chemistry. As with GAD, mindfulness also seems to be good exercise for the networks linking the limbic and cortical systems.

Cognitive Restructuring: While psychoeducation sets the "frame" for the patient and exposure tackles improvements in the neurodynamic regulation of fear and worry, a third aspect of treatment—cognitive restructuring—addresses the problem of conscious interpretation. A common idea among panic suffers while having an attack is that the symptoms will persist indefinitely and inevitably grow in intensity. The only way through the experience, according to the patient's existing narrative, is to make the feared sensations stop through any means possible. An alternative idea—that anxiety symptoms are normal and expectable events that crest and recede on their own—can be explored and demonstrated. When engaged in the cognitive component of the treatment, therapist and patient together identify the hot thoughts that maintain and increase anxiety. Alternative thoughts are then considered, often through a Socratic-style dialogue between therapist and patient.

Normally, nonpanickers reappraise a situation their amygdalas find objectionable and use their PFCs to provide a sober assessment of the potential danger. This regulatory activity prevents the amygdala from triggering the HPA axis. The patient's hippocampus accesses memories and context, allowing for such thoughts as "I've been in this situation before. Nothing bad happened." When treating patients with panic disorder and agoraphobia, cognitive restructuring is critical. In one study, exposure reduced agoraphobia but not panic and cognitive therapy reduced panic but not agoraphobia (van den Hout et al., 1994). In vivo exposure with cognitive restructuring is critical for the treatment of agoraphobia.

Patients who have symptoms of agoraphobia and who are afraid of and avoid specific settings or activities as a result have to be coached to seek them out again for the sake of getting over the problem. Severely agoraphobic patients sometimes can be brought to the feared location or activity through progressive approximations. For example, after an earthquake caused part of the San Francisco Bay Bridge to collapse, many commuters were confronted with having to find new routes to and from work. In the process, the avoidance strategies of many residents with agoraphobic symptoms were disrupted and exposed. One woman came for treatment because, although the Richmond-San Rafael Bridge was by far the shortest route from her home in Berkeley to her job in San Rafael, she had years ago acquired a panicker's conviction that of all the bridges in the Bay Area, the Richmond Bridge was the likeliest to collapse in an earthquake. Accordingly, she endured the horrendous traffic on the Bay Bridge (which she was convinced would be the least likely to go down) and the Golden Gate, and in fact daily left home an hour earlier in order to get to her office safely. She did all this in order to avoid a reoccurrence of the panic attack she had had 10 years earlier on the Richmond Bridge.

When events proved her crystal-ball defense against being caught on the wrong bridge ineffective, the patient simply did not know what to do. She was still afraid of the Richmond Bridge but, working with the therapist, was able to structure exposure trials in small increments: approaching the bridge and then turning around; taking public transportation across it; riding across the bridge while her son drove. Just as important, she was able to restructure her cognitions so that she could counter the implicit force of her previous avoidance tactics. The patient described having to talk to herself "to keep me from taking the old route toward work." Eventually she drove herself across the Richmond Bridge with tolerable anxiety. She was elated not only to have her commute shortened but also by the feeling that she had stared panic in the face and made it blink.

Relapse Prevention: Relapse prevention is an indispensable part of the treatment of panic disorder (Zuercher-White, 1997). With any remaining avoidant behaviors, the likelihood of setbacks increases. Relapse prevention should include in vivo exposure long enough to insure that patients have habituated to the fearful situation and preferably to the situation where the fear first started (Craske & Rodriguez, 1994).

Panic disorder is frequently chronic because of the difficulty of completely extinguishing strong conditioned responses. Panickers should be told that they may experience relapses. Becoming ill, getting very tired, and beginning to use avoidance defenses can all provoke setbacks. Sometimes some preventive education about the likelihood of such events—as well as reminders that the patients has successfully used treatment on this occasion and can always do so again—can help in the event of future problems. By being well prepared for a recurrence of symptoms, patients feel better about termination (Otto & Whittal, 1995). Some therapists taper treatment, offer checkups, or invite patients to tape their final session. Yet even among patients with the best of intentions and dedicated practice of what was learned in therapy, sometimes the attacks come back on their own.

Self-Efficacy: Some researchers have argued that self-efficacy is the most important variable operating in anxiety disorders (Bandura, 1988; Williams, 1996). The perception of being unable to cope with anxiety and master a potentially threatening situation increases anxiety. When self-efficacy increases, anxiety decreases. Once patients think they are able to deal with the situation and the feelings that come up in response to it, their mastery over anxiety increases.

Alfred Bandura (1988) cites well-known studies in the social psychology literature that involve administering epinephrine to subjects who were led to believe they were either in a positive (controllable) or negative (uncontrollable) situation. Their belief that they were in an uncontrollable situation generated reports of sometimes intense anxiety. Subjects who were led to believe that they were in a controllable situation enjoyed it.

Central to self-efficacy theory is the importance of successful completion. As patients see themselves able to accomplish increasingly challenging tasks, they gain a sense of self-control and mastery, with corresponding declines in the level of anxiety.

Countertransference: Countertransference is an issue and an opportunity for therapists treating people suffering from either GAD or panic disorder. No doubt the therapist's amygdala plays a part here. Besides its role in making us anxious, the amygdala is also a central element in attachment schemas (e.g., in making nonconscious emotional appraisals about what other people's facial expressions are telling us). When the amygdala recognizes anxiety in another person's expression, it requires that the rest of the brain, and the sympathetic nervous system in particular, pay attention. Our sensitivity to alarms in the social environment is a legacy of our evolutionary history; it is a capacity that permits one person to put anxiety *into* another, without either person being aware of what is transpiring (Schore, 2002). Working with an anxious patient, we can experience anxiety directly—as when we notice that we have not heard anything the patient has said for the last three minutes—and also indirectly—as we notice ourselves becoming irritable or impatient with the patient's ongoing tendencies to control, catastrophize, attribute anxious experiences to somatic causes, and demand reassurance.

Once again, these ruptures in the therapeutic relationship can be make-or-break moments in the therapy. It is never safe to assume that patients do not notice our anxiety or negativity (Safran & Muran, 2003). Even if patients miss these signals, negative reactions in the therapist are really opportunities to talk about rupture and repair of the relationship. One way of using these negative reactions is to judiciously share with patients what it feels like to try to help them. Panickers in particular pose special countertransference problems. They must weather the rush of stress hormones, dysregulation of their autonomic physiology, and the left hemisphere's confabulatory explanations that these internal events are in fact natural reactions to an impending disaster. As if this were not enough, patients with panic disorder more often than not have a comorbid Axis I disorder as well. Comorbidities may remit when panic is treated successfully, but when the comorbid diagnosis includes severe depression, concomitant treatment may be required. Both substance abuse and eating disorders are common in panickers. Abuse of stimulating, depressive, or hallucinogenic substances can induce panic attacks by dysregulating the anxiety arousal and suppressive systems (see Chapter 6). Therapists should always consider treating substance abuse first. This adds up to a complicated picture and one that again challenges therapists to maintain a hopeful and optimistic stance with patients. It certainly requires us to give thoughtful consideration to our own self-care plan of exercise, enjoyable social contacts, and relaxation.

Both GAD and panic patients experience high anxiety, regard their situations as urgent, and expect that we will too. How the therapist responds to these signals is often closely noted and interpreted by patients. Clinicians should bear in mind that neither intense episodes of anxiety nor panic attacks constitute real emergencies; we should not respond to them as if they were. Part of the job in anxiety treatment is deciding when the little boy is just calling wolf again and when there really is something to worry about.

Common Elements: Although CBT has a specialized language for certain processes in therapy, several authors have observed that CBT processes are little different from those of other effective therapies. In essence, these common processes involve repeated exposure to stress in a supportive interpersonal context (Winnicott's "holding environment"). Confronting unresolved problems in the patient's attachment schema and anxiety regulation routines results in the ability to tolerate increasing levels of arousal when adequate support is also available. Psychotherapy builds bridges between cortical circuits and enhances the patient's capacity to regulate subcortical modules in the brain. The opportunity to endure and repair ruptures in a vital relationship builds trust and enhanced self-confidence in the therapeutic dyad. As Lou Cozolino puts it: "As a therapist one of my primary goals has been to shift my patients' experience of anxiety from an unconscious trigger resulting in avoidance into a conscious cue for curiosity and exploration" (2002, p. 33).

BETH AND THE BASE

Beth was a 28-year-old graduate student in history when she came into one of our mental health departments because she had had a panic attack in class. She was evaluated by a postdoctoral psychology resident, Scott. She told him that she had been having panic attacks since she was a teenager but that they had "kind of come and gone" since then. Beth also talked about her family during the intake hour. She described her father as "a bastard," a rageful man who often tormented the family with his angry outbursts. Beth felt constantly anxious around him. Growing up, her mother tried to soothe Beth's anxiety around her father but would retreat to her bedroom in tears during her husband's rages. Beth learned to do the same.

Scott sat down for a supervision session with Kathleen after his first appointment with Beth. Since the problem seemed to start with Beth's relationship with her father, Scott wanted to focus the therapy on that, feeling that if his patient could get in touch with her feelings of abandonment or disappointment, she could master her anxiety and stop panicking.

Kathleen suggested otherwise. She recommended that they frame the treatment using the four key principles embedded in our acronym "BASE"—brain, alliance, systematic, evidence-based practice. "Start with the *b,* " she told Scott. "Panic is a brain-based disorder. What's the brain doing here, and what does it need in order to stop doing it? Beth is saying that what she wants help with is her panic problem, not her relationship with her father. So let's think about the neurodynamics of the disorder for a while and then we'll consider the psychodynamics." Kathleen talked about how panickers generally have overactive amygdalas that can be potentiated by slight provocations. Their orbitofrontal cortexes have not developed the power to fully inhibit the amygdala. There was no reason to believe that Beth's brain was different from that of other panickers in this regard. Asking Beth to "explore" the relationship with her father at this point would have a good chance of furthering her dysregulated emotions by reenforcing her already oversensitized amygdala. Scott agreed to check this out with his patient and confirm that what she wanted to focus on was stopping the panic attacks. He told Beth a little about what was happening to her brain when she experienced a panic attack, and she clarified that what she really wanted out of therapy was relief from the onslaught of intense panic symptoms. "I'm up for trying anything that will help with that," she said. "What's best?" A good basis for an alliance about helping the patient achieve her own goals in treatment had been established.

Scott referred Beth to a panic group in the clinic, where she met other panickers and could see them improve as they completed their "homework" (utilizing a systematic multimodal treatment approach, the s in BASE). Beth felt the CBT approach described in group made sense, and she agreed to try it. She and Scott proceeded to develop a treatment plan that included cognitive restructuring, relaxation procedures, identifying avoidance behaviors, and then applying interoceptive exposure (which the evidence, the e in BASE, suggests is a critical treatment component). With the support and guidance of Scott and her classmates, Beth got engaged in the treatment. She used the relationships and exercises to reactivate her OFC in helping keep her anxieties within a moderate range and to challenge the unrealistic and anxiety-provoking ideas she entertained about the sensations of anxiety. Learning diaphragmatic breathing and starting to meditate helped her relax. She was not crazy about the exposure components that required her to experience many of the physical signs of anxiety and panic ("I get so dizzy getting whirled around like that!"). But she noticed how much better she was doing—after 8 weeks of treatment, she had not had a panic attack in a month—and agreed that this part of treatment must be important. Beth was feeling increasingly confident and getting a lot out of treatment when her father had a disabling stroke. At the end of treatment, she was no longer panicking but was not sure how things were going to go for her having to be involved in her father's care. Scott suggested she see how it went and call him if he could be of further help.

CHAPTER 8

Posttraumatic Stress Disorder

W ITH POSTTRAUMATIC STRESS disorder (PTSD), specific details of an incident may become indelibly associated with the trauma itself. For example, a common hazard for American troops in Iraq is the so-called IED, or improvised explosive device, that terrorists and opposition forces frequently set as booby traps to blow up vehicles or destroy the curious. These devices may account for up to 40% of the U.S. casualties in Iraq. Brad, an Iraqi War veteran, was driving a Humvee talking to his buddy Miguel at the lead in a convoy passing through disputed territory. Suddenly there was an explosion. Brad looked over and saw, in slow motion, Miguel engulfed in fire. Brad crashed the Humvee into some parked cars and dragged Miguel out of the compartment. Somebody was shooting at them, and Brad half carried and half threw himself and his friend under a truck, out of the line of fire. Then he passed out. One year later in Vallejo, California, a world away from the war, Brad was talking to his wife as she drove them to the supermarket when she slammed on the brakes in response to an unanticipated red light. Brad was flooded by a rush of panic-level anxiety and flashbacks. He was home, he was safe. It was all over. But half or more of his brain did not believe it.

The observation that trauma leaves dysregulated psychological residue in its wake is not new. Charcot studied soldiers with strange conversion hysterias in the nineteenth century, and Freud laid out one of the first theories of about how trauma impacts the victim's psyche. Trauma studies have flourished in bad times and as a consequence of natural disasters. During World War I, large numbers of soldiers in combat began to fall victim to a disorder for which there were no physical findings or diagnostic tests. The symptoms included tiredness, irritability, giddiness, lack of concentration, acute headaches, disorientation, and even amnesia. Some physicians argued that the only cure was complete rest, and officers suffering from the condition were frequently sent home to recuperate. Foot soldiers were looked on more suspiciously and frequently accused of malingering. Often enough, if these men were not taken seriously, they then suffered a "nervous breakdown," deserted, or killed themselves.

Military physicians assumed these soldiers were suffering from a nervous disorder or "shell shocked" (an acute brain injury resulting from being too close to an exploding shell). The fact that many who were not exposed to percussive force became ill and others developed these symptoms only after leaving battle remained a troubling inconsistency. Between 1914 and 1918, some 80,000 British soldiers—about 2% of the total fighting force—were diagnosed with shell shock. During the war, 306 British soldiers were executed for cowardice; many of them suffered from the syndrome. On November 6, 2006, the UK Government gave these soldiers a posthumous conditional pardon (ShotAtDawn.org.uk 2008).

The British learned the lessons of diagnosing and treating wartime PTSD better than their American colleagues. U.S. psychiatrists during World War II, often analytically trained or influenced, faced massive amounts of psychological trauma that was clearly a consequence of combat experience in the real world. An airman who had seen the head of the crewman next to him blown to bits was not concerned with internalized conflict. Many physicians had no idea what to do with these cases, especially at the outset of the war. After a much-publicized incident in which General George S. Patton berated and slapped a GI in the hospital for combat fatigue, a more concerted effort was made to treat these casualties humanely. Nevertheless, the War Department pressured physicians to get enlisted men and women back on duty as quickly as possible.

On the home front, at 10:15 on the evening of November 28, 1942, the Cocoanut Grove nightclub in Boston was virtually filled to capacity when a fake palm tree on the second floor caught fire. Patrons scrambled to get out the same way they had come in, through the main entrance. Bodies piled up on both sides of the revolving door, jamming it so badly that when firefighters arrived they had to dismantle it to get inside. In the fire, 492 people died and hundreds more were injured. Survivors exhibited many of the same symptoms as their countrymen on the battlefield. Erich Lindemann, a Boston psychiatrist, studied the survivors and their relatives and published what has become a classic paper (Lindemann, 1944) that opened a new era in trauma research.

Many studies were conducted on Vietnam veterans who experienced complex stress-related symptoms after returning home. The mental health community created a diagnostic title for the set of symptoms, "post-Vietnam syndrome," and debate erupted for the first time among mental health professionals about the ethics of treating these soldiers so they could be sent back to battle.

DIAGNOSIS

In 1980, when the third edition of the *Diagnostic and Statistical Manual of Mental Disorders* was published, posttraumatic stress disorder appeared for the first time as a diagnostic classification. The *DSM-IV* (APA, 1994) broadened the definition of PTSD. In addition to including those who directly experienced a life-threatening trauma, others who were vicariously involved in a traumatic incident, or were horrified about what happened to others, warranted the diagnosis if they exhibited the symptoms. According to the text revision of *DSM-IV* (*DSM-IV-TR*, 2000), the diagnosis of PTSD requires that the person have experienced, witnessed, or been confronted with an event that involves actual or threatened death or serious injury, or a threat to their own (or others') physical integrity. In addition, in responding to the event the person felt intense fear, helplessness, or horror. Finally, some form of persistent reexperiencing of the event through intrusive images, or memories or physiologic reactions must also be part of the person's reactions.

The three main symptom categories for PTSD center around the reactions noted above. They include:

1. *Reexperiencing* such as "flashbacks," nightmares, recurrent and intrusive recollections of the event including images, thoughts, or perceptions. The sufferer may act or feel as if the trauma were reoccurring through hallucinations, illusions, or dissociative flashbacks.
2. *Avoidance*, including numbing, thoughts, feelings, or conversations, associated with the trauma. The sufferer's memory of the important aspects of the trauma may be blunted. There is a tendency toward feeling detached from others and having a restricted range of affect including feeling unable to have loving feelings or engage in alternating feelings of numbness. The person he may feel that his future is limited.
3. *Hyperarousal*, including difficulty falling or staying asleep and difficulty concentrating during the daytime. The sufferer may be hypervigilant and/or have an exaggerated startle response. He may feel intense distress or physiological reactions on exposure to either internal or external cues that symbolize or resemble an aspect of the traumatic event. Finally, he may exhibit anger problems or irritability.

If patients experience these symptoms from 2 days to 4 weeks after a critical event, according *DSM-IV-TR*, they should be diagnosed with acute stress disorder. If the symptoms persist beyond 4 weeks, the diagnosis should be PTSD.

RISK FACTORS

Despite the numbers of people who experience or witness trauma, not everyone exposed to acutely painful events develops PTSD. In fact, according to one estimate, only 9% of the exposed population develop the disorder (Breslau, Davis, et al., 1998). People from lower socioeconomic backgrounds are more prone to develop PTSD, as are individuals with a family history of psychiatric illness; people with a prior history of trauma and/or substance abuse; and those with a military history that includes combat (Dohrenwend, 1998; McNaully, 2003).

It has been estimated that the lifetime prevalence of exposure to a traumatic stressor for the general population may be as high as 39.1% (Breslau et al., 1998). Women are at greater risk for sexual violence, and they are more likely than men to develop chronic PTSD (Breslau, Kressler, et al., 1998). Certain occupations—such as roofers, lumberjacks, and fishermen—face a higher incidence of trauma and PTSD. Some occupations—such as firefighters, police officers, and child sexual abuse specialists—are more prone to develop secondary traumatic stress as a result of witnessing or responding to people subjected to trauma.

People who have a dissociative experience, (referred to as peritraumatic dissociation), during or after the traumatic event, have an increased risk for having a future PTSD response (Candel & Merckelbach, 2004). Another significant risk factor for subsequent PTSD is lack of social support following a traumatic event (Bowler, Mergler, Huel, & Cone, 1994; Ozer, Best, Lipsey, & Weiss, 2003; Solomon, Mikulincer, & Avitzur, 1988).

Studies that have searched for genetic vulnerabilities have found that PTSD is more prevalent among monozygotic (identical) twins than among dizygotic (fraternal) twins (Skre et al., 1993). Genetic studies have shown that various symptom clusters (about 30% of the arousal symptoms; 20% of reexperience, or "flashback," symptoms; and 30% of the avoidant symptoms) may be genetically linked (True & Lyons, 1999). The issue of genetic predisposition to PTSD was explored in 4,000 twin pairs consisting of Vietnam veterans and their monozygotic twins (Goldberg et al., 1990; True et al., 1993). True and colleagues reported that there was a correlation of 13% to 30% for reexperiencing PTSD symptoms, 30% to 34% for avoidance symptoms, and 28% to 32% for the arousal-type symptoms between the combat-exposed twins and the unexposed twins.

Disassociation is on the extreme-but-not-uncommon end of the spectrum of PTSD symptomotology. Research has shown that individuals who have a tendency to dissociate during and after a trauma are more likely to develop PTSD (Yehuda & McFarlane, 1995). Similarly, trauma therapists report that people who freeze or withdraw in the aftermath of exposure often suffer the most traumatic symptoms later on (John Briere, personal communication). Allen (2001) describes a spectrum of disassociation that he has referred to as a "continuum of disassociation." Traumatized people can experience:

- *Mild disassociation or absorption,* involving a breakdown in the ability to notice outside events and extending to an altered sense of self.
- *Moderate disassociation,* involving an experience of unreality extending to feelings of depersonalization and derealization whereby the person feels as if he or she is watching themselves from afar.
- *Extreme disassociation,* involving a state of unresponsiveness. The person can act catatonic and have no sense of self or time.

Patients with PTSD often show up in emergency rooms and primary care physicians' offices with medical complaints. For example, rape and incest survivors are reported to have more frequent gastrointestinal distress, vaginal discharge, dysuria, headaches, and abdominal pain (Felitti, 1991), and PTSD sufferers in general show an increased risk for obesity (Felitti et al., 1998). Sufferers are reported to have more physical limitations and a higher likelihood for chronic medical conditions (Ullman & Siegel, 1996). Individuals with PTSD also have a higher likelihood of presenting with unexplained symptoms (Goulding, 1994) and increased occurrences of unspecified pain complaints (Wolfe, Schrurr, Brown, & Furey, 1994). There is some evidence that PTSD sufferers experience serious later problems related to the diagnosis. Many studies report increased rates of suicide, premature death, somatization, and sexual revictimization among PTSD sufferers later in life.

The *timing* of the traumatic event is thought to increase the potential for developing the disorder. For example, if the traumatic event occurs suddenly and without warning, the chances of developing PTSD is greater (Carlson & Dalenberg, 2000). This occurs presumably both because of the inherent "uncontrollability" of the event and because suddenness gives the victims no chance to defend themselves in any way from the force of the trauma, perhaps increasing the sense of vulnerability and helplessness.

With prior warning, victims can better control their response and even diminish the impact or damage.

It is quite common that patients with PTSD will develop a comorbid mental disorder. In the population of PTSD sufferers, 51% develop alcohol abuse or dependence, 47% major depression, 43% a conduct disorder, 29% develop a simple phobia, and 28% develop social anxiety disorder (Cash, 2005). The incidence of panic disorder and GAD is also higher in this population (Longan et al., 2003). As if the complex of posttraumatic and comorbid symptoms was not enough, PTSD sufferers also have higher than normal rates of brain injury, posttraumatic grief, and complex trauma within specific relationships occurring over a period of time (such as in abuse or domestic violence). PTSD patients who also abuse alcohol and other drugs typically should undergo concurrent treatment for substance abuse/dependence and PTSD (Ouimette, Moos, & Brown, 2003). Suicide potential is a serious concern for patients with PTSD. Estimates are that up to one-third of PTSD patients treated in an outpatient setting have engaged in self-harm behaviors (Zlotnick, Mattia, & Zimmerman, 1999).

NEURODYNAMICS

Unfortunately, the brain makes it hard to forget some of life's most nightmarish experiences. How early in life individuals are exposed to trauma and how much trauma they are exposed to influence later susceptibility to PTSD. The earlier and more prolonged the trauma, the greater the neurodynamic and psychological damage (DeBellis et al., 1999a, 1999b). Recall the basic rule of neurodynamics (*cells that fire together wire together*) and the finding that trauma leaves a residual impact on the brain. It makes sense—and has been repeatedly demonstrated to be the case experimentally—that *cumulative* trauma increases the likelihood of developing PTSD (Yehuda et al., 1995). Indeed, soldiers who experienced combat were more likely to develop PTSD if they also experienced childhood abuse (Bremner, Southwick, Johnson, Yehuda, & Charney, 1993). Rape victims who experienced previous assault are at increased risk of developing PTSD following a rape (Resnick, Yehuda, Pitman, & Foy, 1995).

These findings are consistent with a large study conducted at the Kaiser Permanente Medical Centers by Vince Feletti on aversive childhood experiences (see also Chapter 4 in this volume). Felleti found that the greater the number of aversive childhood experiences, the higher the incidence of psychological and medical problems and comorbid conditions. We would extend this finding to individuals with histories of previous trauma. Even when these earlier experiences did not result in a full-scale posttraumatic disorder, individuals are put at greater risk for developing PTSD later in the event of repeated traumatization.

Studies of adult PTSD patients who have experienced trauma during childhood or as an adults in combat, have been shown to have reduced hippocampal volume (Bremner et al., 1997). Adult women victimized during childhood by sexual predators have significantly reduced left hippocampal volume (Stein, Koverola, Hanna, Torchia, & McClarty, 1997). Hippocampal shrinkage may explain to some degree the clinical symptoms that accompany such abuse. Consistent with the effects of chronic stress (discussed in Chapter 6), hippocampal damage in PTSD probably is caused by spikes in cortisol levels. Using magnetic resonance imaging to measure hippocampal volume, Bremner has shown a reduced volume for combat-related PTSD (Bremner et al. 1995) and PTSD related to childhood physical and sexual abuse (Bremner et al., 1997). Bremner and colleagues showed that twins with combat-related PTSD had 9% less hippocampal volume on average than their twins who were not exposed to combat (Bremner, 2000). Bremner argues that these results support the notion of a combined genetic and environmental contribution to smaller hippocampal volume.

In an interesting counterpoint to the glucocorticoid-cascade hypothesis that identifies cortisol as the villain in reducing the hippocampal volume of PTSD patients, Gilbertson and colleagues (2002) explored the "vulnerability" hypothesis. According to this alternative view, people who already have smaller hippocampi are more likely to develop PTSD eventually. These people overreact to traumatic events.

In an effort to determine if reduced hippocampal volume is a cause or an effect of the disorder, Gilbertson and colleagues (2002) assessed Vietnam veterans and their monozygotic twin brothers. Subjects with combat-related PTSD were compared to their siblings who had neither the diagnosis nor combat experience. Both sets of twins had smaller hippocampal volumes. These results suggest that both the vulnerability hypothesis and the glucocorticoid-cascade hypothesis appear to be viable, depending on victims' characteristics and the circumstances and the nature of the trauma. Whether it's the case that reduced hippocampal volume is a predisposing factor or a neurodynamic effect of the trauma, the research suggests that the hippocampus is an important player in the posttraumatic syndrome.

Although the hippocampus is damaged by acute stress, the amygdala is likely to become more active as a result of it. Instead of damaging the amygdala, increased cortisol levels appear to hypersensitize it. People with PTSD show increased amygdalar activation and decreased activation of the orbital medial prefrontal cortex when looking at frightening faces (Shin et al., 2005). The flashbacks that occur for patients who suffer from PTSD tend to reside in the memory networks associated with the amygdala (LeDoux, Romanski, & Xagorasis, 1989). Researchers have found increased blood flow in the amygdala, reflecting overactivity in patients with PTSD (Pissiota et al., 2000; Semple et al., 2000). Correspondingly, there is reduced gray matter volume in the medial prefrontal cortexes of these patients (Carrion et al., 2001; De Bellis et al., 2002). The reduction in this area of the brain may reflect its inability to inhibit the overactivity of the amygdala. PTSD is marked by elevated levels of norepinephrine as well as cortisol and by subjects' hypervigilance, exaggerated startle responses, and quickened heartbeats—symptoms caused by an activated amygdala and which *reactivate* the amygdala in an escalating loop. Higher levels of norepinephrine have been associated with irritability and anxiety.

The high states of arousal related to the activation of PTSD symptoms such as flashbacks are associated with the right hemisphere, limbic, and medial frontal regions of the brain. High arousal is also associated with decreased activation of the expressive language centers in the left hemisphere (Rauch et al., 1996). PTSD sufferers experience intense anxiety mixed with irritability, agitation, and an exaggerated startle reflex; and these symptoms are likely to negatively affect the PTSD victim's social relationships and support networks. People around the PTSD sufferer may feel uncomfortable and consciously or unconsciously begin avoiding the victim. Unfortunately, PTSD sufferers themselves are often agoraphobic, taking great pains to avoid the places or situations that remind them of the trauma. The tendency of conditioned learning to generalize can precipitate a general withdrawal from others or situations. (Recall Little Albert, who was conditioned to fear a white rat, and quickly became equally afraid of many white things, including Santa Claus's beard; see also Chapter 7 in this volume.)

The traumatic memories underlying PTSD are deeply imprinted in the various memory systems by the amygdala and other neurodynamic systems (Cahill & McGaugh, 1998). Traumatic events become encoded directly in implicit emotional memory, avoiding slow conscious processing by taking what LeDoux described as the "low" route out of the amygdala. These memories are easily activated and are resistant to cortical integration. This is especially likely to be the case where the trauma was sudden, severe, or prolonged over a period of time and resulted in glucocorticoid damage to the hippocampus.

More because of the emotional intensity of flashbacks than their mimetic accuracy, a large number of decontextualized environmental stimuli can evoke them—for example, the lights suddenly going out in the hallway of her apartment building can evoke flashbacks in a PTSD sufferer who was raped in the dark. Retelling the situational details surrounding the experience of flashbacks can be therapeutic. The immediate response of the amygdala is inhibited or modulated by other long-term memory systems, bringing with it, in this example, the recollection that the hall lights are on a timed switch. The existence of explicit memories alongside implicit ones allows PTSD patients to assimilate and contextualize such experiences (Brewin, Dalgleish, & Joseph, 1996).

Because the release of cortisol is relatively slower than the release of epinephrine and norepinephrine, cortisol levels in PTSD are lower than they are with chronic stress. They also show a greater dynamic range. PTSD is associated with hyperactivity in the hypothalamic-pituitary-adrenal (HPA) axis, which can inhibit reduced cortisol levels through negative feedback. PTSD patients may also undergo an increase in dopamine enervation in the prefrontal cortex. This is thought to play a role in preparing sufferers for the potential advent of future stressors (Charney, Deutch, Southwick, & Krystal, 1995).

The reported damage to the hippocampus among PTSD patients via cortisol has been shown to be associated with verbal memory deficits (Bremner, Krystal, Southwick, & Charney, 1995). Consistent with the evidence of hippocampal damage in PTSD patients, suffers also frequently report declarative and autobiographical memory problems. For example, inpatient adolescents who have experienced trauma were reported to have autobiographical memory loss, with the degree of loss correlated with the number and severity of traumatic events (de Decker et al., 2003). People with low plasma-GABA levels were found to be more prone to PTSD (Vaiva et al., 2004). Yehuda and colleagues (1995) found deficits in semantic memory related to adult veterans with PTSD compared to controls. Other research has explored the working memories of people with PTSD utilizing positron emission tomography (PET) technology. Clark and colleagues (2003) found significantly less activation of the left dorsolateral prefrontal cortex, an area of the brain closely associated with working memory, in PTSD patients compared to controls.

The issue of asymmetrical hemispheric activation in people with PTSD has also been explored. Schiffer, Teicher, and Papanicolaou (1995) found that people with a childhood history of abuse tend to use their left hemisphere when thinking about neutral memories. When they recall early upsetting memories, they use their right hemispheres. Control subjects tended to have more integrated and bilateral responses in recalling both neutral and traumatic memories. The abused subjects appeared to have developed normal right-hemispheric functioning, but their left-hemispheric functioning appeared to be developmentally arrested. A similar pattern was found by van der Kolk (2003) in regard to asymmetrical frontal lobe functioning in PTSD subjects.

Trauma victims have been shown to have greater right-hemisphere activation, especially during flashbacks. PTSD patients show increased metabolism in the right prefrontal and limbic region (Rauch et al., 1996a, 1996b); and adults with a history of childhood trauma show a greater shift to right-hemisphere activation when asked to redirect their thoughts from neutral to unpleasant memories (Schiffer, Teicher, & Papanicolaou, 1995). Traumatic memories generally are encoded without significant left-hemisphere involvement and input from the associated language systems. These memories tend to be strongly sensory, somatic, and emotional (Krystal, Bremner, Southwick, & Charney, 1998). As a result, the records of these events may be generalized and decontextualized. Consistent with these findings on asymmetrical hemispheric activation are results of research using PET technology to measure regional cerebral blood flow with PTSD patients. This research shows decreases in regional cerebral blood flow in the left inferior front (including Broca's area) and the middle temporal cortex (Rauch et al., 1996). As noted previously, this may be one of the many reasons trauma victims have trouble talking about what happened and a factor in why so many instances of traumatization go unreported.

The sleep disturbance common among patients with PTSD typically results from alteration of their sleep architecture (the stages of sleep). The lighter levels of sleep (stages 1 and 2) and rapid-eye-movement (REM) (dream) sleep *increase* among PTSD sufferers, while the level of the deepest level of sleep (stage 4) declines (Friedman, 1997). This means that, in addition to the loss of sleep due to insomnia, the type of sleep produced is of poor quality. PTSD patients are likely to wake up feeling sleep deprived and fatigued.

Using electroencephalograph technology, researchers have shown that patients with PTSD respond to a broader range of environmental stimuli for a longer period of time, as if that stimuli were novel. Sufferers have an impaired ability to dismiss irrelevant stimuli as unimportant (Metzger, Gilbertson, & Orr, 2005). Their poor habituation and lowered thresholds contribute to hyperactivity.

As we noted Chapter 5, McEwan (2004) has developed a broad concept of how we achieve balance under sustained or heavy stress. Allostatic processes allow our bodies work to maintain adaptive functioning and achieve equilibrium while facing significant stressors. The overall accumulation of stress in our bodies constitutes the "allostatic load." PTSD symptoms develop when the normal allostatic maintenance systems fail to shut off after the stressor is gone (McEwan, 1998).

COGNITIVE AND EMOTIONAL FACTORS

Over the last 30 years, psychiatrist and researcher Mardi Horowitz (1986) has made major contributions to the dynamic and cognitive-theoretical understanding of PTSD. In Howowitz's view, victims of a trauma must utilize past cognitive schemta to integrate information about the trauma. Each individual is endowed with a "completion tendency," whereby he or she attempts to match new information with models of the world or schemata already developed. When trauma victims attempt to integrate new information, their experience alternates between the intrusion of some aspects of the trauma intruding into awareness and a sense of overall numbness produced by avoidance and denial (Horowitz, 1986). When denial fails, it gives way again to intrusive thoughts, flashbacks, and nightmares. In more favorable cases, this period of cycling denial and flooding is short, and victims move toward resolution by integrating the confusing emotions and thoughts.

Peter Lang (1985, 1987) developed the concept of "fear networks," which are a product of semantic and other highly organized memories. He argued that there are three components of fear: physiological arousal, subjective reactivity, and behavioral avoidance. These components are only loosely coupled and can vary independently of each other. Edna Foa built a theory of PTSD on this concept of fear networks and proposed that the activation of such networks leads to the expression of PTSD symptoms (Foa et al., 1989). According to this model, memories of the trauma are stored in the fear networks and are activated periodically by environmental cues. Although from a psychodynamic perspective, the overall goal is to help sufferers find meaning and healthy defensive frunctioning through support and interpretation, the more uncontrollable and unpredictable the trauma, the more fragmenting the effects of activated fear networks are likely to be. The degree of memory disorganization alone makes integration more difficult. Correspondingly, the less denial, disassociation, and avoidance patients engage in, the greater their potential for relatively rapid integration of the trauma experience and its aftermath (Cash, 2005). The goal of therapy is to help patients organize the traumatic memory narratives, leading to diminished symptom intensity (Foa & Meadows, 1998; Foa, Molna, & Cashman, 1995).

One limitation of the fear network model is that it appears to be conceived of as a system of semantic and other highly organized memories.

It does not take stock of the implicit memory system. According to a different model, the so-called dual representational theory, trauma information can be stored as verbally accessible memories on the conscious memory level or situationally accessible memories unconsciously. Whereas verbally accessible memories can be accessed in therapy through deliberate recall, situationally accessible memories operate more like procedural memories. They are accessible only through cues that activate the unconscious network (Brewin, Dalgleish, & Joseph, 1996).

McKeever and Huff (2003) have proposed a diathesis-stress model to account for the fact that the majority of people exposed to traumatic stressors do not develop PTSD. The term *diathesis* means susceptibility to a disease or disorder. By adding risk factors—including biological diathesis, residual diathesis, and ecological factors—a "psychological breakpoint" or threshold for PTSD is passed, and the disorder destabilizes the person's premorbid psychological functioning.

Patients with PTSD have cognitive and neuropsychological deficits. They typically show an attentional bias toward, or are fixated on, traumatic stimuli in their environment (Cash, 2005). It has also been reported that patients with PTSD have significant deficiencies in sustained attention and mental manipulation, and experience high levels of retroactive interference. Overall they have difficulty remembering both new and old information because they are easily distracted. These symptoms are consistent with frontal cortical dysfunction (Vasterling et al., 1998). Effective therapeutic approaches for such deficits should be methodologically simple and not rely solely on cognitively sophisticated interpretations of the meaning of the trauma or the patient's reponses to it. Exposure and repetition are critical, as we shall see in the next section.

THERAPEUTIC APPROACHES

One approach to the treatment of PTSD is to focus on helping patients face their reactions to the traumatic event, and gradually integrate the experience into the patient's premorbid psychological functioning. A second approach focuses on helping the patient move away from relying on the pathological defenses and secondary traumatic reactions that are often highly problematic for victims and those around them. CBT comes down on the side of helping patients face the trauma, and a principal feature of therapy guided by this approach is the use of exposure. The timing of when to implement exposure is important. Immediately after the trauma, it is a good practice to avoid involving patients in exploring or recounting details of the trauma. By being asked for a very detailed account of the events too early, patients may code into memory more about the trauma than would otherwise occur. Too early exposure heightens reactivity at a time when the amygdala is already overactive. The hippocampus usually requires some time to recover from the neurochemical cascade of stress hormones and transmitters that occurred during the trauma, and its functions are critical in reconstructing a more accurate and durable version of the experience. Coding in the emotionally charged details of the trauma is not a good practice.

Support for this manner of proceeding comes from research conducted with trauma victims who have been administered propranonol, a drug that inhibits adrenaline and appears to diminish the encoding of memory, immediately after the trauma. These subjects were less prone to develop PTSD than other subjects who had also been traumatized. Subjects had less intense traumatic memories because the hippocampus did not encode the events for longer-term storeage until a later point in the treatment. Immediately after a traumatic event, victims may be supported through a crisis intervention model (Slaikeu, 1990). Specifically, therapists can provide psychological first aid to stabilize, calm, and orient the victim. The five steps to this approach include:

1. **Make psychological contact.** Offer the victim acceptance, understanding, and support. In essence, the therapist offers a calm and reassuring presence.
2. **Explore the dimensions of the problem.** Perform a quick assessment of the victim's functioning level and what he or she experienced. Deal with immediate needs (including suicidality).
3. **Examine possible solutions.** Help the victim to set immediate goals to address needs by offering solutions and encouraging self-direction.
4. **Assist in taking concrete action.** Help the victim take steps toward achieving immediate goals.
5. **Follow up with the victim.** Establish a follow-up contract; at this time go over the outstanding needs and the patient's successes in achieving concrete goals.

A variety of debriefing approaches may be employed with trauma victims. The most popular of these approaches is critical incident stress debriefing, which has been widely used by large organizations, such as the Red Cross (Litz & Gray, 2004). Critical incident stress debriefing typically is offered 24 to 72 hours after traumatic incidents. The evidence base of this approach has been questioned. It appears, on its face, to violate the advice that discussing the details of traumatic events should be put off until the traumatized brain has a chance of optimizing hippocampal resources.

Mitchell and Everly (2000), in discussing an alternative approach, emphasize the importance of these seven steps:

1. Reducing the person's initial distress
2. Preventing psychological disorders such as PTSD
3. Promoting emotional processing through ventilation and normalization
4. Preparing for future experiences
5. Identifying the need for future treatment
6. Avoiding premature diagnostic labeling
7. Providing education about stress, coping with stress, and opportunities for future treatment

After memories have been encoded, exposure therapy helps patients integrate dysregulated memory systems. Emotional engagement with traumatic memories is a critical part of recovery (Zoellner, Fitzgibbons, & Foa, 2001). From a practical perspective, exposure may necessitate imaginal or imagery-based exposure, including visualizing and narrating parts of the trauma story, writing or reading about the trauma or role playing (Taylor, 2004). Avoidance of engagement serves to maintain PTSD symptoms, and a secondary gain of exposure as a therapeutic strategy is that it helps patients stop their escape and avoidance behaviors. This approach in fact is sometimes referred to as escape prevention. It allows patients to minimize the contribution of avoidance to the perpetuation of PTSD symptoms (Cash, 2005).

The CBT approach to PTSD combines exposure with an emphasis on targeting core dysfunctional cognitions (Moore, Zoellner, & Bittinger, 2004). Given that patients with PTSD engage in automatic dysfunctional information processing, helping them identify this automatic processing and reframe and contextualize their symptoms aids in the restoration of a sense of healthy self-organization. Therapists can also help their patients make full and consistent use of their dual (implicit and explicit) memory system. By talking about thoughts, feelings, and bodily sensations, patients dampen the nonconscious power of the amygdala and restore the experience of nuanced contextualization of life that the hippocampus and right hemisphere make possible.

Since the early 1990s, eye movement desensitization and reprocessing (EMDR) has gained popularity as a trauma treatment (Shapiro, 1995). Initially regarded as a curiosity, EMDR has been adopted as a staple by many experienced therapists. There is some empirical support for EMDR's efficacy

(Parnell, 1997), but most trauma experts remain skeptical of the method, and there is no satisfactory neurodynamic explanation for its effectiveness.

Whether EMDR disrupts the configuration of traumatic memories through accelerated information processing and helps patients reprocess and integrate those memories is unclear. The typical EMDR methods of using eye movements and bilateral knee slapping may effectively encourage an "expectancy set" in patients that something therapeutic is going to occur. In any event, it is apparent that many patients respond to the EMDR therapist's offer of a supportive relationship and to the practice of virtual exposure. Ultimately, these may be the most effective ingredients of EMDR.

Horowitz (2001) has combined a cognitive and dynamic approach to the treatment of PTSD and other stress response syndromes. Working through the denial, numbing, and avoidance that are normal reactions to trauma involves attending to defensive coping and resistance. Horowitz recommends addressing patients' defensive measures, dysfunctional beliefs, and disturbed linkages of self and stressor events. The overall goal of Horowitz's cognitive-dynamic approach is to help patients reschematize and reformulate the traumatic event so that it can be adaptively integrated.

Group therapy for patients with PTSD can assist them in overcoming a sense of hopelessness and isolation (van der Kolk, 1993). The approach should be supportive and avoid the retelling of the traumatic events. Group members can learn coping skills from one another and see their peers getting better. They can benefit from supportive relationships and work together to reduce the debilitating effects of the demoralization and other psychological symptoms that are frequently experienced in trauma's aftermath (Foy, Erickson, & Trice, 2001).

Psychoeducational approaches are important as a way of informing the patient what to expect in the way of symptoms. Also, giving patients self-help books adds a level of support (Beckner & Arden, 2008).

With respect to psychopharmacological adjuncts to the psychotherapy of PTSD, selective serotonin reuptake inhibitors are considered the treatment of choice (Friedman, 1997). Sertraline (Zoloft) has been found to be effective in treating the anger and irritability symptoms associated with PTSD, benefits that apparently led the Food and Drug Administration to designate this agent as a specific treatment for PTSD.

Positive growth can come out of a traumatic experience. Updegraff and Taylor (2000) report that up to half of trauma victims report some sort of positive outcome posttrauma. Posttraumatic growth (Tedeschi, 1999) involves finding meaning in the trauma experience and its aftermath as well as recognizing positive changes in one's sense of self, one's relationships, and even one's philosophy of life. The patient's sense of self can change as he acknowledges his connection with the world. This means acknowledging vulnerability and awakening from the delusion of invulnerability. This acknowledgment of an emotionally complex reality endows some sufferers with an enhanced sense of control and a sense of true strength, engendering that most useful of all emotions: hope. Changes in relationships reflect an enhanced sense of relatedness to others. Being able to connect empathetically with others allows sufferers to deepen intimacy and share their most personal feelings and thoughts. Sufferers' philosophy of life coevolves with an opening to the pain of the trauma and a compassionate coming to grips with the beauty, vulnerability, and relatedness of being human. Therapeutic healing may ultimately involve a wider spirituality.

As patients engage in the process of trying to make sense of what happened to them, their immediate narrative may or may not suffice. As the PTSD symptoms subside, they may be inclined to stand back and take a wider look at their place in the world and try to derive meaning from that wider perspective. As the emotional pain of the trauma recedes, a new sense of connectedness with people and the world may emerge. The old self ("old me") is lost; the new self ("new me"), like the Buddha's "beginner's mind," is at once naive and more appreciative of the interdependence of all parts of the world.

Sandra Bloom (1998) has pointed out that people who experience danger have a natural inclination to gather together for safety. This natural tendency can provide a "social transformation" of trauma. When the trauma is widespread—as happens in natural disasters, such as Hurricane Katrina—a gathering and a common purpose that seeks to repair the multitude of problems facing a community can induce parallel healing for individuals. For example, Mark Kloss, father of an abducted and murdered young daughter, founded and directed a foundation to educate people about child abduction. Mothers who lost loved ones to drunken drivers formed MADD (Mothers Against Drunk Driving).

Increasing cognitive complexity and self-complexity bolsters one's stress protective capacities (Tennen & Affleck, 1998). Self-complexity increases as we expand the number of different perspectives we have on ourselves. In their book *Trauma and Transformation*, Tedeschi and Calhoun (1995) offer seven principles of growth after trauma:

1. Growth occurs when one's psychological schemas are changed by traumatic events. Old schemas are destroyed and replaced by new schemas. "I almost died! Why?"

2. Some assumptions are resistant to disconfirmation. These assumptions buffer us from initial distress from the trauma but reduce the possibilities for schema change and growth.
3. Positive evaluations of self must follow trauma for growth to occur. This reconstruction can be as limited as "I am a survivor."
4. Different types of events are likely to cause different types of growth, whether the events were caused by others or oneself.
5. Certain personality characteristics are associated with the possibility of growth. For example, hardiness, optimism, and self-efficacy allow one to see growth more readily.
6. Growth occurs when the trauma serves as a central pivotal change in one's life. It allows one to shift perspective to a new era.
7. Wisdom results from growth. One sees what is possible and what is not.

BRAD AND THE BASE

Brad, the young Iraqi War veteran whose trauma story we recounted at the beginning of this chapter, came into one of our clinics for help. A year after his discharge, he was still experiencing nightmares, hypervigilance, irritability, and depression. He knew what his problem was and what it was called, and he did not want to go to a VA hospital (which often provides specialized mental services for veterans) because he was mad at the government. Our postdoctoral psychology resident, Katie, did the intake evaluation.

Brad told Katie that the last time he took his two children to McDonald's, he had a full-blown panic attack. "Nowadays all they have to do is *ask* me to take them and the thought of it makes me puke." He had started driving on different streets to avoid the place because "I can smell the meat cooking right away." It had gotten so that when someone barbecued in Brad's neighborhood, he had to go inside the house and close the windows. "I hate it that the kids and Sue see me this way. Compared to this, losing my arm was no big deal. Maybe it would have been better if I'd died in that Humvee too."

Katie's supervisor, Mark, suggested they formulate the case from a BASE perspective. That would mean thinking about the brain for starters. Katie would have to enlist Brad in understanding the disorder in a way that would make the approach sensible and understandable. Mark told Katie to tell Brad that the olfactory bulb in his brain (and hers too) lies very close to the amygdala, the brain's "panic button." That was a big reason why just the smell of a Big Mac could trigger memories of those horrible few minutes with Miguel and the smell of burning flesh.

"In order to get that amygdala to settle down, he has to get the rest of his head in the game," Mark said. He suggested that Katie try to help Brad understand that the amygdala is not the part of the brain that does our best thinking. "The best it can come up with is fight or flight."

None of this would go anywhere, Mark said, without the next element in BASE—the alliance. He suggested that Katie tell Brad that she would like to help him learn to deal with his fears a little differently. By bringing them up in a weakened form, they could do for his brain what a flu shot does for the immune system. But even in a weakened form, the fears had to be strong enough that when he confronted the real deal outside the clinic, Brad's defenses would know how to handle them differently. His natural defenses would revive and attack the panicky feelings, and things would start getting back to normal. Mark said, "Don't even try to kid him; he's too smart to be taken in. Tell him he'll really have to be motivated to do it, and not avoid talking to you about his doubts and frustrations as you progress."

Mark asked Katie how she felt about proposing that Brad also get a med evaluation, to see if he and the psychiatrist would agree that some medication to help him sleep and possibly an antidepressant such as Zoloft (sertraline) would be in order. He reminded her that this was the *s* in BASE: systematic and integrated biopsychological treatment.

Finally, Mark suggested again that Katie level with Brad about how hard this would be and how they would both have to be into it. Brad would have to be willing to try giving up some of the old "flight" strategies, such as driving on different streets, avoiding people, and playing dead the rest of his life. "That's the *e*," Mark said. "It stands for evidence-based treatment, and in this case that means exposure, changing the defenses, to put Brad's brain back in order."

Katie went through this with Brad and said, looking him in the eye, that if he was up for this, she was too, and she thought they would get somewhere with it. He said he guessed he owed it to everybody, including himself, to try.

CHAPTER 9

Obsessive-Compulsive Reactions

The infliction of cruelty with a good conscience is a delight to moralists—
that is why they invented hell.

—Bertrand Russell

"I N THE EAST," the bellicose army officer jokingly told his colleague, "they torture captives by putting rats up their arses!" The listener recoiled, shocked. His name was Ernst Lanzer, and to his dismay, he found he kept thinking about the rats and could not get them out of his mind. *What if such a thing should happen to someone I loved?* He started imagining rats gnawing at his father and his fiancée. Lanzer became traumatized by these fantasies; he lost sleep, looked exhausted, began acting strangely, and was dominated by a feeling that he must do certain things in a particular "just so" way in order to get relief. He intermittently felt convinced he would be released from this hell if he just complied with the instructions coming from some corner of his head. At his wits' end, Lanzer sought out a neurologist who was rumored to be getting miraculous results with some cases. The year was 1909. After less than a year of treatment, the doctor pronounced Lanzer cured. The physician was Sigmund Freud, and when he wrote up the case as a paradigm of obsessional anxiety neurosis, Freud changed his patient's name to "the Ratman" (Freud, 1959/1909). It is the only case for which Freud's original process notes survive.

Such cases had been known since ancient times. From the Middle Ages onward in Europe, obsessional symptoms had been seen as signs of satanic possession. Sufferers complained of blasphemous, sexual, or sadistic fantasies and feeling as if something alien were inside them, forcing them to perform rituals. A common treatment was exorcism. By the time the Ratman visited

Freud in Vienna, obsessions and compulsions had (at least in some circles) become secularized and medicalized. They were thought of as symptoms of a nervous disease. But for many sufferers, their symptoms continued to have a shameful and moral importance that transcended the idea of a "disease." Freud himself saw the syndrome as fraught with meaning: a battle between wishes to preserve a loved one and impulses to destroy them.

Some 70 years after the publication of the Ratman's case, another psychiatrist, Robert Spitzer, rewrote the narrative again (American Psychiatric Association, 1980). Obsessive-compulsive reactions, according to Spitzer, could be classified into two major types. Obsessive-compulsive *disorder* involved symptoms with frequently obscure meanings. Sometimes sufferers had interesting symptoms such as Lanzer's, but more often they were more mundane: having to wash repeatedly, or leave the bedroom closet door half open before going to sleep. The obsessions could be vividly horrible or so vague they seemed more like everyday worries. Patients could not always identify what about their obsessions was so enthralling or troubling. OCD, in Spitzer's view, was an anxiety disorder, like generalized anxiety disorder, and the rituals were what the sufferer resorted to as an anxiolytic.

Spitzer's second type of obsessive-compulsive reaction was obsessive-compulsive *personality disorder* (OCPD). OCPD is more Freudian than anything else in the third edition of the *Diagnostic and Statistical Manual of Mental Disorders* (American Psychiatric Association, 1980). Its symptoms read like a a list of the personality characteristics commonly known as "anal": pervasive preoccupations with orderliness, perfectionism, control, obligations, productivity, and morality; and an inability to throw anything away. In psychoanalytic psychology, the obsessional type became a paradigm of a particular kind of battle between cleanliness and a fascination with sexual and toilet functions (or some fusion of the two), and likewise a struggle between dependency and autonomy. Obsessional character in the classical psychoanalytic view was as common in the psychology of men as hysterical character was in women. Spitzer's decision to include OCPD in the *DSM* may be testimony to the fact that whereas the more flamboyant hysterical reactions have become less common with the passage of time, there are still abundant examples of the obsessional type walking among us, wearing suits.

DIAGNOSIS

In distinguishing between OCD and OCPD, Spitzer noted that while sufferers of the former experience their symptoms as dystonic or "weird," patients with the personality disorder experience their symptoms as ego syntonic. In this chapter we look primarily at OCD. Its diagnosis, according to the text revision of the *DSM-IV*, requires that the patient be suffering either obsessions or compulsions, or both together (American Psychiatric Association, 2000). Obsessions are recurrent and persistent thoughts, impulses, or images experienced as intrusive and inappropriate, causing sufferers anxiety and distress. The intrusive thoughts or images do not relate simply to worries about real-life problems, and sufferers summon defenses against them, trying to ignore or suppress the thoughts or images or to neutralize them with some other thought or action. Sufferers, according to the *DSM*, must recognize that these experiences are a product of their own minds and not reality based.

Compulsions are repetitive behaviors or thoughts and images that people feel driven to perform in response to the obsessive intrusion. The compulsion is often governed by idiosyncratic and rigid rules: it must be done *just so*, and not otherwise. The behaviors or operations are aimed at reducing or avoiding distress, or warding off disastrous consequences (but not in a logical or realistic way). To meet diagnostic criteria, the compulsions must consume an hour or more a day and themselves cause distress or functional impairment. In some cases (such as repeated hand-washing or nail-biting), compulsions can be painful, and they often result in feelings of diminished self-esteem that are similar to depression.

Common obsessive thoughts are fears of being homosexual or a pedophile; Ratman-like thoughts of loved ones being shot or cut; and fears of contamination from objects such as doorknobs or toilet seats. In addition to hand-washing, other common compulsions include repeated clearing of the throat, counting systems (e.g., in units of 4), aligning objects in a precise order, and excessive precautions taken to ward off harm (e.g., repeatedly checking the stove to make sure the burner has been turned off). Often enough, however, rituals seem to function more to reduce tension than avoid harm. Many OCD patients cannot say *why* an impending threat or why a special ritual must be performed. Following stereotyped rituals to completion just seems to produce a sense of relief, and they are repeated until that just-so feeling is obtained. Although obsessions are felt as involuntary and are strongly linked to anxiety and distress, ritualizing (both overt and covert) is voluntary, controlled behavior. The ritual has a reparative and relief-bringing function.

OCD sufferers are aware that their thoughts and behavior are not rational but feel bound to comply with the felt imperative in order to fend off feelings that range from discomfort and dis-ease, to anxiety of panic-like proportions or dread. Because sufferers are acutely aware of this irrationality and feel helpless to stop it, untreated OCD may be experienced as an extremely vexing, frustrating, and demoralizing disorder. Some clinicians still tend to regard OCD as an exotic clinical syndrome, but it is not rare. Two to 3% of the U.S. population is estimated to have the disorder within the diagnostic range, and 10% have notable OCD symptoms. Males often develop OCD at an earlier age, but more females suffer from it overall. Fifty percent of adult sufferers say they first experienced symptoms as children or teens—developmental periods when shame is most frequently used as a method of enforcing social conformity. Perhaps for this reason, many OCD sufferers try to hide their symptoms and do not seek treatment. This situation has changed somewhat in recent years because of high-profile successes in treating the disorder with CBT psychotherapy and medication.

ASSESSMENT

If OCD is suspected in adults, some screening questions can help clarify the situation:

- Do you ever have ideas, images, or impulses that seem silly, weird, nasty, or horrible?
- Are you unusually concerned about cleanliness or worry about contamination?
- Do you have to wash your hands repeatedly?
- Do you need to check locks, switches, or calculations repeatedly?
- Do you need to do things in a special way and have things in exact order?
- Do you need to repeat certain actions over and over until it feels just right?
- Do you worry about doing something impulsive that might cause embarrassment or harm?

Assessing OCD includes getting an understanding of the patient's presenting problem, their history, family history, past treatments, patterns of substance use, comorbid symptoms, and mental status. If the patient has a comorbid problem, such as panic disorder, and that diagnosis appears to be primary, the primary problem should become the first area of intervention. Whether patients have had suicidal thoughts or present with other risk factors should be explored. A not-infrequent obsessional fear is of harming another person, often a child or adult family member; if there is some actual potential for carrying out the harm, it is very unlikely that the patient has OCD, because sufferers never act on their violent obsessions (Kaiser Permanente, 2001b).

Not everyone with rituals has OCD. The person who checks the stove and the door three times before leaving home does not have OCD unless there are other symptoms. The OCD diagnosis requires that the obsessions or compulsions cause significant distress. Shame may make patients reluctant to speak of magical connections between thoughts and behaviors, or to disclose compulsions, such as toilet rituals, that seem bizarre. Important to keep in mind here is that many such details, important for treatment, will not be divulged unless asked about. Once again, although some OCD sufferers perceive a clear relationship between a threat (the house burning down) and a ritual (turning the doorknob three times), others cannot do so and may be perplexed and ashamed of behavior and mental operations that seem "crazy." In the *DSM* definition of the disorder, this experience of the compulsions as dystonic or conflictual is part of what makes OCD what it is (American Psychiatric Association, 2000). The rituals seem to have a life of their own, and although they may make little sense to the sufferers, they produce a strong sense of relief upon completion.

It is often helpful to include a more formal method of assessing patients presenting with OCD symptoms. Kaiser Best Practices recommends the Yale-Brown Obsessive-Compulsive Scale (or Y-BOCS; Goodman, et al., 1989a, 1989b). The standard Y-BOCS includes a checklist of symptoms, how much time the patient spends on them, his or her perceived control over them, and how much distress they cause the patient.

OCD SUBGROUPS

The current diagnostic scheme for recognizing and categorizing OCD brings together a variety of different symptom groups that may at some future date be recognized as separate disorders. Some of the most common current diagnostic subgroups (categorized by symptoms) are:

- Obsessive *fears of contamination* (for example by toxic substances), coupled with avoidance of the feared substances and compulsive washing if the patient comes into contact with them
- Obsessive *worry about forgetting* with the paired compulsion of constant checking (e.g., repeatedly checking the Internet to see if an alimony check has cleared the bank)
- Repetitive *fears of performing horrific aggressive or sexual acts*, or intrusive thoughts of an aversive, aggressive, or sexual nature. Compulsions

related to these thoughts may require the patients to confess or solicit reassurance that they will not (or did not) carry these out; avoid objects (such as knives) with an aggressive connotation; count in certain units up to a certain number; or praying rituals.

- Obsessive *hypochondriacal concerns* paired with the compulsion to repeatedly obtain medical reassurance
- *Repetitive fears of imagined disasters* often paired with ritualized and magic defenses, such as putting things in a certain order or place, to ward off a catastrophe
- Extreme or ponderous *slowness in behavior* due to counting or ordering

COMORBID CONDITIONS

Major depressive disorder, phobias, social anxiety disorder, and panic disorder commonly co-occur with OCD. Sufferers are more likely to abuse alcohol and prescription antianxiety drugs. OCD also seems to be closely associated with tic disorders such as Tourette's syndrome, and Tourette's sufferers should be asked about concurrent OCD rituals that may look like Tourette's but have a psychological function and meaning. Repetitive touching, repeating special words, and rituals such as licking and spitting are fairly common in OCD. Whether hoarding should be included as a subtype of OCD or represents a separate disorder is a matter of debate (Kaiser Permanente, 2001b). Recent neuroscientific work has made some headway in tracing the neurodynamic roots of hoarding and sheds some light on the diagnostic question—an issue we return to later in this chapter.

The psychotherapeutic treatment we discuss in the "Treatment" section is stressful (and, yet, can be very rewarding) for patients. Unfortunately, there is no reliable way of identifying patients likely to benefit from therapy in advance, at least not in terms of comorbidities. Comorbid depression, for example, is not a contraindication. *Severe* depression may negatively impact treatment. A large proportion of OCD patients are also depressed on first presentation. If OCD is truly the primary diagnosis, patients are likely to resolve their depression along with their OCD in successful treatment. Therapists should discuss specialized treatment with patients who are actively abusing substances, and it is a good practice to get a consultation with the treating clinician if the patient is currently in a recovery program. Typically, patients should be treated for the substance abuse first. Where patients are medicating themselves in hopes of managing their OCD, treatment should be initiated after a period of sobriety (Kaiser Permanente, 2001b).

ETIOLOGY AND NEURODYNAMICS

Researchers devoted to the study of obsessive-compulsive disorder are split into two camps regarding the causes of the disorder. One holds that it is a psychological disorder; the other thinks its origins are neurodynamic. The latter view is gaining ground. Even within the neurodynamic camp, there is a spectrum of opinion. Some favor the localization hypothesis and look at particular sites as being preeminently important; others look at general factors (such as neurotransmitters) or complex causes (such as the interaction between different neurodynamic modules) as primary. Recent imaging studies are fascinating and suggestive, but do not decisively support one of these hypotheses over the others.

Neuroimaging findings of OCD are among the most robust in the psychiatric literature (Chamberlain, Blackwell, Fineberg, Robbins, & Sabhakian, 2005). Results point to involvement of areas of the orbitofrontal cortex (OFC), caudate nucleus, thalamus, and anterior cingulate gyrus (ACG) (Grados, et al., 2003). Based on a review of the literature, Chamberlain and his colleagues (2005) believe that OCD is a disorder centered in the lateral orbitofrontal loop. They interpret the symptoms as a product of a failure in cognitive and behavioral inhibitory processes.

Imaging studies show abnormalities in blood flow and metabolism in coprocessing involving the OFC and the caudate nuclei. These areas are involved in formulating plans and generating abstract thoughts. Schwartz (1996) suggests that OCD is caused by a failure in processes that coordinate initiation of a complex action (e.g., "I'll pick up the keys I just dropped") with processes that break down the action into the steps needed to accomplish the action ("Start rotating my spine 5 degrees from the vertical toward the target on the floor"). This breakdown may occur as a consequence of chemical miscommunication. The medial frontal lobes, a module that notices when things are amiss, sends a signal to the thalamus when it is alerted to do so by an environmental or internal cue. The thalamus responds, notifying the OFC that the signal was received and implicitly asking for interpretation about the larger picture. When the OFC gets back to the thalamus, the basal ganglia (the caudate nucleus, and the globus pallidus) help form an activation loop (Baxter, 1992), participating in the decision about whether to identify the stimulus as an error signal or let it go.

OCD patients—so this theory goes—kindle and rekindle a neural feedback network in a way that is difficult to inhibit. It is possible that miscommunications between the OFC, the caudate nucleus, and the thalamus underlie the disorder. As a feedback loop of worry signals reverberates throughout the system, the OFC resorts to compulsive defenses to control it. In some sufferers, these ritualized (i.e., procedural) defenses may have a charged meaning in nonconscious implicit memory; but, as mentioned, in many other cases the rituals seem not to have any meaning at all. For OCD sufferers, the subjective affect is a feeling of incompleteness and doubt, and an impulse to consciously focus on relatively simple actions that would otherwise be executed without conscious monitoring.

Studies have found structural, functional, and neurotransmitter differences between OCD sufferers and controls. (For a good review of current imaging and neurotransmitter studies on OCD, see Kaiser Permanente, 2007b.) Successful therapy for OCD is associated with *turning down* the activation of the OFC and the caudate nucleus (Rauch, et al., 1994). Cognitive behavioral therapy has been shown to positively affect glucose metabolic rates with OCD patients (Schwartz, 1996). The fact that OCD frequently responds to treatment with serotonin reuptake inhibitors such as fluoxetine (Prozac) leads some researchers to suspect that, at bottom, OCD is a product of defective serotonin transmission or reception. As with the other theories of causation, it is impossible to know at this point if this is a cause of the disorder or actually an effect of something else. OCD sometimes develops secondary to some systemic or neurological condition such as head trauma or infection (e.g., Sydenham's chorea). Recently, a specific type of bacterial infection (group A streptococcal) has been found to cause OCD in a group of children, which may open one more route to understanding the disorder's pathogenesis.

Baxter and colleagues at UCLA studied 18 patients who underwent a 10-week course of behavior therapy for obsessive-compulsive disorder. Like patients who had responded well to fluoxetine, the psychotherapy patients showed reductions in metabolic activity in the caudate nucleus (Baxter, et al., 1992). Moreover, the *extent* of metabolic change correlated significantly with the degree of improvement. The two caudate nuclei (one in each hemisphere of the brain) sit astride the thalamus in the core of the brain. It has been demonstrated that the caudate is very involved in learning and memory (Graybiel, 2005), particularly when the individual is receiving feedback (Packard & Knowlton, 2002). In OCD, the caudate may not adequately filter the transmission of information regarding worrying events or ideas between the thalamus and the OFC.

In another study, Brody and associates found that the intensity of pretreatment metabolism in the left OFC (which helps extinguish habitual, compulsive responses) correlated positively with the responses of 18 OCD patients to behavior therapy (Brody et al., 1998). A comparison group of patients who received fluoxetine, by contrast, showed a significant negative correlation between clinical response and left orbitofrontal metabolism. As we'll see in Chapter 10, these findings of complementary effects of psychotherapy and medication have also been found in patients with depressive disorders. They suggest that pretreatment imaging might ultimately be useful to predict whether certain patients will respond better to pharmacotherapy or CBT.

National Institute of Mental Health (NIMH) researchers looking at the human serotonin transporter gene, hSERT, may have found a mutation common to OCD sufferers. Another study looked at the impact on genetically engineered mice lacking a specific gene. This gene produces a protein that is important to healthy functioning in the striatum, a part of the brain linked to planning and the initiation of appropriate actions. Mice in the experiment groomed themselves an average of three times as long as ordinary mice, wearing off their fur (Welch et al., 2007). More support for a genetic hypothesis comes from researchers at Cambridge's Brain Mapping Unit who have identified distinctive brain structures in both OCD sufferers and their immediate family members (Baer, Jenike, & Minichiello, 1986).

These discoveries may lead us to an understanding of the genetic susceptibility to OCD and give us a better understanding of what suppresses the expression of the disporder in genetically vulnerable individuals. Correlational research suggests that the triggers for OCD may lie in attachment schema and other early childhood experience. From the attachment and social learning perspectives, the disorder in children is associated with parenting that instills religious scrupulosity, an excessive sense of responsibility, or exposure to experiences that seem, at face value, to stimulate magical hypothesizing (e.g., a child's wishing that his father would die violently coinciding with the father being killed in a car accident).

PSYCHOTHERAPEUTIC TREATMENT

The theory-based case study approach of the early psychoanalytic studies of obsessional neuroses has been largely supplanted by large-N designs looking at the efficacy of specific interventions. Interestingly, research has centered on OCD and shied away from tackling the treatment of OCPD. The latter may be better treated by psychodynamic psychotherapy. Cognitive behavioral therapy (CBT) and pharmacotherapy, especially employing serotonin reuptake inhibitors, have both been shown to be effective with OCD sufferers. Perhaps as a result of the emergence of treatments of known efficacy, more OCD patients are seeking help. The image of OCD is changing somewhat in the popular media, from a disorder associated with sin, possession, and madness to one in which the symptoms are looked at with humor and perspective. Appealing characters with OCD have appeared as staple characters on *Sesame Street* and in popular novels such as *Motherless Brooklyn* (Lethem, 1999). Although the complete elimination of OCD symptoms is uncommon, both psychotherapy and medication typically give sufferers relief from obsessions and compulsions, and both interventions have been shown on PET scans to correct the abnormalities in cerebral glucose metabolism that are characteristic of the disorder (Kaiser Permanente, 2007b).

OCD AND CBT

As discussed in Chapter 6, exposure is a powerful way of changing brain systems that have settled into nonconscious "attractor" neurodynamic patterns. Attractor systems operate on the principle of Hebbian learning— that the more one's brain does something, the more it is likely to do it again—often with a dash of genetic predisposition to start with. Looking up the Spanish word for dog (*perro*), for example, results in slightly altering our nervous system in a way that makes it more likely that the next time we need to know the term, we just "remember" it. In psychopathological reactions of the kind seen in OCD, a type of reconditioning called exposure response prevention (ERP) is a critically important element. Although effective, it is not particularly popular, and that is a major reason why a quarter to one-third of the patients who try it do not comply with CBT treatment for OCD.

Psychoeducation: After one or two sessions and after completing the steps discussed in the diagnosis section, the therapist provides some education about the disorder, its causes, and what has worked for others. If using CBT and in particular ERP techniques, the therapist should help patients understand why this approach is necessary, what will be expected of them, and what they can expect from the therapist. (For some tips on how to do this, see the BASE feature in Chapter 7.) Patients are first taught some basics about the interaction between their behavior and their brain and what results they can expect from treatment. Sometimes just naming the disorder helps: the troubling thoughts and the guilty or shameful feelings or the anxiety they engender are part of a disorder called OCD. As patients come to understand some of the causes of OCD, it becomes obvious how the therapy can help them. It is always a good practice not to assume that we are accurately interpreting patients' appraisals, however, and it is advisable to ask intermittently: "Are you with me so far?" or "What do you think?" If appropriate, the therapist can recommend some further reading about the disorder. Recommended books include: Foa and Kozak's *Mastery of Obsessive-Compulsive Disorder: Patient Workbook* (1997); Foa and Wilson's *Stop Obsessing* (1991); Schwartz's *Brain Lock: Free Yourself from Obsessive-Compulsive Behavior* (1996); Arden and DelCorso's *Healing Your OCD Workbook* (in Press) and Steketee and White's *When Once Is Not Enough* (1990). For scrupulosity and religious obsessions, Ciarrocchi's *The Doubting Disease* (1995) is recommended.

Exposure Response Prevention: From psychoeducation, the therapist moves to help patients create a list of feared stimuli, or triggers, and rank them on a "Subjective Units of Distress Scale" (SUDS), with 0 denoting no fear and 100 pure terror and dread. The SUDS level of the initial exposure activities should be agreed to by patient and therapist. Typically, it is a good idea to start with a SUDS score between 40 and 60. Building on success, the bar can be gradually raised, always with the patients' consent. The eventual aim is to hit a SUDS high enough to initiate affective flooding in patients and begin effective deconditioning. To be effective, ERP requires patients to experience their obsessions and the situations that trigger their compulsions many times over. The gold standard is conducting ERP in vivo (i.e., in situations that are as real life as possible). This may require moving the treatment outside the office and/or having patients do it at home and report back.

"Imaginal exposure" (imagined confrontations with an obsessionally feared event or object) depends on imagining as vividly as possible the stimuli that provoke obsessional thoughts and then refraining from making the compulsive response. It is a less effective but often more practical substitute for actual exposure. Kaiser's OCD Best Practices guideline wryly offers the following example of an obsession for which the treatment of choice would be imaginal exposure: the fear of contamination by dead raccoons 13 minutes before or after the hour. This is to say that imaginal techniques are a good practice when the difficulties of arranging to experience the real thing are too great. They are also helpful when what triggers the compulsive defenses are thoughts or images.

With both imaginal and in vivo exposures, the therapist encourages patients to *focus on their fears*, writing them down or recording them on a portable tape recorder. The journals or tapes can be brought into therapy and played or read out loud, with patients letting themselves reexperience the distressing affects in diminishing cycles until they are much lessened as measured by the SUDS. All through this process the therapist plays a supportive role and offers plenty of positive reinforcement to facilitate patients' willingness to face their fears. The therapist is often the person in the therapeutic partnership who keeps hope alive and bolsters patients' confidence when they hit a plateau or suffer a resurgence of the OCD cycle.

ERP requires deliberate *contact* with a feared stimulus and deliberate *abstaining* from the compulsive defensive activity that has been used to gain relief. Exposure is most effective when it arouses high levels of anxiety and goes on long enough for the anxiety to diminish or (best case) subside. Called *habituation*, this reaction produces a decrease in the somatic, neuro-dynamic, and psychological processing of anxiety in relation to the feared object or event. Without ERP, exposure simply reinforces in a Hebbian fashion the fear circuitry involved in the obsessive-compulsive cycling and the cortical schemas associated with the compulsive defenses.

For example, one of us worked with a patient we will call Gil, who had contamination fears that were particularly intense in regard to using public restrooms (which he avoided, often at the cost of considerable discomfort). Gil came in anxious to do something about the problem because there was a woman at his office he liked and he wanted to ask out. He felt he had been stuck long enough and was looking for help getting over his problem. After teaching Gil something about OCD, his brain, and the treatment, the therapist and Gil took some time to discuss Gil's reactions. With a sigh and some nervous laughter, Gil said, "Let's do it." Before starting the ERP, the therapist took several sessions to do some cognitive work on Gil's ideas about hygiene, contamination, and communicable diseases. Together, the two worked out some ways of challenging unrealistic thoughts about the erroneous idea that germs equal death. These tactics—basically a brief Socratic dialogue challenging the irrational over estimation of the danger of germs—were at Gil's disposal when he would need OFC processing to help deal with spikes in discomfort based on activation of subcortical anxiety.

When both the therapist and Gil agreed that they were well prepared for the ERP process, the therapist asked Gil to walk down the hall, use the men's room, and not wash his hands afterward. The therapist added that even if he successfully refrained from washing but just wiped his hands on a paper towel, he would still be putting a barrier between himself and the feared contact, lowering the therapeutic effectiveness of the exercise. "Your mission, if you choose to accept it, is to 'contaminate' your body, face, and as many items as you can in your house with your hands." Each time Gil used a different restroom, noting his reactions and assigning a SUDS score to his anxiety level. The Kaiser guideline suggests that if an exposure task is too difficult for the patient, an intermediate step consists of postponement of the ritual for a determined amount of time, usually not more than an hour (Kaiser Permanente, 2001b). In Gil's case, that would have meant not washing his hands for a prescribed amount of time. Gil, however, soldiered on, taking on the full exposure, giving up the relief of his compulsive response and also doing homework outside the hours. In seven sessions, happy and a little amazed, Gil announced that he had taken his new friend to the movies and used the men's room with "a SUDS of about 10."

The Kaiser guideline states that both exposure and response prevention are essential for best treatment response. Each seems to target different symptoms, and either alone results in markedly less improvement (Kaiser Permanente, 2001b). In addition to conducting ERP with the therapist, homework is an important part of the treatment. Ideally, patients should practice exposure and response prevention assignments for an hour daily (unless distress subsides sooner). As patients improve and the work moves into a termination phase, it is good practice to include information about relapse and how to prevent it. Patients should know that OCD tends to be reactivated by stress and that practicing ERP and habitualizing the practice of deconstructing unrealistic thoughts pays dividends in preventing relapse. If symptoms become distressing over any length of time, patients should come back for some booster sessions.

Practicing after termination can also mean further improvement. It may be helpful for patients to start a meditation practice to bolster facing troubling thoughts without getting overly attached to them or wasting energy on suppressing something that will go away on its own.

Cognitive Therapy: Cognitive therapy for OCD closely resembles the use of cognitive restructuring techniques discussed with regard to depression (see Chapter 10), panic, and generalized anxiety disorder (see Chapter 7). Three levels of cognitive experience—intrusive thoughts, appraising thoughts, and core beliefs and assumptions—are addressed. Thought records are typically used for this activity, which is designed to motivate change in, among other things, patients' catastrophic thinking and overestimation of threats. Cognitive therapy has been found to be particularly helpful in addressing guilt and scrupulosity (Kaiser Permanente, 2001b), but these elements may also be targeted:

- **Inflated responsibility.** The person feels powerful enough to cause or prevent harm.
- **Overestimation of the importance of thoughts.** Thoughts equal action.
- **The importance of controlling one's thoughts.** Stopping thoughts equals salvation.

- **Overestimation of danger.** A bad event will inevitably occur, and its consequences will inevitably be calamitous.
- **Intolerance of uncertainty.** Worries about making the wrong decision.
- **Perfectionism.** There is a perfect state and it must be achieved.

Other Interventions and Considerations: As in all other forms of psychotherapy, sensitivity to special patient characteristics such as resistance is a basic ingredient for success. OCD tends to be a chronic condition, and improvement rather than cure is the more likely outcome. The treatment requires that patients deliberately evoke and endure emotional distress in the short term in order to obtain long-term benefit. Compliance with treatment is essential for improvement, and lack of compliance on either the therapist's or the patient's part is a common reason for failure. According to the Kaiser guideline, neither thought-stopping nor imaginal exposure has been demonstrated to be an effective intervention (Kaiser Permanente, 2001b). Thought stopping is actually contraindicated in the exposure model of treatment. It could be useful, however, in disrupting mental rituals in the compulsive/defensive part of the cycle.

PHARMACOLOGICAL TREATMENT

Due in part to the fact that patients with OCD typically are expert at finding ways to avoid the full anxiety-provoking impact of their obsessions (an activity that prolongs the disorder), for mild to moderate levels of severity, psychotherapy alone is a good practice. But the more severe an OCD sufferer's problems, the more likely it is that medication should be considered as a part of the treatment. Where there is acute anxiety at the outset (anxiety that is not due to a comorbid panic disorder), short-term medications may be considered until psychotherapy starts to help. As noted, depression is a frequent concomitant of the disorder, and both depression and OCD may respond to an SSRI. Medications are likely to act faster and more effectively on the depression. To the extent that depression is a motivating factor in the patient's seeking help for OCD, this more rapid therapeutic effect on the mood component should be discussed before starting medication. The concern here would be that the OCD may be causing the depression, and if not treated, improvement in the depressive symptoms would be temporary.

A frequent problem in medicating OCD patients—or, patients with anxiety problems in general—is their unusual sensitivity to side effects. It is usually a good practice to discuss the side effects with patients in advance and try to obtain some sense of their history about this and a sense of what side effects are likely to be the most difficult for them to tolerate. Alternative medications (including no medications), dosages, therapeutic effects, and how long they may expect to be taking the medication typically help patients feel a sense of participation and buy-in regarding psychopharmacological treatment. This is also a good time to discuss the importance of following the medication instructions and to remind patients that with medication, as with psychotherapy, improvement is common but cures are rare.

The most studied and effective psychopharmacological agent for treating OCD sufferers are the SSRIs. They are the first-line agents. Side effects are relatively mild and totally reversible, and some side effects fade in 6 to 8 weeks. Common side effects impact the gastrointestinal system (nausea, diarrhea, vomiting), the central nervous system (restless or anxious feelings, jitteriness), and include dizziness, dry mouth, sexual dysfunction, and insomnia. There are also frequently side effects when an SSRI is withdrawn after 5 weeks or more of treatment. These include dizziness, headache, vertigo, nausea, fatigue, flu-like symptoms, insomnia, nervousness, paresthesiae, and tingling or "electric shock feelings."

HOARDING

Hoarding is sometimes considered a type of OCD and other times a disorder on its own. Saxena and colleagues (2004) examined the neurodynamics of hoarding in a group of 45 OCD patients, of whom 12 were hoarders. Study participants were compared with healthy controls in terms of regional cerebral glucose metabolism as measured via PET scans. Compared to both the nonhoarder OCD patients and controls, hoarders demonstrated significantly lower glucose metabolism in the posterior cingulate cortex and the occipital cortex. They also showed significantly lower metabolism in the anterior cingulate gyrus (ACG) and the thalamus. Recall that one of the functions of the ACG is recognizing errors and helping the orbitofrontal cortex make choices to correct them—both skills notably lacking in the otherwise puzzling behaviors of intelligent hoarders. Saxena and colleagues concluded that hoarding constitutes a neurobiologically distinct form of OCD.

Hoarding may or may not respond to ERP treatment, depending in part on whether the patient's behavior is ego syntonic. Often enough, hoarders' symptoms are more distressing to family members or others than to hoarders themselves. Even highly resistant patients may respond to making the creation of an uncluttered living space the goal of treatment, with secondary goals being improved executive functioning. Once the work is in progress, it becomes unavoidable that meeting the goals requires hoarders to get rid of some of the accumulated objects, and this can be the deal-breaker as far as treatment is concerned. Work also needs to take stock of hoarders' tendency to add new possessions with the left hand as the right hand learns to let them go.

CULTURAL CONSIDERATIONS

There is evidence that OCD symptoms transcend nationality and ethnicity (Thomsen, 2000). As we have already noted, they transcend the vogues and changes in worldview that have kept company with OCD for more than 1,000 years of European culture. Nevertheless, cultural sensitivity is required of all therapists treating patients from a culture or religious background that differs from their own. Understanding speakers whose primary language is something other than English is just one of the issues. There are also cultural nuances that touch on many aspects of treatment: subtle differences in the meaning of nonverbal communications, the perception of medical roles and responsibilities, and the understanding of what it is that psychotherapists do. Moreover, OCD is a disorder that may be inseparably involved with patients' religious and moral ideas about "right" and "wrong." Although one of the joys of clinical work is learning about such differences (and everyone in healthcare has a particular obligation to learn about other cultures in addition to their own), it is usually a good practice just to *ask*. How do patients understand their disorder? What do they think will help? If there are cultural differences between the therapist and patients, what can patients tell us about how the disorder might be understood in their original cultural context, and how would it be "treated"? The reader is referred to Ann Fadiman's *The Spirit Catches You and You Fall Down* (1998) for a moving case study of the consequences of leaving these meanings out of treatment.

JACK AND THE BASE

A man we will call Jack came to see one of our postdoctoral psychology residents, Ellen, about his chronic unhappiness and work stress. An intelligent and meticulously groomed 40-year-old man, Jack worked as a free-lance writer. This pursuit gave him long periods of freedom, during which he worried about money, felt worthless, and reflected angrily on past events. When he worked, it tended to be maniacally intense and 24/7. Jack seemed unable to say no to the demands of his employers. He felt an ongoing rage at not being appreciated for the remarkable

---

(Continued)

products he created. His marriage provided some sanctuary from the troubles experienced in his professional and social life. His wife seemed to genuinely understand and appreciate him, and willingly assumed the burden of bringing home the bacon. But Jack had one complaint about the marriage too: his wife had lost all interest in sex and was spending more and more time at work.

In telling his story to Ellen, Jack paused at one point, looked down, and seemed embarrassed. She asked him if there was anything else he wanted to talk about or work on while he was here. Jack looked up at the ceiling, sighed, and said he guessed there was but he did not want to talk about those things now. He focused instead on his aging parents, toward whom he felt an embittered rage, and with whom he seemed to enact the same kind of angry self-sacrificial pattern that infuriated him with his employers. He described the beautiful house he shared with his wife. Everything—the rugs, the kitchen, the garden—sounded perfect, "just so."

When Ellen met with her supervisor, Claudia began to establish a BASE perspective. Ellen was thinking that a good working diagnosis might be adjustment disorder with mixed emotional features or perhaps dysthymia because Jack seemed depressed. Staying with the diagnosis and overall conceptual system, Claudia asked her if Jack had said anything about ritualizing behaviors. Ellen looked a little startled, "I don't think so. Why do you ask?" "I'm not sure," Claudia said, "but he just seems like he might have OCD or maybe the personality disorder form of it. If it were OCPD, you know, there wouldn't necessarily be ritualized compulsions, but I just get a sense there might be. Why don't you ask him?"

Before the next meeting with Jack, Ellen looked over the list of assessment questions that appears earlier in this chapter. She decided to bring them into the hour with Jack, and started with the first one: "Do you ever get ideas, or imagine things or have impulses that seem silly, or nasty or horrible or anything like that?" Jack said, simply, "Yes" and fell silent. Using her sense of humor, Ellen replied, "Well, don't go on and on about it!" Jack smiled and said, "Okay, it isn't like there's anything here to be ashamed of. Lots of people have OCD. It's been all over the news lately. But this is *me*, and it's kind of embarrassing."

Ellen asked if he would be comfortable telling her about the compulsive side first—"The things you do that you feel compelled to do, even if they don't make sense, because of the obsessions—you know the ideas, or whatever."

"Well, for starters, there's the linen closet. Every towel in there—and there's 23 of them, believe me, I know—is folded and sorted by size, and they get washed twice a week whether they've been used or not. Then it takes me forever to get them folded just right and sorted back in there. I have to have them done right. I guess that's a little obsessive." He was pensive for a moment. "That's not such a big deal," he said, "but for the last two years my wife and I have never eaten in a restaurant, and I feel bad about that because that's something she loves. But I just don't trust their level of hygiene and I'm too uncomfortable to do it."

Ellen asked if there was anything else. Jack looked embarrassed again. "Yeah, there's this," he said, pulling his hands out of his jacket and holding them out in front of him so she could see that his fingernails had been chewed to the quick, in fact into the flesh. "That looks painful," she said. "Yeah," he said, "I've got to stop it. A few months ago it got infected and I promised myself I'd stop but I haven't been able to."

In the next supervisory hour with Claudia, Ellen talked about the discoveries that had emerged from the last hour with Jack. Claudia told her about the controversy in OCD research between theories of causation that were purely psychological and those that were primarily neurodynamic. On the psychological side, it sounded like there was a lot going on in Jack's life that might have to do with attachment issues. His behavior sounded like that of a kid who is very ambivalent about his attachment figures—furious at them but at the same time thinking about them all the time as if he were not secure enough to let them go.

"On the brain end of things," Claudia said, "there's no one theory that's clearly superior, but they're all in the same ballpark. There's some evidence that a particular area of the brain—the caudate nuclei –does a poor job filtering out irrelevant information and the prefrontal cortex is compelled to attend to it, making plans and generating abstract thoughts. You know, like SSRIs are helpful with OCD? I'd put my money on complex causes, interaction between different regions—that's why we call it *neurodynamics*, right?"

In the next session, Ellen worked hard to develop a working alliance. Jack said he didn't really have "any of the stuff I've read about" as far as obsessions. "I just get real uneasy and feel like I have to do some of these things to make things right." Ellen began to address the psychoeducational component with Jack in hour 3. In hour 4, she proposed that they start trying to help Jack engage his frontal lobes to get better control over his feelings before moving on to the obsessions and compulsions. That would mean doing some cognitive analysis and using thought records before the ERP. Although this step was consistent with evidenced-based practice (the *e* in the BASE), Jack said, "No, I want to get right into it, even though it's scary."

Ellen revised her plan, based on Jack's preferences. They would try the ERP and cognitive analysis concomitantly, and keep an eye on how well things were going as they proceeded. The exposure Ellen recommended was in vivo; it was to be performed consistently and repetitively when Jack felt as if he had to perform one of his compulsions. By refraining and noting what came up for him and what he had been feeling just before he felt the compulsion, they began to unlock some mysteries. What Ellen did not say was that this would not have been practical without the good working relationship she had already established with her patient. Her first evidence-based OCD treatment was fully launched.

CHAPTER 10

Depression

The Dark amid the Blaze

Oh dark, dark, amid the blaze of noon, Irrecoverably dark! total eclipse, Without all hope of day.

—John Milton, *Samson Agonistes*

ELANA K. IS long and tall (almost 6 feet in height), a pretty 32-year-old African-American woman who works in publishing in San Francisco. She came to see a therapist because "I just don't feel like myself anymore." Since breaking up with a boyfriend a year ago, Elana has been sleeping a lot and mostly letting the answering machine pick up because "I don't feel like seeing anyone or even talking." A couple of times recently she has caught herself wishing that God would just take her off this earth and end her pain. The thought made her realize that her friends were right; she needed to talk to someone. "I feel tired all the time, and I'm fat. The things I used to love, like my job, which would really get me going . . . I don't know . . . it's blah . . . ." Elana's therapist knew she was talking about depression.

A depressive disorder differs from the unhappy or sad moods that almost always occur in relation to interpersonal losses and disappointments in love, work, or fortune. Not all clinically depressed patients are sad, and many sad patients are not necessarily clinically depressed. In some patients, experiences of anxiety, apathy, or irritability may figure more prominently than sadness in their distress. *Anhedonia*—a loss of the capacity to experience pleasure or enjoyment—is commonly present; and problems remembering experiences that are unrelated to sadness and pessimism are common too. There are often subtle interactions between biological events and disorders of mood—for example, hormonally mediated mood alterations in perimenopause may mimic, perhaps even cause (in the sense of initiating a pattern that becomes a neurodynamic attractor), dysthymia.

Each year, about 14 million American adults suffer from clinical depression. The burden of suffering associated with these disorders is staggering. Depression is the second most common mental disorder in the United States and the most frequent reason people seek treatment in outpatient clinics or psychiatric hospitals. An estimated 1 in 20 men will have a clinically significant depressive episode in their lifetimes, and the figure is twice as high for women (Kessler, et al., 2005). Depression is foremost among the psychological problems that can be fatal. Like Elana, depressed people often have feelings of wanting to die. A third will consider suicide, and 8% will make a suicide attempt.

Added to the incalculable loss of those who succeed in killing themselves are the more tangible costs of treating this disorder. Billions of dollars are spent each year just on indirect (and often ineffective) treatments. Patients who are depressed are more likely to smoke, eat carelessly, and avoid exercise. Depressed people with a serious health condition, such as diabetes or heart disease, typically will have more difficulty complying with treatment requirements. The prevalence of depression among primary care patients has been estimated to be twice as high as it is in the general population. It is the cause of more visits to primary care physicians than any complaint other than hypertension. The U.S. Preventive Services Task Force recommends formal depression screening for all adult patients seen in primary care. Depression is also the most common cause of disability in the nation (Murray & Lopez, 1997). In terms of lost productivity and disability, estimates are that the depression-spectrum disorders cost the U.S. economy $44 billion a year.

DIAGNOSING DEPRESSION

Despite remarkable advances in our understanding of brain function and neurobiology, psychiatric diagnosis remains in many ways the *terra incognito* on the map of modern medicine. In virtually all cases, psychiatric diagnoses are made without laboratory or imaging tests of underlying pathology. Alone among specialties, psychology and psychiatry continue to rely on intuition and expert consensus in diagnosing functional disorders (Duncan, Miller, & Sparks, 2004). The diagnosis of depression is established by clinical interview and may be supported by simple self-report rating scales, such as the D-ARK (Depression Arkansas) or the

PHQ9 (Patient Health Questionnaire 9-Item Version). The clinician determines whether symptoms of depression (see Table 10.1) are present and how they are affecting the patient's functioning. The presence of suicidal ideation (or intent), psychotic symptoms, whether the patient is oriented, his level of alertness, cooperation, the quality of his communications, and notable aspects of his motor functioning are factors that should also be taken stock of. Any indication of a potential medical cause for the mood disorder requires referral to and collaboration with a primary care provider or a neurologist.

As we observed in Chapter 4, making *Diagnostic and Statistical Manual* (*DSM*) diagnoses is very much a good news/bad news situation for psychotherapists. Many diagnostic distinctions—for example, between major depression and dysthymia—are not psychotherapeutically useful. They add nothing to our understanding of how the disorder should be treated. Nor, ironically, do the common diagnoses tell us anything about what the *causes* of the disorder may be. Nevertheless, until something better comes along, using the *DSM* allows us to be more systematic (part of what the s stands for in "BASE"). Like *Bird Watching for Dummies*, if you do not know what you are seeing, the *DSM* can help you figure it out.

UNIPOLAR DEPRESSIVE DISORDERS

Major depressive disorder, dysthymia, and depressive disorder not otherwise specified are subgroups of unipolar depression. As noted, distinctions between these categories are not particularly important. Differentiating between unipolar and bipolar depressive episodes, however, can be critical; and *all patients presenting with depressive symptoms should be screened for cycling moods and frank manic or hypomanic episodes*. Because our healthcare systems often privilege major depression for reimbursement purposes, it is important when working with insurance companies and when referring for medication to diagnose the patient accurately in *DSM* terms. Specific symptom clusters for major depressive disorder are shown in Table 10.1.

RISK FACTORS FOR SUICIDE

About one-third of people with a depressive disorder have suicidal thoughts as a part of the disorder. Whenever depression is suspected, some attention should be given to assessing the patient's capacity for self-harm. It is good practice to directly question patients about suicidal thoughts, impulses, plans and whether they ever made a suicide attempt.

Table 10.1

DSM–IV Criteria for Major Depressive Disorder (MDD)

Five (or more) of tho following symptoms have been present during the same 2-week period and represent a change from previous functioning; at least one of the symptoms is either (1) depressed mood or (2) loss of interest or pleasure.

Note: Do not include symptoms that are clearly due to a general medical condition, or mood-incongruent delusions or hallucinations.

- Depressed mood most of the day, nearly every day, as indicated by either subjective report (e.g., feels sad or empty) or observation made by others (e.g., appears tearful). Note: In children and adolescents, can be irritable mood
- Markedly diminished interest or pleasure in all or almost all activities most of the day, nearly every day (as indicated by subjective account or observation made by others).
- Significant weight loss when not dieting or weight gain (e.g., a change of more than 5% of body weight in a month) or decrease or increase in appetite nearly every day. Note: In children, consider failure to make expected weight gains
- Insomnia or hypersomnia nearly every day
- Psychomotor agitation or retardation nearly every day (observable by others, not merely subjective feelings of restlessness or being slowed down)
- Fatigue or loss of energy nearly every day
- Feelings of worthlessness or excessive or inappropriate guilt (which may be delusional) nearly every day (not merely self-reproach or guilt about being sick)
- Diminished ability to think or concentrate, or indecisiveness, nearly every day (either by subjective account or as observed by others)
- Recurrent thoughts of death (not just fear of dying), recurrent suicidal ideation without a specific plan, or a suicide attempt or a specific plan for committing suicide
- The symptoms do not meet criteria for a Mixed Episode
- The symptoms cause clinically significant distress or impairment in social, occupational, or other important areas of functioning
- The symptoms are not due to the direct physiological effects of a substance (e.g., a drug of abuse, a medication) or a general medical condition (e.g., hypothyroidism)
- The symptoms are not better accounted for by bereavement, i.e., after the loss of a loved one, the symptoms persist for longer than 2 months or are characterized by marked functional impairment, morbid preoccupation with worthlessness, suicidal ideation, psychotic symptoms, or psychomotor retardation

Source: American Psychiatric Association, 1994. reprinted by permission.

Contrary to the social intuition of many therapists, patients are often relieved to be asked these direct questions and by the therapist's reassurance that suicidal thinking is a common symptom of the depressive disorder itself that will go away with successful treatment. If they do nothing more, self-report measures given at the initial interview and intermittently thereafter assure the therapist of current information about suicidality. On the PHQ9, any response other than "0" to item 9 may indicate suicidal ideation or intent, and the clinician should follow up. It is also a good idea to keep in mind these risk factors:

- Hopelessness
- Caucasian race
- Male gender
- Advanced age
- Living alone
- Access to firearms

History

- Prior suicide attempts
- Family history of suicide attempts
- Family history of substance abuse

Diagnostic

- General medical illness
- Psychosis
- Substance abuse

COGNITIVE DISTORTIONS

Depressed people disproportionately recall sad experiences when they are depressed. As we noted in Chapter 4, this tendency occurs because of state-based memories. Mood-congruent cognitive schema (such as pessimism and the relative ease of accessing sad memories) are consistent with and perpetuate depression. Patients literally cannot remember when things were better. The mood of depressed patients is also fueled by their "thinking errors." All these elements, along with the behavioral ones to be mentioned, come together as a powerful neurodynamic attractor pattern that can be difficult to escape from. Some common types of thinking errors include:

- **Polarization.** It is all or nothing, good or bad, wonderful or rotten.
- **Overgeneralization.** One unfortunate incident at work is a springboard to conclude that the job is not worth having anymore.
- **Personalization.** The depressed person believes herself to be the object of intense scrutiny and (usually denigrating) attention from peers, partners, and even strangers.

- **Mind reading.** The depressed person knows what you were thinking (even if you were not thinking anything in particular).
- **Shoulds and Should nots.** Rigid and inflexible rules inhibit the individual's capacity to adapt to the environment.

SEASONAL AFFECTIVE DISORDER

In response to signals that it is dark or light outside, the brain activates connections with the pineal gland. If it is dark, the pineal gland secretes melatonin, a sedative hormone whose chemical structure is similar to that of serotonin (in fact, it is synthesized from serotonin). An overabundance of melatonin results in a decline in serotonergic levels in the bloodstream. This may be the basis for seasonal affective disorder. People with this disorder often find themselves becoming more depressed during seasons with fewer hours of daylight. A disproportionate number of people in the northwestern United States or northern Europe suffer from seasonal affective disorder because of overcast skies and shorter days in the winter. Some people suffering from depression keep their drapes drawn because they "don't want to let the outside world in" and are unaware that low levels of light are linked with mood. Depressed patients should be encouraged to maximize their exposure to natural sunlight.

CO-OCCURRING CONDITIONS

Major depressive disorder (MDD) commonly occurs in individuals who also have bipolar disorder, certain personality disorders, eating disorders, or are using or withdrawing from alcohol or other drug addiction. The incidence of depression is much higher among people who have medical problems. Age can play a part as well. The physical symptoms of patients over 60 frequently mask or tend to eclipse the fact that depression is the primary cause of distress. In fact, late-life depression is a significant predicator of suicide, especially in older men. Memory deficits and problems in executive functioning (as suggested by the patient's appearance, finances, or domestic arrangements) are hallmarks of late-life depression. The therapist evaluating older patients may consider psychological or neuropsychological testing. Given the complex role of the hippocampus in depression, memory problems should be regarded as potentially a cause, as well as an effect, of depressed mood.

As we mentioned, depression is typically associated with asymmetric hemispheric activation, with relative inhibition of the left prefrontal cortex

(PFC) and relative activation of the right PFC (Davidson, Ekman, Saron, Senulis, & Friesen, 1990). Patients who have suffered a left-hemisphere stroke develop what is referred to as a catastrophic effect and become very depressed, while patients with a right-hemisphere stroke develop a laissez-faire attitude and demonstrate more acceptance and much less depression.

MIXED DEPRESSION AND ANXIETY

The limitations of the *DSM* system frequently show up in the practice of psychotherapy with patients who come in with mixed depression and anxiety. It is important to find out whether patients believe they are depressed, and if so, why. The heightened sensitivity of the amygdala to cortisol may make anxiety more likely during depression. Typically, if another disorder—such as social anxiety anxiety disorder, posttraumatic stress disorder, generalized anxiety disorder, or obsessive-compulsive disorder—is the primary diagnosis, the patient's depression is likely to remit with successful treatment of the anxiety disorder (Kaiser Permanente, 2006).

SUBSTANCE ABUSE DISORDERS

Many people use drugs as a consequence of depression; conversely substance abuse is a leading cause of depression. Good practice for patients who are depressed and using substances is to consider both disorders primary and focus on engaging and retaining them in therapy and to encourage them to accept a referral for specialized chemical dependency treatment.

WHAT CAUSES DEPRESSION?

The list of specific symptoms for major depression is shown in Table 10.1. In neurodynamic terms, we can group these symptoms into four systems-related categories:

1. Mood changes (dysphoria, hopelessness, sociality, anhedonia, anxiety)
2. Circadian dysregulation (low drive, energy, appetite, sleep, libido)
3. Motor deficits (slow movement, restlessness, agitation)
4. Cognitive impairment (poor attention, working memory, executive function, ruminations)

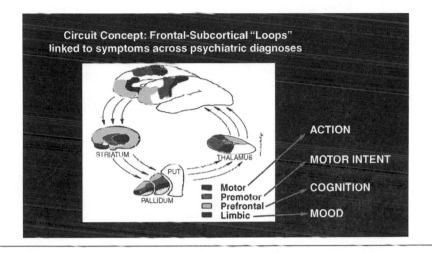

Figure 10.1 Systems-Related Symptom Categories of Depression (*Source:* Mayberg, 2006)

In terms of localized brain sites, the symptoms of depression implicate the neurodynamic modules shown in Figure 10.1—which is to say, depression is a broadly systemic disorder. As we learned in Chapter 2, distributed and systemic factors underlie most important psychological experiences. Problems can arise either from dysfunction in a particular site or from the interactions between several or many sites. For decades, the dominant model of depression has privileged the role of neurotransmitters such as serotonin. Elements of this model are shown in Figure 10.2.

HEMISPHERIC ASYMMETRY

The neurotransmitter model of depression provides a seemingly economical explanation of how antidepressants work, but neuroscience raises questions about its adequacy. That depressive symptoms are associated with *hemispheric asymmetry* is an important finding that has been supported by several studies (Baxter et al., 1985, 1989; Davidson & Slagter, 2000;). Generally, the right hemisphere is associated with negative emotions and the left hemisphere with positive feelings. Also, the right hemisphere is associated with *withdrawal behavior* and the left with *approach behaviors*. These characteristics are particularly relevant to the behavioral activation treatment component of cognitive behavioral therapy (CBT).

Language, making interpretive sense of events, and generating positive, optimistic emotions are all products of robust left-hemispheric functioning.

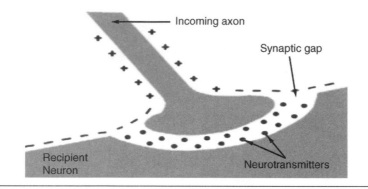

Figure 10.2 Neurotransmitter Model of Depression

Much of what we see with depressed patients—their experience of the enthralling power of somber affects, interpretive capacities hobbled by melancholia—is consistent with right-side dominance. Instead of doing something about their situation, depressed patients seem beguiled by a global negative perspective and passively withdrawing. Right-hemisphere functioning favors global thinking.

If allowed to go on unchecked, the kindled neural networks of depression are self-perpetuating. The more they fire together without balanced input, the more likely they are to fire again, and the more bogged down patients such as Elana become. Imaging studies of depressed subjects show restricted blood flow to the right-hemisphere modules that help us identify and interpret the facial expressions of others. Our ability to use the emotional inputs of others to regulate our own emotional state depends on this capacity, and without it our reliance on our internal reactions is intensified. People become less interesting, and their capacity to help us modulate sadness and pessimism fades. One patient treated with a highly sophisticated neurodynamic intervention called deep brain stimulation (which we discuss later) talked about her emergence from the isolation of years of profound depression. "It was overwhelming to be able to process emotion on somebody's face. I'd been numb to that for so long" (Dobbs, 2006, p. 5).

The ventromedial prefrontal cortex also appears to become more active during sadness (Damasio, 1999).

ANTERIOR CINGULATE CORTEX

The difficulty many depressed patients have noticing details may be caused by sharply diminished activity in their anterior cingulate cortex, or ACC (Lane, 1998). The ACC is the frontal part of the cingulate cortex, which surrounds the corpus callosum, the part of the brain that connects the two hemispheres. The ACC helps regulate autonomic functions, such as blood pressure, and sophisticated cognitive functions as well. Anticipating rewards, decision making, empathy, and subjective emotional experience are all functions in which the ACC plays a critical role. It is a central station for integrating top-down and bottom-up stimuli and triaging processing tasks to other areas in the brain.

The ACC seems to be especially involved when effort is needed to carry out a task in early learning and problem solving (Allman et al., 2001). Many studies attribute functions such as error detection, anticipation of tasks, motivation, and modulation of emotional responses to the ACC (Bush et al., 2000.; Nieuwenhuis et al., 2001). The ACC also contains spindle neurons associated with comprehending the responses of others, and appears to be a neurodynamic component underlying empathy and mindsight. We take up the ACC's role in depression in the later discussion of deep brain stimulation.

GENETICS, NEUROGENESIS, AND STRESS

In examining the neurodynamic causes and effects of depression, we once again encounter the hippocampus—that peanut-size dynamo in the core of the brain that's vital to the encoding of memories and their emotional significance. As we have noted previously, stress causes our hypothalamic-pituitary-adrenal (HPA) system to turn up the production of cortisol. As discussed in Chapters 6 and 8, prolonged exposure to cortisol affects the hippocampus somewhat like prolonged exposure to high blood levels of alcohol affect the liver. It is not a good thing. Long-term elevation in cortisol level shrinks the dendrites and axons of hippocampal neurons. If the stress continues, neurons begin to die in large numbers and the volume of the hippocampus shrinks. Some studies have shown a 10% to 20% decline in volume in chronically depressed patients. This decrease in hippocampal volume in chronically depressed patients (Sheline, Wang, Gado, Csernansky, & Vannier, 1996) may be accompanied by increased amygdalar volume (Sheline, Gado, & Price, 1998), making anxiety and fear a factor for this group as well.

The apparent potency of cortisol's effects on the hippocampus and amygdala may lie in cortisol's power to inhibit the production of *brain-derived neurotropic factor,* a key element in neuroplasticity and neurogenesis. Brain-derived neurotropic factor (BDNF for short), is a sort of naturally occurring neurofertility drug that stimulates the growth of new dendritic branches and releases the reproductive capacity of existing neurons, resulting in the creation of new neurons. Karege, Perret, Bondolfi, Schwald, Bertschy, and Aubry (2002) review the animal research that demonstrates that stress decreases BDNF levels in brain regions associated with depression. Interestingly, about one-third of the population carries a variety of the gene that affects BDNF production in the neuron. This allelle produces a version of BDNF that cannot escape the cell body, diminishing BDNF's benevolent impact relative to that produced by the standard gene, which is released from the neuron through the dendrites (Ramin, 2007). The one-third of the population with this allele are more susceptible to the negative effects of stress on BDNF production.

Perhaps because it is based on genetic and as well as neuroscientific evidence, this BDNF theory of depression predicts what we as therapists so often see: depression running in families. The theory assumes that depression, like anxiety, comes about as a result of a breakdown in the body's allostatic processes for downregulating the stress response. It suggests that stress and our special susceptibility to it may be why the incidence of depression has increased exponentially over the last century. Our culture seems to become more stressful on a daily basis. One-third of us carry a gene that makes us more susceptible to the biochemistry of stress than are others; and stressors are distributed inequitably across the population by socioeconomic class, race, and gender groupings. Elevated cortisol levels during depression attack not only the hippocampus but the prefrontal cortex as well. Cognitive deficits, impairment in working memory, and the diminished capacity to make executive decisions—signal characteristics of depressive disorders—are the result.

How do antidepressants work in the model of depression that emphasizes the role of BDNF and other genetic causes? When the stress response abates, BDNF production resumes, and depleted dendrites and axons once again reach out and sprout foliage in a neural springtime (Ramin, 2007). Antidepressant treatment seems to block the effects of cortisol on BDNF, shielding the hippocampus and other brain centers that are vulnerable to its corrosive effects. Chen, Dowlatshahi, MacQueen, Wang, and Young (2001) found increased BDNF in the brains of patients who had been diagnosed with major depression and treated with antidepressants. It appears, then, that some antidepressant medications *stimulate the production of BDNF and enrich our neuroplastic capacities* as well as inhibit the reuptake of neurotransmitters. Fred Gage, at the Salk Institute of Biological Studies, suggests that the link between selective serotonin reuptake inhibitors (SSRIs), BDNF production, and neurogenesis may account for the fact that it takes 3 weeks for antidepressants such as paroxetine (Paxil) and sertraline (Zoloft) to work: that is how long it takes old neurons to reproduce and newly born ones to get wired in to the neurocircuitry (Ramin, 2007).

Neuroscience has generated new evidence that there is much more to the physiology of clinical depression than is dreamed of in the old "Prozac model" of antidepressant action. The hippocampus seems to be involved, as well as variability in neuroplastic processes (Reid & Stewart, 2001). There is also newly suggestive (and tantalizing) evidence that hippocampal neurogenesis is an important element in how we recover from depression (Castren, 2005). In one study, Karl Deisseroth, a neuroengineer and psychiatrist at Stanford, used high-speed cameras to photograph electrical activity in an interhippocampal module called the dentate gyrus. Deisseroth showed that activity in this area slows in rats exhibiting the behavioral and cognitive equivalents of human depression and resumes normal levels after administration of antidepressant medications (Minkel, 2007).

Deisseroth suggests that "one of the mysteries of depression is how there can be so many different causes . . . and so many different treatments" (quoted in Minkel, 2007). Helen Mayberg, neurologist and neurosurgeon at Emory University, comments that research such as this "tells us the hippocampus is very involved, but it doesn't tell us it's the origin of the problem" (quoted in Minkel, 2007). The hippocampus connects many different roads leading from and into the areas of the brain shown in Figure 10.1. Future neuroscientific exploration will map these roads more closely, and our understanding of why antidepressants and psychotherapy work will be transformed by these new understandings. Better still, brain-based approaches will allow us to generate new and more effective psychotherapeutic and psychopharmacological treatments. Figure 10.3 shows the position of the left and right hippocampi in the brain.

DEEP BRAIN STIMULATION

Mayberg (Mayberg et al., 2005) has designed and tested an experimental treatment for intractable depression called *deep brain stimulation* (DBS). The treatment suggests a different and promising model of the causes of depression. Over the course of her career, Mayberg honed in on an area of the ACC called *Area 25* as being an important switching station in the neurodynamics of depression. Area 25 is both smaller and more activated in most depressed patients. When undepressed people are asked to think about sad things, Area 25 activates; its overactivity is diminished in depressed patients after successful depression treatment. Moreover, because the ACC is wired into both top-down and bottom-up regulatory

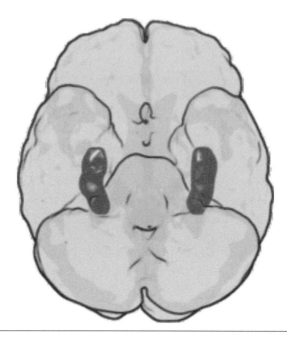

Figure 10.3   Position of the Left and Right Hippocampi in the Brain

modules, it plays a role in modulating fear, memory, error recognition, motivation for reward, sleep, and other functions that become dysregulated in depression.

Mayberg was working closely with a surgeon who performed surgical implantations of pacemakers in the brains of Parkinson's patients to diminish their tremors. Together, they developed a similar procedure for inhibiting the overactivity of Area 25 of depressed patients. Implantating a power supply and pacemaker in patients' upper chests, the surgical team threads a tiny wire from the power supply up into Area 25, next to the corpus callosum. Four-volt electrical pulses from the pacemaker inhibit Area 25.

Candidates for the experimental DBS implant had failed every other attempt to treat their profound, intractable depression. These were patients for whom nothing worked. Mayberg herself did not perform the surgery but was present and talked with subjects (who were treated with a local anesthetic only) as they had the DBS unit implanted and switched on. *New York Times* reporter David Dobbs interviewed Mayberg about what happened with one of the experimental procedure's participants, Deanna Cole Benjamin, during the procedure:

[Mayberg] had told Deanna that if anything felt different, she should say so. Mayberg wasn't going to tell her when the device was activated. "Don't try to decide what's important," Mayberg told her. "If your nose itches, I want to know." Now and then the two would chat. But so far Deanna hadn't said much.

"So we turn it on," Mayberg told me later, "and all of a sudden she says to me, 'It's very strange,' she says, 'I know you've been with me in the operating room this whole time. I know you care about me. But it's not that. I don't know what you just did. But I'm looking at you, and it's like I just feel suddenly more connected to you.'"

Mayberg, stunned, signaled with her hand to the others, out of Deanna's view, to turn the stimulator off.

"And they turn it off," Mayberg said, "and she goes: 'God, it's just so odd. You just went away again. I guess it wasn't really anything.'" (Dobbs, 2006a, p. 5)

Valerie Voon, a research psychiatrist who was part of Mayberg's original team in Toronto, says: "I can't emphasize enough that we need a large, randomized study to confirm this as a treatment" (Dobbs, 2006, p.2). But one year after the implantation procedure, it was looking good: two-thirds of the DBS patients remained greatly improved (Mayberg et al., 2005).

Patients who have recovered from chronic profound depression do not typically want go to Paris or Disneyland or otherwise make up for years of deprivation. Instead, they look forward to being able to start taking care of some of the ordinary things they had neglected because of their depression. One subject said, "It is as though I have been locked in a room with 10 screaming children. Constant noise; no rest; no escape. Whatever just happened, the children have just left the building" (Mayberg, personal communication, 2007). Finally this patient has the energy and planfulness to clean out the garage or the sewing room.

Mayberg's work is a significant advance not only in terms of the DBS procedure but in the elegance of her neurodynamic model. What Mayberg calls the bowl-of-soup model of traditional psychiatry—in which depression is a "chemical imbalance" and treatment is adding a few "extra ingredients" to the mix—will be replaced by a model that seems equal to the task of describing the complexity of human psychology. Depression is beginning to be seen as the dysregulation of mutually influencing interactions between brain modules associated with vegetative functions, mood, mindsight, error correction, and overall energy and activation.

From the neurodynamic perspective, there are a variety of ways of helping someone suffering from depression. Psychotherapy targets the relational deficits poignantly captured by Mayberg's patient, Deanna. Therapy can also help the patient challenge the core orbitofrontal cortex cognitions that support the loop of pessimistic prediction and passive engagement that results in the kind of self-confirming negative experience that is so prominent in depression. By helping patients see the attentional triggers and negative biases that go with depression, and by supporting their engagement in activities that have a fair chance of producing pleasurable results, therapists help patients reactivate their own mood-regulatory attractors.

Neurochemicals and antidepressants such as the SRRIs continue to have an important role in the brain-based model of depression treatment. What is changing is our understanding of *how* antidepressants work and *why* psychotherapy and pharmacotherapy are complementary in many cases, depending on the patient. PET imaging studies of the brains of patients who have undergone successful CBT treatment reveal neurodynamic changes, with some modules (as Mayberg predicted) being activated and others inhibited. After psychotherapy, areas related to body state awareness and cognitive reappraisal are *activated*. The hippocampus and dorsal cingulate are more active after treatment as well. Area 25, the part of the ACC targeted by Maryberg's surgical process, is *inhibited*. Areas associated with self-referencing and personal salience are also *inhibited* after successful treatment, as is activity in the dorsal, ventral, and medial PFC (Goldapple et al., 2004; Dobbs, 2006b). Mayberg (personal communication, 2007) notes that through DBS of area 25 the ACC is taken offline and the PFC is given a chance to function unimpeded. Addtionally, since people who are depressed tend to overactivate their right frontal lobe and underactivate their left frontal lobe, behavior that activates the left frontal lobe is likely to be therapeutic, as we will describe below.

These effects of psychotherapy can be thought of as reducing activation in areas relating to overthinking while improving the capacity for the encoding of new experience. As Mayberg points out, this constellation of effects suggests that the patients who responded to CBT did so because they were more cognitively oriented to begin with. If responders were engaged in trying to *think their way out* of their depression (Dobbs, 2006), the cognitive analysis of CBT could help them improve the efficiency of their thinking and get out of the rut of the negative cognitive bias.

The imaging patterns characteristic of patients successfully treated with CBT contrast with patterns seen in imaging studies of patients successfully treated with antidepressants. Patients who improved after the initiation of SSRIs showed *increased activity* in the PFC and *more inhibition* in the hippocampus and cingulate cortex (Goldapple et al., 2004). As with the psychotherapy patients, Area 25 was inhibited relative to pre-treatment levels. How do we understand the apparently opposite and self-canceling effects of antidepressants and psychotherapy on the depressed brain? If the hypothesis that the CBT responders were busier thinkers to begin with bears out, it may be that the SSRI responders were just different from them. The psychotherapy research suggests the degree to which the patient has been a neglected variable in all forms of mental health treatment. If the SSRI responders are less cognitively involved in their depression at the outset of treatment, it may be that medication helps them bring more of their cognitive potential to bear on mood regulation.

Mayberg offers a more complex neurodynamic explanation. The *relationship* between brain modules matters more than the functioning of any one module per se. Both therapists and psychopharmacologists, in this view, are engaged with the brain in the way that a conductor interacts with an orchestra. Psychopharmacology works on the level of neuron-to-neuron communication, making sure that each instrument in the ensemble plays its part in tune and at the right time. In psychotherapy, the therapist coordinates a neurodynamic ensemble by focusing not so much on the part of one or two instruments but on the effects of the functioning of the many different parts that become involved in the therapeutic relationship. The therapist concentrates on aspects of functioning—for example, emotion regulation—that are products of elaborate networks. Mayberg (personal communication) describes psychotherapy working from "the top down" and medicine working from the "bottom up." Together, the effects of joint psychotherapeutic-psychopharmacological treatment push and pull the system back into a healthy allostatic pattern (Dobbs, 2006a).

TREATMENT

Many interventions can help depressed patients, and about 80% of those seeking help improve over time. Psychotherapy, antidepressant medication, and psychoeducation are all mainstream approaches. Bibliotherapy, light therapy and exercise, pastoral counseling, behavioral activation and coaching, and even the application of electromagnetic stimulation to the skull have also been shown to help people with unipolar depressive disorders. The psychotherapy outcomes research suggests that the efficacy of these quite different approaches may arise from patient variables (Bohart, 2000) and a good therapeutic alliance (Miller et al., 2004).

The first step in building this alliance is to think through with patients what their goals are, what tasks they can and are willing to complete, and what their preferences are regarding treatment. Some patients want pills, and the sooner the better. Others will not even consider them. In cases where patients are more severely depressed or have been helped by antidepressants in the past, combining the two modalities is a good practice. It is also a good practice to help patients understand how a particular treatment works, and what they can expect from the therapist, before getting to the work per se. The key here is to approach patients respectfully and with genuine concern for their preferences and needs in a helping relationship. Maintaining this respectful regard should characterize the whole treatment. Enacting the part of a good-enough parent, the therapist above all else needs accurate empathy regarding patients' emotional and cognitive experiences. Given the prevalence of insecure attachment styles among our patients, it may require special effort on the therapist's part to communicate this understanding to patients and to establish a climate where patients can express feelings (positive *and* negative) about the therapist and how things are going in the treatment (Lambert & Baley, 2002; Wallin, 2007). The more successful the therapist is in creating this climate, the more likely it is that the treatment will be successful. To sidestep or shortcut this process is to increase the odds of premature termination, which are already high with depressed, pessimistic patients.

COGNITIVE BEHAVIORAL TREATMENT

Elana, the patient we met at the beginning of this chapter, had heard good things about cognitive behavioral treatment for depression. "One of my friends is a therapist and she said I should make sure whoever I see knows how to do it." Her brother had been depressed and had attended a CBT group at a health maintenance organization. "That helped Ron, and I think that's what I want too." Although the evidence suggests that no one psychotherapeutic approach is superior to all others in helping depressed people recover, CBT has an excellent track record in outcome trials. Many of its elements are common to other approaches as well, but CBT has a number of advantages. The research suggests that CBT, which is typically more structured and directive than psychodynamic approaches, is well suited to patients such as Elana, who are relatively nonresistant (Beutler et al., 1991). *CBT is less likely to work with more resistant patients; a psychodynamnic approach might be a better fit for such patients.* Mayberg's suggestion that patients who are more cognitively involved in trying to resolve their depression at the outset of treatment may be excellent candidates for CBT also warrants consideraton. An advantage of CBT is that it is relatively easy for patients to understand the "fit" between the therapeutic methods and tasks and the neurodynamic processes underlying depression.

After getting acquainted with Elana and assuring her that he was familiar with cognitive behavioral therapy, the therapist asked her what changes had occurred in her life recently and whether they had been accompanied by behavioral changes. Elana said, "Now that you mention it, a lot has happened." While she had identified the breakup with her boyfriend as a turning point in her mood, she had experienced a number of other losses as well. Her maternal grandmother, the family's matriarch and a primary source of love, stability, and affection, had died of congestive heart failure two years before. Like her grandmother, Elana was a caretaker torn between a loving sense of obligation toward family members, whose problems involved significant substance abuse, and smoldering anger toward them. After the grandmother's death, Elana had in effect adopted a niece and nephew, providing for their monetary and parental needs, which her seriously ill sister could not handle.

Taking care of family meant she no longer had time to sing in the choir at her church, and somehow widened the split she felt between home and the "very white" office world in which she worked. "Sometimes I feel like two different people," she said. Elana mentioned that the boyfriend she had broken up with a year ago was white and had worked at a San Francisco law firm down the street from her office. They had loved each other very much and were on the verge of engagement when Elana started to feel that "I already had too many obligations in my life and I just couldn't face taking on getting married." She felt better being alone and, if possible, "I would rather just have stayed in bed."

In relating all this, Elana started to cry, and the therapist felt both connected to her and that she welcomed his attempts to comfort her. When she felt a little better, they talked again about how the events in her life, her mood, and changes in her lifestyle might be linked. Based on all this, the therapist felt optimistic that CBT was a good way to go for this patient. He told Elana that he begins treatment with information about why CBT is effective in reversing the effects of depression on the brain. He told her it was important that she understand why this approach made sense in terms of her own personal goals for the treatment. This is particularly important in CBT because it is a method that asks patients to *do something*, not just talk about it, outside the hour as well as in it. Obviously, patients' appetites for learning the details of their neurodynamics varies from one person to the next, and this part of the treatment can be expanded or abbreviated as needed. But some version of "this is your brain on depression," and "this is why we're going to do what we're about to do" is important for building the alliance.

Elana was curious and interested. The therapist talked about the typical neurodynamics of the disorder in terms of the specialized roles of three brain modules: the "top" elements (i.e., the left and right hemispheres of the cortex), the "bottom" elements (the hippocampus and the amygdala), and "the middle man" (the ACC). The therapist felt that Elana needed to know that different parts of the brain think differently and regulate emotions differently.

In terms of the "top" elements, the left hemisphere has been shown to be more positive and more planful, *and it can talk*. The right side tends to be more negative and more global, and it is silent—not bad things in themselves but depressing if they are not counterbalanced by robust left-side functioning. In depression, what usually happens is that the right side becomes more active and the left side more inhibited. We can actually see this going on in the brains of depressed people, and see it change after treatment, so things get back in balance. Elana's therapist told her that to help make this happen, they would look together at how Elana's *thinking* had been changed by her *mood*, with the goal of restoring the balance of functions so that her top-level thinking could help her feel better and not so pessimistic.

In terms of the "bottom" elements, the therapist explained that the hippocampus and the amygdala work together, each is important and yet very different from one another. The hippocampus helps create new memories out of experience, and it also helps us figure out new routes to our destinations, even old ones. It helps locate us in time and space. Its partner, the amygdala, is the brain's panic button and the module that stamps that all-important first impression on our interactions with other people. What are we feeling about them? What are they feeling about us, and what are their intentions toward us? The amygdala provides immediate first-draft answers to these questions.

There are recent findings that shrinkage in the volume of both the hippocampus and the amygdala are stress-related—and as the therapist just learned about Elana, there had been plenty of recent stress in her life. Starting two years ago with the loss of her grandmother, she took on the additional responsibility of caring for her nephew and niece. It seemed to the therapist that Elana's feelings about work became more negative at this same time. The therapist asked Elana about the role of ongoing stressors in her life, such as coping with racism and the racial divide. It seemed to him that the divide started to bother her more after her grandmother's death. Elana said, "It's like losing her kind of started a landslide." There were behavioral changes, such as quitting the choir and not seeing friends as much. Then she started feeling more overwhelmed by the pressures of being in a biracial relationship and pessimistic about its future, but when she ended it, there was another loss. All these stresses clearly affected her. The therapist said, "What usually happens in the brain when we get depressed is that one of the 'bottom' elements, the hippocampus, say, becomes less active; and the other one, the amygdala, actually becomes more active, sending a steady stream of negative emotional input up to the top, continuously telling the cortex there's something out there to worry about, something negative."

Elana just nodded.

"The 'middle man,'" the therapist said, "is the ACC, which gets a great deal of input from both the bottom and the top. The ACC is like a middle manager that ends up getting it from both sides." Elana smiled and said, "That's me!" In depressed people, the ACC seems to get overly active, probably trying to keep things in balance, but this is not something that it can necessarily do on its own. One of the things the ACC does is monitor our functioning for mistakes, and it activates when it finds one. When we are depressed, everything we have done in life starts to look wrong. The ACC is also important in sorting and coding experiences that may or may not go into long-term storage. When the ACC hyperactivates, and its bottom partners are overworking and literally shrinking under the impact of stress themselves, it is harder for us to pay attention to the new experiences coming in. This feeds our tendencies to remember only those events that have the same feeling or tone we are experiencing in the present. "So if we're depressed now," the therapist said, "we tend to remember the sad things, the failures, and to dwell on them and forget about the joy."

"That is really interesting," Elana said. "The brain is amazing." Her mood seemed brighter. The therapist thought that her positive response to this psychoeducation component was an indication that her depression, though troublesome, was going to respond well to treatment.

"Yeah, it is," her therapist said, "But I know you didn't come here to learn about the brain but because you want to feel better. Let's see how CBT can help you with that."

CBT involves capturing some of the thoughts (often called *automatic thoughts*) that are part of the stream of consciousness. They are the words and images that pop into our head from moment to moment. For example, on the way to drop off the kids at soccer practice, you notice that the gas gauge is nearing empty. There's a gas station on the way, but stopping would be cutting it close. Some of the automatic thoughts that might run through your head at this point are "If I don't stop, I'll run out of gas and I'll be stuck," "The kids want to get to soccer to see their friends and I don't want to rush them by stopping now," "The last time I was at that station I think the cashier ripped me off."

Each of these thoughts tends to be associated with a particular course of action. In addition to automatic thoughts, Beck (1972; Beck, Rush, Shaw, & Emery, 1979) and other CBT practitioners hypothesize that we also have *core beliefs*. These may be self-appraisals ("People always like me") or judgments about other people ("Men are only interested in one thing") or about life in general ("Whenever something good happens, you can count on something bad happening too"). Core beliefs come into play in making significant or repetitive life decisions, and they tend to be tied up in a complex fashion with moods.

Greenberger and Padesky (1995) illustrate these concepts through a case study of Ben, a retiree who became depressed after his wife was diagnosed with breast cancer (and successfully treated for it) and a good friend and golfing partner died. After his friend's death, Ben withdrew from seeing friends, explaining that "We're at an age where everybody's dying; what's the point in investing time with people anyway?" In Beckian terms, this is an automatic thought. Greenberger and Padesky tied it to an important core belief in Ben's psychology that was based on something his father had often said: "Play with your friends when the sun's shining, because when the sun begins to set you need to go home alone." When his friend died and he feared his wife might too, Ben decided (probably nonconsciously) that this was the beginning of sunset in his own life, and it was time to go home alone.

CBT has been dismissed as the power of positive thinking, but Beck and his colleagues understand that real problems are not resolved just by thinking happy thoughts—any more than they are by getting insight into childhood patterns. "Cognitive therapy suggests instead that people consider as many different angles on a problem as possible. Looking at a situation from many different sides—positive and negative and neutral—can lead to new conclusions and solutions" (Greenberger & Padesky, 1995, p. 23).

Although CBT emphasizes the impact of cognitions on mood, it typically also includes exploration of the how somatic, behavioral, and environmental changes affect mood as well. With roots in behaviorism, CBT practitioners are sensitized to the importance of not letting therapy remain "just talk." They coach patients to undertake *behavioral experiments* to test core beliefs (and then observe the effects on mood). They encourage patients to use *behavioral activation*, planning and living out a return to activities patients once found pleasurable or think they might enjoy now. Activating patients' behavior may in turn induce activation of their left hemisphere, which is likely to be inhibited in depressed patients. Recall that the left hemisphere is associated not only with positive affect but with *approach behaviors* as well. Getting patients to reactivate those neurodynamic attractors in the left hemisphere is likely to exert a positive effect on its own—and if the activity turns out well as a result of the approach, so much the better.

Reducing stress, learning to counterattack codependency with assertiveness, spending more time with supportive people, taking reasonable precautions to enhance personal safety, and using outside resources may all play a part in good CBT practice. An additional legacy of CBT's origins in experimental psychology laboratories is the emphasis the method places on turning patients into neutral observers of their own behavior, with a willingness to collect data to test hypotheses about themselves and the world. Again, this predominantly left-hemispheric activity may be as important as anything relating to the conscious content of the hypothesis testing. CBT tasks patients with more clearly defining their emotional states, enhancing integration, and rebalancing left-right processing. In Elana's case, the therapist suggested she try using a thought record. The thought record is a single-page form that guides data collection about fluctuating feelings and the events, behaviors, and thoughts connected to them. A common version of this protocol that is used at one Kaiser Permanente clinic is shown in Table 10.2.

Elana, unlike some patients, liked using the thought record. "I like structured ways of doing things," she said. Her therapist explained the tasks involved in completing the record, taking as an example Elana's thoughts and feelings about her first therapy session. Although many patients talk nonspecifically about emotional states, saying they feel "uncomfortable" or "numb," Elana described her response near the end of the hour as "hopeful"—a good prognostic sign for a depressed patient. CBT helps patients become more specific about and aware of emotional nuances. In thought records, patients rate the percent of the intensity of a feeling in the mood column and then circle the "hot thought" that provokes the most intense affect or mood. The goal is to get patients into the habit of bringing thoughts and feelings out of working memory into longer-term storage for conscious examination and analysis. That lets both sides of the PFC do a better job of mood and emotion regulation. Implicitly, it also facilitates reempowering the left-hemisphere functions of language and interpretive hypothesizing. The "automatic thoughts" column, for example, requires patients to use their explicit memory, language skills, and

Table 10.2

Thought Record

Name: _____   Date: _____

Situation	Mood	Automatic Thoughts	Evidence That Supports My Hot Thought	Evidence That Does NOT Support My Hot Thought	Alternative or Balanced Thoughts	Re-rate Mood
Who, What, When, Where	1. Specify 2. Rate 0–100	What was going through my mind just before I started to feel this way? Circle hot thought.				0–100

appraisal system in a real-life context. Padesky suggests we ask patients to consider these questions about automatic thoughts:

- What does this say about me if it is true?
- What does this mean about me, my life, my future?
- What am I afraid might happen? What is the worst thing that could happen if it is true?
- What does this mean about how the other person(s) feel(s)/think(s) about me?
- What does this mean about the other person(s) or people in general?
- What images or memories do I have in this situation? (Greenberger & Padesky, 1995, pp. 47–62).

CBT AND BRAIN-BASED THERAPY

CBT has repeatedly been shown to be more effective with depressed patients compared to no treatment and to other forms of psychotherapy, but its contribution to outcome is not as great as factors pertaining to the patient and elements that are common to all psychotherapies (Lambert & Ogles, 2004). Outside the realm of psychotherapy outcome research, CBT has been shown to affect the brain in predictable directions. Mayberg (Mayberg et al., 1999) summarizes the effects of CBT as a reregulation of the neurodynamics of cortical and subcortical emotion regulation. Results of one imaging study of CBT are shown in Figure 10.4.

CBT is effective because it enhances regulatory and attentional processes in the left prefrontal cortex. As a somewhat structured series of exercises involving therapist and patients, it helps create an interpersonal climate of cooperation and trust for depressed patients, most of whom will be currently experiencing relationship problems and impaired confidence in their interpersonal competence. CBT and mindfulness have been combined in the treatment of such special populations as suicidal borderline patients (Linehan, 1993). By engaging patients' conscious-cognitive resources in examining transitory and more stable feelings and assumptions, CBT builds the high road of mood regulation.

Behavioral activation is one of the most powerful techniques in the CBT therapist's repertoire. It is based on the observation that depressed people behave in ways that will sink them deeper into depression. Neurodynamically, they are more likely to be relying on right hemispheric processing and using withdrawal as a primary strategy. Depressed patients often prefer isolating themselves from others, postponing exercise, and oversleeping. In people without a mood disorder, behaviors such as these are

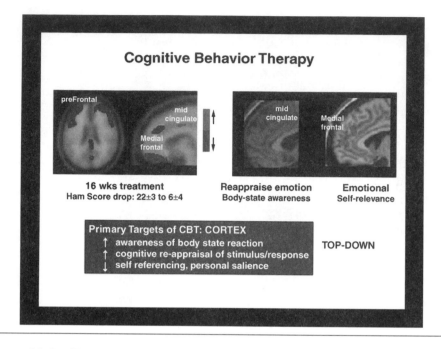

Figure 10.4 Changes in Brain Function as a Result of Cognitive Behavioral Therapy (*Sources:* Goldapple et al., 2004, reprinted by permission; Mayberg, 2006)

likely to result in a darkening mood and perspective. Action is an important therapeutic prescription for depression, and the willingness to prescribe it is one of the major things that sets CBT apart from psychodynamic approaches. Inaction prolongs right hemisphere overactivation. Action can shift the balance back to the left hemisphere, which is correlated not only with action but positive feelings.

One way of approaching behavioral activation with depressed patients who "just don't feel like it" is to use behavioral experiments. With or without the help of thought records, patients are encouraged to remember (and preferably write down) their expectations about how a particular event is going to turn out, go do it, and then go home and record what actually happened and what they actually felt. The technique promotes getting to know the links between poor weather forecasting, staying indoors to avoid the rain, and missing what actually turned out to be a nice sunny day.

Recall the reactions of Mayberg's patients who, after years of intractable profound depression, just wanted to resume the business of living. Working with patients, we can suggest that resuming their engagement with real-life problems can make the depression go away faster. Setting short-term goals and increasing productive and pleasurable activities (e.g., going fishing, to the movies, to a musical event, or salsa dancing) are often helpful as well. The cautionary note here is it is possible to get carried away with the pleasures of coaching and lose track of a second, equally important dimension of behavioral activation: building the alliance with patients. It is more important for therapists to notice how patients are feeling and reacting to the intervention than to be thinking about how beneficial this intervention is going to be for the patient's brain. Lambert (Lambert & Okiishi, 1997; Lambert & Baley, 2002; Miller et al., 2004) and Bohart (2000) continually remind us that it is good practice to ask patients what they think and feel about the activity in the hour (or the homework, as the case may be), and whether it is aligned with the patient's goals in therapy.

Behavioral activation should emphasize developing or reinvigorating social interactions and support. As we noted in Chapter 2, those systems in the brain that have been described as the "social brain" get dysregulated in depression. Social interaction can stimulate attachment schema and social support from friends, reintroducing patients to the warmth and security of families and teams. Psychoeducation about the effects of isolation may motivate patients, but they are more likely to benefit from the actual experience of activating left-hemisphere approach behavior and positive affect. From the therapist's chair, this often involves asking patients to behave counterintuitively. Patients might like to know the good advice that Alcoholics Anonymous offers its members in early recovery: "Fake it until you make it." Engaging in an activity can prime the pump. This is true not only for engaging in pleasurable activities but in social relationships as well. People who have a broad-based social support system live longer, recover from illnesses faster, and fall ill less frequently than people with few social contacts.

INTERPERSONAL THERAPY

Interpersonal therapy (IPT) (Klerman, Weissman, Rounsaville, & Chevron, 1984) has also done well in research trials comparing the efficacy of treatments based on method. The major premise of IPT is that social relationships play a key part in the etiology of most depressions, and helping patients clarify and resolve relational issues is the focus of therapy. IPT is less structured and asks less of patients outside the therapeutic hour than does CBT, and may therefore be a better method for more resistant patients. It is likely to be particularly helpful with patients who have issues involving role disputes, extended grief and loss, role transitions, and social isolation. It tends to be a brief, focused therapy. Neuroimaging studies (Brody et al., 2004) compared IPT to paroxetine (Paxil) treatment in depressed patients. The results suggest that this form of psychotherapy works on the same top-down neurodynamics as does CBT, reregulating the prefrontal cortex, the hippocampus, and the ACC's Area 25.

Severity and Treatment Choice

The evidence supports the enhanced efficacy of combined medication and neurodynamic interventions in treating severe and refractory depression. In mild to moderate depression, psychotherapy interventions often produce better outcomes than medication alone and are the treatment of choice. CBT has been shown to be efficacious for preventing relapse in chronic or severely depressed patients.

Pharmacological Treatment

No antidepressant is clearly more effective than another. Studies indicate that from 50% to 60% of clinically depressed people improve on SSRIs or tricyclics (while about 30% improve on placebos; Quitkin et al., 2000). SSRIs have become the preferred type of antidepressant because they typically provoke fewer side effects and there is less risk that patients can fatally overdose on these medications. Tricyclic antidepressants *can* be taken in lethal overdoses, and *they should not be taken by patients at risk for suicide.* Similarly, tricyclic antidepressants are generally to be avoided with older patients because of the risks of contributing to falls.

Artful psychopharmacology, adequate dosing, and allowing adequate response time are three of the four keys to optimal psychopharmacotherapy outcome. The fourth key to success with medication is *the relationship with the prescribing clinician.* Depressed patients typically are pessimistic and burdened by guilt, encumbered by low motivation, lacking in both self-direction and social support. For any one of these reasons, patients may give up on antidepressant treatment, therapy, or both. Education of patients and their families can help, but undoubtedly the relationship between clinicians and patients is the most important element.

Recent research highlights the importance of the relationship factor in prescribing, as well as psychotherapeutic, relationships. It is interesting to see the emergence and recognition of this factor in the current climate and how it was masked during the period we have called the *pax medica.* For example, the landmark National Institute of Mental Health (NIMH) Treatment of Depression Collaborative Research Program reported that imipramine with clinical management was significantly more beneficial than placebo with clinical management for depressed patients (Elkin, Parloff, Hadley, & Autry, 1985). The original research design overlooked the potential effect of the person of the psychiatrist on patient's treatment outcome, assuming that all psychiatrists are equally interpersonally skilled. In a recent reanalysis of the data, McKay, Zac, and Wampold (2006) made the surprising (except to brain-based therapists) discovery that the variance due to the psychiatrist was actually greater than the variance due whether the patient received a placebo or an antidepressant (9.1%: 3.4%; or on another measure, 6.7%: 5.9%). The best-performing psychiatrist got better outcomes with placebos than the worst-performing psychiatrist got with imipramine.

Despite their current popularity, alternative agents such as St. John's wort (*Hypericum perforatum*) and SAMEe (sadenosylmethionine) have not been shown to be effective in the research. Dosage varies from one commercial product to another, and serious drug interactions are possible. Antidepressants are often prescribed for bipolar patients, but only experienced psychopharmacologists should do so. *Antidepressants can trigger mania, hypomania, and rapid cycling in bipolar patients*, and there are too many cases when the diagnosis of bipolar disorder is made only *after* an unfortunate experience with antidepressants. Expectant or lactating mothers also need special psychopharmacological expertise. Inadequate evidence about potential risks to the fetus or newborn from antidepressants make clinical expertise vital when prescribing them.

Kaiser Psychiatry's Depression Best Practices team recommends that most patients stay on an initial course of antidepressants at the full therapeutic dose for 6 to 9 months (Kaiser Permanente, 2006). After the first episode of treatment, if the patient is doing well, the medication should be discontinued, since only 50% of patients will have another episode. If the full depressive episode recurs during or shortly after the discontinuation, the initial episode has probably not run its course and medication should be reinitiated, typically for another 4 to 9 months. Discontinuation should be tapered over several weeks and slowed further if there are signs of withdrawal. Tapering is especially important with paroxetine (Paxil).

Figure 10.5 shows an imaging study of patients who responded and did not respond to SSRI treatment. As noted, the medication, like psychotherapy, lowers activity in Area 25; but in contrast to therapy, antidepressants activate the prefrontal cortex.

When Should a Therapist Refer for a Medication Evaluation?

A referral for medication is called for when patients present with certain characteristics, including:

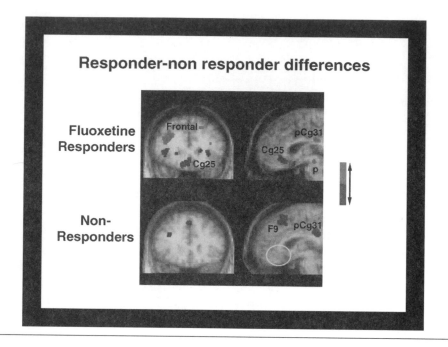

Figure 10.5 Imaging Study of the Brains of Fluoxetine (Prozac) Responders and Nonresponders

- Suicidal preoccupations or impulses
- Psychotic symptoms
- Significant functional impairment in memory or attention
- Impairment in the capacity to maintain vital relationships (e.g. parenting)
- Marked sleep disturbance
- Major changes in appetite and weight

In severe cases, antidepressants should be initiated without delay. The presence of stressors does not preclude a medication trial. In acute cases of adjustment disorder, a brief course of symptom-specific brief medications, such as trazodone (Desyrel) for transient sleep disturbance and short-term use of benzodiazepines for acute, situationally based comorbid anxiety may be therapeutic. For patients with major depressive disorder, antidepressants should be considered. Antidepressants can be an effective treatment for some patients with dysthymic disorder, but psychotherapy is the treatment of choice.

Cultural and Ethnic Factors

Among many ethnic and racial groups, somatic complaints are a culturally sanctioned way of expressing emotional distress. Depressed patients who report many or primarily physical symptoms may be resistant to both psychotherapy and medications. Asking patients about their concerns at the start of treatment can help. Where the therapist's and patient's racial or ethnic background differ, it is generally a good practice to inquire about the patient's feelings about the differences, and to do so on more than one occasion, if for no other reason than to clarify that this is a legitimate topic of conversation about which many people have strong feelings.

Integrated Care

All therapists see many depressed patients. A strong working relationship with one or more prescribing clinicians will help psychotherapists deliver the best outcomes for patients. We can help patients through the early period of adjusting to medication, especially before they experience any positive benefit from it. Combining psychotherapy with pharmacotherapy can enhance medication adherence, improve maintenance of treatment gains, and reduce the chance of relapse. If the psychopharmacologist neglects to do so, therapists can refer depressed patients for a medical workup to rule out the presence of conditions such as hypothyroidism, anemia, cancers (particularly of the pancreas), stroke, and dementia, as any of these conditions produce symptoms mimicking depressive disorders. If patients are taking medication for a medical problem (e.g., propranolol [Inderal] for hypertension), it may cause depression as a side effect.

Recent imaging studies make it clear that psychotherapy and antidepressant medication perform complementary functions to restore appropriate mood regulation. One model of this process is shown in Figure 10.6.

Because Elana's depression fit the *DSM*'s "five of nine symptoms" test for major depressive disorder, and because the mood disorder was adversely affecting relationships and her work, the therapist discussed a referral for a medication evaluation. A reasonable skeptic, Elana agreed to get more information and after the consultation, she started taking sertraline (Zoloft). When the therapist checked with her about how she felt about the process, she said, "What did it for me was that the doctor explained how it's not just a drug. She said it's a medicine and it only works if I have the kind of depression that will be helped by it. I just wish it didn't take three weeks to find out if it's going to work."

In Elana's thought records, what emerged as a core belief intimately related to her moods was that *love is always conditional.* "If you don't make

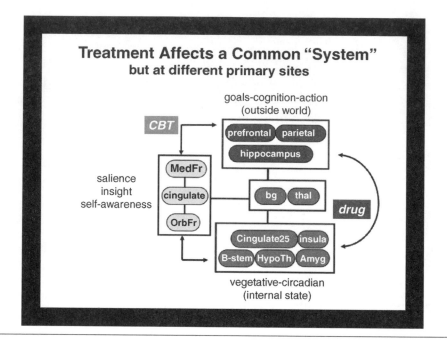

Figure 10.6 Integrated CBT-Antidepressant Treatment *Source:* After Mayberg, 2006; reprinted by permission).

yourself indispensable, you'll be disposed of." Deep worries about abandonment were activated by the loss of her grandmother and by the preemptive strike she launched against her ex-boyfriend. In a therapy that lasted 23 weeks, Elana created a more mature and coherent autobiography for herself. Using CBT methods and a good alliance with the therapist, she was able to partially rewire the neural networks involved in her attachment patterns and rebalance the books between right- and left-hemispheric functioning. More plainly, "I feel great; now I'm going to lose some weight."

CHAPTER 11

Exercise, Sleep, and Mindfulness

"There are twelve hours in the day, and above fifty in the night."

—Marie de Rabutin-Chantal

I N THE *PAX medica*, psychology inherited Freud's legacy of a disembodied model of the mind and behavior, while psychiatry became increasingly preoccupied with pharmacological interventions. In the process, something important dropped out of *all* the mental health professions. Because of the special biology of the brain, the mind not only affects the quality of internal life and the behaviors available to us but is itself structurally affected by these factors. The results of imaging studies discussed in Chapter 10 make this point quite dramatically. Mind, brain, and behavior are cocreators of our moods, memories, and habits.

Although we require that our patients share with us the most intimate details of their relational life, many therapists still hesitate to inquire into more mundane—but equally impactful—factors, such as sleep and exercise. These domains also shape the biology of the brain. If patients do not exercise or get adequate sleep, is it safe to assume that they will start doing so after completing treatment for anxiety or depression? We maintain that *focusing on these areas is an important part of therapy itself.* Taking care of the brain's biological needs contributes to the overall goal of treatment, which is helping patients achieve a more balanced and happier state of mind. In this final chapter we focus on three areas that can help promote a healthy brain and a healthy psyche: exercise, sleep, and mindfulness. Promoting patients' formation of healthy habits in these areas beneficially effects mood and affect regulation after termination.

EXERCISE

People who exercise on a regular basis are better able to deal with stress and are less anxious and depressed. The biochemical changes occurring as a result of physical exertion mute anxiety and raise the levels of endorphins, a biochemical intervention that often compares favorably to the effects of prescribed medication. Exercise enhances oxygenation of the blood, lowers its acidity (pH), and results in an overall increase in energy level. Interestingly, aerobic exercise improves the blood supply to the brain, enhancing the growth of cranial capillaries (Kolb, 1995).

The so-called runner's high is the result of the release of endorphins, which are natural brain opioids. The euphoric mellow feeling we get after exercise may also be enhanced by reductions in cortisol. For depressed patients, exercising forces the brain stem's amnergic system to increase output because more norepinephrine is needed to rev up the heart rate. This charge-up of norepinephrine occurs also in the brain. As noted earlier, some antidepressant medications work to increase the transmission of noreprinphrine.

Since the early 1990s, more than 100 studies have looked at the relationship between exercise and depression, and there are good meta-analytic reviews of the results as well (Calfas & Taylor, 1994; North et al., 1990). These studies confirm that exercise results in a moderate improvement in depressive symptoms. The longer the program, the more intense the exercise, and the more days per week it is engaged in, the greater the antidepressant effects (North et al., 1990).

Exercise has also been shown to be a moderately effective intervention for anxiety (Calfas & Taylor, 1984). As with depression, an aerobic exercise program that engaged participants who had not been exercising regularly and that kept them engaged for more than 10 weeks showed the greatest effectiveness. In some measure, the anxiolytic effects of exercise may be the result of changes in blood chemistry monitored by the amygdala.

Blood levels of the hormone thyroxine, produced by the thyroid, increase by about 30% during exercise and remain elevated for some period of time afterward. Elevations of thyroxine are associated with the subjective experience of increased energy. When thyroxine is low (as occurs in hypothyroidism), energy is reduced, and this decline tends to be associated with depression. Blood levels of insulin begin to decrease approximately 10 minutes into an aerobic exercise session and continue to decrease after 70 minutes of exercise. Regular exercise also increases a cell's resting sensitivity to insulin. Exercise can have a profound positive effect on one's vulnerability to diabetes, a disorder associated with significant adverse mental health consequences.

Cortisol aids in the conversion of proteins and lipids to usable carbohydrates, replenishing energy supplies for facing problems and challenges. However, as we have noted throughout this book, chronically elevated cortisol levels are an important ingredient in many dysphoric states of mind. Chronically high levels of the neurohormone detrimentally affect the hippocampus, the amygdala, and the prefrontal cortex (PFC) (see Chapters 6 and 7). When these physiological aspects of the stress response are combined with the sedentary lifestyles lead by many of our patients, the potentially adverse effects of elevated cortisol are heightened. Cortisol prepares us for physical action; the lack of it prolongs elevated cortisol levels in the bloodstream and inhibits the reestablishment of allostasis at a less stressful set point. Patients whose craving for carbohydrates increases at such times have an additional factor to contend with if they are not working off this accumulated fuel through exercise. The combined lack of physical activity, sustained high levels of cortisol, and increased carbohydrate consumption impedes the action of insulin and promotes glucose uptake. High insulin and high cortisol, in turn, lead to fat deposits and atherosclerotic plaques in coronary arteries, increasing the potential for heart disease.

Fascinating recent research on the neurodynamic effects of exercise has zeroed in on the hippocampus. Fred Gage is one of the pioneering neuroscientists who discovered neurogenesis (Gage, 2000; Alborn, Nordborg, Peterson, & Gage, 1998). In animal studies using mice as subjects, Gage demonstrated that although all his subjects showed growth of new cells in the hippocampus, the more athletic subjects—those who jogged more minutes on the treadmills—produced up to three times as many as their sedentary colleagues. Healthier hippocampi are associated not only with better memories but faster cognitive processing. Exercise may be one of the more reliable ways to attain these goals.

If patients can find a form of exercise they actually enjoy or that involves a perk, such as socializing with a "gym buddy," the chances of pursuing the routine goes up substantially. Some routines involve commitment to a schedule while others can be performed spontaneously. Stretching, walking, or performing an aerobic exercise such as running or bicycle riding all promote relaxation and a greater sense of well-being.

SLEEP

Sleep has been studied extensively for more than 80 years. Researchers have identified three types and numerous stages of sleep. The major types are slow wave, fast wave, and dream (rapid eye movement [REM]) sleep. Although we generally go through REM periods every 90 minutes in the course of a night's sleep, most of REM is skewed to the later portion of our sleep cycle. It comprises 25% of overall sleep time in healthy adults. In contrast, the slowest-wave sleep occurs earlier in the cycle.

Sleep Stages

Stage 1 is a transition state between waking and sleeping. Brain waves are fast; they are referred to as low-amplitude and high-frequency waves. Subjects awakened from this stage of sleep report that they were not really asleep.

In stage 2, sleep is light, and the brain waves are referred to as theta waves. Many insomnia patients complain that they do not sleep when in fact they are experiencing stage 2 sleep. We spend half of the night in stage 2 sleep. Stage 2 sleep increases during periods of stress relative to slow-wave or deep sleep.

Stages 3 and 4 are considered deep sleep. It is in this phase of the cycle that we produce slow brain waves (delta waves). Deep sleep gives our immune system a boost while allowing body functions to slow down. If deprived of deep sleep, our immune system tends to be suppressed and our bodies ache. Because stress increases the release of noreinephrine and epinephrine, deep-sleep deprivation also promotes a decrease in slow-wave sleep. In the sleep deprived, the first stage of sleep to rebound is deep sleep, perhaps indicating its importance in overall alliostasis.

Like stage 1 sleep, REM sleep is composed of low-amplitude and high-frequency brain waves. The amount of time we spend in REM decreases as we age. In REM, most body functions are at almost wakeful levels of activation. Metabolism goes up during REM sleep, and energizing neuro-transmitters are active. REM sleep is called paradoxical sleep for this reason. We may dream that we are running, and most of our organs function as if we were doing exactly that.

Although it is never used for diagnostic purposes in psychiatry, one of the most reliable biological markers for depression is early-onset REM sleep. The normal sleep cycle and the cycle typical of depressives is shown in Figures 11.1 and 11.2, respectively.

The neurodynamic dysregulation involving the sleep cycle in depression may be related to another biological marker, hyperactivity in the frontal lobes, particularly in the right hemisphere. One of the functions of REM sleep is thought to be the facilitation of transferring the content learned from the day into longer-term memory storage. In one study, researchers concluded that they detected replays of the day's events occurring in the neocortex and the hippocampus. Repeated cycles of neural activation

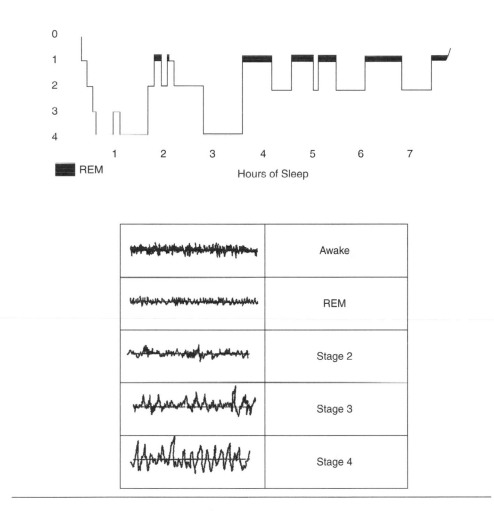

Figure 11.1   The Normal Sleep Cycle

alternating between the hippocampus and neocortex were synchronized, as if the two regions were having a dialogue (Ji & Wilson, 2007). Other reviews of the evidence cast down on the relationship between REM and memory consolidation. As Marcos Frank and Joel Benington summarize the research, "despite a steady accumulation of positive findings over the past decade, the precise role of sleep in memory and brain plasticity remains elusive" (Frank & Beninington 2006, p. 477).

Many depressed patients complain about sleep problems, perhaps because, from a neurodynamic perspective, they are impacted by two changes in brain functioning: overactivation of the right frontal lobe processing and

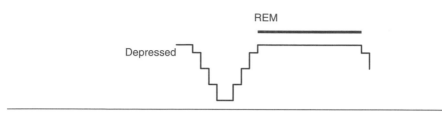

Figure 11.2   Early Onset and Prolonged REM Sleep in Depression

diminished functioning in the hippocampus, which facilitate or accompany the individual's withdrawal from the world. Energy flows away from these brain modules and toward the prefrontal cortical areas concerned with thinking and emotional processing—both relatively involutional processes. When sleep is disrupted, the dysregulation may intensify this withdrawal process, expressed in overactivation of the right hemisphere and its negative emotions, and underactivation of the left hemisphere, with its sunnier affects. Often a goal that is as important as getting patients back out into the world and into the relational surroundings of marriage, family, job, and avocations is helping them get back to sleep. People who are depressed frequently experience early-morning awakening and awaken during REM sleep. Too much REM sleep contributes to depression, and REM deprivation has been shown to help alleviate depression. Sleep-deprived people generally recover about half of the REM they have lost when given a chance to resume normal sleeping patterns, and REM rebound occurs only after they regain slow-wave sleep.

Overall, sleep patterns are rhythmically tied to the light of the day and the dark of night. Light is taken in through the eyes and retina, which send the information to the pineal gland to stop producing melatonin, thereby signaling the brain that it is daytime and not time for sedation. In contrast, when it is dark outside, our retina sends information to the pineal gland that it should produce melatonin to induce sedation.

Our circadian rhythm is tied to both exposure to light and body temperature (Czeiler & Khalsa, 2000). Ideally, when we go to sleep at night, our body temperature is dropping. Just before we rise from bed, our body temperature is on the rise. When we get out of bed, the exposure to light and movement of our body promotes a rise in body temperature.

Sleep Problems

Virtually everyone has had insomnia at some point in life. For many people it is an ongoing problem. Approximately half the population reports trouble sleeping once a week, and 15% have trouble sleeping two or more nights a week. Sleep problems are especially common among people experiencing anxiety or depression (Ford & Kamerow, 1989). When we are tense and preoccupied, it is difficult to "unwind" and sleep. Stress raises the levels of the activating neurotransmitters norepinephrine and epinephrine, which normally subside at night. Patients who are experiencing stress, anxiety, or depression may keep themselves charged up and tense by thinking about what is waiting for them the next day. Since the problem is widespread and medical help is typically pharmacological in nature, it is a good practice to have some tips at hand regarding behavioral interventions for insomnia.

According to both the American Psychiatric Association (1994) and the American Sleep Disorders Association (1997), the symptoms of primary insomnia include:

- A subjective complaint of problems initiating and maintaining sleep, daytime fatigue associated with the sleep disturbance, and other significant distress or impairment in social or occupation functioning
- A duration of a month or more (*Diagnostic and Statistical Manual of Mental Disorders*, 4th ed.) or 6 months (International Classification of Sleep Disorders)
- The sleep disturbance includes a sleep latency of more than 30 minutes or awakening more than 30 minutes before desired time and before cumulative sleep time exceeds 6.5 hours
- The experience occurs 3 or more nights per week

These symptoms are indicative of primary insomnia and are similar to the sleep problems seen in patients with generalized anxiety disorder (GAD) and some forms of depression (Hauri & Fischer, 1986). Indeed, a significant number of patients seek treatment for insomnia. Ironically, *excessive worry* about the lack of sleep contributes to the problem for GAD-related insomnia.

There are two types of insomnia, early insomnia and sleep-maintenance insomnia. Patients with early insomnia have difficulty getting to sleep. In sleep-maintenance insomnia, they have difficulty staying asleep. They may fall asleep without difficulty but wake up in the middle of the night and have trouble getting back to sleep. To diagnose either type of insomnia, at least 1.5 hours must elapse while lying in bed trying to sleep.

People tend to overestimate the time that it takes for them to get to sleep. If stressed, even a little time awake feels like hours. A person troubled by not being able to sleep will probably overestimate the time they went without sleep. The issue is not just sleep loss but the meaning patients assign to it, what they tell themslves about why they lost sleep (and what the consequences will be) that determines the ill effects of sleep loss. Although patients with GAD may feel otherwise, there are no clear consequences from not getting to sleep during the first several minutes. In fact, researchers in sleep labs usually regard people who can get to sleep in under 15 minutes as having a unique form of sleep disorder. In such cases, this shortened sleep latency time is the result of a rebound effect, making up for sleep lost the previous night.

Sleep-maintenance insomnia problems can also be overestimated. Most people wake up in the middle of the night. But if it takes patients more than 1 hour to get back to sleep, they probably have sleep-maintenance insomnia. Moderate sleep loss generally has been shown to negatively affect mood. The negative impact on mood will be greater among people who become angry and concerned about sleep loss than on those who just take it in stride. A positive emotional valence—for example, a parent of a newborn who sees it as just one aspect of the love and concern she feels for her baby—can take the focus off sleeping per se. In contrast, insomniacs often overreact and overestimate both the actual dimensions of the problem and its seriousness.

Many people with insomnia have difficulty regulating their body temperature. Because of less physical activity in the daytime, some insomnia patients tend to have a body temperature that increases at night when it should be dropping. Thus, failing to exercise during the day results in less of a dip in body temperature in the night. To correct these problems, patients should be encouraged to keep their rooms cool during bedtime and to exercise in the late afternoon. When they get up in the morning, they should be exposed to the light so that their bodies can adjust to the correct body temperature cycle.

Most people feel worse immediately upon awakening from a sleep-deprived night. As their body temperature rises, they are exposed to light, they engage in activity, and they generally feel better. The way we think about our sleep deprivation after a "sleepless night," however, affects how we feel the rest of the day. If we regard it as a major problem, our mood will be dampened and we are likely to continue to feel poorly.

Since most sleep research takes place in universities, we know much about the effects of sleep deprivation on college students. It has been shown that those who are sleep deprived but have managed at least 5 hours of sleep suffer no significant drop in cognitive functioning. However, subjects who get fewer than 5 hours of sleep show measurable negative cognitive effects.

More support for the 5-hour hypothesis comes from an interesting source. A prominent sleep researcher and avid sailboat racer assessed the performance of around-the-world racers (Dement, 1976). He found that sailors who slept fewer than 5 hours placed poorly in the race, because they made navigational mistakes. Racers who managed just 5 hours of sleep placed higher than either of the other two groups. Many researchers now regard 5 hours of sleep as the minimum biological requirement. For this reason, 5 hours is sometimes referred to as core sleep. It is during core sleep that we receive all of our slow-wave sleep and half of our REM sleep. Despite losing 50% of our optimal REM total, we get almost normal amounts of stages 3 and 4 sleep.

Common Causes of Insomnia: Many factors contribute to insomnia, including, aging, medical conditions, and drugs. As we age, the quality of our sleep deteriorates. We wake up more and spend more time in light sleep. To complicate this problem, many older people spend time indoors and are exposed to less natural light, which dysregulates their circadian rhythms. Also, loss of social cues, such as eating dinner in the early evening or waking up at set times, negatively impacts the sleep cycle.

Lifestyle factors such as diet, bedtime schedules, and environmental factors contribute to patients' insomnia. Some agents and practices to be considered and inquired about when evaluating sleep problems include the following:

- Caffeine
- Nicotine
- Alcohol
- Sugar
- Heavy meals before bedtime
- Hunger
- Exercise just before bedtime
- No exercise at all
- Daytime naps
- Computer use in the late evening
- Warm bedrooms
- Sporadic and novel noise
- Light
- Poor mattress
- Poor air quality in the bedroom
- High body temperature

Some people try to improve their sleep by using techniques that actually exacerbate sleep problems. Alcohol precipitates a reduction in the deepest stage of sleep (stage 4) and REM sleep. It can also contribute to mid-sleep cycle awakening because the alcohol is wearing off during the night.

Several medical conditions are associated with insomnia. Therapists are advised to ask patients about the presence of any of these if insomnia is a complaint. Some of the conditions contributing to insomnia are:

- Arthritis
- Asthma
- Bronchitis
- Cancer
- Epilepsy
- Fibromyalgia
- Heart disease
- Huntington's disease
- Hypertension
- Hyperthyroidism
- Kidney disease
- Parkinson's disease

A number of treatments also have been found to cause insomnia. Many physicians do not take the time to warn patients that insomnia is a side effect of prescribed medication. A few of the medications that contribute to insomnia include:

- Appetite suppressants
- Asthma medications
- Decongestants
- Corticosteroids
- Diuretics
- Heart medications
- Kidney medications
- Parkinson's medications

How Therapists Can Help: Patients willing to consider behavioral suggestions for improving their sleep should first make sure that their beds are for two purposes only: sleep and sex. If they toss and turn for more than 1 hour, they should get up and go to another room. Getting out of bed allows their body temperature to drop and may shake up the neurodynamics of lying in bed thinking about the fact that they are still awake.

The effectiveness of behavioral approaches to improving sleep rests on the patient preferences and on the strength of the therapeutic alliance. But just as cognitive-behavioral therapy (CBT) has been shown to affect brain metabolism, behaviorally oriented sleep treatments can retune a badly misaligned sleep neurophysiology and contribute to the recovery of depressed patients.

Paradoxically, patients should not try too hard to go to sleep. Placing too high a value on sleep results in worrying about not getting enough. Research has shown that trying to fall asleep promotes muscle tension and elevated heart rate, blood pressure, and stress hormones. A vivid example of how this occurs was demonstrated in one study that offered participants a chance to compete with others for a cash prize awarded to whomever could get to sleep the quickest. Participants took twice as long as they usually did to fall asleep (Jabobs, 1999).

Patients whose insomnia is having a serious negative impact on their lives may be interested in and encouraged to try more formal behavioral treatment for sleep disorders. Sleep scheduling is an important behavioral practice for helping patients reestablish normal sleep schedules. By adjusting the time they go to bed—for example, by staying up considerably later than usual—patients will build up "sleep pressure" to go to sleep and stay asleep through the night. People who are sleep deprived fall asleep earlier the next night to "catch up" on lost sleep. Where waking up has become a neurodynamic attractor for patients and they assign considerable importance to the problem, it is usually a good practice to establish a schedule that is commensurate with reconditioning the system. The common practice of sleeping in in the morning is only likely to make it more difficult to sleep the next night. Sleep scheduling, by contrast, requires that patients get up in the morning at the usual time no matter how much sleep they managed to get the previous night. Somewhat counterintuitively, rather than going to bed *earlier*, they will be going to bed *later*.

The second component of the more formal CBT approach to insomnia is cognitive analysis. Negative sleep thoughts (NSTs) can promote temporary insomnia to the status of long-term insomnia. NSTs are essentially inaccurate ideas about sleep that create a self-fulfilling prophecy. If patients believe these NSTs, they will have more difficulty falling asleep again because of the buildup of stress. NSTs will result in negative emotions, such as anger, and result in activating the biochemical changes associated with these emotions. The NSTs are the first link in a chain of events that ends in insomnia.

Ask patients to identify their false thoughts and replace them with accurate information about sleep. For example, if people wake up in the middle of the night, they may interpret their wakefulness in one of these ways:

- This isn't great but at least I've got my core sleep.
- If I don't get a good night's sleep tonight, I will tomorrow night.
- I may get back to sleep; I may not. Either way, it isn't the end of the world.

Adopting these thoughts will paradoxically enable patients to get back to sleep if they wake up. By adopting accurate thoughts about sleep, patients can take the pressure off themselves and relax enough to get to sleep. In addition, patients may tell themselves that while they are lying in bed, they might as well use the time to relax. Relaxation methods, such as diaphragmatic breathing, are helpful to quiet the mind down. Teaching patients to practice relaxation during the daytime will help them sleep at night. Relaxation methods work best if practiced twice daily, once during the day and once before bed. They serve to reduce the effect of stress.

Patients should be encouraged to calculate how many hours they actually sleep on average and then add 1 hour to the total. Use this formula to schedule how much sleep time patients should allow themselves. For example, if patients have averaged 5 hours of sleep for the past month, despite staying in bed for 8 hours, they can allow themselves 6 hours of potential sleep time. If their normal wakeup time has been 6:00 A.M., they can go to bed at 11:30 P.M. They should employ this schedule for at least 4 weeks. Their goal will be to fill up most of that bedtime with sleep. Eventually their body temperature will adjust and the sleep pressure will build up so that they can make another adjustment to add another hour and sleep for 7 hours.

This approach is useful for people who have chronic insomnia, not for people who have experienced a night or two of poor sleep. For chronic insomniacs, the task is to repair the sleep cycle architecture. If a patient's sleep cycle is out of sync, sleep scheduling helps move it back into a normal pattern and more normal neurodynamics. By practicing sleep scheduling, patients will be increasing sleep efficiency.

Sleep is a normal biorhythm mediated by neurodynamic systems that are light sensitive. Patients with insomnia should also be advised to avoid activities, such as computer use, before bedtime because such activities stimulate the PFC to override drowsiness. Looking at the computer screen for extended periods of time is essentially looking at a light source, and light triggers daytime neurodynamic patterns. The pineal gland is signaled to suppress or secrete the sleep hormone melatonin based on the presence of light taken in through the retina. Patients should be encouraged to use soft light a few hours before going to sleep.

Researchers at Stanford University studied the effect of exercise on sleep in adults ages 55 to 75 and found that those who exercised 20 to 30 minutes in the afternoon reduced the time that it took to go to sleep by one-half Dement, 1976). Two meta-analytic studies have shown that exercise increases overall sleep efficiency (Kubitz et al., 1996; O'Connor & Youngstedt, 1995). These studies demonstrate that, with exercise, there is an increase not only in sleep time but in slow-wave sleep. Exercising 3 to 6 hours in advance of bedtime is a good practice because the exercise elevates heart rate and body temperature, yet allows body temperature to drop before bedtime. Patients may want to know that aerobic exercise not only has a calming and antidepressant effect but that it also helps promote sleep, especially if completed before the early evening.

Patients who complain of early-morning awakening may be helped by being exposed to bright light in the early morning. This will insure that melatonin production will be low throughout the day and that their body temperature will be the lowest when they sleep. Patients with sleep-maintenance insomnia should be exposed to bright light in the late morning. This promotes lowered body temperature in the middle hours of their sleep cycles and the likelihood of staying asleep.

Similarly, it is a good sleep-promoting practice for patients to keep their body temperature low at night. A cool bedroom will promote the deepest sleep. Warm bedrooms, by contrast, promote light sleep. Hot baths may also be helpful as a wind-down activity. Although they raise body temperature while in the tub, the temperature drops sharply by bedtime.

Diet also has a major effect on sleep. Foods rich in tryptophan (an amino acid that converts to serotonin) contributes to sedation, while protein-rich foods (such as fish) make one less sleepy. Consuming simple carbohydrates such as white bread is also contraindicated. Complex carbohydrates, such as whole wheat bread, are helpful. Whereas simple carbohydrates increase insulin, leading to increased tryptophan and ultimately more serotonin, this conversion occurs on a short-term basis only. Simple carbohydrates result in increased blood glucose, and patients may awaken during the sleep cycle. By consuming complex carbohydrates, patients will trigger serotonin conversion on a long-term basis and a slow and sustained rise in glucose.

Vitamin levels can also affect sleep. Deficiencies of B vitamins, calcium, and magnesium may inhibit sleep. Taking a calcium-magnesium tablet at night will promote relaxation and may also help restless leg syndrome, a condition characterized by an irresistible urge to move one's body to stop uncomfortable or odd sensations. The condition typically affects the legs, but may also involve the arms and torso.

Since our brains are geared to pay attention to novelty, patients should be advised to minimize nonrepetitive sights and sounds that invite attention. The television should go off well before bedtime because it will periodically grab attention and wake people up. "White noise," such as a fan, is monotonous and serves as a good muffler for other noises, such as barking dogs. Some people keep a fan on all night long to provide white noise. Another useful technique is the use of good-quality earplugs to filter out noises.

SOPORIFICS

We live in a society still caught in the throws of the *pax medica*, which inspires in many of us the hope that we can find the answer to complex neurodynamic problems in a pill. Millions of people treat their insomnia with over-the-counter sleep drugs or physician-prescribed benzodiazepines. Over-the-counter sleep aids such as Sominex and Excedrin PM contain diphenhydramine (Benadryl) and do produce some sedation. But it has been shown that these sleep aids also rely on a significant placebo effect. Upon waking the next morning, patients who use these agents may experience the "groggies" and have more difficulty concentrating.

Primary care physicians often prescribe sleep medications, such as zolpidem tartrate (Ambien), or a nonbenzodiazepine medication, such as trazodone (Desyrel), for sleep problems. Although a substantial number of sleep problems are mediated by overall neurodynamic dysregulations (such as is the case with depression), it is often possible to help patients sleep better by using behavioral techniques instead of medications. If consulted for advice, therapists should let patients know that over-the-counter sleep aids suppress important stages of sleep. They can also lead to tolerance and withdrawal. In other words, more of the drug will be needed to achieve the same effect.

Two major surveys of hundreds of studies on the effectiveness of treatment for insomnia have shown that sleep medications are relatively ineffective (quoted in Jacobs, 1999). Benzodiazapines are half as effective as behavioral approaches. Benzodiazepines are not effective as a long-term treatment for insomnia because they produce tolerance and withdrawal. Most patients who take them on a regular basis will experience daytime grogginess and shallow sleep and suffer from withdrawal when they try sleeping without them, making it even harder to sleep. Patients who are taking sleep medications should not stop them abruptly, however. Withdrawal should be a gradual, self-paced tapering process. At Kaiser we recommend that withdrawal from benzodiazepines be supervised by a physician. These two guidelines are important:

1. Week 1: Reduce the dose one night during the week. It is advisable to choose an easy night, such as a weekend night, for initiating the process.
2. Week 2: Reduce the dose two nights per week, spacing the nights apart to ensure that they are not consecutive.

Continue this pattern until patients achieve sleep with no medication.

We recommend informing patients of all of the ideas for improving sleep that we've mentioned in this section, throwing a broad net to catch all factors. A summary list includes the following suggestions:

- Beds are for sleeping and sex. Do not watch television, balance the checkbook, discuss finances with your spouse, or argue in bed. Make the bed carry only one association: sleep.
- If you do not sleep and find yourself tossing and turning, get up and go to another room.
- Do not try too hard to go to sleep. It will frustrate you and have a paradoxical effect. Try telling yourself "It's okay if I get just a few hours sleep tonight. I will catch up tomorrow night." This change in expectation will free you to relax and get to sleep. The harder you try the harder it will be to induce sleep. That is how the brain works!
- Avoid drinking large quantities of liquid at night. Drinking a lot will lower the sleep threshold and cause you to wake up to urinate.
- Avoid bright light at least a few hours before going to sleep. Do not work on the computer into the late evening.
- Do all planning for the next day before you get into bed. If you think of something you need to remember, get up and write it down. This will help postpone thinking or worrying about anything until the next day.
- Avoid daytime naps. Naps are a way to steal sleep from the nighttime.
- Try eating a light snack with complex carbohydrates before bed. Foods rich in tryptophan are advisable. Do not eat anything with sugar or salt before bed.
- Avoid protein snacks at night because protein blocks the synthesis of serotonin and promotes alertness.
- Exercise 3 to 6 hours before going to bed.

- If noise bothers you, use earplugs.
- Avoid alcohol within 2 hours of bedtime.
- If you are troubled by chronic insomnia, try the sleep scheduling technique.
- Try using relaxation exercises (see "Mindfulness, below"). To help you go to sleep or go back to sleep if you awaken during the night.

MIA AND THE BASE

When Mia came in for a consultation regarding sleep problems and what she suspected was chronic fatigue, it quickly became apparent that her attitude about sleep was contributing to sleep loss and stress. The problem started when her old supervisor got promoted and a new one transferred into her unit. A Medicaid eligibility worker, Mia said she had already felt stressed as a consequence of turnover in her unit and the "constantly changing" eligibility guidelines. One of her new supervisor's first actions was to announce that she would be auditing 10 cases from each worker.

Mia worried the audit would show how far behind she was and that her work was not good enough. She started having trouble getting to sleep and dropped the Weight Watchers regimen she had been using successfully to guide her nutrition for the last three years. At night, she worked on her computer to teach herself the new programs being introduced at work. To get to sleep, she started taking over-the-counter sleep aids and drank a glass or two of wine while she watched the 11 o'clock news on television. Mia thought she needed 8 hours of sleep every night and had maintained that standard for years. But now she was consistently losing 2 hours of sleep each night. She started to worry that she would make mistakes because of her sleep loss.

When she came in for counseling and met Susan, one of our interns, Mia was preoccupied with making more mistakes as a result of the lost hours of sleep. Worrying about it was keeping her tossing and turning. "I need this job," she said, "and that audit's coming up in three weeks. I just feel like I'm freaking out about it." Mia felt she needed a quick fix in the form of sleep medication. Susan went to her supervisor, Robert, to discuss the referral for a medication evaluation.

Robert suggested that before making a decision about a medical evaluation, they look at the BASE issues in Mia's case. A discussion of the system concepts, the s in the acronym, led them to focus on the diagnosis of Mia's sleep problem. Looked at in this way, it appeared that Mia's attempts to deal with the problem were actually exacerbating it, and it might be helpful to lower her anxiety level about the consequences. What she was suffering from was an anxiety-induced sleep problem. Robert also suggested that Susan think about whether Mia met the criteria for GAD.

Robert and Susan decided to work with Mia to develop sleep hygiene techniques consistent with evidence-based practice. Robert explained to Mia that several factors contributed to her brain's inability to get to sleep, including her computer use, its consequent suppression of melatonin production, the changes in her diet, the confounding influence of over-the-counter sleep aids, her lack of exercise, and late-evening alcohol use. Mia also contributed to her sleeplessness by worrying about her sleep loss. Eliminating these factors instead of introducing medication became the target of the treatment.

Mia agreed to enroll in a sleep class at Kaiser and was surprised to learn that she was getting enough core sleep to keep her functioning reasonably well, even if it was less than she felt she needed. She Googled this finding to confirm it and then began to feel some relief that perhaps sleeplessness would not automatically lead to failing the audit and losing her job. She worried a little less about her mistakes and found that she actually made fewer of them. Encouraged, she made other changes in her pre-bedtime behavior, giving up her glasses of wine and the 11 o'clock news. She met again with Susan to share some of this information. They worked out a schedule for doing as much as she could to clean up the backlog of open files at work and also to schedule time when she was not going to worry about it. To her satisfaction, her sleep improved steadily over the next week.

MINDFULNESS

As noted, Walter Cannon first drew our attention to the fight-or-flight response; its counterpoint is what Herbert Benson (2000) called the relaxation response. The relaxation response involves activating the parasympathetic nervous system that lowers heart rate and metabolism, and slows down breathing. The sympathetic nervous system activates our body during the fight-or-flight response; the parasympathetic nervous system calms us down during the relaxation response. A number of techniques can be employed to evoke this response, including self-hypnosis, visual imagery, and meditation. Many of these techniques involve a focus on breathing.

Relaxation in the form of meditation with yoga includes stretching, which promotes physiological as well as psychological relaxation. A considerable amount of energy is wasted in maintaining muscle tension. Chronic stress builds up in muscles, making tendons thicken and shorten due to the overdevelopment of connective tissue. Stress also contributes to overactivity of the sympathetic nervous system, resulting in tension buildup in an already taxed system. One quick way to get rid of that buildup of tension is to stretch. Our muscles are endowed with a rich blood supply. Both exercise and stretching promote better blood flow to our muscles and result in the energized feeling of relaxation. By stretching our muscles, we force the used and deoxygenated blood back for refueling in the lungs. Enriched blood flow refreshes and invigorates muscles and facilitates the release of tension.

Jon Kabat-Zinn has been a pioneering force in bringing one relaxation and attention-training methodology into mainstream medicine and psychology. After getting a PhD in molecular biology, Kabat-Zinn felt he wanted to do something more with his life than pursue an academic or scientific career. He found his own Buddhist meditation to be a useful tool in focusing his attention and clearing his mind. In 1979 Kabat-Zinn began teaching Mindfulness-Based Stress Reduction at the Stress Reduction Clinic at the University of Massachusetts Hospital. This 8-week course combines meditation and Hatha yoga to help patients cope with stress, pain, and illness by using "mindfulness," or moment-to-moment awareness (Kabat-Zinn, 1990). Concurrently, Kabat-Zinn and his colleagues conducted a number of studies on the effects of mindfulness on the brain's emotion regulation system (particularly under stress) and on the body's immune system (Davidson, Kabat-Zinn, et al., 2003).

While CBT is usually taught in the form of a specific treatment for a specific disorders, mindfulness presents itself as an approach that is helpful with many aspects of life (the "full catastrophe," as Kabat-Zinn calls it). The psychotherapy outcome literature suggests a similar conclusion: it's not necessary to break down suffering into the bite-sized categories of the *Diagnostic and Statiscal Manual* in order to help someone overcome it. Likewise, brain imaging studies of the neurodynamic changes of successful CBT and IPT treatment tend to show similar effects, regardless of specific variations in technique. Imaging studies of mindfulness show significant increases in activation of the left prefrontal cortex, a pattern previously associated with positive affect, in meditators compared with nonmeditators (Davidson & Kabat-Zinn, et al., 2003). Significant increases in antibody titers to influenza vaccine were also found among subjects in the meditation group compared with those in the wait-list control group. The magnitude of increase in left-hemispshere activation predicted the magnitude of antibody titer rise to the vaccine. Mindfulness meditation has now been used with borderline patients in dialectic behavior therapy (Linehan, 1993), patients with depression (Segal, Williams, & Teasdale, 2001), patients with obsessive-compulsive disorder (Baxter et al., 1992), and those with general medical problems, such as chronic pain (Kabit-Zinn, 1990).

Richard Davidson and colleagues (2000) have described the neural circuits of various affective styles and of emotional reactivity and resilience. In his Laboratory for the Study of Affective Neuroscience in Madison, Wisconsin, Davidson has shown how mindfulness training alters neural function and bolsters nonreactivity. Among other findings, he discovered a left-frontal shift occuring when we focus on an emotionally provoking activity. When we are accessing narrative functions, which normally are activated by psychotherapy, there is also a shift to the left prefrontal cortex. This shift tends to evoke positive affects and positive appraisals of experience. Further, since the left PFC is action-oriented and the right is oriented to withdrawal, this shift also implies approaching life rather than avoiding it.

One of the key tests of affective style is the individual's capacity to regulate negative affect, dysphoric experiences in which both the amygdala and the right hemisphere typically play important roles. Activation of the middle PFC is associated with both the experience of self-observation and mindfulness meditation (Cahn & Polich, 2006). This area has been described as the center of *metacognition* (thinking about thinking), or awareness. The anterior cingulate cortex (ACC) also seems to be activated during mindfulness meditation. Long-term meditators show increased thickness of the medial prefrontal cortex and also enlargement of the right insula (Lazar et al., 2005), areas closely associated with empathy and self-awareness.

Mindfulness takes as the focus of its reflective practice two subjects: breathing and the changing to-ing and fro-ing of the mind from thought to thought, feeling to feeling. The focus on breathing seems to promote a sense of the connection between the body and the mind, or an embodied mind. The superior temporal cortex is the part of the brain that pays attention to breathing and primes the body to get ready for the next breath cycle. Its activation may contribute to a sense of reflective coherence and an integration of the inner and the outer self. Subjectively, attending to one's breathing leads to a sense of neurodynamic harmony between autonomic and cortical functioning. Siegel (2007) has suggested that mindfulness promotes a kind of internal attunement that harnesses the social circuits of mirror neurons. It develops our sense of empathy for ourselves as well as others. Insofar as this leads to greater self-awareness, mindfulness refines our capacity for self-regulation.

Converging evidence from the literature in neuroscience and mindfulness suggests that just *labeling* affect may build our capacity for managing negative affective experience (Cresswell et al., 2007). Mindfulness-based cognitive therapy encourages patients to use words to label emotional states, such as "here is anger;" in "here is sadness"(Segal, Williams, & Teasdale, 2002). Affective labeling appears to activate the right ventrolateral PFC and attenuates the amygdala (Harri et al., 2000; Lieberman & Eisenberger, 2005).

This pattern of neural activation represents a top- (cortical) down (limbic-amygdala) inhibition (Aron et al., 2004), similar to that seen in brain imaging studies of depressed patients who have undergone successful psychotherapy. The process of verbal labeling of affective states reduces anxiety and negative affect (Kalisch et al., 2005; Lieberman et al., 2004; Ochsner et al., 2002). Highly proficient practioners of mindfulness show reduced activation of the PFC and the right amygdala, effects not seen in subjects regarded as low in mindfulness. These positive effects also seem to correlate with enhancements in the neural affect regulation pathways (Cresswell et al., 2007). These studies of mindfulness support the most important finding of the psychotherapy literature: many things can help mental suffering. As psychotherapists, we have learned that having access to a good relationship with a learned healer helps people. The brain is back in Western psychology, and neuroscience is building bridges to the East as well. As an adaptation of Buddhist practice, mindfulness has moved away from religious enlightenment and toward the relief of suffering and the attainment of happiness. Brain imaging will help identify which practices within this tradition are most effective in transforming the "destructive emotions" of anger, despair, and fear. Their effectiveness depends not on some miraculous agency but rather on the will and talent of the sufferer to overcome problems and on the astonishing plasticity of the human brain.

References

Abeles, M. (1991). *Corticonics: Neural circuits of the cerebral cortex*. Cambridge: Cambridge University Press.

Abercrombie, H. C., Thurow, M. E., Rosenkranz, M. A., Kalin, N. H., & Davidson, R. J. (2003). Cortisol variation in humans affects memory for emotionally laden and neutral information. *Behavioral Neuroscience, 117*, 505–516.

Adler, H. M. (2002). The sociophysiology of caring in the doctor-patient relationship. *Journal of General Medicine, 17*, 883–890.

Adolphs, R. (2003). Cognitive neuroscience of human social behavior. *Nature Reviews Neuroscience, 4*, 165–178.

Adolphs, R., Tranel, D., & Damasio, A. (1998). The human amygdala in social judgment. *Nature, 393*, 470–474.

Aguirre, G. K., Singh, R., & D'Esposito, M. (1999). Stimulus inversion and the responses of face and object-sensitive cortical areas. *NeuroReport, 10*, 189–194.

Ahern, G. L., Schomer, D. L., Kleefield, J., Blume, H., Rees-Cosgrove, G., Weintraub, S., & Mesulam, M. M. (1991). Right hemisphere advantage for evaluating emotional facial expressions. *Cortex, 27*, 193–202.

Ainsworth, M. D. S. (1968). Object relations, dependency, and attachment: A theoretical review of the infant mother relationship. *Child Development, 40*, 969–1025.

Ainsworth, M. D. S., Blehar, M. C., Waters, E., & Wall, S. (1978). *Patterns of attachment: A psychological study of the strange situation*. Hillsdale, NJ: Erlbaum.

Allen, J. G. (2001). *Traumatic relationships and serious mental disorders*. Hoboken, NJ: Wiley.

Allman, J. M. (2001). The anterior cingulate cortex: The evolution of an interface between emotion and cognition. *Annals of the New York Academy of Sciences, 935*, 107–117.

Ambrose, S. H. (2001). Paleolithic technology and human evolution. *Science 291*(5509): 1748–1753.

American Psychiatric Association (1980). *Diagnostic and statistical manual of mental disorders* (3rd ed.). Washington, DC: Author.

American Psychiatric Association (1994). *Diagnostic and statistical manual of mental disorders* (4th ed. rev.). Washington, DC: Author.

American Psychiatric Association (2000). *Diagnostic and statistical manual of mental disorders* (Text Revision). Washington, DC: Author.

American Sleep Disorders Association (1997). *International Classification of Sleep Disorders: Diagnostic and Coding Manual*. Revised ed. Rochester, MN: American Sleep Disorders Association.

Andreason, N. C. (2001). *Brave new brain: Conquering mental illness in the era of the genome*. New York: Oxford University Press.

Andrews, G., & Harvey, R. (1981). Does psychotherapy benefit neurotic patients? A re-analysis of the Smith, Glass, and Miller data. *Archives of General Psychiatry, 38*, 1203–1208.

Apfeldorf, W. J., Shear, M. K., Leon, A. C., & Portera, L. (1994). A brief screen for panic disorder. *Journal of Anxiety Disorders, 8*(1), 71–78.

Arbib M. A. (2002). Language evolution: The mirror system hypothesis. In M. A. Arbib (Ed.), *The Handbook of Brain theory and Neural Networks: Second Edition* (pp. 606–611). Cambridge, MA: MIT Press.

Arbib, M. A., Érdi, P., & Szentágothai, J. (1998). *Neural organization: Structure, function, and dynamics*. Cambridge, MA: MIT Press.

Arden, J. B. (1996). *Consciousness, dreams, and self: A transdisciplinary approach*. Madison, CT: International Universities Press/Psychosocial Press.

Arden, J. B. (in press). *Healing your anxiety workbook*. Boston: Fair Winds.

Arden, J. B. (1998). *Science, theology, and consciousness*. Westport, CT: Praeger.

Arden, J. B. & DelCorso, D. (in press). *Healing your OCD workbook*. Boston: Fair Winds.

Arden, J. B. (2002). *Surviving Job Stress*. Franklin Lake, N.J.: Career Press.

Armstrong, D., & Winstein, K. J. (2008, January 17). Exaggerated effectiveness of antidepressants. *Wall Street Journal*, p. D1.

Arnsten, A. F. T. (2000). Genetics of childhood disorders: XVIII, ADHD. Part 2: Norepinephrine has a critical modulatory influence on pre-frontal cortical function. *Journal of the American Academy of Child and Adolescent Psychiatry, 39*(9), 374.

Aston-Jones, G., Valentino, R. J., Van Bockstaele, E. J., & Meyerson, A. T. (1994). Locus coeruleus, stress, and PTSD: Neurobiology and clinical parallels. In M. M. Murburg (Ed.), *Catacholamine function in posttraumatic stress disorder: Emerging concepts.* (pp. 17–62). Washington, DC: American Psychiatric Press.

Baddeley, A. (1992). Working memory. *Science, 255*, 556–559.

Baddeley, A. (1994). The remembered self and the enacted self. In V. Neisser & R. Fivush (Eds.), *The remembering self: Construction and accuracy in the self-narrative* (pp. 236–242). Cambridge, UK: Cambridge University Press.

Baer, L., Jenike, M. A., & Minichiello, W. E. (1986). *Obsessive compulsive disorders: Theory and management*. Littleton, MA: PSG Publishing.

Bailey, C. H., & Kandel, E. R. (1995). Molecular and structural mechanisms underlying long-term memory. In M. S. Gazzania (Ed.), *The cognitive neurosciences* (pp. 19–36). Cambridge, MA: MIT Press.

Bandura, A. (1988). Self-efficacy conception of anxiety. *Anxiety Research, 1*: 77–98.

Barber, C. (2008). The medicated Americans. *Scientific American Mind, 19*(1).

Barlow, D. H. (1990). Long-term outcome for patients with panic disorder treated with cognitive-behavioral therapy. *Journal of Clinical Psychiatry, 51(12, suppl. A)*, 17–23.

Barlow, D. H. (1997). Cognitive-behavioral therapy for panic disorder: Current status. *Journal of Clinical Psychiatry, 58*(suppl. 2), 32–36.

Barlow, D. H. (2004). Psychological treatments. *American Psychologist, 59*, 869–878.

Barlow, D. H., Craske, M. G., Cerny, J. A., & Klosko, J. S. (1989). Behavioral treatment of panic disorder. *Behavior Therapy, 20*, 261–282.

Barlow, D. H., Gorman, J. M., Shear, M. K., & Woods, S. W. (2000). Cognitive-behavioral therapy, imipramine, or their combination for panic disorder: A randomized controlled trial. *Journal of the American Medical Association, 283*(19), 2529–2536.

Barlow, D. H. (2000). Unraveling the mysteries of anxiety and its disorders from the perspective of emotion theory. *American Psychologist, 55*(11), 1247–1263.

Barlow, D. H. (1997). Cognitive-Behavioral Therapy for panic disorder: Current status. *Journal of Clinical Psychiatry, 58* (Suppl. 2): 32–37.

Barlow, D. H. (1996). Health care policy, psychotherapy research, and the future of psychotherapy. *American Psychologist, 51*(10): 1050–1058.

Barlow, D. H. (1990). Long-term outcome for patients with panic disorder treatment with Cognitive-Behavioral Therapy. *Journal of Clinical Psychiatry, 51* (12, Supp. A): 17–23.

Barlow, D. H. & Craske, M. G. (1994). *Mastering your anxiety and panic II*. San Antonio, TX.: Graywind Publication/The Psychological Corporation.

Bron-Cohen, S. (1995). *Mindblindness*. Cambridge, MA: MIT Press.

Bartels, A., & Zeki, S. (2004). The neural correlates of maternal and romantic love. *NeuroImage, 21*, 1155–1166.

Bartels, A., & Zeki, S. (2000). The neural basis of romantic love. *Neuro Report, 17*, 3829–3834.

Baxter, L. R., Jr., Phelps, M. E., Mazziotta, J. C., Schwartz, J. M., Gerner, R. H., Selin, C. E., et al. (1985). Cerebral metabolic rates for glucose metabolism in mood disorders. *Archives of General Psychology, 42*, 441–447.

Baxter, L. R., Jr., Phelps, M. E., Mazziotta, J. C., Guze, B. H., Schwartz, J. M., & Selin, C. E. (1987). Local cerebral glucose metabolic rates in obsessive-compulsive disorder. *Archives of General Psychiatry, 44*, 211–218.

Baxter, L. R., Jr. (1992). Neuroimaging studies of obsessive-compulsive disorder. *Psychiatric Clinics of North America, 15*(4), 871–884.

Baxter, L. R., Jr., Schwartz, J. M., Bergman, K. S., Szuba, M. P., Guze, B. H., Mazziotta, J. C., et al. (1992). Caudate glucose metabolic rate changes with both drug and behavior therapy for obsessive-compulsive disorder. *Archives of General Psychiatry, 46*, 681–689.

Baxter, L. R., Jr., Schwartz, J. M., Phelps, M. E., Mazziotta, J. C., Guze, B. H., Selin, C. E., et al. (1989). Reduction of prefrontal cortex glucose metabolism common in three types of depression, *Archives of General Psychiatry, 46*, 243–250.

Beck, A. T. (1972). *Depression: Causes and treatment*. Philadelphia: University of Pennsylvania Press.

Beck, A. T. (1976). *Cognitive therapy and emotional disorders*. New York: International Universities Press.

Beck, A. T., Rush, A. J., Shaw, B. F., & Emery, G. (1979). *Cognitive therapy of depression*. New York: Guilford Press.

Bebee, B., & Lachmann, F. M. (2002). *Infant research and adult treatment. Co-constructing interactions*. New York and London: Analytic Press.

Beebe, B., & Lachman, F. M. (1988). Mother-infant mutual influence and precursors of psychic structure. In A. Goldberg (Ed.), *Progress in self psychology* (Vol. 3, pp. 3–25). Hillsdale, NJ: Analytic Press.

Beebe, B., & Lachman, F. M. (1994). Representation and internalization in infancy: Three principles of salience. *Psychoanalytic Psychology, 11*, 127–166.

Beebe, B. & Lachman, F. M. (2002). *Infant research and adult treatment*. New York: The Analytic Press.

Beckner, V. & Arden, J. B. (2008). *Conquering Post Traumatic Stress Disorder* Boston: Fairwinds Press.

Bell, M. A., & Fox, N. A. (1992). The relations between frontal brain electrical activity and cognitive development during infancy. *Child Development, 63*, 1142–1163.

Benes, F. M. (1989). Myelination of cortical-hippocampal relays during late adolescence. *Schizophrenia Bulletin, 15*(4), 585–593.

Benson, H. (2000). *The relaxation response*. New York: HarperCollins.

Benton, D. (1992). Vitamin-mineral supplantation and intelligence of children: A review. *Journal of Ortho Medicine, 7*: 31–38.

Berthoz, S., Armony, J. L., Blair, R. J. R., & Dolan, R. J. (2002). An fMRI study of intentional and unintentional (embarrassing) violations of social norms. *Brain, 125*, 1696–1708.

Bergin, A. E., & Garfield, S. L. (Eds.) (1971). Handbook of psychotherapy and behavior change: An empirical analysis. New York: Wiley.

Bernhardt, P. C., Dabbs, J. M., Jr., Fielden, J. A., & Lutter, C. D. (1998). Testosterone changes during vicarious experience of winning and losing fans at sporting events. *Physiology and Behavior, 65*(1), 59–62.

Bever, T. G. & Chiarello, R. J. (1974). Cerebral dominance in musicians and non musicians. *Science, 185*, no. 150, 537–539.

Beutler, L. E., Engle, D., Mohr, D., Daldrup, R. J., Bergan, J., Meredith, K., et al. (1991). Predictors of differential and self-directed psychotherapeutic procedures. *Journal of Consulting and Clincal Psychology, 59*, 333–340.

Beutler, L. E., & Harwood, T. M. (2000). *Prescriptive psychotherapy: A practical guide to systematic treatment selection*. New York: Oxford University Press.

Bjornebekk, A., Mathe, A. A., & Brene, S. (2005, March 15). The antidepressant effect of running is associated with increased hippocampal cell proliferation. *International Journal of Neuropsychopharmacology*, 1–12.

Black, J. E. (1998). How a child builds its brain: Some lessons from animal studies of neural plasticity. *Preventative Medicine, 27,* 168–171.

Blakemore, S.-J., & Firth, V. (2004). How does the brain deal with the social world? *Neuroreport, 15,* 119–128.

Blonder, L. X., Bowers, D., & Heilman, K. M. (1991). The role of the right hemisphere in emotional communication. *Brain, 114,* 1115–1127.

Bloom, S. L. (1998). By the crowd they have been broken, by the crowd they shall be healed: The social transformation of trauma. In R. G. Tedeschi & C. L. Calhoun (Eds.), *Posttraumatic growth: Positive changes in the aftermath of crisis* (pp. 179–213). Mahwah, NJ: Erlbaum.

Bohart, A. C. (2000). The patient is the most important common factor: Patients' self-healing capacities and psychotherapy. *Journal of Psychotherapy Integration, 10*(2).

Bokhorst, C. L., Bakermans-Kranenburg, M. J., Fearon, R. M., Van IJzendoorn, M. H., Fonagy, P., & Schuengel, C. (2003). The importance of shared environment in mother-infant attachment security: A behavioral genetic study. *Child Development, 74,* 1769–1782.

Bögels, S. M., Alberts, M., & de Jong, P. J. (1996). Self-consciousness, self-focused attention, blushing propensity and fear of blushing. *Personality and Individual Differences, 21,* 573–581.

Bonnano, G. A. (2004). Loss, trauma, and human resilience. Have we underestimated the human capacity to thrive after extremely aversive events? *American Psychologist, 59,* 20–28.

Boone, O., Grillon, C., Vythilingam, M., Neumeister, A., & Charney, D. S. (2004). Adaptive and maladaptive psychobiological responses to severe psychological stress: Implications for the discovery of novel pharmacotherapy. *Neuroscience & Biobehavioral Reviews, 28,* 65–94.

Botvinick, M., Jha, A. P., Bylsma, L. M., Fabian, S. A., Solomon, P. E., & Prkachin, K. M. (2005). Viewing facial expressions of pain engages cortical areas involved in the direct experience of pain. *NeuroImage, 25,* 312–319.

Bowen, M. (1978). *Family therapy in clinical practice.* New York: Jason Aronson.

Bower, G. H., & Siver, H. (1998). Cognitive impact of traumatic events. *Development and Psychopathology, 10,* 625–654.

Bowlby, J. (1969/1999). *Attachment and loss, Vol. 1: Attachment.* New York: Basic Books.

Bowlby, J. (1973). *Attachment and loss, Vol. 2: Separation.* New York: Basic Books.

Bowlby, J. (1980). *Attachment and loss, Vol. 3: Loss, sadness and depression.* New York: Basic Books.

Bowler, R. M., Mergler, D., Huel, G., & Cone, J. E. (1994). Psychological, psychosocial, and psychophysiological sequela in a community affected by a railroad chemical disaster. *Journal of Traumatic Stress, 7,* 601–624.

Bremner, J. D., Krystal, J. H., Southwick, S. M., & Charney, D. S. (1995). Functional neuroanatomical correlates of the effects of stress on memory. *Journal of Psychiatry, 156,* 360–366.

Bremner, J. D., Randall, P., Vermetten, E., Staib, L., Bronen, R. A., Mazure, C., et al. (1997). Magnetic resonance image-based measurement of hippocampal volume in posttraumatic stress disorder related to childhood physical and sexual abuse: A preliminary report. *Biological Psychiatry, 41,* 23–32.

Bremner, J. D., Southwick, S. M., Johnson, D. R., Yehuda, R., & Charney, D. S. (1993). Childhood physical abuse and combat-related posttraumatic stress disorder in Vietnam veterans. *American Journal of Psychiatry, 150*(2), 235–239.

Bremner, J. D., & Narayan, M. (1998). The effects of stress on memory and the hippocampus throughout the life cycle: Implications for childhood development and aging. *Development and Psychopathology, 10,* 871–885.

Breslau, N., Davis, G., Andreski, P., Federman, B., & Anthony, J. C. (1998). Epidemiological findings on posttraumatic stress disorder and co-morbid disorders in the general population. In B. P. Dohrenwald (Ed.), *Adversity, stress, and psychopathology* (pp. 319–330). New York: Oxford University.

Breuer, J. & Freud, S. (1955). Studies on hysteria. In J. Strachey (Ed. & Trans.), *The standard edition of the complete psychological works of Sigmund Freud.* (Vol. 2). London: Hogarth Press (Originally published 1895.)

Brewin, C. R., Dalgleish, T., & Joseph, S. (1996). A dual representation theory of post traumatic stress disorder. *Psychological Research, 103,* 670–686.

Brody, A. L., Butler, R. W., Braff, D. L., Rauch, J. L., Jenkins, M. A., Sprock, J., et al. (1990). Physiological evidence of exaggerated startle response in a subgroup of Vietnam veterans with combat-related PTSD. *American Journal of Psychiatry, 147*(10), 1308–1312.

Brody, A. L., Saxena, S., Mandelkern, M. A., Fairbanks, L. A., Ho, M. L., & Baxter, L. R., Jr. (2001). Brain metabolic changes associated with symptom factor improvement in major depressive disorder. *Biological Psychiatry, 50*(3), 171–178.

Brody, A. L., Saxena, S., Schwartz, J. M., Stoessel, P. W., Maidment, K., Phelps, M. E., et al. (1998). FDG-PET predictors of response to behavioral therapy versus pharmacotherapy in obsessive-compulsive disorder. *Psychiatry Research: Neuroimaging, 84,* 1–6.

Brody, A. L., Saxena, S., Stoessel, P., Gillies, L. A., Fairbanks, L. A., Alborzian, S., et al. (2001). Regional brain metabolic changes in patients with major depression treated with either paroxetine or interpersonal therapy. *Archives of General Psychiatry, 58,* 631–640.

Brothers, L. (1996). Brain mechanisms of social cognition. *Journal of Psychopharmacology, 10,* 2–8.

Brothers, L. (1997). *Friday's foot print.* New York: Oxford Press.

Brown, G. W., & Harris, T. O. (Eds.) (1989). *Life events and illness.* New York: Guilford Press.

Brüne, M. (Ed.) (2003). *The social brain: Evolution and pathology.* Sussex, UK: Wiley.

Brunson, K. L., Avishai-Eliner, S., Hatalski, C. G., & Baram, T. Z. (2001). Neurobiology of the stress response early in life: Evolution of a concept and the role corticotrophin releasing hormone. *Molecular Psychiatry, 6,* 647–656.

Buchanan, T. W., & Adolphs, R. (2004). The neuroanatomy of emotional memory in humans. In D. Reisberg & P. Hertel (Eds.), *Memory and emotion* (pp. 42–75). New York: Oxford University Press.

Burns, D. (1999). *Feeling good: The new mood therapy*. New York: Avon Books.

Bush, G., Luu, P., & Posner, M. I. (2000). Cognitive and emotional influences in anterior cingulate cortex. *Trends in Cognitive Science, 4*, 215–222.

Cadoret, R. J., Yates, W. R., Troughton, E., Woodworth, G., & Stewart, M. A. (1995). Genetic-environmental interaction in the genesis of aggressivity and conduct disorders. *Archives of General Psychiatry, 52*, 916–924.

Cahill, L., & McGaugh, J. L. (1998). Mechanisms of emotional arousal and lasting declarative memory. *Trends in Neuroscience, 21*(7), 294–299.

Calfas, K. J., & Taylor, W. C. (1994). Effects of physical activity on psychological variables in adolescents. *Pediatric Exercise Science, 6*, 406–423.

Calson, E. B., & Dalenberg, C. J. (2000). A conceptual framework for the impact of traumatic experiences. *Trauma, Violence, & Abuse, 1*, 4–28.

Candel, I., & Merckelbach, H. (2004). Peritraumatic disassociation as a predictor of posttraumatic stress disorder: A critical review. *Comprehensive Psychiatry, 45*, 4450.

Cannon, W. B. (1915). *Bodily changes in pain, hunger, fear and rage: An account of recent researches into the function of emotional excitement*. New York: Appleton.

Carpenter, G. (1974). Mother's face and the newborn. *New Scientist, 21*, 742–744.

Carrion, V. G., Weems, C. F., Eliez, S., Ptwardhan, A., Brown, W., Ray, R. D., et al. (2001). Attenuation of frontal asymmetry in pediatric posttraumatic stress disorders. *Journal of Consulting and Clinical Psychology, 54*, 303–308.

Carr, L., Iacoboni, M., Dubeau, M. C., Mazziotta, J. C., & Lenzi, G. L. (2003). Neural mechanisms of empathy in humans: A relay from neural systems for imitation to limbic areas. *Proceedings of the National Academy of Sciences, USA, 100*, 5497–5502.

Carr, L., Iacoboni, M., Dubcau, M. C., Maziotta, J. C., & Lenzi, G. L. (2003). Neural mechanisms of empathy in humans: A relay for neural systems for imitation to limbic areas. Proceedings of the National Academy of Sciences, *100*(9), 5497–5502.

Carr, R. E., Lehrer, P. M., Hechron, S. M., & Jackson, A. (1996). Effect of psychological stress on airway impedance in individuals with asthma and panic disorder. *Journal of Abnormal Psychology, 105*(1): 137–141.

Carr, R. E., Lehrer, P. M., & Hechron, S. M. (1995). Predictors of panic-fear in asthma. *Health Psychology, 14*(5): 421–426.

Carter, C. S. (2003). Developmental consequences of oxytocin. *Physiology & Behavior, 79*, 383–397.

Carter, C. S., Braver, T. S., Barch, D. M., Botvinick, M. M., Noll, D., & Cohen, J. D. (1998). Anterior cingulated cortex, error detection, and the online monitoring of performance. *Science, 280*, 747–749.

Carver, C. S., & Scheier, M. F. (2002). Optimism. In C. R. Snyder & S. J. Lopez (Eds.), *Handbook of positive psychology* (pp. 231–243).

Casey, B. J., Castellanos, F. X., & Giedd, J. N. (1997). Implications of right frontostriatal circuitry in response ot inhibition and attention-deficit/hyperactivity disorder. *Journal of the American Academy of Child and Adolescent Psychiatry, 36*, 374–383.

Cash, A. (2005). *Posttraumatic stress disorder*. Hoboken, NJ: Wiley.

Castren, E. (2005). Is mood chemistry? *National Review of Neuroscience, (3)*: 241–6 PMID 15738959.

Chajet, E., & Algom, D. (2003). Selective attention improves under stress: Implications for theories of social cognition. *Journal of Personality and Social Psychology, 85*, 231–248.

Chamberlain, S. R., Blackwell, A. D., Fineberg, N. A., Robbins, T. W., & Sahakian, B. J. (2005). The neuropsychology of obsessive compulsive disorder: The importance of failures in cognitive and behavioural inhibition as candidate endophenotypic markers. *Neuroscience and Biobehavioral Reviews, 29(3)*, 399–419.

Chaminade, T., Meltzoff, A. N., & Decety, J. (2002). Does the end justify the means? A PET exploration of the mechanisms involved in human imitation. *NeuroImage, 15*, 318–328.

Charney, D. S., Deutch, A. Y., Southwick, S. M., & Krystal, J. H. (1995). Neural circuits and mechanisms of post-traumatic stress disorder. In: M. J. Friedman, D. S. Charney, & A. Y. Deutch (Eds.), *Neurobiological and clinical consequences of stress: From normal adaptation to post-traumatic stress disorder* (pp. 271–287). Philidelphia: Lippincott, Williams & Wilkins.

Checkly, S. A. (1999). Functional MRI study of the cognitive generation of affect. *American Journal of Psychiatry, 156(2)*, 209–215.

Chen, B., Dowlatshahi, D., MacQueen, G. M., Wang, J. F., & Young, L. T. (2001). Increased hippocampal BDNF immunoreactivity in subjects treated with antidepressant medication. *Biological Psychiatry, 50*, 260–265.

Chiron, C., Jambaque, I., Nabbout, R., Lounes, R., Syrota, A., & Dulac, O. (1997). The right brain is dominant in human infants. *Brain, 120*, 1057–1065.

Christianson, S. A. (Ed.) (1992). *Handbook of emotion and memory*. Hillsdale, NJ: Erlbaum.

Chungai, H. (2001). Local brain functional activity following early deprivation: A study of postinstitutionalized Romanian orphans. *Neuro Image, 14*, 1290–1301.

Chugani, H. T. (1998). A critical period of brain development: Studies of glucose utilization with PET. *Preventative Medicine, 27*, 184–188.

Chugani, H. T., & Phelps, M. E. (1991). Imagining human brain development with positron emission tomography. *Journal of Nuclear Medicine, 32(1)*, 23–26.

Chugani, H. T., Phelps, M. E., & Mazziotta, J. C. (1987). Position emission tomography study of human brain functional development. *Annals of Neurology, 22*, 487–497.

Ciarrocchi, J. W. (1995). *The doubting disease*. New York: Paulist Press.

Clark, C. R., McFarlane, A. C., Morris, P., Weber, D. L., Sonkkilla, C., Shaw, M., et al. (2003). Cerebral function in posttraumatic stress disorder during verbal working memory updating: A positron emission tomography study. *Biological Psychiatry, 53,* 474–481.

Cohen, N. H. (1984). Preserved learning capacity in amnesia: Evidence for multiple memory systems. In L. R. Squire & N. Butters (Eds.), *Neuropsychology of memory* (pp. 83–103). New York: Guilford Press.

Cohen, N. J., & Squire, L. R. (1980). Preserved learning and retention of pattern-analyzing skill in amnesia: Dissociation of knowing how and knowing that. *Science, 210,* 207–209.

Cohen, S. (2004, November). Social relationships and health. *American Psychologist,* 676–684.

Cohen, S., Tyrell, D. A. & Smith, A. P. (1991). Psychological stress and susceptibility to the common cold. *New England Journal of Medicine, 325,* 606–612.

Cohn, J. K., & Tronick, E. K. (1982). Communication rules and sequential structure of infant behavior during normal and depressed interaction. In E. K. Tronik (Ed.), *Social interchange in infancy.* Baltimore, MD: University.

Coon, D. J. (1994). "Not a creature of reason": The alleged impact of Watsonian behaviorism on advertising in the 1920s. In: J. T. Todd & E. K. Morris, *Modern perspectives on John B. Watson and classical behaviorism.* Westport, CT: Greenwood Press.

Corina, D. P., Vaid, J., & Bellugi, V. (1992). The linguistic basis of left hemisphere specialization. *Science, 255,* 1258–1260.

Cowan, W. M., & Kandel, E. R. (2001). A brief history of synapses and synaptic transmission. In W. M. Cown, T. C. Sudhoff, & C. F. Stevens (Eds.), *Synapses* (pp. 1–87). Baltimore: Johns Hopkins University.

Cozolino, L. (2002). *The neuroscience of psychotherapy.* New York: Norton.

Cozolino, L. (2006). *The neuroscience of human relationships: Attachment and the developing social brain.* New York: Norton.

Craig, A. D. (2004). Human feelings: Why are some more aware than others. *Trends in Cognitive Science, 8,* 239–241.

Craske, M. G. (1991). Models and treatments of panic: Behavioral therapy of panic. *Journal of Cognitive Psychotherapy: An International Quarterly, 5*(3), 199, 214.

Craske, M. G. & Barlow, D. H. (1993). Panic disorder and agoraphobia. In D. H. Barlow (Ed.), *Clinical handbook of psychological disorders* (2nd ed.), New York: Guilford Press.

Craske, M. G., Meadows, E., & Barlow, D. H. (1994). *Therapist's guide for your mastery of anxiety and panic II and agoraphobia supplement.* New York: Graywind.

Craske, M. G., & Freed, S. (1995). Expectation about arousal and nocturnal panic. *Journal of Abnormal Psychology, 104*(4): 567–575.

Craske, M. G., & Barlow, D. H. (1990). Nocturnal panic: Response to hyperventilation and carbon dioxide challenge. *Journal of Abnormal, 99*(3): 302–307.

Craske, M. G., & Barlow, D. H. (1993). Panic disorder and agoraphobia. *In Clinical Handbook of Psychological Disorder: A step by step treatment manual* (2nd Ed.) D. H. Barlow (Ed.) New York: Guilford.

Craske, M. G., Brown, T. A., & Barlow, D. H. (1991). Behavioral treatment of panic disorder: A two year follow-up. *Behavior Therapy, 22,* 289–304.

Craske, M. G., Meadows, E., & Barlow, D. H. (1994). *The therapist for the mastery of your anxiety and panic II & Agorphobia Supplement.* San Antonio, TX.: Graywind Publications/The Psychological Corporation.

Craske, M. G. & Rodriquez, M. I. (1994). Behavioral treatment of panic disorders and agoraphobia. *Progress in Behavior Modification, 29:* 1–26.

Critchley, H. D., Wiens, S., Rotshtein, P., Öhman, A., & Solan, R. J. (2004). Neural systems supporting interoceptive awareness. *Nature Neuroscience, 7,* 189–195.

Crufurd, D. I. O., Creed, F., & Jayson, M. D. (1990). Life events psychological disturbance in patients with low-back pain. *Spine, 15,* 490–492.

Cumberland-Li, A. (2003). The relation of parental emotionality and related dispositional traits to parental expression of emotion and children's social functioning. *Motivation and Emotion, 1,* 27–56.

Cummings, J. L. (1985). *Clinical neuropsychiatry.* New York: Grune & Stratton.

Czeisler, C. A. & Khalsa, S. B. S. (2000). The human circadian timing system and sleep-wake regulation. In M. Kryger, T. Roth, W. Dement (Eds.), *Principles and practice of sleep medicine* (3rd Ed., pp. 353–375). Philadelphia, PA: W. B. Saunders.

Damasio, A. (1999). *The feeling of what happens: Body and emotion in the making of consciousness.* New York: Harcourt.

Damasio, A. (2003). *Looking for Spinoza's joy, sorrow, and the feeling brain.* New York: Harcourt.

Damasio, A. R. (1994). *Descartes' error.* New York: Putnam and Sons.

Darwin, C. (1859). *On the origin of species by means of natural selection, or the preservation of favoured races in the struggle for life.* London: John Murray.

Darwin, C. R. *The descent of man, and selection in relation to sex* [1871]. Boston: Adamant, 2005.

Davidson, R. J. (1992). Anterior cerebral asymmetry and the nature of emotion. *Brain and Cognition, 20,* 125–151.

Davidson, R. J., Ekman, P., Saron, C. D., Senulis, J. A., & Friesen, W. V. (1990). Approach-withdrawal and cerebral asymmetry: Emotional expression and brain physiology I. *Journal of Personality and Social Psychology, 58,* 330–341.

Davidson, R. J. & Slagter, H. A. (2000). Mental Retard. Dev. Disabilities. Res. Rev. *6,* 116–170.

Davidson, R. J., Kabat-Zinn, J., Schumacher, J., Rosenkranz, M., Muller, D., Santorelli, S. F., et al. (2003). Alterations in brain and immune function produced by mindfulness meditation. *Psychosomatic Medicine, 65,* 564–570.

Davidson, R. J., Jackson, L., & Kalin, N. H. (2000). Emotion, plasticity, context, and regulation. *Psychological Bulletin, 126:* 890–909.

Davis, M. (1992). The role of the amygdala in fear and anxiety. *Annual Review of Neuroscience, 15,* 353–375.

Davis, L. & Siegel, L. J. (2000). Posttraumatic stress disorder in children and adolescents: A review and analysis. *Clinical Child and Family Psychology Review*, 3(3), 135–154.

Dawson, G. (1994a). Development of emotional expression and emotion reguation in infancy. In G. Dawson & K. W. Fischer (Eds.), *Human Behavior and the Developing Brain* (pp. 346–379). New York: Guilford Press.

Dawson, G. (1994b). Frontal electroencephalographic correlates of individual differences in emotion expression in infants: A brain systems perspective on emotion. In N. A. Fox (Ed.), *The development of emotion regulation: Biological and behavioral considerations. Monographs of the Society for Research in Child Development*, 59(2–3, Serial No. 240), 135–151.

DeBellis, M. D., Baum, A. S., Birmaher, B., Keshavan, M. S., Eccard, C. H., Boring, A. M., et al. (1999a). A. E. Bennett research award. Developmental traumatology, Part I: Biological stress symptoms. *Biological Psychiatry* 45(10), 1259–1270.

DeBellis, M. D., Keshavan, M. S., Clark, D. B., Casey, B. J., Giedd, J. N., Boring, A. M., et al. (1999b). A. E. Bennett research award. Developmental traumatology, Part II: Brain development. *Biological Psychiatry* 45(10), 1271–1284.

De Bellis, M. D., Keshavan, M. S., Shifflett, H., Iyengar, S., Beers, S. R., Hall, J., et al. (2002). Brain structures in pediatric maltreatment-related posttraumatic stress disorder: A sociodemographically matched study. *Biological Psychiatry*, 52, 1066–1078.

De Bellis, M. D., Keshavan, M. S., Clark, D. B., Casey, B. J., Giedd, J. N., Boring, A. M., et al. (1999). Developmental traumatology part II: Brain development. *Biological Psychiatry*, 45, 1271–1284.

De Bellis, M. D., Baum, A. S., Birmaher, B., Keshavan, M. S., Eccard, C. H., Boring, A. M., et al. (1999). Developmental traumatology part I: Biological stress systems. *Biological Psychiatry*, 45, 1259–1270.

de Decker, A., Hermans, D., Raes, F., & Eelen, P. (2003). Autobiographical memory specificity and trauma in inpatient adolescents. *Journal of Clinical Child and Adolescent Psychology*, 32, 22–31.

D'Esposito, M., Detre, J., Alsop, D., Shin, R., Atlas, S., & Grossman, M. (1995). The neural basis of the central executive system of working memory. *Nature*, 378, 279–281.

de Jong, P. J., Peters, M. L., & De Cremer, D. (2003). Blushing may signify guilt: Revealing effects of blushing in ambiguous social situations. *Motivation and Emotion*, 27, 225–249.

Dement, W. C. (1976). *Some Must Watch While Others Must Sleep*. New York: Norton.

DeSteno, D., Dasgupta, N., Bartlett, M. Y., & Cajdric, A. (2004). Prejudice from thin air: The effect of emotion on automatic intergroup attitudes. *Psychological Science*, 15, 319–324.

Devinsky, O. (2000). Right cerebral hemisphere dominance for a sense of corporeal and emotional self. *Epilepsy and Behavior*, 1, 60–73.

deWolff, M. S., & van IJzendoorn, M. H. (1997). Sensitivity and attachment: A meta-analysis of parental antecedents of infant attachment. *Child Development, 68,* 571–591.

Diamond, D. M., & Rose, G. (1994). Stress impairs LTP and hippocampal-dependent memory. *Annals of the New York Academy of Sciences, 746,* 411–414.

Dias, R., Robbins, T. W., & Roberts, A. C. (1996). Dissociation in prefrontal cortex of effective and attentional shifts. *Nature, 380,* 69–72.

Dickerson, S., & Kemeny, M. (2004). Acute stressors and cortisol responses: A theoretical integration and synthesis of laboratory research. *Psychological Bulletin, 130,* 355–391.

Diorio, D., Viace, V., and Meany, M. I. (1993). The role of the prefrontal cortex (cingulated gyrus). in the regulation of hypothalamic-pituitary-adrenal responses to stress. *Journal of Neuroscience, 13,* 3839–3847.

Dobbs, D. (2006a). A depression switch? *New York Times Magazine,* http://www.nytimes.com/2006/04/02/magazine/02depression.

Dobbs, D. (2006b). Profile: Helen Mayberg. Turning off depression (reprinted from Scientific American Mind, August/September, 2006). http://daviddobbs.net/page2/page7/page7.html.

Dohrenwend, B. P. (Ed.) (1998). *Adversity, stress and psychopathology.* New York: Oxford University.

Dolan, R. J. (1999). On the neurology of morals. *Nature Neuroscience, 2*(11), 927–929.

Douglas, R. J., & Pribram, K. H. (1966). Learning and limbic lesions. *Neuropsychologia, 4,* 197–220.

Drake, R. A. (1984). Lateral asymmetry of personal optimism. *Journal of Research in Personality, 18,* 497–507.

Drummond, P. D., & Mirco, N. (2004). Staring at one side of the face increases blood flow on that side of the face. *Psychophysiology, 41,* 281–287.

Duman, R. S. (2004). Role of neurotrophic factors in the etiology and treatment of mood disorders. *NeuroMolecular Medicine, 5*(1), 11–25.

Dunbar, R. I. (1996). *Grooming, gossip, and the evolution of language.* Cambridge, MA: Harvard University.

Duncan, B. I., Miller, S. D., and Sparks, J. A. (2004). *The heroic patient.* San Francisco: Jossey-Bass.

Dunn, J., & McGuire, S. (1994). Young children's nonshared experiences: A summary of studies in Colorado and Cambridge. In E. M. Hetherington, D. Reiss, &   R. Plomin (Eds.), *Separate Social Worlds of Siblings: The impact of nonshared environment on development* (pp. 111–128). Hillsdale, NJ: Erlbaum.

Eccles, J. C. (1984). The cerebral neocortex: A theory of its operation. In E. G. Jones &   A. Peters (Eds.), *Cerebral cortex: Functional properties of cortical cells* (Vol. 2). New York: Plenum Press.

Edelman, G. M. (1987). *Neural Darwinism: The theory of neuronal group selection.* New York: Basic Books.

Edelman, G. M. (1989). *The remembered present: A biological theory of consciousness.* New York: Basic Books.

Eggermont, J. J. (1998). Is there a neural code? *Neuroscience and Biobehavioral Reviews, 22,* 355–370.

Einon, D. F., & Morgan, M. J. (1977). A critical period for social isolation in the rat. *Developmental Biology, 10,* 123–132.

Einon, D. F., Morgan, M. J., & Kibbler, C. C. (1977). Brief periods of socialization and later behavior in the rat. *Developmental Psychobiology, 11,* 213–225.

Eisenberger, N. I., & Lieberman, M. D. (2004). Why rejection hurts: A common neural alarm system for physical and social pain. *Trends in Cognitive Sciences, 8,* 294–300.

Ekman, P. (1983). Autonomic nervous system activity distinguishes among emotions. *Science, 221,* 1208–1210.

Ekman, P., & Oster, H. (1979). Facial expression of emotion. *Annual Review of Psychology, 39,* 1125–1134.

Elbert, T., Pantev, C., Wienbruch, C., Rockstroh, B., & Taub, E. (1995). Increased cortical representation of the fingers of the left hand in string players. *Science, 270,* 3053-7–30.

Elkin, I., Parloff, M. B., Hadley, S. W. & Autry, J. H. NIMH treatment of depression collaborative research program: background and research plan (1985). *Archives of General Psychiatry 42:* 305–316.

Elkin, I., Shea, M. T., Watkins, J. T., Imber, S. D., Sotsky, S. M., Collins, J. F., et al. (1989). The National Institute of Mental Health (NIMH). Treatment of Depression Collaborative Research Program. *Archives of General Psychiatry, 46,* 971–982.

Ellis, A. (1996). *Reason and emotion in psychotherapy.* Secaucus, NJ: Lyle Stuart.

Ellis, A. (1962). *Reason and emotion in psychotherapy.* Secaucus, NJ: Lyle Stuart.

Ellard, K., Beurepaire, J., Jones, M., Piper, D., Tennant, C. (1990). Acute chronic stress in duodenal ulcer disease. *Gastroenterology, 99,* 1628–1632.

Erickson, P. S., Perfileva, E., Bjork-Erickson, T., Alborn, A. M., Nordborg, C., Peterson, D. A. & Gage, F. H. et al. (1998). Neurogenesis in the adult human hippocampus. *Nature Medicine, 4,* 1313–1317.

Eysenck, H. J. (1952). The effects of psychotherapy: An evaluation. *Journal of Consulting Psychology, 16,* 319–324.

Fadiman, A., *The spirit catches you and you fall down.* (1998). New York: Farrar, Straus and Giroux.

Feldman, T. E., Greenbaum, C. W., & Yirimiya, N. (1999). Mother-infant affect synchrony as an antecedent of the emergence of self-control. *Developmental Psychology, 35*(5), 223–231.

Felitti, V. J. (1991). Long-term medical consequences of incest, rape, and molestation. *Southern Medical Journal, 83,* 328–331.

Felitti, V. J., Anda, R. F., Nordenberg, D., Williamson, D. F., Spitz, A. M., Edwards, V., et al. (1998). Relationship of childhood abuse and household dysfunction to many of the leading cause of death in adults: The Adverse

Childhood Experiences (ACE) Study. *American Journal of Preventative Medicine, 14,* 245–258.

Felton, D. L., Ackerman, K. D., Wiegand, S. J. & Felton, S. Y. (1987). Noradrenergic sympathetic innervation of the spleen: I. Nerve fibers associate with lymphocytes and macrophanges in specific compartments of the splenic white pulp. *Journal of Neuroscience Research, 18,* 28–36.

Feng, J., Spence, I., & Pratt, J. (2007). Playing an action video game reduces gender differences in spatial cognition. *Psychological Science, 18,* 850–855.

Field, S. (1994). The effects of mother's physical and emotional unavailability on emotional regulation. In N. A. Fox (Ed.), *The development of emotional regulation: Biological and behavioral considerations. Monographs of the Society for Research in Child Development, 59* (2–3, Serial No. 240), 208–227.

Field, T. (1998). Maternal depression effects on infants and early interventions. *Preventative Medicine, 27,* 200–203.

Field, T., Fox, N. A., Pickens, J., & Nawrocki, T. (1995). Relative right frontal EEG activation in 3- to 6-month-old infants of "depressed" mothers. *Developmental Psychology, 31,* 358–363.

Field, T., Schanberg, S. M., Scafidi, F., Bauer, C. R., Vega-Lahr, N., Garcia, R., et al. (1986). Effects of tactile/kinesthetic stimulation on pre-term neonatics. *Pediatrics, 77,* 645–658.

Field, T. M. (1997). The treatment of depressed mothers and their infants. In L. Murray & P. J. Cooper (Eds.), *Postpartum depression and child development* (pp. 221–236). New York: Guilford Press.

Field, T. M., Healy, B., Goldstein, S., & Bendell, D. (1988). Infants of depressed mothers show "depressed" behavior even with nondepressed adults. *Child Development, 59,* 1569–1579.

Field, T. M., Woodson, R., Greenberg, R., & Cohen, D. (1982). Discrimination and imitation of facial expression by neonates. *Science, 218,* 179–181.

Fife, W. P., & Moon, C. M. (1998). The role of mother's voice in the organization of brain function in the newborn. *Acta Paediatrica, 397*(Suppl.), 86–93.

Fifer, W. & Moon, C. (1995). The effects of fetal experience with sound. In J. P. Lecanuet, W. Fifer, N., Krasnergor, B. W., Smotherman (Eds.), Fetal development: A psychobiological perspective. (pp. 351–366). Hillsdale, NJ: Erlbaum.

Fischer, K., Shaver, P. R., & Carnochan, P. (1990). How emotions develop and how they organize development. *Cognition and Emotion, 4,* 81–127.

Fivush, R. (1998). Children's recollections of traumatic and nontraumatic events. *Development and Psychopathology, 10,* 699–716.

Foa, E. B., & Kozak, M. J. (1997). *Mastery of obsessive-compulsive disorder: Patient workbook.* San Antonio: Psychological Corporation.

Foa, E. B., & Wilson, R. (1991). *Stop obsessing.* New York: Bantam.

Foa, E. B. & Meadows, E. A. (1998). Psychosocial treatments fro posttraumatic stress disorder. In R. Yehuda (Ed.) *Review of Psychiatry,* Vol. 17. Psychological trauma (pp. 179–204). Washington, D.C.: American Psychiatric Assoication.

Foa, E. B., Molinar, C., & Cashman, L. (1995). Change in rape narratives during exposure therapy for Posttraumatic Stress Disorder. *Journal of Traumatic Stress, 8*, 675–690.

Foa, E. B., Steketee, G. & Rothbaum, B. O. (1989). Behavioral/Cognitive conceptualizations of post-traumatic stress disorder, *Behavior Therapy, 20*, 155–176.

Fonagy, P., Gergely, G., Jurist, E. L., & Target, M. (2006). *Affect regulation, mentalization, and the development of self*. New York: Other.

Fonagy, P., & Target, M. (1997). Attachment and reflective function: Their role in self-organization. *Development and Psychopathology, 9*, 679–700.

Fonagy, P., Target, J., Steele, M., Steele, H., Leigh, T., Levinson, A., et al. (1997). Crime and attachment: Morality, disruptive behavior, borderline personality disorder, crime and their relationship to security of attachment. In L. Atkinson & K. J. Zucker (Eds.), *Attachment and psychopathology* (pp. 223–274). New York: Guilford Press.

Ford, D. E. & Kamerow, D. B. (1989). Epidemiologic study of sleep disturbances and psychiatric disorders: An opportunity for prevention? *Journal of the American Medical Association, 262*, 1479–1484.

Fosha, D. (2000). *The transforming power of affect: A model for accelerated change*. New York: Basic Books.

Foy, D. W., Erickson, C. B., & Trice, G. A. (2001). Introduction to group intervention for trauma survivors. *Group Dynamics: Theory, Research, and Practice, 5*, 246–251.

Fraley, R. C., & Shaver, P. R. (1997). Adult attachment and the suppression of unwanted thoughts. *Journal of Personality and Social Psychology, 73*, 1080–1090.

Frank, M. G. & Benington, J. H. (2006). The role of sleep in memory consolidation and brain plasticity: Dream or reality? *The Neuroscientist, 12*: 6, 477–488.

Franklin, T. R., Acton, P. D., Maldjian, J. A., Gray, J. D., Croft, J. R., Dackis, C. A., et al. (2002). Decreased gray matter concentration in the insular, orbitofrontal, cingulated, and temporal cortices of cocaine patients. *Biological Psychiatry, 51*, 134–142.

Freedman, M., Black, S., Ebert, P., & Binns, M. (1998). Orbitofrontal function, object alternation and preservation. *Cerebral Cortex, 8*, 18–27.

Freeman, W. (1987). Simulation of chaotic EEG patterns with a dynamic model of the olfactory system. *Biological Cybernetics, 56*, 139–150.

Freeman, W. (1995). *Societies of brains: A study in the neuroscience of love and hate*. Hillsdale, NJ: Erlbaum.

Freeman, W. J. (1992). Tutorial in neurobiology. *International Journal of Bifurcation and Chaos, 2*, 451–482.

Freud, S. (1953). Project for a scientific psychology. In J. Strachey (Ed. & Trans.), *The standard edition of the complete psychological works of Sigmund Freud* (Vol. 1, pp. 295–397). London: Hogarth Press. (Originally written 1895.)

Freud, S. (1958). Recommendations to physicians practicing psychoanalysis. In J. Strachey (Ed. & Trans.), *The standard edition of the complete psychological works of*

Sigmund Freud (Vol. 12, pp. 111–120). London: Hogarth Press. (Originally published 1912.)

Freud, S. (1958a). *An outline of psychoanalysis.* In J. Strachey (Ed. & Trans.), *The standard edition of the complete psychological works of Sigmund Freud* (Vol. 23, pp. 139–208). London: Hogarth Press. (Originally published 1939.)

Freud, S. (1958b). Lecture XXXI: The dissertation of psychical personality. In J. Strachey (Ed. & Trans.), *The standard edition of the complete psychological works of Sigmund Freud* (Vol. 23) London: Hogarth Press. (Originally published 1912.)

Fried, I., Wilson, C. C., MacDonald, K. A., & Behnke, E. J. (1998). Electric stimulates laughter. *Nature, 391*–650.

Friedman, M. J. (1997). Drug treatment for PTSD: Answers and questions. *Annals of the New York Academy of Sciences, 821,* 359–468.

Frith, C. D., & Frith, U. (1999). Interacting minds: A biological basis. *Science, 286,* 1692–1695.

Fumark, T., Tillfors, M., Marteinsdottir, I., Fischer, H., Pissiolta, A., Langström, B., et al. (2002). Common changes in cerebral blood flow in patients with social phobia treated with citalopram or cognitive-behavioral therapy. *Archives of General Psychiatry, 59,* 425–433.

Fuster, J. M. (1997). *The prefrontal cortex.* Philadelphia: Lippincott-Raven.

Fuster, J. M., Bodmer, M., & Kroger, J. K. (2000). Cross-modal and cross-temporal association in neurons of the frontal cortex. *Nature, 405,* 347–351.

Gage, F. H. (2000). Mammalian neural stem cells. *Science, 287:* 5457, 1433–1438.

Galin, D., Johnstone, J., Nakell, L., & Herron, J. (1979). Development for the capacity for tactile information transfer between hemispheres in normal children. *Science, 204,* 13301–1331.

Gallese, V. (2001). The "shared manifold" hypothesis: From mirror neurons to empathy. *The Journal of Consciousness Studies, 8*(5–7), 33–50.

Gallese, V., Fadiga, L., Fogassi, L., & Rizzolatti, G. (1996). Action recognition in the premotor cortex. *Brain, 119,* 593–609.

Gallese, V., & Keysers, C. (2001). Mirror neurons: A sensorimotor representation system. *Behavioral and Brain Sciences, 24,* 983–984.

Gallese, V. (2001). The 'shared manifold' hypothesis: From mirror neurons to empathy. *Journal of Conscientiousness Studies, 8,* 33–50.

Gardener, H. (1987). *The mind's new science: A history of cognitive revolution.* New York: Basic Books.

Gardiner, R., Jr. (1997), Sociophysiology as the basic science of psychiatry. *Theoretical Medicine, 18,* 355–356.

Gauthier, I., Tarr, M. J., Moylan, J., Skudlarski, P., Gore, J. C., & Anderson, A. W. (2000). The fusiform "face area" is part of a network that processes faces at the individual level. *Journal of Cognitive Neuroscience, 12,* 495–504.

Gazzaniga, M. (2008). *Human: The science of what makes us unique.* New York: HarperCollins.

Gazzaniga, M. S., Bogen, J. E., & Sperry, R. W. (1962). Some functional effects of sectioning the cerebral commissures in man. *Proceedings of the National Academy of Sciences, 48,* 1765–1769.

Gazzaniga, M. S. (1985). *The social brain.* New York: Basic Books.

Gazzaniga, M. S. (1995). Consciousness and the cerebral hemispheres. In M. S. Gazzaniga (Ed.), *The cognitive neurosciences* (pp. 1391–1400). Cambridge, MA: MIT Press.

Gazzaniga, M. S., Eliassen, J. C., Nisenson, L., Wessinger, C. M., & Baynes, K. B. (1996). Collaboration between the hemispheres of a callosotomy patient: Emergent right hemisphere speech and the left brain interpreter. *Brain, 119,* 1255–1262.

Gazzaniga, M. S., & LeDoux, J. E. (1978). *The integrated mind.* New York: Plenum Press.

Gazzaniga, M. S., Wilson, D. H., & LeDoux, J. E. (1977). Language, praxis, and the right hemisphere: Clues to some mechanisms of consciousness. *Neurology, 27,* 1144–1147.

George, M. S., Ketter, T. A., Parekh, P. I., Gill, D. S., Maragell, L., Pazzaglia, P. J., et al. (1995). Depressed subjects have decreased rCBF activation during facial emotional recognition. *International Journal of Neuropsychiatric Medicine, 2,* 45–55.

Gerschwind, N., & Galaburda, A. M. (1985). Cerebral lateralization: Biological mechanisms, associations, and pathology: A hypothesis and program for research. *Archives of Neurology, 42,* 428–459.

Gershon, M. (1999). *The second brain.* New York: HarperCollins.

Gilbertson, M. W., Shenon, M. E., Ciszewski, A., Kasai, K., Lasko, N. B., Orr, S. P., et al. (2002). Smaller hippocampal volume predicts pathologic vulnerability to psychological trauma. *Nature Neuroscience,* 1242–1247.

Globus, A., & Scheibel, A. B. (1967). Pattern and field in cortical structure: The rabbit. *Journal of Comparative Neurology, 131,* 155–172.

Globus, G., & Arpai, J. P. (1993). Psychiatry and the new dynamics. *Biological Psychiatry, 35,* 352–364.

Globus, G. G. (1992). Toward a noncomputational cognitive neuroscience. *Journal of Cognitive Neuroscience, 4,* 299–310.

Goleman, D. (2006). *Social Intelligence: The New Science of Human Relationships.* New York: Bantam Books.

Goldapple, K., Segal, Z., Garson, C., Lau, M., Bieling, P., Kennedy, S., et al. (2004). Modulation of cortical-limbic pathways in major depression: Treatment-specific effects of cognitive behavior therapy. *Archives of General Psychiatry, 61,* 34–41.

Goldberg, E. (2001). *The Executive Brain: Frontal lobes and the civilized mind.* New York: Oxford University Press.

Goldman-Rakic, P. S. (1993). Working memory and the mind. In *Mind and brain readings from Scientific American magazine, September* (pp. 66–77). New York: Freeman.

Goldman-Rakic, P. S. (1987). Development of cortical circuitry and cognitive function. *Child Development, 58,* 601–622.

Goldstein, R. Z. (2002). Drug addiction and its underlying neurobiological basis: Neuroimaging evidence for the involvement of the frontal cortex. *American Journal of Psychiatry, 159,* 1642–1652.

Goleman, D. (2006). *Social intelligence: The new science of human relationships.* New York: Bantam.

Golomb, J., deLeon, M. J., Kluger, A., George, A. E., Tarshish, C., & Ferris, S. H. (1993). Hippocampal atrophy in normal aging: An association with recent memory impairment. *Archives of Neurology, 50*(9), 967–973.

Gould, R. A., Otto, M. W., & Pollack, M. H. (1995). A meta-analysis of treatment outcome for panic disorder. *Clinical Psychology Review, 15*(8), 819–844.

Goodman, G. S., Ghetti, S., Quas, J. A., Edelstein, R. S., Alexander, K. W., Redlich, A. D., et al. (2003). A prospective study of memory for child sexual abuse: New finding relevant to the repressed-memory controversy. *Psychological Science, 14,* 113–118.

Goodman, W. K., Price, L. H., Rasmussen, S. A., Mazure, C., Delgado, P., Heninger, G. R., et al. (1989a). The Yale-Brown Obsessive Compulsive Scale (Y-BOCS): Part I. Development, use, and reliability. *Archives of General Psychiatry, 46*(11), 1006–1011.

Goodman, W. K., Price, L. H., Rasmussen, S. A., Mazure, C., Delgado, P. Heninger, G. R., et al. (1989b). The Yale-Brown Obsessive Compulsive Scale (Y-BOCS): Part II. Validity. *Archives of General Psychiatry, 46*(11), 1012–1016.

Goren, C. C., Sarty, M., & Wu, P. Y. K. (1975). Visual following and pattern discrimination of face-like stimuli by newborn infants. *Pediatrics, 56,* 544–549.

Gottman, J., & Katz, L. K. (1996). Parental meta-emotion philosophy and the emotional life of families: The theoretical models and preliminary data. *Journal of Family Psychology, 10,* 243–268.

Gould, E., McEwen, B. S., Tanapat, P., Galea, L. A. M., & Fuchs, E. (1997). Neurogenesis in the dentate gyrus of the adult tree shrew is regulated by psychosocial stress and NMDA receptor activation. *Journal of Neuroscience, 17*(7), 2492–2498.

Gould, E., Reeves, A. J., Graziano, M. S., & Gross, C. G. (1999). Neurogenesis in the neocortex of adult primates. *Science, 286,* 548–552.

Gould, E., Tanapat, P., Hastings, N. B., & Shors, T. J. (1999). Neurogenesis in adult: A possible role in learning. *Trends in Cognitive Science, 3,* 186–191.

Gould, E., Tanapat, P., Rydel, T., & Hastings, N. (2000). Regulation of hippocampal neurogenesis in adulthood. *Biological Psychiatry, 48,* 715–720.

Goulding, J. M. (1994). Sexual assault history and physical health in randomly selected Los Angeles women. *Health Psychology, 13,* 130–138.

Grados, M. A., Walkup, J., & Walford, S. (2003). Genetics of obsessive-compulsive disorders: New findings and challenges. *Brain and Development, 25*(Suppl. 1), S55–S61.

Granger, D. A., Granger, G. A. & Granger, S. W. (2006). Immunology and Developmental Psychopathology. In D. Cicchetti & D. Cohen (Eds.) *Developmental Psychopathology Vol. 2, Developmental Neuroscience,* (pp. 677–709). New York: Wiley.

Graybiel, A. M. (2005). The basal ganglia: Learning new tricks and loving it. *Current Opinion in Neurobiology, 15,* 638–644.

Greenberger, D., & Padesky, C. (1995). *Mind over mood: Change how you feel by changing the way you think.* New York: Guilford Press.

Greene, J. D., Lowenberg, K., Nystrom, L. E., Darley, J. M., & Cohen, J. D. (May, 2008). Saving lives vs. keeping promises: An fMRI investigation of consequentialist and deontological moral judgment. Manuscript in preparation.

Greene, J. D., Sommerville, R. B., Nystrom, L. E., Darley, J. M., & Cohen, J. D. (2001). An fMRI investigation of emotional engagement in moral judgment. *Science, 293,* 2105–2108.

Greenson, R., *The technique and practice of psychoanalysis.* New York: International Universities Press, 1992.

Gribsby, J. & Hartlaub, G. (1994). Procedural learning and the development and stability of character. *Perceptual and Motor Skills, 79,* 355–370.

Grigsby, J., & Osuch, E. (2007). Neurodynamics, state, agency, and psychological functioning. In C. Piers, J. P. Muller, & J. Brent (Eds.), *Self-organizing complexity in psychological systems.* Lanham, MD: Rowman & Littlefield.

Grigsby, J., & Stevens, D. (2000). *Neurodynamics of personality.* New York: Guilford Press.

Grigsby, J., & Stevens, D. (2002). Memory, neurodynamics, and human relationships. *Psychiatry, 65,* 13–34.

Gundel, H., Lopez-Sala, A., & Ceballos-Baumann, A. O. (2004). Alexithymia correlates with the size of the right anterior cingulate. *Psychosomatic Medicine, 66,* 132–140.

Gunnar, M. R., Tout, K., deHaan, M., Pierce, S., & Stansburg, K. (1997). Temperament, social competence, and adrenocortical activity in preschoolers. *Developmental Psychobiology, 31,* 65–85.

Gunnar, M. R. & Vazquez, D. (2006). Stress neurobiology and developmental psychopathology. In D. Cicchetti & D. Cohen, Developmental Psychopathology Vol. 2, *Developmental Neuroscience,* (pp. 533–577), New York: Wiley.

Guzowski, J. F., Setlow, B., Wagner, E. K., & McGaugh, J. (2001). Experience-dependent gene expression in the rat hippocampus after spatial learning: A comparison of the immediate-early genes Arc, c-fos, and zif 268. *Journal of Neuroscience, 21*(14), 5089–5089.

Hariri, A. R., Bookheimer, S. Y., & Mazziotta, J. C. (2000). Modulating emotional responses: Effects of a neocortical network on the limbic system. *NeuroReport, 11,* 43–48.

Hampson, E. (2008). Endocrine contributions to sex differences in visuospatial perception and cognition. In J. B. Becker, K. J. Berkley, N. Geary, E. Hampson, J. P. Herman, & E. A. Young (Eds.), *Sex differences in the brain: From genes to behavior* (pp. 311–325). New York: Oxford University Press.

Harlow, J., (1868). Recovery from passage of an iron bar through the head. *Publication of the Massachusetts Medical Society 2*, 329–346.

Hart, A. J., Whalen, P. S., Shin, L. M., McInerney, S. C., Fischer, H., & Rauch, S. L. (2000). Differential response in the human amygdala to racial out-group vs. in-group face stimuli. *NeuroReport 11*, 2351–2355.

Harter, S. (1988). Developmental processes in the construction of the self. In T. D. Yawkey & J. E. Johnson (Eds.), *Integrative processes and socialization: Early to middle childhood* (pp. 45–78), Hillsdale, NJ: Erlbaum.

Harter, S., Bresnick, S., Bouchey, H. A., & Whitsell, N. R. (1997). The development of multiple role-related selves during adolescence. *Development and Psychopathology, 9*, 835–854.

Hauri, P. J. & Fischer, J. (1986). Persistent psychophysiologic (learned) insomnia. *Sleep, 9*, 38–53.

Hawkins, J., & Blakeslee, S. (2004). *On intelligence.* New York: Holt.

Hebb, D. O. (1949). *The organization of behavior: A neuropsychological theory.* New York: Wiley.

Heller, W., Etienne, M. A., & Miller, G. A. (1995). Patterns of perceptual asymmetry in depression and anxiety: Implications for neuropsychological models of emotion and psychopathology. *Journal of Abnormal Psychology, 104*, 327–333.

Herschkowitz, N., Kegan, J., & Zilles, K. (1997). Neurobiological basis of behavioral development during the first year. *Neuropediatrics, 28*, 296–306.

Higgin, E. S. (2008). The new genetics of mental illness. *Scientific American Mind.* June/July, pp. 41–47.

Hock, R. (2005). *forty studies that changed psychology: explorations into the history of psychological research.* 5th ed. New Jersey: Prentice Hall.

Horowitz, M. J. (2001). *Stress response syndromes: Personality styles and interventions* (4th ed.), Northvale, NJ: Jason Aronson.

Horowitz, M. J. (1986). *Stress response syndromes.* Lanham, MD: Jason Aronson.

Hovarth, A. O., & Bedi, R. P. (2002). The alliance. In J. C. Norcross (Ed.), *Psychotherapy relationships that work. Therapist contributions and responsiveness to patients.* (pp. 37–70) New York: Oxford Univesity Press.

Howard, K. I., Kopta, S. M., Krause, M. S., & Orlinsky, D. E. (1986). The dose-effect relationship in psychotherapy. *American Psychologist, 41*, 159–164.

Hubel, D. H., & Wiesel, T. (1963). Receptive fields of cells in striate cortex of very young, visually inexperienced kittens. *Journal of Neurophysiology, 26*, 994–1002.

Hugdahl, K. & Davidson, (Eds.) (2003). *At asymmetrical brain.* Cambridge, MA: MIT Press.

Iacoboni, M. (2003). Understanding intentions through imitations. In S. Johnson (Ed.), *Taking action: Cognitive neuroscience perspectives on intentional acts* (pp. 107–138). Cambridge, MA: MIT Press.

Iacoboni, M., & Lenzi, G. L. (2002). Mirror neurons, the insula, and empathy. *Behavioral and Brain Sciences, 25*, 107–138.

Iacoboni, M., Lieberman, M. D., Knowlton, B. J., Molnar-Szakacs, I., Moritz, M., Throop, C. J., et al. (2004). Watching social interactions produces dorsomedial prefrontal and medial parietal BOLD fMRI signal increases compared to a resting baseline. *NeuroImage, 21,* 1167–1173.

Icker, B. R., Pham, T. M., Sanders, L. A., Albeck, D. S., Mohammed, A. H., & Grandholm, A. C. (2000). Long-term environmental enrichment leads to regional increases in neurotrophin levels in rat brains. *Experimental Neurology, 164*(1), 45–52.

Insel, T. R., & Young, L. J. (2001). The neurobiology of attachment. *Nature Reviews Neuroscience, 2,* 129–136.

Insel, T. R. (2003). Is social attachment an addictive disorder? *Physiology & Behavior, 79,* 351–357.

Jacobs, G. D. (1999). *Say good night to insomnia.* New York: Holt.

Jacob, B., Schall, M., & Scheibel, A. B. (1993). A quantitative analysis of Wernicke's area in humans: Gender, hemisphere, and environmental factors. *Journal of Comparative Neurology, 327,* 97–111.

Jacobs, B. L., van Prag, H., & Gage, F. H. (2000). Depression and the birth and death of brain cells. *American Scientist, 88,* 340–345.

James, W. (2007). *Principles of psychology* (Vols. 1–2). New York: Cosimo Classics. (Original work published 1890.)

Ji, D., & Wilson, M. A. (2007). Coordinated memory replay in the visual cortex and hippocampus during sleep. *Nature Neuroscience, 10,* 100–107.

Johnsen, B. H., & Hugdahl, K. (1991). Hemispheric asymmetry in conditioning to facial emotional expressions. *Psychophysiology, 28,* 154–162.

Johnson-Laird, P. N. (1983). *Mental models: Towards a cognitive science of language, inference, and consciousness.* Cambridge, MA: Harvard University Press.

Kaas, J. H. (1987). The organization of the neocortex in mammals: Implications for theories of brain function. *Annual Review of Psychology, 38,* 129–151.

Kaas, J. H. (1989). Why does the brain have so many visual areas? *Journal of Cognitive Neuroscience, 1,* 121–135.

Kabat-Zinn, J. (1990). *Full catastrophe living: Using the wisdom of your body and mind to face stress, pain, and illness.* New York: Delta.

Kagan, J. (1992). Behavior, biology, and the meanings of temperamental constructs. *Pediatrics, 90,* 510–513.

Kagan, J. (1994). *Galen's prophecy: Temperament and human nature.* New York: Basic Books.

Kagan, J. (1998). In N. Eisenberg (Ed.), *Handbook of child psychology* (pp. 177–236). New York: Wiley.

Kagan, J., & Snidman, N. (2004). *The long shadow of temperament.* Cambridge, MA: Harvard University Press.

Kaiser Permanente Northern California Regional Psychiatry and Chemical Dependency Best Practices. (2001a). Anxiety Best Practices Workgroup. *Clinical practice guideline for the treatment of panic disorder* (2nd ed.—summary, revised). Oakland, CA: Kaiser Permanente.

Kaiser Permanente Northern California Regional Psychiatry and Chemical Dependency Best Practices. (2001b). Anxiety Best Practices Workgroup. *Clinical practice guideline for the treatment of obsessive-compulsive disorder in adults: Summary.* Oakland, CA: Kaiser Permanente.

Kaiser Permanente Northern California Regional Psychiatry and Chemical Dependency Best Practices. (2006). Depression Best Practices Workgroup. *Clinical practice guideline for the treatment of depression.* Oakland, CA: Kaiser Permanente.

Kaiser Permanente Northern California Regional Psychiatry and Chemical Dependency Best Practices. (2007a). Anxiety Best Practices Workgroup. *Clinical practice guideline for the treatment of panic disorder* (3rd ed.). Oakland, CA: Kaiser Permanente.

Kaiser Permanente Northern California Regional Psychiatry and Chemical Dependency Best Practices. (2007b). Anxiety Best Practices Workgroup. *Clinical practice guideline for the treatment of obsessive-compulsive disorder in adults: Update April, 2007.* Oakland, CA: Kaiser Permanente.

Kaiser Permanente Northern California Regional Psychiatry and Chemical Dependency Best Practices (2008). Anxiety Best Practices Workgroup. *Clinical practice guideline for the treatment of social anxiety disorder.* Oakland, CA: Kaiser Permanente.

Kalin, N. H., Larson, C., Shelton, S. E., & Davidson, R. J. (1998). Asymmetric frontal brain activity, cortisol, and behavior associated with fearful temperament in rhesus monkeys. *Behavioral Neuroscience, 112,* 286–292.

Kalin, N. H., Shelton, S. E., & Lynn, D. E. (1995). Opiate systems in mother and infant primates coordinate intimate contact during reunion. *Psychoneuroendocrinology, 20*(7), 735–742.

Kalin, N. H., Shelton, S. E., & Snowdon, C. T. (1993). Social factors regulating security and fear in infant rhesus monkeys. *Depression, 1,* 137–142.

Kaminer, T. (1999). *Maternal depession, maternal speech, and infant gaze at four months. Unpublished doctoral dissertation* St John's University, New York

Kandel, E. R. (1997). *Journal of Cell Physiology, 173,* 124–125.

Kapur, N., Scholey, K., Moore, E., Barker, S., Brice, J., Thompson, S., et al. (1996). Long-term retention deficits in two cases of disproportionate retrograde amnesia. *Journal of Cognitive Neuroscience, 8,* 416–434.

Karege, F., Perret, G., Bondolfi, G., Schwald, M., Bertschy, G., Aubry, J. M. (2002). Decreased serum brain-derived neurotrophic factor levels in major depressed patients. *Psychiatry Research, 109*(2): 143–8.

Karen, R. (1998). *Becoming attached: First relationships and how they shape our capacity to love.* New York: Oxford University Press.

Katz, F. K., & Woodin, E. (2002). Hostility, hostile development, and conflict engagement in marriages: Effect on child and family functioning. *Child Development, 73,* 636–656.

Katz, L. C., & Shatz, C. J. (1996), *Science, 274,* 113–1138.

Kaye, K. (1982). *The mental life of babies: How parents create persons.* Chicago: University of Chicago Press.

Kehoe, P., & Blass, E. M. (1989). Conditional opioid release in ten-day-old rats: Reversal of stress with maternal stimulation. *Developmental Psychobiology, 19*(4), 385–398.

Kempermann, G., Kuhn, H. G., & Gage, F. H. (1997). More hippocampal neurons in adult mice living in an enriched environment. *Nature, 386,* 493–495.

Kemperman, G., Kuhn, H. G., & Gage, F. H. (1998). Experience induced neurogenesis in the senescent dentate gyrus. *Journal of Neuroscience, 18,* 3206–3212.

Kensinger, E. A., & Corkin, S. (2004). Two routes to emotional memory: Distinct neural processes for valence and arousal. *Proceedings of the National Academy of Sciences of the USA, 101,* 3310–3315.

Kessler, R. C., Chiu, W. T., Demler, O., & Walters, E. E. Prevalence, severity and comobidity of 12-month DSM-IV disorders in the National Comorbidity Survey Replication. (2005). *Archives of General Psychiatry, 62:* 617–627.

Kessler, R. C., McGonagle, K. A., Zhao, S., Hughes, M., Eshleman, S., Wittchen, H-V., Kender, K.S. (1994). Lifetime and 12-month prevalence of DSM-III-R psychiatric disorders in the United States: Results from the National Cormorbidity Survey. *Archives of General Psychiatry, 51:* 8–19.

Kiecolt-Glaser, J. (1999). Marital stress: Immunological, neuroendocrine, and autonomic correlates. *Annals of the New York Academy of Science, 840,* 656–663.

Kihlstrom, J. E. (1987). The cognitive unconscious. *Science, 237,* 1445–1452.

Kilts, C. D., Egan, G., Gideon, D. A., Ely, T. D., & Hoffman, J. M. (2003). Dissociable neural pathways are involved in the recognition of emotion in static and dynamic facial expressions. *NeuroImage, 18,* 156–168.

Kimura, D. (1999). *Sex and cognition.* Cambridge, MA: MIT Press.

Kingstone, A., Tipper, C., Ristic, J., & Ngan, E. (2004). The eyes have it! An fMRI investigation. *Brain and Cognition, 55,* 269–271.

Kitts, C. D., Egan, G., Gideon, D. A., Ely, T. D., & Hoffman, J. M. (2003). Dissociable neural pathways are involved in the recognition of emotion in static and dynamic facial expressions. *Neuro Image, 18,* 156–168.

Kivimaki, M., Ferrie, J. E., Brunner, E., Head, J., Shipley, M. J., Vahtera, J., et al. (2005). Justice at work and reduced risk of coronary heart disease among employees: The Whitehall II Study. *Archives of Internal Medicine, 165,* 2245–2251.

Klein, M. (1975). *The collected writings of Melanie Klein: Vol. 1. Love, guilt and reparation and other works 1921–1945.* London: Hogarth Press. (Original works published 1921–1945.)

Klein, D. F. (1993). False suffocation alarms, spontaneous panics and related conditions: An integrative hypothesis. *Archives of General Psychiatry, 50:* 306–317.

Kleinschmidt, A., Bess, M. F., & Singer, W. (1987). Blockade of "NMDA" receptors disrupts experience-based plasticity of kitten striate cortex. *Science, 238,* 355–358.

Klerman, G. L., Weissman, M. M., Rounsaville, B. J., and Chevron, E. S. (1984). *Interpersonal psychotherapy of depression: A brief focused specific strategy.* New York: Basic Books.

Knight, R. T., & Grabowecky, M. (1995). Escape from linear time: Prefrontal cortex and conscious experience. In M. S. Gazzaniga (Ed.), *The cognitive neurosciences* (pp. 1357–1371). Cambridge, MA: MIT Press.

Kolb, B., & Whishaw, I. O. (1998). Brain plasticity and behavior. *Annual Review of Psychology, 49*, 43–64.

Kolb, B. (1995). *Brain Plasticity and Behavior.* Mahwah, NJ: Lawrence Erlbaum Associates.

Koski, L., Iacoboni, M., Dubeau, M. C., Woods, R. P., & Mazziotta, J. C. (2003). Modulation of cortical activity during different imitative behaviors. *Journal of Neurophysiology, 89*, 460–471.

Kranowitz, C. S. (2005). *The Out-of-Sync Child: Recognizing and Coping with Sensory Processing Disorder.* New York: Penguin.

Krumholz, H. M., Butler, J., Miller, J., Vaccarino, V., Williams, C. S., Mendes de Leon, C. F., et al. (1988). The prognostic importance of emotion support for elderly patients hospitalized with heart failure. *Circulation, 97*, 958–964.

Krystal, J. H., Bremner, J. D., Southwick, S. M., & Charney, D. S. (1998). The emerging neurobiology of dissociation: Implications for treatment of post traumatic stress disorder. In J. D. Bremner & C. R. Marmar (Eds.), *Trauma, memory, and dissociation* (pp. 321–363). Washington, DC: American Psychiatric Press.

Kusurkar, R. A. (2004). Sir Charles Sherrington (1857–1952). *Journal of Postgraduate Medicine, 50*, 238–239.

Kubitz, K. K., Landers, D. M., Petruzzello, S. J., & Han, M. W. (1996). The effects of acute and chronic exercise on sleep. *Sports Medicine, 21*(4), 277–291.

LaBar, K. S. (2007). Beyond fear: Emotional memory mechanisms in the human brain. *Current Directions in Psychological Science, 16*, 173–177.

Laberge, B., Gauthier, J., Cote, G., Plamondon, J., & Cormier, H. J. (1992). The treatment of coexisting panic and depression: A review of the literature. *Journal of Anxiety Disorders, 6*: 169–180.

Lambert, M. (2006). Invited address. Kaiser-Permanente Northern California Region Annual Psychiatry and Chemical Dependency Services Conference. April 26, San Francisco.

Lambert, M. J. (Ed.) (2004). *Handbook of psychotherapy and behavior change* (5th ed.) New York: Wiley.

Lambert, M. J., & Barley, D. E. (2002). Research summary on the therapeutic relationship and psychotherapy outcome. In J. D. Norcross (Ed.), *Psychotherapy relationships that work: Therapist contributions and responsiveness to patients.* (pp. 17–32) New York: Oxford University Press.

Lambert, M. J., & Bergin, A. E. (1994). The effectivness of psychotherapy. In A. E. Bergin & S. L. Garfield (Eds.), *Handbook of psychotherapy and behavior change* (4th ed., pp. 143–189). New York: Wiley.

Lambert, M. J., & Lambert, J. M. (1999). Use of psychological tests for assessing treatment outcome. In Mark E. Maruish (Ed.), *The use of psychological testing for treatment planning and outcomes assessment. Vol. 1: General considerations* (4th ed.) Mahwah, NJ: Erlbaum.

Lambert, M. J., & Ogles, B. (2004). The efficacy and effectiveness of psychotherapy. In M. J. Lambert (Ed.), *Bergin and Garfield's handbook of psychotherapy and behavior change* (5th ed., pp. 139–193). Hoboken, NJ: Wiley.

Lambert, M. J., & Okiishi, J. C. (1997). The effects of the individual psychotherapist and impliations for future research. *Clinical Psychology Science and Practice, 4,* 6–75.

Lane, R. D. (1998). Neural correlates of levels of emotional awareness: Evidence of an interaction between emotion and attention in the anterior cingulate cortex. *Journal of Cognitive Neuroscience, 10,* 525–535.

Lang, P.J. (1987). Fear and anxiety: Cognitive, memory, and behavior. In D. Magnusson, & A. Ohman (Eds.) *Psychopathology: An interactional perspective* (pp. 159–176). San Diego: Academic Press.

Lang, P.J. (1985). The cognitive psychophysiology of emotion: Fear and anxiety. In A. H. Tuma, & J.D. Maser (Eds.) *Anxiety and Anxiety Disorders* (pp. 131–170).

Larsen, R. J., Kasimatis, M., & Frey, K. (1992). Facilitating the furrowed brow: An unobtrusive test of the facial feedback hypothesis applied to unpleasant affect. *Cognition and Emotion, 6,* 321–338.

Lazar, S. W., Kerr, C. W., Wasserman, R. H., Gray, J. R., Greve, D. N., Treadway, M. T., et al., (2005). Meditation experience is associated with increased cortical thickness. *Neuroreport, 16*(17), 1893–1897.

LeDoux, J. E. (1994). Emotion, memory, and the brain. *Scientific American, 270,* 32–39.

LeDoux, J. E. (1996). *The emotional brain: The mysterious underpinnings of emotional life.* New York Simon and Schuster.

LeDoux, J. E. (2002). *The synaptic self: How are brains become who we are.* New York: Penguin.

LeDoux, J. E. (1995). Emotion: Clues from the brain. *Annual Review of Psychology, 46,* 209–235.

LeDoux, J. E., Iwata, J., Cicchetti, P., & Reis, D. J. (1988). Different projections of the central amygdaloid nucleus mediate autonomic and behavioral correlates of conditioned fear. *Journal of Neuroscience, 8,* 2517–2529.

LeDoux, J. E., Romanski, L. M., & Xagorasis, A. E. (1989). Indelibility of subcortical emotional memories. *Journal of Cognitive Neuroscience, 1,* 238–243.

LeDoux, J. E., Sakaguchi, A., & Reis, D. J. (1984). Subcortical efferent projections of the medial geniculate nucleus mediate emotional responses conditioned to acoustic stimuli. *Journal of Neuroscience, 4,* 683–698.

Lenartowicz, A., & McIntosh, A. R. (2005). The role of anterior cingulate cortex in working memory is shaped by functional connectivity. *Journal of Cognitive Neuroscience, 17,* 1026–1042.

Leppanen, J. & Hietanen, J. (2003). Affect and face perception. *Emotion, 3*, 315–326.

Lethem, J. (1999). *Motherless Brooklyn.* New York: Random House.

Levenson, R., & Reuf, A. (1997). Emotional knowledge and rapport. In W. Ickes (Ed.), *Empathic accuracy* (pp. 44–72). New York: Guilford Press.

Lewis, M. D. (1995). Cognition-emotion feedback and the self-organization of developmental paths. *Human Development, 38*, 71–102.

Lewis, T., Amini, F., & Lannon, R. (2000). *A general theory of love.* New York: Random House.

Ley, R. (1985). Blood, breath, and fears: A hyperventilation theory of panic attacks and agoraphobia. *Clinical Psychology Review, 5*: 271–285.

Ley, R. (1989). Dyspeic-fear and catastrophic cognitions in hyperventilatory panic attacks. *Begavioral Research and Therapy. 27*(5): 549–554.

Ley, R. (1988). Panic attacks during sleep: A hyperventilation probability model. *Journal of Behavioral and Experimental Psychiatry. 19*(3): 181–192.

Libet, B. (1981). Timing of cerebral process relative to concomitant conscious experience in man. In G. Adam, I. Meszaros, & E. I. Banyai (Eds.), *Advances in physiological sciences.* Elmsford, NY: Pergamon Press.

Lieberman, M., & Eisenberger, N. I. (2005). A pain by any other name (rejection, exclusion, ostracism).still hurts the same: The role of dorsal anterior cingulate cortex in social and physical pain. In J. Cacioppo (Ed.), *Social neuroscience: People thinking about people.* Cambridge, MA: MIT Press.

Lieberman, M., & Ochsner, K. (2001). The emergence of social cognitive neuroscience. *American Psychologist, 56*, 717–734.

Lindemann, E. (1944). Symptomatology and management of acute grief. *American Journal of Psychiatry, 101*, 141–148.

Linehan, M. (1993). *Cognitive-behavioral treatment of borderline personality disorder.* New York: Guilford Press.

Liotti, M., & Tucker, D. M. (1992). Right hemisphere sensitivity to arousal and depression. *Brain and Cognition, 18*, 138–151.

Litz, B. T., & Gray, M. J. (2004). Early intervention for trauma in adults: A framework for first aid and secondary prevention. In B. T. Litz (Ed.), *Early intervention for trauma and traumatic loss* (pp. 87–111). New York: Guilford Press.

Loftus, E. F. (2003). Make believe memories. *American Psychologist, 58*, 867–873.

Loftus, E. F., Milo, E. M., & Paddock, J. R. (1995). The accidental executioner: Why psychotherapy must be informed by science. *Counseling Psychologist, 23*(2), 300–309.

Lombroso, P. J., & Sapolsky, R. (1998). Development of the cerebral cortex: Stress and brain development. *Journal of the Academy of Child and Adolescent Psychiatry, 37*, 1337–1339.

Long, B. C., & van Stavel, R. (1995). Effects of exercise training on anxiety: A meta-analysis. *Journal of Applied Sport Psychology, 7*, 167–189.

Lovgren, S. (2005, August 1). Chimps, humans 96 percent the same, gene study finds. *National Geographic News*, 1.

Lynch, M., & Cicchetti, D. (1998). Trauma, mental representation, and the organization of memory for mother-referent material. *Development and Psychopathology, 10,* 235–257.

Main, M. (1995). Attachment: Overview, with implication for clinical work. In S. Goldberg, R. Muir, & J. Kerr (Eds.), *Attachment theory: Social, developmental, and clinical perspectives* (pp. 407–474). Hillsdale, NJ: Analytic Press.

Main, M. (1996). Introduction to the special section on attachment and psychopathology: 2. Overview of the field of attachment. *Journal of Consulting and Clinical Psychology, 64,* 237–243.

Main, M., & Goldwyn, R. (1994). Adult attachmnent scoring and classificaton system. Unpublished manuscript, University of California, Berkeley.

Main, M., & Hesse, E. (1990). Parents' unresolved traumatic experiences are related to infant disorganized status: Is frightened and/or frightening parental behavior the linking mechanism? In M. T. Greenburg, D. Cicchetti, & E. M. Cummings (Eds.), *Attachment in the preschool years: Theory, research, and intervention* (pp. 161–182). Chicago: University of Chicago Press.

Main, M., & Solomon, J. (1986). Discovery of an insecure/disorganized attachment pattern. In T. B. Brazelton & M. Yogman (Eds.), *Affective development in infancy* (pp. 95–124). Norwood, NJ: Ablex.

Main, M., & Solomon, J. (1990). Procedures for identifying infants as disorganized/disoriented during the Ainsworth Strange Situation. In M. T. Greenburg, D. Cicchetti, & E. M. Cummings (Eds.), *Attachment in the preschool years: Theory, research, and intervention* (pp. 121–160). Chicago: University of Chicago Press.

Maitland, S. B., Herlitz, A., Nyberg, L., Backman, L., & Nilsson, L. G. (2004). Selective sex differences in declarative memory. *Memory and Cognition, 32,* 1160–1169.

Margraf, J., Barlow, D. H., Clark, D. M., & Telch, M. J. (1993). Psychological treatment of panic: Work in progress on outcome, active ingredients, and follow-up. *Behavior Research and Therapy, 31*(1), 1–8.

Marmot, M. G., & Shipley, M. J. (1996). Do socio-economic differences in mortality persist after retirement? 25-year follow-up of civil servants in the first Whitehall Study. *British Medical Journal, 313,* 1177–1180.

Martin, A., Wiggs, C. L. & Weisberg, J. (1997). Modulation of human medial temporal lobe activity by form, meaning, and experience. *Hippocampus, 7,* 587–593.

Mayberg, H. S. (2006). Medication, psychotherapy and DBS in the treatment of depression: A functional neuroimaging perspective. Invited address. Annual Kaiser Permanente Psychiatry and Chemical Dependency Services Conference, San Francisco, April 22, 2006.

Mayberg, H. S., Liotti, M., Brannan, S. K., McGinnis, S., Mahurin, R. K., Jerabek, P. A., et al. (1999). Reciprocal limbic-cortical function and negative mood: Converging PET findings in depression and normal sadness. *American Journal of Psychiatry, 156,* 675–682.

Mayberg, H. S., Lozano, A. M., Voon, V., McNeely, H. E., Hmani, C., Schwalb, J. M., et al. (2005). Deep brain stimulation for treatment-resistant depession, *Neuron, 45*, 651–660.

McCabe, A., & Peterson, C. (1991). Getting the story: A longitudinal study of parental styles in eliciting narratives and developing narratives and developing narrative skill. In A. McCabe & C. Peterson (Eds.), *Developing narrative structure* (pp. 217–253). Hillsdale, NJ: Erlbaum.

McCraty, R., Atkinson, M., Tomasion, D., & Tiller, W. A. (1998). The electricity of touch: Detection and measurement of cardiac energy exchange between people. In K. H. Pribram & J. King (Eds.), *Brain and values: Is biological science of values possible?* (pp. 359–379). Hillsdale, NJ: Erlbaum.

McEwen, B. (1999). Development of the cerebral cortex XIII: Stress and brain development—II. *Journal of the American Academy of Child and Adolescent Psychiatry, 38*, 101–103.

McEwen, B. S. (1992). Paradoxical effects of adrenal steroids on the brain: Protection versus degeneration. *Biological Psychology, 31*, 177–199.

McEwen, B. S. (1998). Stress, adaptation, and disease: Allostasis and allostatic load. *Annals of the New York Academy of Science, 840*, 33–44.

McEwen, B. S. (2004). Structural plasticity of the adult brain: How animal models help us understand brain changes in depression and systematic disorders related to depression. *Dialogues in Clinical Neuroscience, 6*, 119–133.

McEwan, B. S., & Stellar, E. (1993). Stress and the Individual- Mechanisms leading to disease. *Archives of Internal Medicine, 153*, 2093–2101.

McEwen, B. S., & Wingfield, J. C. (2003). The concept of allostasis in biology and biomedicine. *Hormones and Behavior, 43*, 2–15.

McFarland, D. (2001). Respiratory markers of conversational interaction. *Journal of Speech, Language, and Hearing Research, 44*, 128–145.

McGaugh, J. L. (1990). Significance and remembrance: The role of neuromodulatory systems. *Psychological Science, 1*, 15–25.

McGaugh, J. L. (2004). The amygdala modulates the consolidation of memories of emotionally arousing experiences. *Annual Review of Neuroscience, 27*, 1–28.

McGaugh, J. L., Introlini-Collison, I. B., Cahill, L. F., Castellano, C., Dalmuz, C., Parent, M. B., et al. (1993). Neuromodulatory systems and memory storage: Role of the amygdala. *Behavioral Brain Research, 53*, 81–90.

McKay, K. M., Zac, E. I., & Wampold, B. E. (2006). Psychiatrist effects in the psychopharmacological treatment of depression. *Journal of Affective Disorders, 92*(2/3), 287–290.

McKeever, V. M., & Huff, M. E. (2003). A diathesis-stress model of posttraumatic stress disorder: Ecological, biological, and residual stress pathways. *Review of General Psychology, 7*, 237–250.

McNally, R. J. (2003a). Progress and controversy in the study of posttraumatic stress disorder. *Annual Review of Psychology, 54*, 229–252.

McNally, R. J. (2003b). Recovering memories of trauma: A view from the laboratory. *Current Directions of Psychological Science, 12*, 32–35.

Meany, M. (2001). Maternal care, gene expression, and the transmission of individual differences in stress reactivity across generations. *Annual Review of Neuroscience, 24,* 1161–1192.

Meltzoff, A. N., & Moore, M. K. (1977). Imitation of facial and manual gestures in human neonates. *Science, 198,* 74–78.

Mesulam, M. M. (1998). From sensation to cognition. *Brain, 121,* 1013–1052.

Metzger, L. J., Gilbertson, M. W., & Orr, S. P. (2005). Electophysiology of PTSD. In J. J. Vaserling & C. R. Brewin (Eds.), *Neuropsychology of PTSD: Biological, cognitive, and clinical perspectives* (pp. 83–102). New York: Guilford Press.

Mikulincer, M., & Shaver, P. R. (2003). The attachment behavioral system in adulthood: Activation, psychodynamics, and interpersonal processes. In M. P. Zanna (Ed.), *Advances in experimental social psychology* (Vol. 35, pp. 53–152). New York: Academic Press.

Miller, G. (2005). New neurons strive to fit in. *Science, 311,* 938–940.

Miller, G. (2005). New neurons strive to fit in. *Science, 35,* 938–940.

Miller, S. D., Duncan, B. L., & Hubble, M. A. (2004). Outcome-informed clinical work. In J. Norcross & M. Goldfriend (Eds.), *Handbook of psychotherapy integration.* New York: Oxford University Press.

Milner, B. (1962). Les trouble de la mémoire accompagnant des lésions hippocampiques bilatérales. In P. Passouant (Ed.), *Physiologie de l'hippocampe* (pp. 257–272). Paris: Centre National de la Recherche Scientifique.

Milner, B. (1965). Memory disturbances after bilateral hippocampal lesions in man. In P. M. Milner & S. E. Glickman (Eds.), *Cognitive processes and brain.* Princeton, NJ: Van Nostrand.

Minkel, J. R. (2007, July 6). Brain pathway may underlie depression: A crescent of electrical activity spotted in rats may allow researchers to map the depressed brain. *Scientific American Mind News,* http://www.sciam.com/article.cfm?id=brain-pathway-may-underlie-depression.

Mitchell, J. P. (2002). Distinct neural systems subserve person and object knowledge. *Proceedings of the National Academy of Sciences, 99*(23), 15238–15243.

Mitchell, J. T., & Everly, G. S., Jr. (2000). Critical incident stress management and critical incident stress debriefings: Evolutions, effects, and outcomes. In B. Raphael & J. P. Wilson (Eds.), *Psychological debriefing: Theory practice, and evidence* (pp. 71–90). New York: Cambridge University Press.

Mitchell, S. A., & Black, M. J. (Eds.) (1995). *Freud and beyond: A history of modern psychoanalytic thought.* New York: Basic Books.

Moore, S. A., Zoellner, L. A., & Bittinger, J. N. (2004). Combining cognitive restructuring and exposure therapy: Toward an optimal integration. In S. Taylor (Ed.), *Advances in the treatment of PTSD: Cognitive-behavioral perspectives* (pp. 13–17). New York: Springer.

Moran, J. M., Macrae, C. N., Heatherton, T. F., Wyland, C. L., & Kelley, W. M. (2006). Neuroanatomical evidence for distinct cognitive and affective components of self. *Journal of Cognitive Neuroscience, 18,* 1586–1594.

Mountcastle, V. B. (1979). An organizing principle for cerebral function: The unit module and the distributed system. In F. O. Schmitt & F. G. Worden (Eds.), *The neurosciences: Fourth study program* (pp. 21–42). Cambridge, MA: MIT Press.

Müller-Schwarze, D. (1984). Analysis of play therapy behavior: What do we measure and when? In P. K Smith (Ed.), *Play in animals and humans* (pp. 271–294). New York: Basil Blackwell.

Murray, C. J. L., Lopez, A. D. (1997). Alternative projections of mortality and disability by cause 1990–2020: Global Burden of Disease Study. *Lancet, 349*: 1498–1504.

Neisser, U. (1987). *Cognitive psychology*. New York: Appleton-Century-Crofts.

Neisser, V., & Fivush, R. (Eds.) (1994). *The remembering self: Construction and accuracy in the self-narrative*. Cambridge: Cambridge University Press.

Neville, H. J., Bavelier, D., Corina, D., Rauschecker, J., Karni, A., Lalwani, A., et al. (1998). Cerebral organization for language in deaf and hearing subjects: Biological constraints and effects of experience. *Proceedings of the National Academy of Sciences of the USA, 95*, 922–929.

Nieuwenhuis, S., Ridderinkhof, K. R., Blom, J., Band, G. P., & Kok, A. Nikolaenko, N. N., Egorov, A. Y., & Frieman, E. A. (1997). Representational activity of the right and left hemispheres of the brain. *Behavioral Neurology, 10*, 49–59.

Nobre, A. C., Coull, J. T., Frith, C. D., & Mesulam, M. M. (1999). Orbitofrontal cortex is activated during breaches of expectation in tasks of visual attention. *Nature Neuroscience, 2*, 11–12.

Nomura, M., Ohira, H., Haneda, K., Iidaka, T., Sadato, N., Okada, T., et al. (2004). Functional association of the amygdala and ventral prefrontal cortex during cognitive evaluation of facial expressions primed by masked angry faces: An event-related fMRI study. *NeuroImage, 21*, 352–363.

Norcross, J. C. (1993). The relationship of choice: Matching the therapist's stance to individual patients. *Psychotherapy, 30*, 402–403.

Norcross, J. D. (2002). Empirically supported therapy relationships. In J. D. Norcross (Ed.), *Psychotherapy relationships that work: Therapist contributions and responsiveness to patients*. New York: Oxford University Press.

Norcross, J. C. (Ed.) (2001). Empirically supported therapy relationships: Summary report of the Division 29 Task Force (2001). *Psychotherapy, 39*(4).

North, T. C., McCullagh, P., & Tran, Z. V. (1990). Effect of exercise on depression. *Exercise and Sport Science Reviews, 18*, 375–415.

Nowicki, S., & Duke, S. (2002). *Will I ever fit in?* New York: Free Press.

Ochs, E., & Capps, L. (1996). Narrating the self. *Annual Review of Anthropology, 25*, 19–43.

Ochsner, K. (2006). How think controls feeling: A social cognitive neuroscience approach. In P. Winkleman & E. Harmon-Jones (Eds.), *Social Neuroscience*. New York: Oxford University Press.

Ochsner, K., & Gross, J. (2005). The cognitive control of emotion. *Trends in Neuroscience, 9*, 242–249.

O'Connor, T. G., Bredenkamp, D., Rutter, M., & the English and Romanian Adoptees (ERA) Study Team. (1999). Attachment disturbances and disorders in children exposed to early severe deprivation. *Infant Mental Health Journal*, 20(1), 10–29.

O'Connor, P. J., & Youngstedt, M. A. (1995). Influence of exercise on human sleep. *Exercise and Sport Science Reviews, 23*, 105–134.

O'Doherty, J., Kringelback, M. L., Rolls, E. T., Hornak, J., & Andrews, C. (2001). Abstract reward and punishment representations in the human orbital frontal cortex. *Nature Neuroscience, 4*(1), 95–102.

Ogawa, J. R., Sroufe, I. A., Weinfeld, N. S., Carlson, E. A., & Egeland, B. (1997). Development and the fragmented self: Longitudinal study of dissociated symptomatology in a nonclinical sample. *Development and Psychopathology, 9*, 855–880.

Olney, J., Lubruyere, J., Wang, G., Wozniak, D. F., Price, M. T., Sesma, M. A. (1991). NMDA antagonist neuotoxicity: Mechanishm and prevention. *Science, 257*: 1515–1518.

Orlinsky, D. E., Grave, K., & Parks, B. K. (1994). Process and outcome in psychotherapy—Noch einmal. In A. E. Bergin & S. L. Garfield (Eds.), *Handbook of psychotherapy and behavior change* (pp. 257–310). New York: Wiley.

Orlinsky, D. E., & Howard, K. J. (1998). Process and outcome in psychotherapy. In S. I. Garfield & A. E. Bergin (Eds.). *Handbook of psychology and behavioral change* (pp. 311–381). New York: Wiley.

Ouimette, P., Moos, R. H., & Brown, P. J. (2003). Substance use disorder–posttraumatic stress disorder comorbidity: A survey of treatments and proposed practice guidelines. In P. Ouimette & P. J. Brown (Eds.), *Trauma and substance abuse: Causes, consequences, and treatment of comorbid disorders* (pp. 91–110). Washington, DC: American Psychological Association.

Otto, M. W. & Whittal, M. L. (1995). Cognitive-Behavioral Therapy and the longitudinal course of panic disorder. *Psychiatric Clinics of America, 18*(4): 803–820.

Ozer, E. J., Best, S. R., Lipsey, T. L., & Weiss, D. S. (2003). Predators of posttraumatic stress disorder and symptoms in adults: A meta-analysis. *Psychological Bulletin, 129*, 52–73.

Packard, M. G., & Knowlton, B. J. (2002). Learning and memory functions of the basal ganglia. *Annual Review of Neuroscience, 25*, 563–593.

Padesky, C. A. (1994). Schema change processes in cognitive therapy. *Clinical Psychology and Psychotherapy, 1*(5), 267–278.

Pakarik, G. (1992). Posttreatment adjustment of patients who drop out early vs. late in treatment. *Journal of Clinical Psychology, 48*(3), 379–387.

Pakarik, G. (1993). Beyond effectivenes: Uses of consumer-oriented criteria in defining treatemtnt success. In T. R. Giles (Ed.), *Handbook of effective psychotherapy* (pp. 409–436). New York: Plenum Press.

Panksepp, J. (1998). *Affective neuroscience: The foundation of human and animal emotions*. New York: Oxford University Press.

Panskepp, J., & Beatty, W. W. (1980). Social deprivation and play in rats. *Behavioral and Neural Biology, 30*, 197–206.

Panksepp, J., Gordon, N., & Burgdorf, J. (2002). Empathy and action-perception resonances of basic socio-emotional systems of the brain. *Behavioral and Brain Sciences, 25,* 43–44.

Papp, L. A., Klein, D. F. & Gorman, J. M. (1993). Carbon dioxide hypersensitivity, hyperventilation and panic disorder. *American Journal of Psychiatry, 150*(8): 1149–1157.

Parent, M. B., West, M. & McGaugh, J. L. (1994). Memory of rats with amygdala regions 30 days after footshock, motivated escape training reflects degree of original training. *Behavioral Neuroscience, 108,* 1080–1087.

Parnell, L. (1997). *Transforming trauma: EMDR: The revolutionary new therapy for freeing the mind, clearing the body, and opening the heart.* New York: Norton.

Payne, J. D., Nadel, L., Britton, W. B., & Jacobs, W. J. (2004). The biophysiology of trauma and memory. In D. Resiberg & P. Hertel (Eds.), *Memory and emotion* (pp. 76–128). New York: Oxford University Press.

Pekarik, G. (1993). Beyond effectiveness: Uses of consumer-oriented criteria in defining treatment success. In T. R. Giles (Ed.), *Handbook of effective psychotherapy* (pp. 409–436). New York: Plenum Press.

Pelphrey, K. A., Sasson, N. J., Reznick, J. S., Paul, G., Goldman, B. D., & Piven, J. (2002). Visual scanning of faces in autism. *Journal of Autism and Developmental Disorders, 32,* 249–261.

Perls, F., Hefferline, R., & Goodman, P. (1951). *Gestalt therapy: Excitement and growth in human personality.* New York: Dell.

Pernanen, K. (1991). *Alcohol in human violence.* New York: Guilford Press.

Perry, B. D., Pollard, R. A., Blakey, T. I., Baker, W. L., & Vigilante, D. (1995). Childhood trauma, the neurobiology of adaptation and "use dependent" development of the brain; How "states" become "traits." *Infant Mental Health Journal, 16*(4), 271–291.

Persinger, M. A., & Makarec, K. (1991). Greater right hemisphericity is associated with lower self-esteem in adults. *Perceptual and Motor Skills, 73,* 1244–1246.

Pettus, A. (2006 July–August). Psychiatry by prescription: Do psychotropic drugs blur the boundaries beween illness and health? *Harvard Magazine,* 38–91.

Pham, T. M., Soderstrom, S., Henriksson, B. G., & Mohammed, A. H. (1997). Effects of neonatal stimulation on later cognitive function and hippocampal nerve growth factor. *Behavioral Brain Research, 86,* 113–120.

Phelps, E. A., O'Connor, K. J., Cunningham, W. A., Gatenby, J. C., Funayama, E. S., Gore, J. C., et al. (2000). Amygdala activation predicts performance on indirect measures of racial bias. *Journal of Cognitive Neuroscience, 12,* 729–738.

Phillips, A. (1993). *On kissing, tickling and being bored.* Cambridge, MA: Harvard University Press.

Pike, A., & Plomin, R. (1996). Importance of nonshared environmental factors for childhood and adolescent psychopathology. *Journal of the American Academy of Child and Adolescent Psychiatry, 35,* 560–570.

Pinker, S. (1997). *How the mind works.* New York: Norton.

Pinker, S. (2008, January 13). The moral instinct. *New York Times Magazine*, 32–58.

Pissiota, A. F., Fernandez, M., von Knorring, L., Fischer, II., & Fredrikson, M. (2002). Neurofunctional correlates of posttraumatic stress disorder: A PET symptom provocation study. *European Archives of Psychiatry and Clinical Neuroscience, 252*, 68–75.

Pissiota, A., Frans, O., Fernandez, M., von Knorring, L., Fischer, H., & Fredrikson, M. (2002). Neurofunctional correlates of posttraumatic stress disorder: A PET symptom provocation study. *European Archives of Clinical Neuroscience, 252*, 68–75.

Pitman, R. K., Orr, S. P., van der Kolk, B. A., Greenberg, M. S., Meyerhoff, J. L., & Mougcy, E. H. (1990). Analgesia: A new dependent variable for the biological study of post traumatic stress disorder. In M. E. Wolf & A. D. Mosnaim (Eds.), *Post-traumatic stress disorder: Etiology, phenomenology and treatment* (pp. 141–147). Washington, DC: American Psychiatric Press.

Pollack, S. (2001). P3b reflects maltreated children's reactions to facial displays of emotion. *Psychophysiology, 38*, 267–274.

Pollack, S., & Tolley-Schell, S. (2003). Selective attention to facial emotion in physically abused children. *Journal of Abnormal Psychology, 112*, 323–338.

Pope, H. G., Hudson, J. I., Bodkin, J. A., & Olivia, P. (1998). Questionable validity of "dissociative amensic" in trauma victims. *British Journal of Psychiatry, 172*, 210–215.

Porges, S. W., Doussard-Roosevelt, J. A., & Maiti, A. K. (1994). Vagal tone and the physiological regulation of emotion. In N. A. Fox (Ed.), *The development of emotional regulation: Biological and behavioral considerations. Monographs of the Society for Research in Child Development, 59*(2–3, Serial No. 240) 167–186.

Post, R. M., & Weiss, S. R. B. (1997). Emergent properties of neural systems: How focal molecular neurobiological alterations can affect behavior. *Development and Psychopathology, 9*, 907–929.

Preston, S. D., Bechara, A., Grabowski, T. J., Damasio, H., & Damasio, A. R. (2002, April). Functional anatomy of emotional imagery. Positron emission tomography of personal and hypothetical experiences. *Journal of Cognitive Neurosciences*, Suppl., 126.

Prochaska, J. L., & DiClemenetc, C. C. (1983). Stages and processes of self-change in smoking: Toward an integrative model of change. *Journal of Consulting and Clinical Psychology, 5*, 390–395.

Prochaska, J. O., & Norcross, J. D. (2002). *Systems of psychotherapy: A transtheoretical analysis* (5th ed.) Pacific Grove, CA: Brooks/Cole.

Puce, A., Allison, T., Gore, J. C., & McCarthy, G. (1995). Face-sensitive regions in human extrastriate cortex studied by functional MRI. *Journal of Neurophysiology, 74*, 1192–1199.

Quitkin, F. M., et al. (2000). *Journal of Neuroscience, 20*, 1225–1311.

Ramin, C. J. (2007). *Carved in sand: When attention fails and memory fades in midlife.* New York: HarperCollins.

Ramnani, N., & Miall, R. C. (2004). A system in the human brain for predicting the actions of others. *Nature Neuroscience, 7*, 85–90.

Rauch, S. L., Jenike, M. A., Alpert, N. M., Baer, L., Breiter, H. C. R., Savage, C. R., et al. (1994a). Regional cerebral blood flow measured during symptom provocation in obsessive-compulsive disorder using oxygen 15-labeled carbon dioxide and positron emission tomography. *Archives of General Psychiatry, 51*, 62–70.

Rauch, S. L., Shin, L. M., Dougherty, D. D., Alpert, N. M., Fischman, A. J., & Jenike, M. (2002). Predictors of fluvoxamine response in contamination-related obsessive compulsive disorder: A PET symptom provocation study. *Neuropsychopharmacology, 27*, 782–791.

Rauch, S. L., van der Kolk, B. A., Fisher, R. E., Alpert, N. M., Orr, S. P., Savage, C. R., et al. (1996a). A symptom provocation study of PTSD using PET and script driven imagery. *Archives of General Psychiatry, 46*, 493–500.

Rauch, S. L., van der Kolk, B. A., Fisler, R. E., Alpert, N. M., Orr, S. P., Savage, C. R., et al. (1996b). A symptom provocation study of PTSD using PET and script driven imagery. *Archives of General Psychiatry, 53*, 380–387.

Reid, I. C. & Stewart, C. A. (2001). How antidepressants work: New perspectives on the pathophysiology of depressive disorder. *British Journal of Psychiatry, 178*: 299–303.

Reiman, E. M., Raichle, M. E., Robins, E., Mintun, M. A., Fusselman, M. J., Fox, P. T., et al. (1989). Neuroanatomical correlates of lactate-induced anxiety attack. *Archives of General Psychiatry, 46*, 493–500.

Reiman, E. M., Raichle, M. E., Butler, F. K., Hersocovitch, P. & Robins, E. (1984). A focal brain abnormality in panic disorder, a severe form of anxiety. *Nature, 310*, 683–685.

Reisberg, D., & Heuer, F. (2004). Memory for emotional events. In D. Reisberg & P. Hertel (Eds.), *Memory and emotion* (pp. 3–41). New York: Oxford University Press.

Resnick, H. S., Yehuda, R., Pitman, R. K., & Foy, D. W. (1995). Effects of previous trauma on acute plasma cortisol level following rape. *American Journal of Psychiatry, 152*(11), 1675–1677.

Rezai, K., Andreason, N. C., Alliger, R., Cohen, G., Swayze, V., & O'Leary, D. S. (1993). The neuropsychology of the prefrontal cortex. *Archives of Neurology, 50*, 636–642.

Rilling, J. K., Gutman, D. A., Zeh, T. R., Panoni, G., Berns, G. S., & Kilts, C. D. (2002). A neural basis for social cooperation. *Neuron, 35*, 395–405.

Rizzolatti, G., & Arbib, M. A. (1998). Language within our grasp. *Trends in Neurosciences, 21*(5), 188–194.

Rizzolatti, G., Fadiga, L., & Gallese, V. (2001). Neurophysiological mechanisms underlying the understanding and imitation. *Nature Reviews Neuroscience, 2*, 66–70.

Rizzolatti, G., Fadiga, L., Gallese, V., & Fogassi, C. (1996), Pre-motor cortex and the recognition of motor action. *Cognitive Brain Research, 3*(2), 131–141.

Robbins, P., & Zacks, J. M. (2007). Attachment theory and cognitive science: Commentary on Fonagy and Target. *Journal of the American Psychoanalytic Association*, 55(2), 909–920.

Rochat, P. (2002). Various Kinds of Empathy as Revealed by the Developing child, not the Monkey's Brain. *Behavioral and Brain Science*, 25, 45–46.

Rogers, C. R. (1942). *Counseling and psychotherapy: Newer concepts in practice*. Boston: Houghton Mifflin.

Rogers, C. R. (1951). *Patient centered therapy*. Boston: Houghton Mifflin.

Rogers, C. R. & Dymond, R. F. (Eds.) (1954). *Psychotherapy and personality change*. Chicago: University of Chicago Press.

Roizen, J. (1997). Epidemiological issues in alcohol-related violence. In M. Galanter (Ed.), *Recent developments in alcoholism* (Vol. 13, pp. 7–40). New York: Plenum Press.

Rolls, E. T. (1999). *The brain and emotion*. Oxford: Oxford University Press.

Rosenblum, L. A., Coplan, J. D., Friedman, S., Basoff, T., Gorman, J. M., & Andrews, M. W. (1994). Adverse early experiences affect noradrenergic and serotonergic functioning in adult primates. *Biological Psychiatry*, 35, 221–227.

Ross, E. D., Homan, R. W., & Buck, R. (1994). Differential hemispheric lateralization of primary and social emotions: Implications for developing a comprehensive neurology for emotions, repression, and the subconscious. *Neuropsychiatry, Neuropsychology, and Behavioral Neurology*, 7, 1–19.

Rudebeck, P. H., Buckley, M. J., Walton, M. E., & Rushworth, M. F. S. (2006). A role for the macaque anterior cingulate gyrus in social valuation. *Science*, 313, 1310–1312.

Rudy, J. W., & Morledge, P. (1994). Ontogeny of contextual fear conditioning in rats: Implications for consolidation, infantile amnesia, and hippocampal system function. *Behavioral Neuroscience*, 108, 227–234.

Rumelhart, D. E., & McClelland, J. L. PDP models and general issues in cognitive science. In D. E. Rumelhart & J. L. McClelland (Eds.), *Parallel distributed processing: Explorations in the microstructure of cognition*.

Russell, Bertrand (1921). *The analysis of mind*. London: Allen & Unwin.

Rutter, M. (1989). Temperament: Conceptual issues and implications. In G. A. Kohstamm, J. E. Bates, & M. K. Rothbart (Eds.), *Temperament in childhood* (pp. 362–479). New York: Wiley.

Rutter, M., Dunn, J., Plomin, R., Simonoff, E., Pickles, A., Maughan, B., et al. (1997). Integrating nature and nurture: Implications of person-environment correlations and interactions in developmental psychopathology. *Development and Psychopathology*, 9, 335–364.

Sabbagh, M. A. (2004). Understanding orbital frontal contributions to the theory-of-mind reasoning. Implications for autism. *Brain and Cognition*, 55, 209–219.

Safran, J. D., & Muran, J. C. (2003). *Negotiating the therapeutic alliance: A relational treatment guide*. New York: Guilford Press.

Sala, F., Krupat, E., & Roter, D. (2002). Satisfaction and the use of humor by physicians and patients. *Psychology and Health*, 17, 269–280.

Sapolsky, R. M. (1987). Glucocorticoids and hippocampal damage. *Trends in Neuroscience, 19*(9), 346–349.

Sapolsky, R. M. (1990, January). Stress in the wild. *Scientific American*, 116–123.

Sapolsky, R. M. (1996). Why stress is bad for your brain. *Science, 273*, 749–750.

Sapolsky, R. M. (1997). The importance of a well-groomed child. *Science, 277*, 1620–1621.

Sapolsky, R. M., Romero, L. M., & Munck, A. U. (2000). How do glucorcorticoids influence stress response? Integrating permissive suppressive, stimulatory, and preparative actions. *Endrocrine Reviews, 21*, 55–89.

Saxena, S., Brody, A. L., Maidment, K. M., Smith, E. C., Zohrabi, N., Katz, E., et al. (2004). Cerebral glucose metabolism in obsessive-compulsive hoarding. *American Journal of Psychiatry, 161*(6), 1038–1048.

Schacter, D. L. (1996). *Searching for memory: The brain, the mind, and the past.* New York: Basic Books.

Schaefer, R. (1992). *Retelling a life: Narration and dialogue in psychoanalysis.* New York: Basic Books.

Schiff, B. B., Esses, V. M., & Lamon, M. (1992). Unilateral facial contractions produce mood effect on social cognitive judgements. *Cognition and Emotion, 6*, 357–368.

Schiffer, F., Teicher, M. H., & Papanicolaou, A. C. (1995). Evoked potential evidence for right brain activity during the recall of traumatic memories. *Journal of Neuropsychiatry and Clinical Neurosciences, 7*, 169–175.

Schmidt, L. A. (1999). Frontal brain electrical activity in shyness and sociability. *Psychological Science, 10*, 316–321.

Schmand, B., Smit, J. H., Geerlings, M. I., & Lindeboom, J. (1997). The effects of intelligence and education on the development of dementia: A test of the brain reserve hypothesis. *Psychological Medicine, 27*, 1337–1344.

Shoenthaler, S., Stephen, A. & Doraz, W. (1991). Controlled trail of vitamin-mineral supplementation on intelligence and brain function. *Personal Differences, 12*: 343–350.

Schore, A. N. (1994). *Affect regulation and the origin of the self: The neurobiology of emotion development.* Hillsdale, NJ: Erlbaum.

Schore, A. N. (1996). The experience-dependent maturation of a regulatory system in the orbital prefrontal cortex and the origin of developmental psychopathology. *Development and Psychopathology, 8*, 59–87.

Schore, A. N. (1997a). A century after Freud's Project—Is a rapprochement between psychoanalysis and neurobiology at hand? *Journal of the American Psychoanalytic Association, 45*, 1–34.

Schore, A. N. (1997b). Early organization of the nonlinear right brain and development of a predisposition to psychiatric disorders. *Development and Psychopathology, 9*, 595–631.

Schore, A. N. (2002). Clinical implications of psychoneurobiological model of projective identification. In S. Alhanati (Ed.), *Primitive mental states* (pp. 1–65, Vol. 2). New York: Karnac.

Schore, A. N. (2003). *Affect regulation and the repair of the self*. New York: Norton.

Schwartz, J. M. (1996). *Brainlock: Free yourself from obsessive-compulsive behavior*. New York: HarperCollins.

Schwartz, J. M., Stoessel, P. W., Baxter, L. R., Jr., Martin, K. M., & Phelps, M. E. (1996). Systematic changes in cerebral glucose metabolic rate after successful behavior modification treatment of obsessive-compulsive disorder. *Archives of General Psychiatry, 53*, 109–113

Scoville, W. B., & Milner, B. (1957). Loss of recent memory after bilateral hippocampal lesions. *Journal of Neurology, Neuroscurgery and Psychiatry, 20*, 11–21.

Searlman, A. (1977). A review of right hemisphere linguistic capabilities. *Psychological Bulletin, 84*(3), 503–528.

Seeman, T. E., & Syme, S. L. (1987). Social networks and coronary heart disease: A comparative analysis of network structural and support characteristics. *Psychosomatic Medicine, 49*, 341–354.

Seeman, T. E., Lusignolo, T. M., Albert, M., & Berkman, L. (2001). Social relationships, social support, and patterns of cognitive aging in healthy, high-functioning older adults. *Health Psychology, 4*, 243–255.

Segal, Z. V., Williams, J. M. G., & Teasdale, J. D. (2001). *Mindfulness-based cognitive therapy for depression: A new approach to preventing relapse*. New York: Guilford Press.

Segal, Z. V., Williams, J. M. G., & Teasdale, J. D. (2002). *Mindfulness-based cognitive therapy for depression*. New York: Guilford Press.

Selye, H. (1979). *The stress of my life*. New York: Van Nostrand.

Semple, W. E., Goyer, P. F., McCormick, R., Donovan, B., Muzic, R. F., Jr., Rugle, L., et al. (2000). Higher blood flow at amygdala and lower frontal cortex blood flow in PTSD patients with comorbid cocaine and alcohol abuse compared with normals. *Psychiatry: Interpersonal and Biological Processes, 63*, 65–74.

Sergent, J., Ohta, S., & MacDonald, B. (1992). Functional neuroanatomy of face and object processing. *Brain, 115*, 15–36.

Shapiro, F. (1995). *Eye movement desensitization and reprocessing: Basic principles, protocols, and procedures*. New York: Guilford Press.

Shaver, P. (1999). In J. Cassidy and P. Shaver (Eds.), *Handbook of attachment theory: Research and clinical applications*. New York: Guilford Press.

Sheline, Y. I., Gado, M. H., & Price, J. L. (1998). Amygdala core nuclei volumes are decreased in recurrent major depression. *Neuro Report, 9*, 2023–2028.

Sheline, Y. I., Wang, P. W., Gado, M. H., Csernansky, J. C., & Vannier, M. W. (1996). Hippocampal atrophy in recurrent major depression. *Proceedings of the National Academy of Sciences, USA, 93*, 3908–3913.

Sherry, D. F., & Schacter, D. L. (1987). The evolution of multiple memory systems. *Psychological Review, 94*, 439–454.

Shima, K., & Tanji, J. (1998). Role of the cingulated motor area cells in voluntary movement selection based on reward. *Science, 282*, 1335–1338.

Shin, L. M., Wright, C. I., & Cannistraro, P. A. (2005). A functional magnetic resonance imaging study of amygdala and medial prefrontal cortex responses to overtly presented fearful faces in posttraumatic stress disorder. *Archives of General Psychiatry, 62,* 273–281.

ShotAtDawn.org.uk. (2008). War pardons receives royal assent. Accessed March 13, 2008. http://www.janpieterchielens.be/shotatdawn/index.html.

Siegel, D. J. (1999). *Developing mind: Toward a neurology of interpersonal experience.* New York: Guilford Press.

Siegel, D. J. (2007). *The mindful brain: Reflection and attunement in the cultivation of well-being.* New York: Norton.

Siegel, D. J., & Hartzell, M. (2004). *Parenting from the inside out.* New York: Jeremy P. Tarcher/Penguin.

Siegel, D. J., & Varley, R. (2002). Neural systems involved in "theory of mind. *Nature Reviews Neuroscience, 3,* 267–276.

Silberman, E. K., & Weingartner, H. (1986). Hemispheric lateralization of functions related to emotion. *Brain and Cognition, 5,* 322–353.

Singer, B. & Ryff, C. D. (1999). Hierarchies of life histories and associated health risks. *Annals of the New York Academy of Sciences, 896,* 96–116.

Skarda, C. A., & Freeman, W. J. (1987). How brains make chaos in order to make sense of the world. *Behavioral and Brain Sciences, 10,* 161–195.

Skre, I., Onstad, S., Torgersen, S., Lygren, S., & et al. (1993). A twin study of DSM-III-R anxiety disorder. *Acta Psychatria Scandinavica, 88,* 85–92.

Slaikeu, K. A. (1990). *Crisis intervention: A handbook for practice and research* (2nd ed.). Needham Heights, MA: Allyn & Bacon.

Smith, E. E. & Kosslyn, S. M. (2007). *Cognitive psychology: Mind and brain.* Upper Saddle River, NJ: Pearson/Prentice Hall.

Solms, M., & Saling, M. (1990). *A moment of transition: Two neuroscientific articles by Sigmund Freud.* London: Institute of Psycho-Analysis/Karnac Books.

Smith, M. L., Glass, G. V., & Miller, T. I. (1980). *The benefits of psychotherapy.* Baltimore: Johns Hopkins University Press.

Solomon, Z., Mikulincer, M., & Avitzur, E. (1998). Coping, locus of control, social support, and combat-related Posttraumatic Stress Disorder: A prospective study. *Journal of Personality and Social Psychology, 55,* 279–285.

Spear, L. P. (2000). The adolescent brain and age-related behavioral manifestations. *Neuroscience and Biobehavioral Reviews, 24,* 417–463.

Sperry, W. W. (1974). Lateral specialization in the surgically separated hemispheres. In F. Schmitt & F. Worden (Eds.), *Third neurosciences study program* (Vol. 3, pp. 5–19). Cambridge, MA: MIT Press.

Springer, S., & Deutsch, G. (1998). *Left brain, right brain: Perspectives from cognitive neuroscience.* New York: Freeman.

Squire, L. R., Knowlton, B., & Musen, G. (1993). The structure and organization of memory. *Annual Review of Psychology, 44,* 453–495.

Sroufe, L. A. (1996). *Emotional development: The organization of emotional life in the early years.* New York: Cambridge University Press.

Stass, D. T., Gallup, G. G, & Alexander, M. P. (2001). The frontal lobes are necessary for a "theory of mind." *Brain, 124,* 279-286.

Stein, M. B., Koverola, C., Hanna, C., Torchia, M. G., & McClarty, B. (1997). Hippocampal volume in women victimized by childhood sexual abuse. *Psychological Medicine, 27,* 951-959.

Stein, P., & Kendall, J. (2003). *Psychological trauma and the developing brain: Neurologically based interventions for troubled children.* Binghamton, NY: Haworth Maltreatment and Trauma Press.

Steketee, G. (1999). *Overcoming obsessive-compulsive disorder: Patient manual.* Oakland, CA: New Harbinger Publications.

Steketee, G., & White, L. (1990). *When once is not enough.* Oakland, CA: New Harbinger.

Sterling, P. & Eyer, J. (1998). Allostatis: A new paradigm to explain arousal pathology. In S. Fisher & J. Reason (Eds.) *Handbook of stress, cognition, and health* (pp. 629-649). New York: Wiley.

Stern, D. N. (1985). *The interpersonal world of the infant.* New York: Basic Books.

Sterr, A., Muller, M. M., Elbert, T., Rockstroh, B., Pantev, C., & Taub, E. (1998). Changed perceptions in Braille readers. *Nature, 391,* 134-135.

Sullivan, R. M. & Gratton, A. (2002). Prefrontal cortical regulation of hypothalamic-pituitary-adrenal function in the rat and implications for psychopathology: Side matters. *Psychoneuroendocrinology, 27,* 99-114.

Szentágothai, J. (1975). The "module-concept" in cerebral cortex architecture. *Brain Research, 95,* 475-498.

Szentágothai, J. (1979). Local neuron circuits of the neocortex. In F. O. Schmitt & F. G. Worden (Eds.), *The neurosciences: Fourth study program* (pp. 399-415). Cambridge, MA: MIT Press.

Szentágothai, J. (1980). Principles of neural organization. In J. Szentágothai, M. Palkovits, & J. Hamori (Eds.), *Advances in physiological sciences Vol. 1, Regulatory functions of the CNS: Principles of motion and organization* (pp. 1-16). Budapest: Akadémiai Kiadó.

Taylor, S. (2004). Efficacy and outcome predictors for three PTSD treatments: Exposure therapy, EMDR, and relaxation training. In S. Taylor (Ed.), *Advances in the treatment of Posttraumatic Stress Disorder: Cognitive-behavioral perspectives* (pp. 13-37). New York: Springer.

Teasdale, J. D., Howard, R. J., Cox, S. G., Ha, Y., Brammer, M. J., Williams, S. C. R., et al. (1987). Human cerebral hemispheres develop at different rates and ages. *Science, 236,* 1110-1113.

Teasdale, J. D., Howard, R. J., Cox, S. G., Ha, Y., Brammer, M. J., Williams, S. C. R., & Checkley, S. A. (1999). Functional MRI study of the cognitive generation of affect. *American Journal of Psychiatry, 156,* 209-215.

Tedeschi, R. G. (1999). Violence transformed: Posttraumatic growth in survivors and their societies. *Aggression and Violent Behavior, 4,* 319-341.

Tedeschi, R. G., & Calhoun, L. G. (1995). *Trauma and transformation: Growing in the aftermath of suffering.* Thousand Oaks, CA: Sage.

Teichner, M. H., Anderson, S. L., Polcari, A., Anderson, C. M., Navalta, C. P., Kim, D. M. (2003). The neurobiological consequences of early stress and childhood maltreatment. *Neuroscience and Biobehavioral Reviews, 27*, 33–44.

Tennen, H., & Affleck, G. (1998). Personality and transformation in the face of adversity. In R. Tedeschi, C. L. Park, & L. Calhoun (Eds.), *Posttraumatic growth: Positive changes in the aftermath of crisis* (pp. 65–98). Mahwah, NJ: Erlbaum.

Teuber, H.-L. (1964). The riddle of frontal lobe function in man. In J. M. Warren and K. Akert (Eds.). *The frontal granular cortex and behavior* (pp. 410–444). New York: McGraw-Hill.

Thatcher, R. W., Walker, R. A., & Giudice, S. (1987). Human cerebral hemispheres develop at different rates and ages. *Science, 236*, 1110–1113.

Thayer, J. F., & Cohen, B. H. (1985). Differential hemispheric lateralization for positive and negative emotion: An electromyographic study. *Biological Psychology, 21*(4), 265–266.

Thomsen, P. H. (2000). Obsessive-compulsive disorder. Pharmacological treatment. *European Child and Adolescent Psychiatry, 9* (Suppl. 1) 76–84.

Tomarken, A. J., & Davidson, R. J. (1994). Frontal brain activation in repressors and nonrepressors. *Journal of Abnormal Psychology, 103*(2), 339–349.

Toradotter, M., Metis, M., Henriksson, B. G., Winblad, B., & Mohammed, A. H. (1998). Environmental enrichment results in higher levels of nerve growth factor MRNA in the rat visual cortex and hippocampus. *Behavioral Brain Research, 93*, 83–90.

Trevarthen, C. (1993). The self born in intersubjectivity: The psychology of an infant communicating. In U. Neisser (Ed.), *The perceived self: Ecological and interpersonal sources of self-knowledge*. Cambridge: Cambridge University Press.

Trevarthen, C. (1996). Lateral asymmetries in infancy: Implications for the development of the hemispheres. *Neuroscience and Biobehavioral Reviews, 20*, 1–16.

True, W. R., & Lyons, M. J. (1999). Genetic risk factors for PTSD: A twin study. In R. Yeduda (Ed.), *Risk factors for posttraumatic stress disorder* (pp. 61–78). Washington, DC: American Psychological Association.

Tucker, D. M. (1992). Developing emotions and cortical networks: In M. R. Gunnar & C. A. Nelson (Eds.), *Minnesota symposium on child psychology Vol. 24, Developmental behavioral neuroscience* (pp. 75–128). Hillsdale: NJ: Erbaum.

Tucker, D. M. (2003). Corticolimbic mechanisms in emotional decisions. *Emotions, 3*(2), 127–149.

Tucker, D. M., Luu, P., & Pribram, K. H. (1995). Social and emotional self-regulation. In J. Grafman & K. Hoyoak (Eds.), *Structure and functions of the human prefrontal cortex* (pp. 213–239). New York: New York Academy of Sciences.

Tucker, D., Penland, J., Sanstead, H., et al. (1990). Nutritional status and brain function in aging. *Journal of Clinical Nutritional, 52*: 93–102.

Turner, E. H., Matthews, A. M., Linardatos, B. S., Tell, R. A., and Rosenthal, R. (2008). Selective publication of antidepressant trials and its influence on apparent efficacy. *New England Journal of Medicine, 358*(3), 252–260.

Ullman, M. T., Miranda, R. A., & Travers, M. L. (2008). Sex differences in the neurocognition of language. In J. B. Becker, K. J. Berkley, N. Geary, E. Hampson, J. P. Herman, & E. A. Young (Eds.), *Sex differences in the brain: From genes to behavior* (pp. 291–309). New York: Oxford University Press.

Ullman, S. E., & Siegel, J. M. (1996). Traumatic events and physical health in a community sample. *Journal of Traumatic Stress, 9,* 703–713.

Updegraff, J. A., & Taylor, S. E. (2000). From vulnerability to growth: Positive and negative effects of stressful life events. In J. H. Harvey & E. D. Miller (Eds.), *Loss and trauma: Loss and trauma: General and close relationship perspectives* (pp. 3–28). New York: Brunner-Routledge.

Urry, H. L., Nitschke, J. B., Dolski, I., Jackson, D. C., Dalton, K. M., Mueller, C. J., et al. (2004). Making a life worth living: Neural correlates of well-being. *Psychological Science, 15*(6), 367–372.

Vaiva, G., Thomas, P., Ducrocq, F., Fontaine, M., Boss, V., Dovos, P., et al. (2004). Low post traumatic GABA plasma levels as a predictive factor in the development of acute posttraumatic stress disorder. *Biological Psychiatry, 55,* 250–254.

Van den Hout, M., Arntz, A., & Hoekstra, R. (1994). Exposure reduced agoraphobia but not panic, and cognitive therapy reduced panic but not agoraphobia. *Behavior Research and Therapy, 32*(4): 447–451.

Van der Knapp, M. S., Valk, J., Bakker, C. J., Schooneveld, M., Faber, J., Willemse, J., et al. (1991). Myelination as an expression of the functional maturity of the brain. *Developmental Medicine and Child Neurology, 33,* 849–857.

van der Kolk, B. A. (1987). Drug treatment of posttraumatic stress disorder. *Journal of Nervous and Mental Disorders, 13,* 203–213.

van der Kolk, B. A. (1993). Group for patients with histories of catastrophic trauma. In A. Alonso & H. I. Swiller (Eds.), *Group therapy in clinical practice* (pp. 289–305). Washington, DC: American Psychological Association.

van der Kolk, B. A. (1994). The body keeps the score: Memory and the evolving psychobiology of post traumatic stress. *Harvard Review of Psychiatry, 1,* 253–265.

van der Kolk, B. A. (1996). The complexity of adaptation to trauma: Self-regulation, stimulation discrimination, and characterlogical development. In B. A. van der Kolk, A. C. Mcfarlane, & L. Weisaeth (Eds.), *Traumatic stress: The effects of overwhelming experience on mind, body, and society* (pp. 182–213). New York: Guilford Press.

van der Kolk, B. A. (2003). The neurobiology of childhood trauma and abuse. *Child and Adolescent Psychiatric Clinics of North America, 12,* 293–317.

Vandenberg, S. G., & Kruse, A. R. (1978). Mental rotations: Group tests of three-dimensional spatial visualization. *Perceptual and Motor Skills, 47,* 599–604.

van IJzendoorn, M. H., & Bakerman-Kranenburg, M. J. (1997). Intergenerational transmission of attachment: A move to the contextual level. In L. Atkinson & K. L. Zucker (Eds.), *Attachment and psychopathology* (pp. 135–170). New York: Guilford Press.

Vasterling, J. J., Brailey, K., Constans, J. I., & Sutker, P. B. (1998). Attention and memory dysfunction in posttraumatic stress disorder. *Neuropsychology, 12*, 125–133.

Vernadakis, A. (1996). Glia-neuron intercommunications and synaptic plasticity. *Progressive Neurobiology, 49*, 185–214.

Vyas, A., Mitra, R., Shankaranarayana Rao, B. S., & Chattarji, S. (2002). Chronic stress induces contrasting patterns of dendritic remodeling in hippocampal and amygdaloid neurons. *Journal of Neuroscience, 22*, 6810–6818.

Wager, N., Feldman, G., & Hussey, T. (2001). Impact of supervisor interactional style on employees' blood pressure. *Consciousness and Experimental Psychology, 6*.

Wallin, D. (2007). *Attachment in psychotherapy*. New York: Guilford Press.

Wamala, S. P., Mittleman, M. A., Horsten, M., Schenck-Gustafsson, K., & Orth-Gomer, K. (2000). Job stress and the occupational gradient in coronary heart disease in women. *Social Science and Medicine, 51*, 481–498.

Watson, J. B. (1930). *Behaviorism* (Rev. ed.). Chicago: University of Chicago Press.

Watson, J. B. (1919). *Psychology from the standpoint of a behaviorist*. New York: Lippincott.

Weiner, I. (1998). *Principles of psychotherapy*. New York: Wiley.

Welch, J. M., Lu, J., Rodriguiz, R. M., Trotta, N. C., Peca, J., Ding, J.-D., et al. (2007, 23 August). Cortico-striatal synaptic defects and OCD-like behaviours in Sapap3-mutant mice. *Nature 448*, 894–900.

Wexler, B. (2006). *Brain and culture: Neurobiology, ideology, and social change*. Boston: MIT Press.

Wexler, B. E., Gottschalk, C. H., Fulbright, R. K., Prohovnik, I., Lacadie, C. M., Rounsaville, B. J., et al. (2001). Functional magnetic resonance imaging of cocaine craving. *American Journal of Psychiatry, 158*, 86–95.

Wheeler, M. A., Stuss, D. T., & Tulving, E. (1997). Toward a theory of episodic memory: The frontal lobes and autonomic consciousness. *Psychological Bulletin, 121*, 331–354.

Whalen, P. J. (1998). Fear, vigilance, and ambiguity: Initial neuroimaging studies of the human amygdala. *Current Directions in Psychological Science, 7*, 177–188.

Whalen, P. J., Kagan, J., Cook, R. G. (2004). Human amygdala responsivity to masked fearful eye whites. *Science, 306*, 2061.

White, M. (2007) *Maps of Narrative Practice*. New York: Norton.

Wilson (Eds.), *Psychological debriefing: Theory practice, and evidence.* (pp. 71–90). New York: Cambridge University Press.

Williams, S. L. (1996). Therapeutic changes in phobic disorders. In R. Scharzer (Ed.) *Self-efficacy: Thought control of action*. Washington, DC: Hemisphere.

Winnicott, D. W. (1953). Transitional objects and transitional phenomena. *International Journal of Psycho-Analysis*, 34, 89–97.

Winnicott, D. W. (1966). *The family and individual development*. New York: Basic Books.

Winnicott, D. W. (1941/1975). The observation of infants in a set situation. Through paediatrics to psycho-analysis. *Collected papers* (pp. 52–70). London: Hogarth Press.

Winnicott, D. W. (1975). *Holding and interpretation*. New York: Basic Books.

Winnicott, D. W. (1958/1975/1992). *Collected papers: Through paediatrics to psychoanalysis*. London: Tavistock, 1958; London: HogarthPress & The Institute of Psycho-Analysis, 1975; London: Karnac Books, 1992.

Winson, J. (1993). The biology and function of rapid eye movement sleep. *Current Opinion in Neurobiology*, 3, 243–248.

Wittling, W., & Pfluger, M. (1990). Neuroendocrine hemisphere asymmetries: Salivary cortisol secretion during lateralized viewing of emotion-related and neutral films. *Brain and Cognition*, 14, 243–265.

Wolf, N. S. (In press). Before and beyond words: The neurobiology of empathy (H. L. Ansbacher & R. R. Ansbacher, Eds.). New York: Norton. (Originally published 1979.)

Wolfe, J., Schrurr, P. P., Brown, P. J., & Furey, J. (1994). Posttraumatic stress disorder and war-zone exposure as correlates of perceived health in female Vietnam war veterans. *Journal of Consulting and Clinical Psychology*, 62, 1235–1240.

Wolpe, J. (1958). *Psychotherapy by reciprocal inhibition*. Stanford, CA: Stanford University Press.

Wong, D., Horng, J., Bymaster, F., Hauser K., & Molloy, B. (1974). A selective inhibitor of serotonin uptake: Lilly 110140, 3-(p-trifluoromethylphenoxy)-N-methyl-3-phenylpropylamine. *Life Sciences*, 15 (3): 471–479.

Wu, J.C., Buschsbaum, M. S., Hersey, T. G., Hazlett, E., Sciotte, N. & Johnson, J. C. (1991). PET in generalized anxiety disorder. *Biological Psychiatry*, 29, 1181–1199.

Yang, T. T., Menon, V., Eliez, S., Blasey, C., White, C. D., Reid, A. J., et al. (2002). Amygdalar activation associated with positive and negative facial expressions. *NeuroReport*, 13, 1737–1741.

Yehuda, R., Keefe, R. S. E., Harvey, P. D., Levengood, R. A., Gerber, D. K., Geni, J., et al. (1995). Learning and memory in combat veterans with posttraumatic stress disorder symptoms in holocaust survivors. *American Journal of Psychiatry*, 152(2), 1815–1818.

Yehuda, R., & McFarlane, A. C. (1995). Conflict between current knowledge about posttraumatic stress disorder and its original conceptual basis. *American Journal of Psychiatry*, 152, 1705–1713.

Young, L. J., Lim, M. M., Gingrich, B., & Insel, T. R. (2001). Cellular mechanisms of social attachment. *Hormones and Behavior*, 40, 133–138.

Zald, D. H. (2003). The human amygdala and the emotional evaluation of sensory stimuli. *Brain Research Reviews, 41,* 88–123.

Zajonc, R. B. (1968). Attitudinal effects of mere exposure. *Journal of Personality and Social Psychology, 9*(2), 1–27.

Zlotnick, C., Mattia, J. I., & Zimmerman, M. (1999). Clinical correlates of self-mutilation in a sample of general psychiatric patients. *Journal of Nervous and Mental Disease, 187,* 296–301.

Zoellner, L. A., Fitzgibbons, L. A., & Foa, E. B. (2001). Cognitive-behavioral approaches to PTSD. In J. P. Wilson, M. J. Friedman, & J. D. Lindy (Eds.), *Treating psychological trauma and PTSD* (pp. 159–82). New York: Guilford Press.

Zuercher-White, E. (1997). *Treating panic disorder and agoraphobia: A step-by-step clinical guide.* Oakland, CA: New Harbinger Publications.

Zuercher-White, E. (1998). *An end to panic: Breakthrough techniques for overcoming panic disorder and agoraphobia.* Oakland, CA: New Harbinger Publications.

AUTHOR INDEX

SUBJECT INDEX

Page numbers followed by *t* indicate a table and *f* indicate a figure.